Dialogue Editing for Motion Pictures

Dialogue Editing for Motion Pictures

A Guide to the Invisible Art

John Purcell

Foreword by Dominick Tavella

AMSTERDAM • BOSTON • HEIDELBERG • LONDON
NEW YORK • OXFORD • PARIS • SAN DIEGO
SAN FRANCISCO • SINGAPORE • SYDNEY • TOKYO

Focal Press is an imprint of Elsevier

Publisher: Elinor Actipis
Associate Acquisitions Editor: Cara Anderson
Assistant Editor: Robin Weston
Publishing Services Manager: George Morrison
Project Manager: Marilyn E. Rash
Copyeditor: Dianne Wood
Proofreader: Jodie Allen
Indexer: Ted Laux
Marketing Manager: Christine Degon Veroulis
Text Printing: Sheridan Books
Cover Printing: Phoenix Color Corp.

Focal Press is an imprint of Elsevier
30 Corporate Drive, Suite 400, Burlington, MA 01803, USA
Linacre House, Jordan Hill, Oxford OX2 8DP, UK

∞ Recognizing the importance of preserving what has been written, Elsevier prints its books on acid-free paper whenever possible.

Library of Congress Cataloging-in-Publication Data
Purcell, John, 1957–
   Dialogue editing for motion pictures : a guide to the invisible art / John Purcell
      p.   cm.
   Includes bibliographical references and index.
   ISBN-13: 978-0-240-80918-2 (alk. paper)
   ISBN-10: 0-240-80918-1 (alk. paper)
1. Motion picuters—Sound effects. 2. Sound motion pictures. I. Title.
   TR897.P7975 2007
   791.43—dc22
                                                                2007010822

British Library Cataloguing-in-Publication Data
A catalogue record for this book is available from the British Library.

For information on all Focal Press publications visit our website at
www.books.elsevier.com.

09   10   11   10 9 8 7 6 5 4 3 2
Printed in the United States of America

Working together to grow
libraries in developing countries

www.elsevier.com | www.bookaid.org | www.sabre.org

ELSEVIER   BOOK AID International   Sabre Foundation

In memory of Grant Maxwell, 1958–2006

Contents

Foreword

I really like this book.

But, I am getting ahead of myself.

To begin, I am a rerecording engineer, more commonly known as a mixer. My job is to take all of the assorted sounds—dialogue, sound effects, music, Foleys—that have been painstakingly assembled for the film's track and create a final, smooth, and hopefully moving and emotional soundtrack that you will hear in the theater or on your TV.

I've been doing it for some thirty years now, and I've mixed just about every kind of film or video you can imagine, from student films to big-budget studio features, commercials, video games, documentaries, on and on. One thing that I have learned through all of this is that in any kind of project, *every word is important*. The loss of a single word in a sentence, sometimes a single syllable, can make the entire sentence unintelligible. Worse still, it can often cause the loss of the next few sentences as the odd audience member furrows his brow and says, "What did she say?"

This brings us to this book's subject, dialogue editing. The job of the dialogue editor is to make every single word as clear as possible. He or she has to remove any and all distractions, noises, or mumbles to make the words as clear as a bell. All of this preparation of the myriad bits and pieces of production sound and ADR is for the mix, that is, for me. Since my time is quite expensive and, usually limited, everyone wants me to spend as little time as possible fixing dialogue problems, and most of my time making it sound beautiful. Remember, *every word is important!*

This is why I think that dialogue editing is usually the most important part of preparing for a mix. I find it ironic that if the work is done well—if the dialogue sounds clean and natural—the dialogue editor's work is usually

---

Note: Dominick Tavella mixes films in New York. Among his many works are *Romance & Cigarettes, State and Main, Chocolat, Far and Away, The Royal Tenenbaums,* and *Vanity Fair.* He received an Oscar® and a BAFTA Award for his work on *Chicago.*

invisible. Directors and editors expect to hear the words they heard on the set and in the cutting room. It's very easy to take notice of added sound effects, or Foleys, or music, because these things are added after the fact; they are embellishments, icing. But the dialogue editing is often not noticed unless there is a problem. Great dialogue editing is invisible, but its importance cannot be overstressed. Remember, *every word is important!*

This book is filled with lots of useful information and advice, but there are a few things that I particularly like about it. I like how John stresses the human factor. The interactions among the different editorial departments, and even among your own crew, can often make the difference between a great job and a lousy one. Listen to him on this.

Another thing I like is this author's approach to the "rules" of editing. If you ask just about any true craftsperson—editor, plumber, designer, or carpenter—he or she will tell you that each job is unique. There may be general approaches to solving a particular dilemma, but each job, even each element of a job, will have different needs from the last one. You have to listen to the work; it will tell you what it wants. John knows this.

So, this is more than a "how-to" book, as it should be. It's also a "why" book. The technical part of any of the film crafts, though daunting, is the easiest to teach. It is much more difficult to explain the subtleties, the "feeling" of when it's right, the elusive search for why it's wrong. This is the agonizing, keep-you-up-at-night part of the job. John does a great job of describing this, and his passion shines through.

As filmmakers, we are creating an artificial world, and asking an audience to pretend along with us for a couple of hours. This is a fragile construct, and we have to be careful to never show the process, never break the illusion of a real space in a real world, by inadvertently revealing the details behind the facade. The dialogue has to be as perfect as we can make it, or we risk losing the audience.

I really like this book. I think every aspiring, or practicing, editor can find a lot of good in these pages. Heck, even I learned a lot.

So enjoy this book, and remember, it's a map, not a turn-by-turn set of instructions. It should help you find your own way. Enjoy the journey, and I'll see you at the movies.

Dominick Tavella

Preface

There are many books about film sound. There are books about sound theory and the role sound plays in a movie. There are practical books that teach you about sound editing, sound design, or sound equipment. There are books for film music composers or those who wish they were composers. And there are books about Foley, sound effects, music editing, and mixing. But you do not hear of many books about dialogue editing.

Every live-action film contains dialogue. Lots of it. After all, that's how most films tell their stories. When you, the dialogue editor, receive a locked film from the picture editor, the sound is a mess. It sounds bad, it's unorganized, it doesn't "act" like a movie. You have just a few weeks to untangle this mess, to create a believable cinematic flow, and to remove the artifacts of the film-making process. You have to fix what you can and rerecord the rest. During this short time you work with a film's dialogue tracks, you must get to know them, cajole and seduce them, and get them to behave the way you want—this is dialogue editing.

This is a book for people who need to edit production sound for dramatic films but were never taught how to do it. Dialogue editing operates under a different set of rules than music editing or effects editing. There are some things you've simply got to know, but unless you're fortunate enough to work with more experienced editors in many different situations, there's no one to teach you the process. This book offers you that education.

Who Can Benefit from Reading This Book?
- Anyone who wants to edit dialogue tracks in a professional manner
- Sound editors who want to better understand dialogue editing and how it fits in with the rest of the postproduction process
- Dialogue editors who want to run a more organized cutting room
- Film students and students of motion picture sound engineering
- Picture editors and assistants
- Anyone who sees dialogue editing as a boring, tedious chore and who could use a bit of inspiration

- Amateur video enthusiasts who want their movies to sound better
- Anyone who's wondered, "How do they do that?"

How a film was shot, recorded, and edited will dramatically influence the dialogue editing process. Much of this book, then, deals with things that at first glance don't appear to be dialogue. There's a lot of talk in this book about *process*—the overview of how things work. You'll find technical overviews of motion picture postproduction: film, tape, NTSC, PAL, 24p, and more. There are summaries of film picture editing, OMF manipulation, and ADR management.

You'll also find a lot of discussion about organization. If you keep your work organized, you stand a better chance of learning what the tracks are trying to tell you. A well-run dialogue editing room helps to make the process rewarding and fun rather than the dreary, repetitive, nerdy chore that some allege it to be.

There's a section in this book that deals with managing your time and another about getting along with the picture department. Brilliant tracks and subtle manipulations aren't enough when you're miserably behind schedule or if you can't get what you need from the picture cutting room.

A Note about Word Choice

In an attempt to make this book as universal as possible, I've included English-language professional film terms used the world over. And in an attempt to be as fair a possible, I've used relatively interchangeable words, well, interchangeably. This is meant to prevent confusion, but like all good intentions, it may backfire.

For example, you'll find the terms "ADR," "looping," and "postsync" used almost indiscriminately. I do explain that *looping* is a specific process that is not the same as ADR (see Chapter 15). However, so many people use ADR, looping, and postsync interchangeably that once you know the difference between them, you might as well use the word that most easily rolls off your tongue and is acceptable to your colleagues. Sometimes, tilting at linguistic windmills is pointless.

You'll notice that I cavalierly exchange "sound designer" with "supervising sound editor" and "sound supervisor." These titles do not mean the same thing, but depending on the crowd you run with, it is difficult to tell one term from the other. Out of fairness, I have sprinkled a bit of one term here and a bit of another term there. In general, I use *supervising sound editor* to describe the person in charge of a film's postproduction sound.

A "mix" (New York) and a "dub" (Los Angeles and London) are the same thing. From lifelong habit, I use *mix*, try though I do to be fair to the *dub* people. Practices vary by location, each film culture having its own system and terminology. The techniques and jargon described in this book have their roots in New York, but there's a smattering of Europe, Los Angeles, and the rest-of-the-world tossed in.

Avid's not the only picture editing workstation in the world. But let's face it, Avid currently maintains a near monopoly, with Apple's Final Cut Pro still a distant second in market penetration. It seems silly to constantly write "Avid or Final Cut Pro or whatever else you use to cut picture," so often I use *Avid* to mean "picture editing workstation." It's easier to read.

In addition, this book is very Pro Tools-centric. Examples must be described and shown on *something*, and Pro Tools' omnipresence makes it an obvious choice. Still, all this DigiSpeak isn't meant as an endorsement, and this is *not* meant to be a book about editing dialogue using the Pro Tools products. The examples that specifically mention Pro Tools can be transferred easily to other workstations.

I've tossed around the terms "location mixer," "sound recordist," "location recordist," and the like to mean "the person responsible for the location sound recording." This rather clumsy randomizing of terms is due to two problems faced in writing a book like this. First, depending on where you live and how big your production is, a different term is used for the role. Second, wanting to keep you, the reader, on my side, I've generally tried to avoid gender-specific terms such as "soundman." All of this results in occasionally inelegant prose, but you're here for the information, not the eloquence.

Finally, on the topic of gender-specific language, please forgive me my use of *he, his, she, her,* and so on, or if it looks like I'm giving the guys too many of the good positions. I've tried to randomly distribute the jobs in my make-believe productions, and I alternate between *he* and *she* with military regularity. But someone may be put off, either by my goofy inconsistency or by my failure to accurately balance the use of gender pronouns. It's not that I didn't try.

Key Words

Every book like this has a glossary of relevant terms. There are many, many excellent books about film sound that offer outstanding definitions of "industry" terms, a few of which are cited at the beginning of the glossary. I won't try to top those. However, some words that apply specifically to dialogue editing are written in **boldface** when they first appear in the text. These words are defined or discussed in the glossary at the end of the book.

This book's objective is to tell you about those things you can't figure out on your own. Dialogue editing may be misunderstood, but it's not magic. If you don't lose sight of the needs of the film and stick to a few rules, you can create brilliant, interesting dialogue. This is a practical guide for getting the most from dialogue tracks, telling a story with production recordings, and making a huge invisible contribution to the narrative success of any film.

Acknowledgments

As much as it's fun to think otherwise, it's impossible to write a book like this without help. Having said that, I'd like to acknowledge the following people.

Thanks to Brooks Harris for his guidance through the minefield of OMF, EDLs, and HD workflows. I'm grateful to Jack Calaway for his personal notes concerning the early days of nonlinear video editing. No one else could have offered such a front-row history of the subject.

I appreciate Mike Poppleton's contributions to the chapter on conformations, as well as his observations about EDLs and OMF. Isaac Sehayak was instrumental in sorting out picture cutting issues, and Daniel Ward and Graeme Nattress offered valuable insight into HD production procedures. Doron Sulliman contributed greatly to the section on Avid OMF exports. Yakov Gilad helped get the project started, and Paul Soucek provided priceless oversight and support as work progressed.

Thanks to Ruth Shek Yasur and Bill Stott for language assistance, and to Yisrael David, Gil Segal, Oliver Masciarotte, Doron Sulliman, and Barbara Alper for helping with screenshot production.

Avid screenshots are courtesy of Edit Studios, Tel Aviv. Pro Tools screenshots are courtesy of The Mix Room Ltd. and DB Studios, Tel Aviv. Sonic Studio, LLC, provided the soundBlade screenshot.

For their invaluable aid in reviewing and fact-checking, I'm grateful to Colin Alexander, Larry Blake, Matt Connolly, Todd Hooker, Justin Kim, Barend Onneweer, Rodger Pardee, and Brandon Walker. To the countless others who provided information, clarification, and direction, my sincere thanks.

CHAPTER 1

What Is Dialogue Editing?

Dialogue editing is one of the least understood aspects of motion picture sound postproduction. Most people have some grasp of the roles of sound effects editors or backgrounds editors or music editors. To most moviegoers, Foley is a charming—yet perhaps a bit silly—process, and it's not hard to understand it once you've seen it. Mixing, too, is a pretty straightforward concept, even if massively complex in actual fact. Few non-pros, however, understand dialogue editing. "Does that mean you take out the dirty words?" is a common response when I tell someone what I do for a living.

A dialogue editor is responsible for every sound that was recorded during the shoot. She takes the more or less finished film from the picture editor, makes sense of the edited sounds, organizes them, finds out what works and what doesn't. The dialogue editor wades through the outtakes to find better articulations, quieter passages, sexier breaths, and less vulgar lip smacks. He replaces washy wide-shot sound with clean close-up takes, establishes depth in otherwise flat scenes, and edits tracks for maximum punch and clarity.

Dialogue editors work to remove the filmmaking from the film. Dolly squeaks, camera noise, crew rustling, and light buzzes must go; otherwise, the magic of the movies is compromised. These editors help present the actors in their best light, quieting dentures, eliminating belly noises, and sobering slurred syllables. And when the production sound can't be saved, the dialogue editor is involved in the ADR process, that is, the rerecording of voices in the studio to replace problem field recordings or to beef up performances.

Dialogue editing is all of these things and more. Dialogue is what makes most films work. The dialogue editor makes the dialogue work.

There are many kinds of films. Some are driven largely by juxtaposition of images, most notably silent classics such as *Potemkin* and *Alexander Nevsky*. Others use a language of camera motion or composition to speak to the viewer, obvious examples being *Citizen Kane* and *Besieged*. Still others use color or shading to make a point. Among the many examples of color in storytelling are films as diverse as *Juliet of the Spirits*, *Women on the Verge of a Nervous Breakdown*, and *The Corpse Bride*. Many films rely heavily on music to express themselves, while others manipulate through sound effects. Filmmakers concoct a personal stew of visual and aural tools to reveal or enhance a story.

But the overwhelming majority of narrative films rely on the spoken word to tell the story, develop characters, and touch hearts. The modern motion picture has more in common with theater than with early montage cinema, in that only a minority of current (especially commercial) films trust image over dialogue. However cinematic or structurally sophisticated, most of the films you work on will tell their story through dialogue.

You can eliminate all (or most) of the sound effects in a scene, the backgrounds can largely be muted, or the music can be dumped. The scene will still work. But for the most part you can't eliminate the dialogue track, even for a moment. The dialogue holds key story information as well as the **room tone**, the "air" that defines the location of the scene.

We've grown so accustomed to the language of film that blind acceptance of the implausible is the norm. After a century of tutoring in film language, we accept the convention of cutting from one speaking character to another and we interpret this unnatural collision as a "conversation." We have no trouble accepting the abnormal **phone split**, in which we hear both sides of a telephone conversation. And we don't shake our heads in disbelief when listening to a conversation in a distant long shot—sounds we rationally know would be out of bounds to us. We *want* to believe that what we see and hear is very real. Only something that patently breaks the rules of the language of film will shatter our confidence and make us question the reality we've been accepting.

Most people know that films are rarely shot in order but rather in a sequence determined by location and set availability, actors' schedules, exotic equipment rental coordination, and (hopefully) overall efficiency. Even within scenes, the shot sequences may not be in script order. Don't be surprised when you find that two people who are apparently talking to each other on screen were not together when the close-ups were shot. This shooting discontinuity makes the dialogue editor's job even more crucial. We must do everything in our power to convince the viewer that these characters actually were talking with each other; we must remove any impediments to the audience's total belief in the reality of the scene.

Many photographic mistakes dash our confidence in a film. Crossing the axis, exposed flying wires, ridiculous costumes or makeup, or absurd anachronisms can take us out of the magic. Many audio mistakes jar us out of the fantasy as well. Poorly matched ADR, grossly inappropriate backgrounds or sound effects (birds out of season or location, incorrect guns or motors, etc.), insensitive use of perspective, or a sloppy mix will drag us out of the film, even if for a moment, and it's a battle to reestablish trust after such a betrayal.

Dialogue editors play a vital role in the subterfuge of moviemaking. It's up to us to turn the many shots and production sounds into a convincing, coherent scene that even the most skeptical filmgoer will watch without being aware of the filmmaking that went into it. Unlike sound effects editors, background editors, or music editors, our magic most certainly goes unseen (or unheard)—if it's performed well. Only our failures attract attention.

So, just what is the dialogue editor's part in this process?

- To organize and manage the material. When you first screen a film, the sound may seem to work, but just beneath the surface it's unorganized and unfocused. One of your biggest jobs is to make sense of it; otherwise, you can't help the dialogue discover itself.
- To smooth the transitions between shots so conversations appear to be happening in the same space, at the same time.
- To fix articulation problems, **overlaps**, and other language issues. This usually involves searching through **alternate takes** to find similar deliveries that can be used for patches.
- To address unwanted, unseemly actor noises such as lip smacks, denture clatter, and hungry belly rumbles. At times any one of these may be appropriate, but each must be challenged, removed, replaced, or at least thought about.
- To pay attention to changes and adds that will enhance the story or motivate characters' actions. This often involves a combination of observation and talking with the director, editor, and writer.
- To remove unwanted external noises, whether crew or dolly noise, unnecessary footsteps, or birds chirping during day-for-night scenes. The list of on-set noises is endless, and each one of them reminds the viewer that we're making a movie.
- To replace sections of dialogue corrupted by distortion, wind, clothing rustle, boom handling, and the like.
- To determine what can't be saved through editing and must be rerecorded through postsynchronization. This is done in conjunction with the ADR supervisor.

- To serve as the arbiter of sync issues in the film. Usually the other departments follow your lead in deciding the film's sync.
- To prepare the dialogue tracks for the dialogue premix (predub). Your tracks not only must sound good but must be presented to the mix in a logical and efficient manner so that the mixer can spend precious time telling a story with the dialogue tracks rather than merely sorting out disasters.
- To assist in the dialogue premix. You more than anyone know the tracks, and you planned a particular interpretation of the scene while cutting them, so you need to be involved at this stage. You also have to be available to make fixes or changes to the dialogue tracks during the premix.
- To separate production effects from the dialogue track in preparation for the **M&E** mix.

Although it's occasionally derided as boring or purely technical by the ill-informed, dialogue editing is the glue that holds the production sound together. No other facet of sound editing requires such a wide array of skills.

Appendix A is an overview of the process of dialogue editing in outline form. At first glance, it may seem overwhelming with its many steps. However, as you learn more about the *process* of dialogue editing, you'll see the outline as more of a commonsense reminder than as an imposing mandate. Keep it handy when you edit dialogue. Use the steps that are relevant to the project you're working on and skip the ones that don't apply. Use the outline to help you organize your project and keep on target.

CHAPTER 2

No One Works in a Vacuum—How to Know Where You Fit into the Filmmaking Process

Introduction

Most of the challenges facing dialogue editors are the result of decisions made on the set. Location mixers must make choices about sound, story, sample rates, timecode, and formats. These decisions will irrevocably affect the future of the production tracks and hence your way of working.

You can't undo incorrect sample rates, weird timecode, or improper timebase references, but if you equip yourself with a knowledge of production workflows, you'll be better able to respond to the problems that come your way. Since you inherit the fruits of the production, you need to understand how films are shot and how the moviemaking chain of events fits together. This way, you can plan postproduction workflows before the shoot, before it's too late to do anything but react to problems.

The way we work today is the offspring of generations of tradition, technological advances, economic pressures, and a good deal of chance. Current cinema workflows are more complicated than ever, and with the introduction of high-definition shooting, postproduction, and distribution, things appear to be truly out of control. But remember that with each significant new technology in the film industry has come a brief period of bedlam that quickly settled into a state of equilibrium. And usually the pressure to get things back to normal is so great that innovative, creative means are quickly devised to rein in the technology and make things better than ever.

How We Got Where We Are

Sound recording and motion picture filming grew up at more or less the same time. When Thomas Edison recited "Mary Had a Little Lamb" in 1877 to demonstrate his tinfoil phonograph,[1] a bitter war of innovation, patent fights, and downright thievery was raging in Europe and the United States to come up with methods of photographing and projecting moving pictures. Most initial attempts at displaying motion were inspired by Victorian parlor toys like the Phenakistoscope and later the Zoetrope (a spinning slotted cylinder that contained a series of photographs or drawings); a strobe effect gave the impression of motion when the pictures were viewed through the slots. Enjoyable though those gadgets were, they weren't viable ways to film and project real life.

Auguste and Louis Lumière's public screening of *La sortie des ouvriers de l'usine Lumière* in 1895 is generally acclaimed as the "birth of cinema," but, then, Christopher Columbus is credited with discovering America. Believe what you will. *La sortie des ouvriers*, about a minute long, was a static shot of workers leaving the Lumière plant. Was this really the first film to be shown? Of course not. As early as 1888, Augustin Le Prince was able to film and project motion pictures. And Edison, who long claimed to be the inventor of cinema, was making movies in 1892.

Since 1892, Birt Acres and Léon Bouly had been independently improving their motion picture systems and their movies. But Bouly couldn't pay the yearly patent fees for his invention and his license expired, while Acres proved a prodigious inventor and filmmaker but managed to slip into relative obscurity. Meanwhile, Antoine Lumière, father of Auguste and Louis, more or less copied Edison's Kinetoscope while taking advantage of Bouly's lapsed patent. The offspring of this effort was the Lumière *Cinématographe*,[2] a camera, projector, and filmprinter all rolled into one. The brothers Lumière shot and commercially distributed numerous short *actualités*, including *l'Arrivée d'un train en gare* (*Arrival of a Train at a Station*) and *Déjeuner de bébé* (*Baby's Lunch*).

In all fairness, the Lumière family had more going for them than just sharp elbows. By 1895, the world was evidently ready to pay money to see factory workers leaving work or a train arriving at a station. Plus, the *Cinématographe* was startlingly lightweight and portable compared to its behemoth competitors.

---

[1] Biographies of Thomas Edison aren't hard to come by, but a rich and simple source of Edison history and archival material is the U.S. Library of Congress web site, which has a section devoted to him. Edison phonograph sound clips and movie excerpts are available, as are countless historical documents (*http://memory.loc.gov/ammem/edhtml/edhome.html*).

[2] Tjitte de Vries. "The Cinématographe Lumière: A Myth?" *Photohistorical Magazine of the Photographic Society of The Netherlands* (1995, *http://www.xs4all.nl/~wichm/myth.html*).

It was clear to all that a method of showing sound and picture was of great commercial interest. In the late 1880s, Edison and his associate, W.K.L. Dickson, linked the Edison cylinder phonograph with a larger tube that was slotted much like the Zoetrope. It wasn't elegant, but it did produce synchronized images and sound.[3] Georges Demeny, in 1891, claimed to produce a synchronous sound system, but like so many assertions in this time of riotous invention, this proved unfounded. There were many other attempts to add sound to the ever more popular moving picture, but at least three impediments came between a successful marriage of sound and picture: reliable synchronization, amplification, and the fact that silent pictures were so effective and popular.

Early Attempts at Sound in Movies

Many early sound movies were merely prerecorded playback tracks to which "silent" actors mimed. By the 1920s, when commercial talkies were a real possibility, sound playback was usually from a phonograph synchronized to the film projector via belts, pulleys, and cogs. The most successful interlocked phonograph/projector system was the Vitaphone, made by Western Electric and Bell Laboratories. But this double-system playback failed completely in the event of a film break or a skip in the record. The projectionist had no choice but to return to the beginning of the reel. Eugene Augustin Lauste patented a form of optical film soundtrack in 1910, but it would be another 20 years before optical recording was adopted for film sound.[4]

Amplification of disk or cylinder recordings posed a hurdle, since early phonographs played their sounds acoustically rather than through amplification—hardly appropriate for large halls. The German Tri-Ergon sound-on-film system, later improved on by American Lee De Forest, enabled a sound reader to convert variations in the optical track into a signal that could be amplified by valve amplifiers newly improved by the Marconi company and others. This was the beginning of a standard for sound reproduction that would last more than 50 years—optical sound printed directly onto the filmprint.

But there was one more hurdle to clear in order to bring sound movies out of the "gee whiz" ghetto and into commercial success. Simply stated, silent pictures worked. By the mid-1920s silent films had established a language and an audience and were rightly considered both entertainment for the

---

[3] Mark Ulano. "Moving Pictures That Talk, Part 2: The Movies Are Born a Child of the Phonograph" (*http://www.filmsound.org/ulano/index.html*).

[4] David A. Cook. *A History of Narrative Film* (New York: Norton, 1981, pp. 241–44).

masses and an intellectual means of expression. Many filmmakers and film theorists vehemently objected to adding the vulgar novelty of sound to this new but advanced art form. The most famous objection came in the form of the 1928 manifesto "Sound and Image" published by Eisenstein, Pudovkin, and Alexandrov.[5] They protested that cinema with sound would become a means of displaying the ordinary and the real, rather than reaching to higher meanings through the newly developed art of *montage*.

It would be naïve to think, however, that the development of cinema sound was held up because of the rantings of a few Soviet intellectuals. In fact, it was the studios that were most opposed to innovation. They had a good thing going, and it was hard for executives to imagine that it would ever change. Silent films were relatively easy and cheap to produce, and studios had invested heavily in the mechanism that enabled them to crank out and distribute them. Also, the costs of refitting movie theaters with sound playback equipment seemed uncomfortably and unnecessarily high. Plus, silent films weren't altogether silent or as inexpensive as met the eye. Often projections were accompanied by live sound effect artists, musicians, singers, or actors, and all these people had to be paid. Studios were interested in reducing these costs, and the most attractive place to start was with the musicians. Devising a way to mechanically play a musical score to a silent film would reduce costs by dismissing the cinema orchestra from every performance. And playback tracks never go on strike.

Talkies

In 1926, Warner Brothers released Alan Crosland's *Don Juan*, with a huge score preformed by the New York Philharmonic Orchestra. The music was played back—in sync—from a Vitaphone record. Thus, the stage was set for a commercially released feature-length talkie to step into history. Crosland's *The Jazz Singer*, which premiered in October 1927, was actually a standard silent movie with a few lines of spoken dialogue, but still it was a huge money maker. It didn't take long for the studios to see the writing on the wall and begin gearing up for sound production and distribution.

Shooting and recording a Vitaphone film was much like producing a live radio show. There was no postproduction, so every sound in a scene had to be recorded live—sound effects, offscreen dialogue, music, everything. Until rerecording was perfected in the 1930s, editing of any kind was all but impossible.

---

[5] Cook, 1981, pp. 265–66.

Postsynchronization was first used in 1929 by King Vidor on the film *Halle-lujah!*[6] Freeing the shooting process from the draconian restrictions that early sound recording techniques imposed, it restored some of the freedom and lightness of the silent era. By the mid-1930s, it was possible to mix several channels of sound without distortion, and postsynchronization of dialogue and other sounds began to allay the fears of those who predicted that sound cinema would inevitably result in naturalistic films.

Sound was still recorded optically, however, so it was very tedious and time consuming to edit and manipulate recorded tracks. Blimps were invented to quiet noisy cameras, microphones became more directional, and optical soundtracks were improved and standardized. The sound Moviola was made available in 1930, so there was now a standardized, sophisticated way to edit picture and optical sound film. In 1932, a process of printing a common serial number on synchronized picture tracks and soundtracks was developed. "Edge numbering," or "rubbering," allowed accurate logging of film elements and reprinting of edited tracks from their original masters. This system of coding film workprint and sound elements has remained more or less unchanged.

In a brief period of time, movie sound got much better. Arc lights lost their deafening hum, so they could be used on sound pictures. Biased recording was introduced, yielding far quieter tracks. Fine-grain film stock resulted in not only better-looking prints but also finer-resolution optical soundtracks, as did UV optical printing. In 1928, the frequency response of motion picture soundtracks was 100 Hz to 4000 Hz. Ten years later it was 30 Hz to 10,000 Hz.[7]

Despite these improvements in sound recording and mixing technology, film sound editing didn't substantively change for more than 20 years. Picture and sound editors worked on Moviolas, later adding flatbed film editing tables such as the Steenbeck, KEM, or console Moviolas. Sound was printed onto 35 mm optical sound film for editing and mixing, and released on 35 mm film with mono optical soundtracks.

The Modern Era

In 1958 magnetic recording came of age and everything changed. Stefan Kudelski introduced the Nagra III battery-operated transistorized field tape recorder, which with its "Neo-Pilot" sync system became the de facto

---

[6] Cook, 1981, p. 268.
[7] Elisabeth Weis and John Belton, eds. *Film Sound: Theory and Practice* (New York: Columbia University Press, 1985, p. 67).

standard of the film industry.[8] Soon production sound was transferred to 35 mm magnetic film, **mag stripe**, which could be easily handled, coded, edited, and retransferred as needed. Dialogue and effects editors were now free to manipulate tracks as never before. During the mix, edited dialogue, effects and backgrounds, Foley, and music elements were combined and recorded onto yet more 35 mm magnetic film (**fullcoat**). (This system continues today on films edited mechanically.) With sound elements on mag, there was no real technical limit to the complexity of the sound design or even the number of tracks, although the cumulative hiss from the mag discouraged playing too many tracks at once. When Dolby noise reduction was introduced in 1975, even this limitation was surmounted.

The system of recording on analogue tape, editing sound and picture on mag stripe, and mixing to fullcoat served the film industry for more than 30 years. It was predictable, stable, and universal, and its hunger for labor kept apprentices and assistants—many of whom would be the next generation of editors— near the action. Then, once again, it all changed. Enter nonlinear picture editors and digital audio workstations.

Now, for far less than the price of a car, you can have unrivaled editing, processing, and management power in a small computer. You can make changes over and over, painlessly creating alternate versions of your work. There's no getting around the fact that the technology is massively better than it was a generation ago, which means that you're much more empowered to make your own choices.

Therein lies the problem. Digital audio workstations and the hugely altered workflow they bring about have turned sound editing on its head. What was once a well-understood, widely accepted process has been given a huge dose of democracy, if not anarchy. The way we work has changed in a revolutionary way, not just in a few evolutionary adjustments. Crews are smaller and roles are less defined, and even the basic workflow is no longer basic. The way you work now depends on where you live, plus a thousand other peculiar variables.

Different Formats, Different Processes

What makes for the present confusion is not that modern editing has been digitized but rather that the picture almost always has to be transferred to video, which has a different timebase from that of film. Countless sample

---

[8] Audio Engineering Society (*http://www.aes.org/aeshc/docs/audio.history.timeline.html*).

rates, pullups, pulldowns, transfer speeds, and timecode types may lead you to believe that digital audio postproduction is a hopeless maze of variables, any of which are poised to trip you up and wreck your health.

Not so. Despite all the options, it all comes down to two variables:

- How was it shot?
- How and where will postproduction take place?

Break down the production into logical categories, like these two fundamental questions, and there will be no doubt as to how to proceed with your postproduction. Master that and the process is no longer cryptic.

Next, we'll look briefly at several ways of shooting and posting films. These examples are simplified, but ought to give you an idea of where moviemaking workflows are similar and where they differ. Don't get frustrated by the details. Study the work models that affect you and glimpse at the others. Audio postproduction details are discussed in Chapters 5, 9, and 10. *What's important at this point is that you have a good understanding of the filmmaking process, since what goes on before and after dialogue editing greatly affects your work.* All of the illustrations presented here are based on the film model (filmprint and mag sound), so it's worth your while to read this section even though you're almost certainly working electronically.

The Film Model Since the advent of magnetic recording in the late 1950s and industry acceptance of magnetic sound film a short time later, the workflow shown in Figure 2.1 has been the model for making movie sound. There are still films produced in this manner or that use big chunks of the model in their production.

The Film Shoot During the shoot, the camera uses synchronous motors to maintain an exact speed of 24 frames per second (fps).[9] On the sound side, the mono Nagra recorder (or stereo Nagra with FM pilot or stereo Nagra with timecode) records a 50 Hz or 60 Hz **pilot tone** onto the tape along with the audio. When it's time to shoot, you'll hear "Roll sound!" from the assistant director. The sound always starts first because (1) it takes longer for a Nagra than a camera to get up to speed, and (2) tape is much cheaper than film so no one complains about a little bit of it being wasted. Once the Nagra is locked

---

[9] Actually, most cameras can run at several fixed speeds, such at 23.98, 24, 25, 29.97, and 30 fps. Many can be adjusted to run at a number of "non-sync" speeds to give the effect of speeding up or slowing down the action. You can't record sync sound at such "unreal" speeds, however.

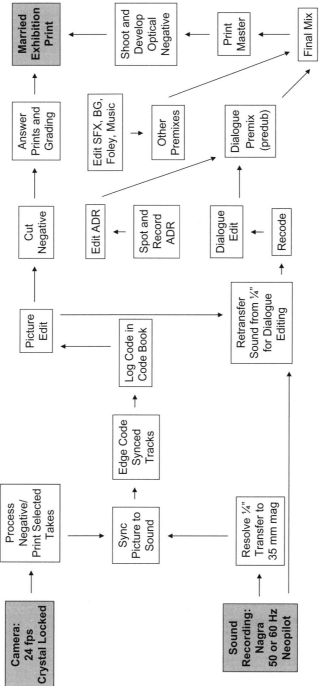

Figure 2-1 Workflow of an analogue project shot on film and edited with the film workprint and magnetic sound film.

at the proper speed, indicated by a flag on the front panel, the location mixer will say something to the effect of "Sound speeding." Next comes the camera.

When the set, the actors, the background actors, and the photography department are absolutely ready, the assistant director will call, "Roll camera!" In comes the clapper/loader, who has written the appropriate scene and take information on the slate. He stands in a place visible to the camera and audible to the microphone and verbally announces the upcoming shot. When the camera is running and locked, the camera assistant will announce, "Camera speeding." At this point, the clapper/loader will call "Marker!" to let the world know that the clap is soon to happen. One gentle smack of the clapper, and the deaf film camera and the blind Nagra have what it takes to find their sync in postproduction.

The Film Lab At the end of a shooting day, or at some other sensible interval, the clapper/loader gathers up the negative, labels it, and sends it to the lab for processing. The lab develops all of the negative, but to reduce costs only the takes selected by the director during the shoot are printed for screening and editing (hence the familiar command: "Cut! Print it!"). These selected takes arrive at the picture cutting room in the form of positive 35 mm workprints, which will soon be organized by scene and slate, or whatever other system the picture editor chooses. But not just yet.

The ¼" Nagra tapes, or sound rolls, are transferred to 35 mm mag stripe. To ensure that they're played back at precisely the same speed they were recorded at, a **resolver** attached to the Nagra compares the pilot tone recorded on the tape with the **mains frequency** (50 or 60 Hz) and slews the tape to the right speed. For the rest of the postprodcution process, whenever sound and picture must be interlocked, the mains frequency serves as the common clock.

The Picture Cutting Room Back in the picture cutting room, the assistant editor uses the slate information and claps to synchronize picture with sound. Then the lab rolls are broken into a more sensible order, usually by scene, and leaders with start marks are added. Each picture/sound pair of rolls is coded with a unique series number, a several digit edge code stamped at left intervals on the workprint. Once printed, the edge code information is entered into the "Code Book," a vast database also housing the **Keykode** and scene/shot/take data for the entire film—vital for locating alternate shots, reprinting shots, and keeping things in order. Now the director and editor will sequester themselves in the cutting room for weeks or months, finally emerging with a locked picture.

For quite a while now, the picture team has been handling the mag stripe that contains the production sound, coating it with perspiration, dirt, and Reuben sandwich detritus. That's why it's common to log the shots used in the final picture edit and retransfer the takes from the original ¼" tapes to a fresh mag. These pristine tracks will be the raw material of the dialogue edit. The dialogue team splits the tracks into many units and works on Moviolas or flatbed editors to add tone, replace problem words, or remove noises. Their finished product will be many (perhaps 20 or more tracks per reel) 1000-ft rolls of mag stripe.

Sound Effects and ADR Meanwhile, the rest of the sound department has been busy. The ADR supervisor spots where new lines must be recorded and prepares the volumes of paperwork necessary to manage the ADR. These lines are recorded in a studio and then edited by the ADR editor. Sound effects and background editors add texture, excitement, space, and emotion to the film. Foley, the "live" sound effects (for example, footsteps, body motion, cloth rustle, and the sounds of objects like plates, locks, and keys), are recorded and edited. Finally, the music—scored as well as acquired and practical—is edited by the music department. Like the dialogue units, these elements arrive at the mix as 1000-ft rolls of mag.

Negative Cutting While the film's sound is becoming beautiful, the picture is having its own adventure. Negative cutters use **key numbers** embedded in the edge of the workprint and negative to conform the original camera negative to the picture edits made by the editor. This glued-together negative is printed to create the first real version of the film, the silent **first answer print**. The director and director of photography use the first answer print to make decisions about the brightness and color of each shot. This process, called color timing or grading, may require several grading sessions and prints before the film has the desired look.

The Mix The sound elements are finished and there's a print to project, so the film is ready to mix. Rarely does a mixer string up all of the elements of a film and mix everything at the same time. Instead, the film undergoes a series of **premixes** (predubs) in which one group of elements is mixed in isolation. Usually the first premix is the dialogue, since production sound serves as the foundation on which all other sounds are built. The timbre, noise level, and attitude of the dialogue premix will determine how subtle, loud, wide, or aggressive the rest of the tracks can play. In the premixes, the editor's tracks are playing from the 1000-ft rolls of mag stripe and are recorded to 1000-ft loads of multitrack fullcoat, onto which up to six tracks can be recorded.

Premixes are about detail, getting the most out of the dialogue or the effects, background, and so on. Here you focus shots to direct the viewer's attention or to enhance the emotion of a scene. The premixes are combined in the final mix to create the best flow, to move the narrative forward, and to create the best "ride" for the audience. During final mix, the playback sources are the multitrack premix recordings. The final mixed sounds are recorded onto multitrack fullcoat **stems**, keeping the final, balanced, beautified dialogue, effects, and music separate on different fullcoats to more easily create different versions of the final film mix, whether for international, television, or airplane distribution. The stems are then combined to make a **print master**, whose number of channels depends on the distribution format (Dolby Stereo, Dolby Digital, SDDS, DTS). The print master goes to a lab where it's converted to an optical negative, which is then joined with the color-corrected printing negative to form a release print. Premiere, popcorn, fame, and fortune follow.

Don't let the whirlwind nature of this description scare you. The details of the audio side of this production methodology will be discussed in much greater detail later. *What's important is to understand the overall workflow of making a movie.* Take another look at Figure 2-1 before we move on to how most films are made today, how the new system compares to the mechanical method, and where lie the traps that can get you into trouble.

Making Movies in the Digital Age

Moviemaking today isn't all that different from when picture meant film and sounds were on mag. But the small differences between then and now can be crippling if ignored. Two steps in the process require great attention. First, the film must be transferred to videotape (which runs at a different speed than film does) while maintaining an absolute reference between a frame of film and its matching video frame to ensure accurate negative matching. Second, you must remember that NTSC video doesn't run at 60 Hz (30 fps) but rather at 59.94 Hz (29.97 fps). If you keep your wits about you regarding the **telecine** transfer and pay attention to NTSC sample rates, you'll find electronic editing pretty straightforward.

We'll now look at seven electronic work models, with postproduction in PAL, NTSC, and high-definition 24p. Again, remember the most basic questions you should ask when approaching a sound for film job:

- How was it shot?
- Where and how will it be posted?

A Brief Pause to Discuss Negative Cutting in the Modern World

Avid's Film Composer and Final Cut Pro's Cinema Tools came into being to allow editors cutting on workstations to create accurate negative cut lists. It's vital that the negative cutters know that a certain video frame refers exactly to a corresponding frame of negative. This is not a good place for approximations.

Negative cutting was more straightforward in the days of sprockets. You simply put the 35 mm workprint into a sync block, read the key numbers from the print (numbers that were printed directly from the original negative onto the workprint), and found the corresponding piece of negative. Simple. Now we edit on workstations, which offer countless creative advantages over film but make negative matching more complicated. Remember, you can't directly load film negative into a workstation; you must first transfer the image to videotape or at least create some sort of a videolike stream and load that. This process is called the telecine transfer and it's done at the lab or at a boutique "dailies facility" working in conjunction with the lab. Since neither PAL nor NTSC video runs at film speed, maintaining a relationship between film frames and video frames is a bit of a black art.

In the NTSC world, the transfer from film (24 fps) to tape (29.97 fps) is accomplished by scanning one frame of negative onto two successive fields of video, then scanning the next frame onto three fields of video, and so on. This cycle, called the 2:3:2 pulldown,[10] continues for frames A, B, C, and D; on the fifth frame the cycle starts over.[11] As long as the transfer engineer takes care to start this "A-frame" cycle at the right place and then carefully logs all of the appropriate information into a **FLEx file**, the Avid can keep track of the redundant fields and deliver a reliable negative cut list. During telecine, and for the rest the postproduction process until the picture is again on film, all picture and sound elements are slowed by 0.1 percent, to the NTSC crystal rate of 59.94 Hz. While the project stays in the video/computer world, sound and picture run at 29.97 fps.

Back on the other side of the ocean, PAL folks don't even try to transfer the 24 fps negative to videotape at its natural speed. Instead, they accelerate it to

---

[10] The 2:3:2 pulldown has many names: 3:2 pulldown, 2:3 pulldown, 2:3:2 pulldown, and so on. It's all the same thing.

[11] A concise explanation of the NTSC 3:2 pulldown can be found in *The Film Editing Room Handbook, Third Edition*, by Norman Hollyn (Los Angeles: Lone Eagle Press, 1999, pp. 105–14).

25 fps and transfer it directly to tape with no interfield shenanigans.[12] The upside of this procedure is that there develops a direct relationship of film frames to video frames (25 film frames = 25 video frames), so it's easy to establish a database that will form the basis of the negative cut list. The downside is that after telecine transfer you're left with a master videotape, usually a Betacam, with a picture running 4 percent fast, so you can't sync with your audio—yet. There are no quick video sound dailies in PAL.

Once the negative is transferred to tape, the speeded-up picture is loaded into the picture editing computer. The workstation is then placed in "film mode," which again slows the film to its native 24 fps, keeping track of which fields the workstation doubled to make the speed change. Now the sound—which never changed speed—is loaded into the workstation and synced with the picture. As in the NTSC model, the picture assistant will create a database that contains scene, take, timecode, sound roll number, and so on. This information will again present itself as a negative cut list for the lab and an edit decision list (EDL) for the sound department. (An EDL is a document that describes every event in a film. It can detail both sound and picture edits, and it's an important tool for dialogue editors. We will encounter EDLs throughout this book.)

Keep in mind that, whether in PAL or NTSC, the sync of the film is determined by the assistant picture editor, who often works late at night, is occasionally not terrifically experienced, and may not be secure enough to ask questions. When you start a project and get a locked film from the picture department, remember how the syncing was done—by a human, not by God. Always question sync.

Working in an NTSC Environment

Pullups, pulldowns, impossible-to-remember sample rates, noninteger frame rates—these are the intricacies of NTSC. Those used to jumping through these hoops take it all for granted. But to those used to working in PAL, undertaking a project in NTSC is intimidating.

Actually, there's only one truth you must respect to avoid the pitfalls of NTSC: *At any given stage in the process, the picture and sound must have the same reference.* Whether you're at "film speed" (44.1/48 kHz, 30 frame TC, 60 Hz line

---

[12] There is a PAL postproduction method in which film negative is transferred to tape at 24 fps before loading the Avid, to allow for sound dailies. However, the 25 fps technique is more common.

reference, 24 fps film) or "pulled down" for video (44.056/47.952 kHz, 29.97 frame TC, 59.94 Hz line reference, 23.976 fps film speed), keep the picture and the sound at the same reference at any given step and you'll have no problems. You can pull up and pull down as many times as you want; just do the same to sound and picture at each step and your NTSC blues will vanish.

A Note about Drop-Frame Timecode

Let's get something straight. "Non-drop-frame timecode" does *not* mean 30 fps and "drop-frame timecode" does *not* mean 29.97 fps. The dropness or non-dropness of a timecode flavor has to do with how it counts, not how fast it runs. A drop-frame calendar (say, the Gregorian) includes leap years to keep it in sync with the solar year, while a non-drop-frame calendar (the Islamic, for instance) has no mechanism to keep it in solar sync. Both calendars run at the same rate—a day is a day, an hour is an hour, a minute is a minute. But one has a built-in "hitch" to force it back into sync with the seasons, while the other doesn't. Christmas always holds a hope of snow, but Ramadan can occur in any season.

SMPTE timecode works much the same way. Both non-drop-frame and drop-frame timecode count 30 frames per second, 60 seconds per minute, and so forth. The difference is that with 29.97 drop-frame timecode an hour of timecode equals an hour of clock time because the counting mechanism has a way of realigning with reality, whereas an hour of 29.97 non-drop-frame timecode is 3 seconds—18 frames longer than a clock hour. Still, despite its seeming inaccuracy, non-drop-frame's simplicity makes it the standard in film production.

Single-System NTSC Production and Editing

There are no secrets to single-system NTSC production. It's very straightforward—the sound is recorded onto the videotape along with the picture, and there's no speed change throughout postproduction. The timecode for the sound and the picture is the same, so it's the most straightforward of all of the processes. Figure 2-2 shows the NTSC single-system workflow.

After the shoot, the video dailies are loaded into the picture workstation, the picture is usually highly compressed to allow for manageable storage. There's nothing to sync, plus sound and picture share the same timecode so list management is not complicated.

When picture editing is finished, the editor makes an **OMF** and sound EDLs for the sound department. The OMF (which will be discussed in Chapter 5)

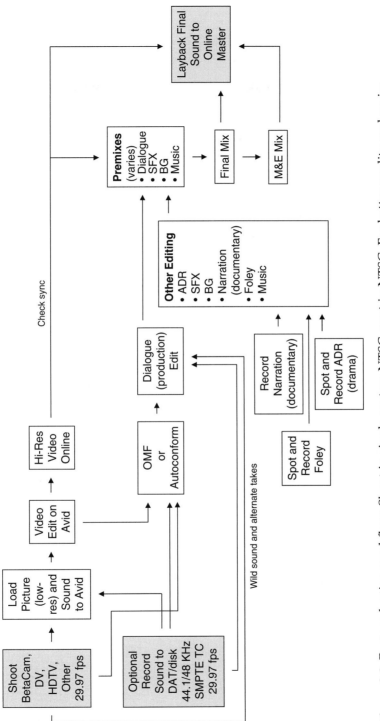

Figure 2-2 Postproduction workflow: Shoot in single-system NTSC, post in NTSC. For better quality and easier postproduction, backup sound can be recorded separately, using the same timecode as the camera's. An OMF of the picture editor's sound files and edits can be used for dialogue, or the sound team can auto-assemble the original production sounds using the master tapes, an EDL from the Avid, and appropriate software.

is a postproduction Rosetta stone that enables the dialogue editor to work directly with the tracks from the Avid. The EDL and the original field recordings are used by the sound team to recreate the picture editor's sound edits—if necessary—by going back to the original recordings. If the sound was initially loaded into the Avid via analogue or if there are other sound problems, the sound assistant will **auto-assemble** (or **PostConform**) the film using the EDLs to automatically recreate all of the picture editor's sound edits with audio from the original tapes.

The dialogue editor also uses the audio EDLs to find alternate sound takes during the editing process. From this point on, electronic postproduction resembles the mechanical film model. It's true that during the mix, sounds will play from a DAW or hard-disk player, and will likely be recorded to a hard-disk recorder rather than to fullcoat, but those differences are cosmetic rather than structural.

Meanwhile, the picture department redigitizes the necessary images, this time with no compression. The online edit, followed by color correction and titles, yields a high-quality picture, into which the mixed sound is inserted.

Shoot Film (24 fps), Record Sound on Tape, Edit Picture and Sound in NTSC

Once again: *At any given stage in the process, the picture and sound must have the same reference,* either 60 Hz (film speed) or 59.94 Hz (video speed). Over the course of production and postproduction, the image and sound will speed up and slow down several times between film and video speed (see Figure 2-3), but as long as they work in tandem, there will be no problems. Really.

At the shoot, the sound recorder is running at 44.1 or 48 kHz and the film camera is running at a fixed 24 fps. The DAT (or ¼" tape) will record 30 fps timecode. When the film is transferred to videotape, it undergoes the 2:3:2 pulldown. This doesn't affect its speed, but since the telecine is referenced to the video clock rate of 59.94 Hz, the picture is slowed by one-tenth of a percent to 23.976 fps. If the original audio field recordings are to be synchronized in the telecine, that DAT player must also be locked to the video reference generator so that it will be running at the same rate as the film.

The video recorder, whether Betacam, U-Matic, or the like, runs at the video reference speed and the timecode on the tape is 29.97 fps, almost always non-drop for film postproduction. Because sound and picture are running at the same speed, the DAT sound can be synced to the picture in the telecine transfer bay, but this would certainly not be my first choice. I'd wait to sync sound and picture in the Avid.

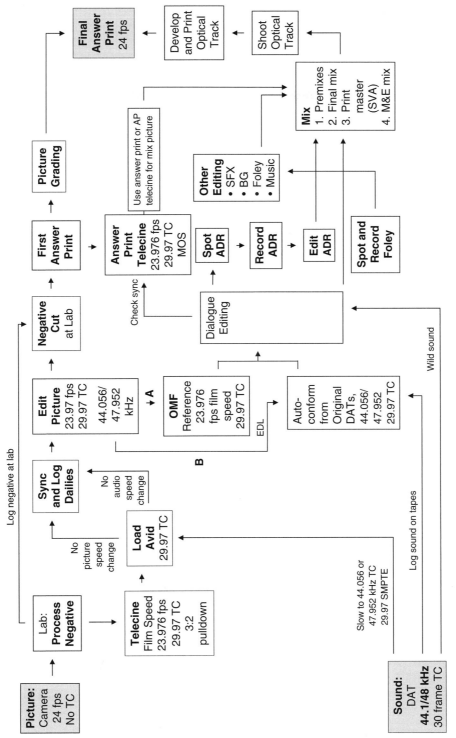

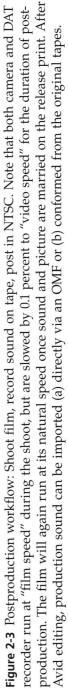

Figure 2-3 Postproduction workflow: Shoot film, record sound on tape, post in NTSC. Note that both camera and DAT recorder run at "film speed" during the shoot, but are slowed by 0.1 percent to "video speed" for the duration of post-production. The film will again run at its natural speed once sound and picture are married on the release print. After Avid editing, production sound can be imported (a) directly via an OMF or (b) conformed from the original tapes.

The assistant picture editor loads the tapes into the Avid/FCP, along with the DAT sound. The TC DAT player must be referenced to video while loading sound into the picture workstation, thus pulling down the sample rate to 44.056 or 47.952 kHz. For the rest of the process, all video and audio equipment are locked to NTSC video reference. Once sound and picture elements are loaded into the Avid, the assistant synchronizes the shots, again providing information so that the computer knows the offset values between sound and picture. This information is used at the end of the editing process to allow for accurate reconforming of audio elements.

The rest of the process resembles the mechanical film model, even though the equipment is a bit more modern. Throughout the remainder of this double-system workflow, picture and sound remain locked to video reference, 59.94 Hz. Even the mix, where you're likely watching a projected film image rather than a videotape, will usually occur at 59.94 Hz. If you're editing at 44.056 or 47.952 kHz and want to add some new synchronous material—music, for example—it must be loaded at video, not film, speed. Otherwise, you'll have two conflicting timebases within your edit list—a good formula for losing sync.

Only when the negative is cut, the film is printed, and the mix is complete is the film projected at its "natural" speed of 24 fps.

Shoot Film (24 fps) or Tape, Record Sound on Hard-Disk Recorder, Edit in NTSC

It's now common to record location sound on hard-disk recorders, forgoing tape altogether. Cantar, Deva, and 774 are among the players in this ever more crowded field. Recording on location without tape offers easier backup, far more tracks, and increased versatility. New generation analogue-to-digital converters, combined with much smarter analogue and digital circuitry, offer better sound than DAT recorders. With sample rates of up to 192 kHz and 24-bit resolution, sound detail and dynamics are vastly improved. Also, the location mixer can add **metadata** notes to the soundfiles and can painlessly provide individual unmixed tracks as well as mixdowns for the picture editor. (See Figure 2-4.) It's almost too good to be true.

Effective use of this new technology, however, entails a bit more than swapping out the old kit for new. Just as picture and sound cutting room procedures and culture had to retool when sprockets fell to digital workstations, so too must the location mixer and editorial team modify some of their work habits to fully exploit the advantages of hard-disk field recorders.

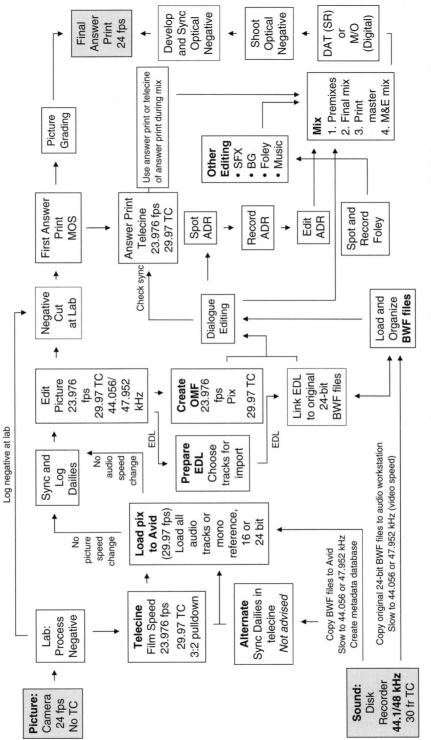

Figure 2-4 Postproduction workflow: Shoot film, record sound on hard-disk recorder, post in NTSC. Original recording soundfiles can be copied directly to the Avid and to the sound department's drives.

A disk-recorded shoot differs little from film production with a DAT recorder. The recorder rolls, the camera comes up to speed, and a clapper is used to synchronize the two. Some hard-disk recorders allow for offloading to an external hard drive, while others permit only transfer to DVD-RAMs. Some can be programmed to name files as they go, while others require naming take by take. Some location mixers name files based on scene and take or camera setup and take (when they have time), while others simply let the recorder name files by recording order. For these reasons, a bit of planning is in order.

If you're shooting in a tape format, whether high definition (HD) or standard definition (SD), and recording sound on hard disk, there are several routes you can take to synchronize the video camera and recorder. You can use radio links to transmit the camera's timecode to the audio recorder, or you can transmit the recorder's timecode to the camera. Both of these techniques have some serious downsides.[13]

The most reliable and common way to get a video recorder/camera and a hard-disk recorder to work in tandem is to attach a very stable free-running timecode generator to the camera and record its output to one of the camera's unused audio channels. At least twice daily, synchronize the camera's time-code generator with the timecode clock on the hard-disk recorder. This pre-serves the integrity of the videotape's longitudinal timecode—making for easier video postproduction—and it can be used on multiple-camera shoots. When the videotapes are digitized and synchronized in the Avid, the audio timecode, which is on an audio channel of the tape, is attached to each video image. Since all tracks of a take have a common timecode, it's easy to sync each track to the corresponding image.

At the end of each shooting day, the sound recordist drops by the location cutting room and transfers the day's spoils to an editing drive. As soon as the picture telecine tapes are back from the lab, the picture assistant can start syncing dailies, as there are no longer DATs to digitize into the Avid.

Working in a PAL Environment

The PAL world, with its 25 fps, 50 Hz fixed realities and never a dropped frame, is decidedly less complicated than its North American cousin.[14] Of

---

[13] For a detailed discussion of incorporating hard-disk recorders into a shoot, see *Aaton Audio: Post Chain, v11* (Aaton, s.a, February 2006, *www.aaton.com*).

[14] For a clear, brief overview of working in PAL, see "PAL Basics: Film Sound for the Rest of the World" by Douglas Murray, in *The Motion Picture Editors Guild Magazine* (vol. 23, no. 2, March/April 2002).

course, filmmaking in an NTSC environment is also a snap once you've caught on. Still, it's very comfortable living in a world in which 25 fps really is 25 fps, not a slightly slow-witted relative.

Single-System PAL

If you're editing a single-system-originated project, shot on videotape or HD with no extra sound recorder, there's virtually no difference working in PAL or NTSC aside from the obvious frame rate. Figure 2-5 shows the PAL workflow.

North Americans, remember that you'll never run into frames 25, 26, 27, 28, or 29 when working in PAL. Source video and source audio will have the same timecode, of course, since this is single system.

If your project was shot at 25 fps on HD or SD video for film blow-up, remember to put your **sync pop** (beep, plop, etc.) two video frames later than you usually would, since it must be 48 *film* frames before the first frame of action. So, rather than placing the sync pop for reel 1 at 00:59:58:00, for example, place it at 00:59:58:02. This way, when the video image is scanned to film, there will indeed be 48 frames between the plop and the beginning of the reel.

Shoot Film (24 fps), Record Sound on Tape, Edit Picture and Sound in PAL

This is still the most common production workflow for low-budget films in the PAL world. (See Figure 2-6.) Things will change as shooting on film gives way to electronic cinematography and location mixers choose hard-disk recorders over tape. For now, though, many films are made this way. Unlike its NTSC relative, in which the picture department has it pretty easy (except for policing the telecine transfer for proper A-framing), double-system PAL is very easy on the sound department but requires a bit of thinking by the picture editor. The fundamental problem is that film runs at 24 fps and PAL video runs at 25. Given this reality, there's no elegant way to maintain proper speed and sync while transferring from film to PAL videotape.

Unlike the highly regular NTSC 2:3:2 pulldown, which is jitterless to normal humans, the PAL 24 → 25 telecine transfer adds one highly visible repeated field every 12 frames. Films transferred to PAL at 24 fps display a telltale twice-per-second bump in what should be smooth motion, such as camera pans or slow car bys.

Timecode on the DAT will be 25 fps, since the project will be edited in a PAL/EBU environment. The speed of the sound will never change, whereas the picture will make a brief foray from 24 fps (90 feet/minute) to 25 fps (93

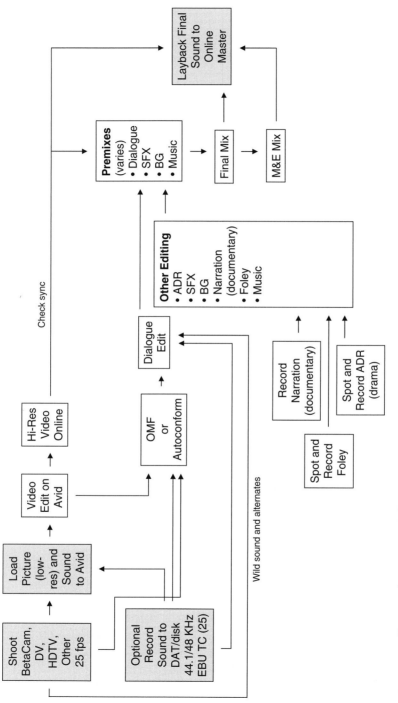

Figure 2-5 Postproduction workflow: Shoot single-system PAL, post in PAL. As with single-system production in NTSC, speed remains constant throughout the process.

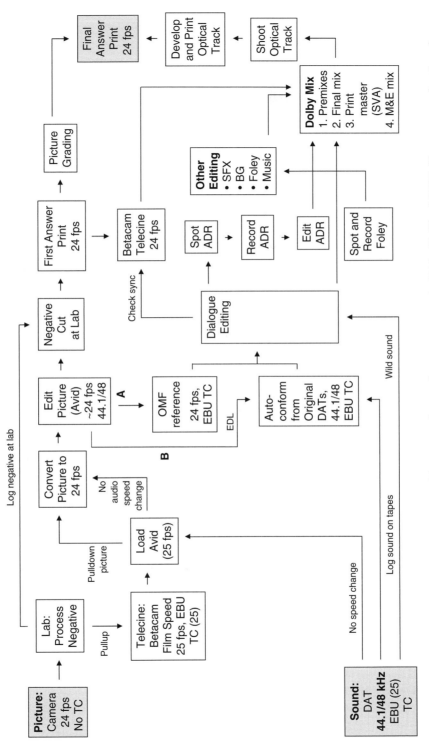

Figure 2-6 Postproduction workflow: Shoot film, record sound on tape, post in PAL. Unlike NTSC film postproduction, here the sound never changes speed throughout the process. As with NTSC projects, edited sound can be imported (a) directly from the Avid, or can be reconformed (b) from the original tapes.

feet, 12 frames/minute) and back. The "picture dumps," the videotapes made from the Avid for the sound department, must run at 24 fps, but negative cutters usually request a 25 fps tape for their purposes. The first answer print is transferred to video at 24 fps, not 25, as picture must stay at its natural speed at this point in the process. As a result, the telecine of the first answer print always displays the telltale bump that comes from repeating a field every 12 frames. The speed is right, but the motion looks goofy.

Shoot Film (24 fps), Record Sound on Hard-Disk Recorder, Edit Picture and Sound in PAL

More and more films are being recorded with hard-disk recorders, so you'll eventually face this work model. (See Figure 2-7.) On the picture side, nothing's changed from the DAT paradigm. The picture still makes its round-trip speed change, ending up at its original 24 fps. Only on the sound side of the story are things a bit more complicated because the larger word lengths available with hard-disk recordings.

Soundfiles that are 24 bit can be loaded into an advanced Avid such as Adrenaline can be imported directly into a digital audio workstation via OMF. Assuming there are no audio problems, you can use the OMF—no need to return to the original files. If, on the other hand, the picture editor worked on an older or more modest Avid, he used 16-bit sound. After picture editing, the original 24-bit files must be relinked to the Avid OMF so that the sound department can take advantage of the larger original word lengths.

Shooting and Posting at 25 fps (in PAL)

Even though it's no longer rocket science to shoot 24 fps film and edit in PAL or NTSC, you can still find a number of producers in the PAL world who choose to shoot their feature films at 25 fps. With this method, the film stays at its natural speed throughout the postproduction process and is slowed down to 24 fps only during projections; also:

- The picture editor can work on virtually any workstation, so no more hunting for Film Composer or Cinema Tools.
- This technique offers an easy way to avoid flicker when shooting a film involving lots of television screens or data monitors.
- Original sound recordings can be easily synchronized to the telecine dailies, since there's no speed change in the transfer.

There are two downsides to shooting at 25 fps. One is not your problem; one is. At 25 fps, film rushes through the camera 4 percent faster than at 24 fps,

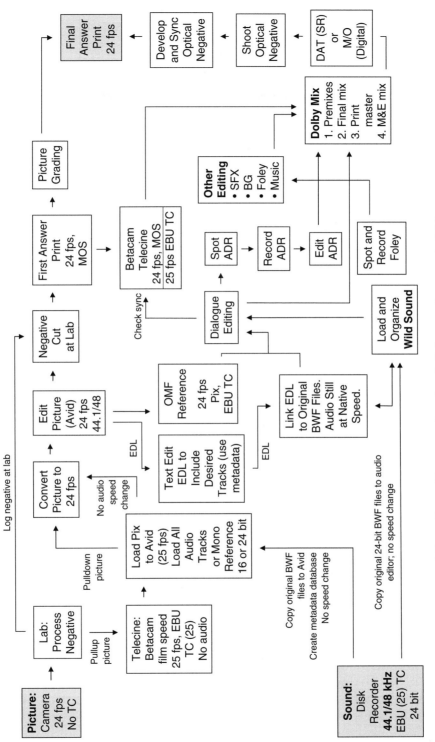

Figure 2-7 Postproduction workflow: Shoot film, record on hard-disk recorder, post in PAL.

so more is used. You don't care about this unless you have a piece of the film's profits. However, there's a sound issue to consider. Shooting and posting at 25 fps doesn't cause a problem until the film is finished and its time to screen the print—at 24 fps. Not only will all action be slower than you're used to seeing (not much you can do about that), but the sound will be heard at a lower pitch. This may not make a discernable difference with dialogue (although everyone will sound a bit sleepy), but you'll notice the difference with music. Everything will be flat, and those with perfect pitch will howl like dogs when hearing "impossible" chords.

The solution? After the mix, during the print mastering process, you can raise the pitch of the entire mix by 4 percent. The 25 fps print will indeed sound sharp, but when played at the world standard 24 fps, the pitch will be correct. Again, however, we have a downside. When pitch-shifting a full mix with dialogue, music, and effects components, you run a decent chance of encountering glitches. Many supervising sound editors forgo the pitch-shift altogether, preferring a certain pitch error to an uncertain artifact problem. A classic no-win situation. If you do choose to pitch-shift, make a copy of the print master prior to pitch correction. This will be your TV audio master, which will of course run at 25 fps. There's nothing dumber than starting with a 25 fps master, pitching up for the filmprint, and then pitching down for TV.

If your project is intended for 24 fps film release, the head plop for each reel will fall two frames later than you expect it to. If this is a TV-only project, the plop will go at its normal place, two seconds before the beginning of program.

Shooting Film and Recording Sound for PAL TV

It's possible to shoot film at 24 fps for 25-frame PAL television, but it's not a director's first choice. The 4 percent additional film stock cost may not appeal to producers, but the nasty PAL 24 → 25 frame speed adjustment or the even more unseemly and noticeable bumps means that most PAL film-for-television productions are shot at 25 fps.

This is good news for the sound department, since it leaves little room for silly mistakes down the production line. You'll record at 48 kHz with **EBU** 25 fps timecode, and unlike its feature film cousin, you can sync the sound directly to the Betacam dailies so that everyone can hear the sync rushes. If the picture department chooses to load the Avid with the sound from the Beta telecine masters rather than from the original DATs, you'll have to do a PostConform (or equivalent) after picture editing, as the sound on the Beta will result in a compromised OMF.

High Definition

High definition (HD) is everywhere. It's increasingly seen in production as an alternative to film negative, and it appears in postproduction, where high-resolution digital files allow for multigeneration visual effects at a price and quality superior to that of traditional optical effects. HD is rapidly being accepted as a consumer television format. Plus, digital cinema is quickly making inroads in the movie distribution market. Unlike video or film formats, HD isn't something you can easily label, however. Basically it's any format that offers higher resolution than SD NTSC or PAL video, and that's not very difficult to do. But there's no such thing as "just HD." Instead, there are scores of formats, frame rates, and resolutions.

Many issues must be taken into account when launching into an HD production. There are just so many variables. Frame rates of 23.976, 24, 29.97, 30, 59.94, and 60 fps are allowed by the Advanced Television Standards Committee. And that's just for NTSC. Add in resolutions and scan technique, and you end up with more than 20 combinations. Table 2-1 lists a few legal HD frame rates for NTSC production.[15]

Since manufacturers have adopted different standards, similar cameras may reference at different rates. Differences between digital recorders only compound the problems. The higher the number of variables, the greater the amount of organizational work that inevitably falls on assistant editors in all departments of a film project. But before breaking into a panic, remember that the same rule that applies to NTSC production applies to HD: *At any given stage in the process, the picture and sound must have the same reference.* If, at each stage of production and postproduction, sound and picture maintain the same reference, you can intelligently wade through the morass of HD filmmaking.

Table 2-1 NTSC High-definition Frame Rates

Resolution	Type of Scanning	Frame Rates (fps)
1920 × 1080	Progressive	23.976, 24, 29.97, 30
	Interlaced	29.97, 30
1280 × 720	Progressive	23.976, 24, 29.97, 30, 59.94, 60

---

[15] Chris Meyer. "Designing for HD: An Essential Checklist" (*www.filmmaking.com*).

Ironically, the best way to approach HD workflow is to treat it like film.[16] If the project was shot on 24p (or 23.98p), create SD work tapes and edit with them as you normally would. For film projects, transfer the negative to HD as though you were working with an SD electronic editing model. In PAL, transfer the negative at 50 Hz (24 fps) to a 24p HD recorder. From this you can make all necessary PAL offline copies. For NTSC, lock the telecine and the 24p recorder to 59.94 Hz (23.976 fps). Standard 29.97 NTSC work copies can be created from this HD master. Just remember to keep the reference the same for sound and picture at all stages in the postproduction process, and you won't have any problems.

When the finished job is scanned to film for release, sound and picture will both be referenced to 60 Hz and will fall into sync. Many filmmakers shooting HD but expecting to release on film choose to shoot at 24p since it's easy to create an excellent filmprint from that. TV formats are also relatively compatible with 24p. Well-heeled productions may shoot 23.98p with sound at 29.97 fps and then edit on a workstation capable of storing and displaying HD images (and equipped with a dizzying amount of storage). You can also shoot at 24p/48 kHz as long as (again!) sound and picture are running at the same rate at any given step of the process.[17]

To survive a production shot on HD, or shot on film and transferred to HD, make a detailed chart of the project's workflow *before* shooting begins. Discuss with the director of photography, the supervising sound editor, and the picture editor what each hopes to accomplish and come up with a plan that doesn't give any player an excuse to change the rules in midstream. Specify frame rates, timecode, and sample rates for each step of the process and make sure that everyone understands and concurs.

Keep the reference rates correct and you'll get through the job. However, remember that HD is a relatively new format whose "common knowledge" rules haven't filtered down to low-budget producers just yet. So expect that everything in the field was done wrong, and be prepared for surprises—another reason for knowing as much as possible about all of the filmmaking workflows.

---

[16] For much more detailed information on HD shooting rates and their implications, see *High Definition and 24p Cinematography* by Paul Wheeler (Oxford: Focal Press, 2003).

[17] Visit *http://24p.com/reference.htm* for an ever-growing series of papers on working in a 24p environment, presented by Michael Phillips and others.

CHAPTER 3

A Quick Look at Picture Editing

More than any other sound editor, the dialogue editor needs to know what happens in the picture department. When we remain ignorant of "that picture stuff," things go wrong and we don't know why. If we don't understand the way picture editors think, we can't understand the tracks they give us. And without a decent grasp of the picture cutting process and the issues facing picture editors, we don't know if we're being snowed or if it really *is* impossible to give us what we need.

The picture editor and the picture department assistants have huge responsibilities. At one level they must organize, absorb, and edit the vast collection of shots from the filming in order tell a story, develop characters, and create sequences that are more than the sum of their parts. At the same time, they must wrangle a huge database of picture and audio offsets so that negative cutters and sound editors can make sense of their edit room decisions. Keep in mind this unlikely balance between wizard/artist and bean counter/IT administrator when you're having a tough time relating to your picture editor.

A Picture Editing Primer (NTSC Version)

The following idealized description of film editing won't make a film editor out of you, but it should give you an idea of the workflow in a modern picture editing room. Pay attention to the organization, methodology, procedures, and issues involved, and you'll be better equipped to communicate with picture editors and more likely to get what you need from them.

Telecine and Digitization

At the end of a day's shooting the negative is rushed to the lab for processing. Once dry it's taken to the **telecine** bay for transfer to videotape. A telecine works much like a projector shining into a video camera that's synchronized to the projector's shutter. A powerful cathode ray tube is the source of light, and the image is scanned rather than merely videotaped. The telecine operator has enormous control over brightness, contrast, and color, but with dailies the transfer is usually **one light**, a term from film printing meaning that no great care was taken to color-correct each shot, but rather a decent, average setup was used. Depending on the needs of the picture editing department, the videotape format may be Betacam SP, Digital Betacam, DVCAM, U-Matic, or S-VHS.

Increasingly, high-budget productions are forgoing transfer to tape and instead creating high-definition files directly from the telecine. It's only a matter of time before this process is democratized and all transfers go straight to disk. Tape or file, the process and the bottleneck issues are the same. In certain circumstances, the audio from the shoot—whether originating on DAT, Nagra-D, DA-88, or hard-disk recorder—is transferred to the videotape during the telecine transfer (not recommended). Otherwise, the sound is transferred and synchronized in the picture-cutting room.

Transferring negative to tape without developing a relationship between film frames and video frames is a waste of time. Remember, sooner or later, a **negative cutter** will have the job of precisely recreating the picture editor's decisions. Unlike the picture editor working in a virtual world with many levels of undo, the negative cutter works with a pair of scissors, with one chance to get it right. This is no place for approximations. For the telecine videotape to be useful, you must know the relationship between any given videotape frame and the corresponding film frame and original audio timecode. If you don't, you'll find yourself in darkness once the picture editing is finished.

Establishing a relationship between the telecine videotape and the original sound recording is no great feat, given that each carries timecode to identify every frame. But what about the original film negative, which holds no timecode? Thankfully, original camera negative film is manufactured with a chunk of data printed twice per foot, outside the sprockets. Machine-readable **Keykode**[1] barcodes contain address information as well as codes for manufacturer, film stock, and lot number. This information replicates the human-readable key number. During telecine transfer, the colorist creates a record of pertinent information from the film negative, the sound recording (if used), and the transfer videotape.

---

[1] Keykode is a trademark of the Eastman Kodak Company.

Generically, the colorist's record is called a **Telecine Log**, but the two most common varieties are **FLEx** (Film Log EDL Exchange Protocol) files, developed by da Vinci Systems, and **ALE** (Avid Log Exchange) files, developed by Digidesign. These make up the database used to track edits throughout the picture editing process. Limited fields of the FLEx files can be recorded to **VITC** lines on the videotape, thus making foot+frame and **pulldown** information machine readable. One Telecine Log printout, shown in Figure 3-1, is provided for each videotape.

Back in the cutting room, the assistant picture editor digitizes the videotapes, using the telecine logs to tell the Avid all there is to know about scenes, takes, camera rolls (the name given to each roll of original negative), Keykode, and pulldown. The Avid now also knows how to decode the 4-frame A-frame sequence so that it can unambiguously match a video frame to its film parent. If the original sound was transferred and synchronized in the

```
000 Manufacturer Aaton No. 021 Equip Keylink Version 9.78 Flex 1006
010 Title LOST IN JORDAN
011 Client Nessie Prods


012 Shoot 2005-05-07 Xfer Date 2006-05-08


100 Edit 0001 Field A1 PAL
110 Scene Take Cam Roll Sound 12:18:54:13.0
120 Scrpt
200 35 25.00 000088 000347+06 Key EH089597 003860+00 p1
300 Assemble 044 At 03:19:00:00.0 For 00:03:42:07.0
400 KLink 25.00 Fps At 12:18:54:13.0


100 Edit 0002 Field A1 PAL
110 Scene Take Cam Roll Sound 12:30:10:04.0
120 Scrpt
200 35 25.00 000088 000352+03 Key EH089597 004209+02 p1
300 Assemble 044 At 03:22:43:11.0 For 00:03:45:09.0
400 KLink 25.00 Fps At 12:30:10:04.0
```

Figure 3-1 Example of a FLEx file made during a telecine transfer session. This information is used to establish a relationship between film negative Keykode and videotape timecode; it will follow the picture through the editing process to facilitate accurate negative cutting.

Figure 3-2 Syncing a shot in an Avid. Once the sync relationship is established between sound and picture for each shot, an offset database facilitates creation of video and audio EDLs and a negative cut list. The picture editor can forget about the many timecodes, since the machine will remember this vital information.

telecine bay, the assistant picture editor will digitize sound along with picture. Even though the audio timecode will match the video timecode (the two are now on the same tape and in sync, after all), the FLEx or ALE file will enable the Avid to generate an EDL[2] that refers to the original DAT or HD timecode or to the metadata-equipped **BWF** soundfile. Without this, you wouldn't be able to **autoconform** the dialogue from the original tapes. If the telecine videotape doesn't include audio, the assistant picture editor will load the sound into the Avid, sync the claps for each take, and supply the missing audio data for each take (**sound roll** number, scene and take, etc.). This is shown in Figure 3-2.

---

[2] An EDL (edit decision list) is an event-by-event description of a video-based program, with all picture and sound edits detailed. We'll discuss the EDL in great detail in Chapter 5.

More and more films are originating their picture on something other than film negative. As DV and HD photography becomes more common, negative cutting will become less a part of the filmmaking process. For now you need to remember that a great deal of picture editing hygiene centers around painless negative cutting.

Organizing the Material

Before beginning to break up the long (up to an hour) digitized dailies rolls into individual scenes and takes, the assistant will check one more time that the metadata accurately reflects the realities of the videotape. Timecode, camera and sound roll numbers, scene, and take labels must be correct at this point; once editing begins it's much harder to find and resolve problems.

The assistant editor organizes every scene and take into **bins** (Avidspeak for folders), as shown in Figure 3-3, arranged however is most comfortable for

	Name	Start	Duration	KN Start	KN Duration	Labroll	Shoot Date
	3/24/3 V	04:26:38:16	58:08	EH 31 6648-5445+12	91+02	00011T	2005-11-03
	3/24/2 V	04:25:37:02	1:02:11	EH 31 6648-5349+09	97+09	00011T	2005-11-03
	3/24/1 V	04:24:41:04	57:09	EH 31 6648-5262+03	89+10	00011T	2005-11-03
	3/23/4 V	04:23:34:12	1:09:14	EH 31 6648-5158+00	108+11	00011T	2005-11-03
	3/23/3 V	04:22:51:09	43:03	EH 31 6648-6233+12	67+06	00011T	2005-11-03
	3/23/2 V	04:21:19:13	1:37:18	EH 31 6648-6090+04	152+11	00011T	2005-11-03
	3/23/1 V	04:20:00:00	1:21:09	EH 31 6648-5966+00	127+02	00011T	2005-11-03
	3/22/6	04:12:16:12	1:21:13	EH 31 6650-9600+08	127+06	00010T	2005-11-03
	3/22/5	04:10:00:00	2:16:12	EH 31 6650-8793+00	213+04	00010T	2005-11-03
	3/22/4	04:06:11:06	2:13:02	EH 31 6648-6551+02	207+15	00009T	05-11-03
	3/22/4 V	04:06:11:06	2:14:19	EH 31 6648-6551+02	210+09	00009T	05-11-03
	3/22/3	04:04:15:08	1:59:03	EH 31 6648-6370+00	186+02	00009T	05-11-03
	3/22/3 V	04:04:15:08	1:59:03	EH 31 6648-6370+00	186+02	00009T	05-11-03
	6P1/25/3 V	04:40:00:00	2:09:22	EH 56 1324-7985+01	202+15	00012T	2005-11-03
	6P1/25/2 V	04:30:31:10	1:23:15	EH 31 6648-5025+01	130+10	00011T	2005-11-03
	6P1/25/1 V	04:29:30:07	1:02:04	EH 31 6648-4929+09	97+02	00011T	2005-11-03
	6BP1/27/2 V	04:47:24:10	42:15	EH 56 1324-7177+08	66+09	00012T	2005-11-03
	6BP1/27/1 V	04:46:46:02	38:08	EH 56 1324-7897+01	59+14	00012T	2005-11-03
	6BP1/26/6	04:45:34:06	1:13:07	EH 56 1324-7784+13	114+08	00012T	2005-11-03
	6BP1/26/6 V	04:45:34:06	1:13:14	EH 56 1324-7784+13	114+15	00012T	2005-11-03
	6BP1/26/5 V	04:44:32:10	1:02:12	EH 56 1324-7688+03	97+10	00012T	2005-11-03
	6BP1/26/4 V	04:44:26:23	6:04	EH 56 1324-7679+10	9+10	00012T	2005-11-03
	6BP1/26/3 V	04:43:24:03	1:04:21	EH 56 1324-7581+08	101+05	00012T	2005-11-03
	6BP1/26/2 V	04:43:13:06	10:07	EH 56 1324-8287+00	16+01	00012T	2005-11-03
	6BP1/26/1 V	04:42:07:24	1:06:07	EH 56 1324-8185+00	103+09	00012T	2005-11-03
	6AP1/28/4 V	04:49:37:02	48:24	EH 56 1324-7384+13	76+08	00012T	2005-11-03
	6AP1/28/2 V	04:48:53:07	46:02	EH 56 1324-7316+06	72+00	00012T	2005-11-03
	6AP1/28/1 V	04:48:05:18	49:16	EH 56 1324-7242+01	77+09	00012T	2005-11-03
	3/24/5 V	04:28:31:03	1:00:08	EH 31 6648-4837+02	94+04	00011T	2005-11-03
	3/24/4 V	04:27:36:24	55:07	EH 31 6648-4752+08	86+06	00011T	2005-11-03

Figure 3-3 Shots in the Avid are organized in bins.

her. Typically, bins are organized by scene. To make editing easier, you can add text descriptions of each take to the existing **metadata**.[3]

The First Assembly

The picture editor screens and logs the shots. He then selects the shots that best serve each moment of the scene to construct an **assembly**. This first assembly is often numbingly long, but it allows editor and director to see for the first time how the shots interact.

Nonlinear picture editing workstations like Avid and FCP allow endless versions of scenes, so editors can easily play with the story, saving different interpretations to present to the director. Such flexibility comes at a cost: Unmanaged, this wildly growing collection of versions becomes unwieldy. To combat this disarray, editors and assistants apply standardized naming schemes to the files.[4] So, for example, a file including the editor's first cut of scenes 33 and 34 may be called "033-034 v100." The second editor's cut would be "033-034 v101." The "v101" tells you which screening the version relates to. Typically, "100" denotes the editor's cuts; "200," the director's cuts; and "300," later studio or public screening edits. Other editors rely on dates to keep track of versions, since the Avid's bin view is easily sorted by date. The specifics of version codes vary by production, but there must always be a means of knowing what the edit refers to.[5]

Sound Enters the Picture

As the editor and director work to find the story and eliminate narrative dead ends, doing their best to hide bad acting and feature the good stuff, many versions are created, all of which are logically (hopefully) logged and saved. Often, an editor will add **temp music** and **temp SFX** to the Avid cut. Temp music will almost never survive to the final soundtrack, since few small-budget films can afford John Williams or Led Zeppelin. It's there to provide

---

[3] These bins may later save your life. If for some reason you can't access the original sound rolls, you can create OMFs (Open Media Framework files) from the Avid bins that contain all of the takes. From these OMF files you can create sessions and extract correctly named soundfiles from them. It's not the easiest procedure, for you or for the picture department. But it's good to know that this option exists.

[4] This is the naming scheme discussed in *The Film Editing Room Handbook, Third Edition*, by Norman Hollyn (Los Angeles: Lone Eagle Press, pp. 167–68).

[5] Learn from this file-coding system. When you save versions of your work, apply a meaningful name that refers to the tape version, the sequence number of your work, and/or the date of the last edit. More about this in Chapter 6.

mood and rhythm and to give a screening audience (as well as the director and editor) a clue as to how the scene will work. When the composer gets involved, he'll likely be told to use the temp music track as an inspiration, to "make it just like this, but *different.*"

Don't be surprised to hear "temporary" sound effects added during the offline. Sometimes you really *do* need to hear a sound effect to understand the feel of a scene. The endlessly ringing phone, the crying baby in the next room, the downstairs neighbors who won't give us any peace . . . these sorts of things must be heard for the scenes to make sense. Moreover, as **focus groups** become ever more common, directors feel that their unfinished films must sound as "finished" as possible. Right or wrong, filmmakers assume that a public audience (or even an audience of studio executives) can't appreciate an unfinished work.

As a result, Avid edits are becoming more and more loaded with temp SFX, temp ADR, temp music, and temp Foley. An entire industry has grown from this mess. Significant chunks of a sound budget now go to temporary mixes, and supervising sound editors are often brought onboard during the picture editing process for the sole purpose of preparing and nursing countless temp mixes. The dialogue editor may or may not become involved with the temp mixes, depending on the size of the production.

As the dialogue editor, you take what comes out of the picture editing room and make sense of it. However, if the picture department loads sounds into the Avid without timecode, you have no access to them except through the OMF.[6] And if (God forbid) the **wild sounds** were loaded via analogue at very low or distorted levels, you're up a creek. Even though the sound department will theoretically replace any Avid-loaded SFX, Foley, dialogue, ADR, or music, you must be able to access what they did in picture, just in case the director falls in love with his cutting room ADR and you're forced to use it.

The only way to give the sound department some level of control over these wild sounds is to arrange for all nonproduction sounds (i.e., everything that didn't originate at the shoot) to be first transferred to a timecode format (usually TC DAT or a soundfile with a timestamp) and *then* digitized into the Avid. These sounds or files can be loaded directly into the Avid session, and as long as the filenames go unchanged you'll have no trouble relinking to the

---

[6] OMF is a means of transferring media between different machines (for example, between a Final Cut Pro picture editor and a Fairlight audio editor). Much more about this in Chapter 5.

original files, which are held for safekeeping in the sound department. This rule applies as well to temporary narration the editor may record into the Avid; record instead to TC DAT and then digitize it into the workstation. If it turns out that the director can't part with the "perfect" sound he recorded in the cutting room (which happens more often than you'd think), you'll be able auto-conform the material as though it were a production sound.

If budget allows, the assistant picture editor will regularly conform the 35mm **workprint** to the editor's Avid edit. This way there will always be a filmprint available for screenings. The temporary soundtrack—whether a rough mix within the Avid or a serious board mix—is transferred to 35mm fullcoat for double-system screening.

Screenings, Recuts, Completion, and Music

The film now undergoes a series of public and private screenings, revisions, and restructurings. At this point, both the composer and the supervising sound editor are onboard. The composer provides musical sketches for the spotted scenes. These are synchronized with the picture, discussed, and fought over. New musical sketches appear, and the process continues until the score is more or less set.

When pictures were cut on film, people thought (and worked) in 1000-ft **editorial reels**. Before the final mix, these were merged into 2000-ft **A/B reels**. In the early days of workstations, picture editors continued this convention—cutting a film in 1000- or 2000-ft reels—largely because the weak computers of the era couldn't handle longer sessions without getting slow or stupid. Today, however, many picture editors prefer to assemble their scenes into one continuous string. This way the entire film or parts thereof can be screened without changing reels. The downside is that once the picture is locked, the picture editor or assistant has to break the film into reels because labs insist on 2000-ft lengths. This is a good time for the supervising sound editor to lend a hand, to ensure that the **changeovers** occur in sound-friendly places (away from music, high-density dialogue, anticipated complex low-frequency backgrounds, etc.).

Wrap-Up

When the film is locked and broken into reels, a bit of work still remains for the picture people. The negative cutter will need a digital dump, or **output tape**, along with a special EDL and **cut list**. If you're working in PAL on a Film Composer or on Final Cut Pro with Cinema Tools, you have to make a 25 fps cut list, shown in Figure 3-4, and output tape for the negative cutter.

```
ASSEMBLE LIST
- - - -
Reel 4 v
Picture 1

                247 events        LFOA:            29834
                0 dupes           total footage:   29834
                0 opticals        total time: 00:19:53:08
```

	Footage	Record TC	Duration	First/Last Key	Tape	Start	Lab Roll	Clip Name
1.	0 83	04:00:00:00 04:00:03:08	84 00:00:03:08	KZ 32 3428-9532+09 9537+12	006	06:37:19:11 06:37:22:19	000018	94B/1.sync.01
2.	84 141	04:00:03:09 04:00:05:16	58 00:00:02:07	KZ 32 3427-4042+01 4045+10	007	07:13:17:00 07:13:19:07	000020	95G/1.sync.01
3.	142 198	04:00:05:17 04:00:07:23	57 00:00:02:06	KZ 32 3428-9541+07 9544+15	006	06:37:25:03 06:37:27:09	000018	94B/1.sync.01
4.	199 1015	04:00:07:24 04:00:40:15	817 00:00:32:16	KZ 32 3412-6498+13 6549+13	006	06:16:22:09 06:16:55:00	000016	95B/2P.U.sync.01
5.	1016 1120	04:00:40:16 04:00:44:20	105 00:00:04:04	KZ 32 3427-4071+07 4077+15	007	07:13:35:20 07:13:39:24	000020	95G/1.sync.01
6.	1121 1222	04:00:44:21 04:00:48:22	102 00:00:04:01	KZ 32 3428-9629+10 9635+15	006	06:38:21:14 06:38:25:15	000018	94C/1.sync.01

Figure 3-4 Excerpt of a cut list produced by an Avid. Armed with this list and a reference videotape, the negative cutter can assemble the original camera negative to match the film editor's cuts.

For the sound department, the assistant picture editor will make a 24 fps output tape and two sets of EDLs (audio only and video only). He'll also make an OMF (usually OMF-2).

This is when you come by to pick up the original tapes and associated sound reports, lined script, and list of characters. If the original sound recordings, whether on DAT or hard disk, aren't available to you, ask the assistant to create a series of OMFs from the bins containing all of the original takes. From this you can create sessions and then extract soundfiles. It's a bit of a hassle to work this way, but if it's all you can manage, smile and move on.

CHAPTER 4

The Sound Department

There's no such thing as a "typical" small feature film, so it's difficult to describe a typical sound team. You may be working with a team of 15 or more people, but more than likely it will be less than 6.

The Players

The following sections describe the important players who should be working on any sound team.

Supervising Sound Editor

The boss. Commonly the only member of the sound team hired directly by the production and usually selected by either the director or the picture editor. The rest of the sound team is often employed by the audio postproduction studio where the work is performed or is subcontracted by the supervising sound editor. (As with all aspects of sound postproduction, the details of employment and chain of command depend on the film as well as the local film culture.)

The supervising sound editor has the enviable task of bringing the film's sound to life, enhancing the narrative, developing characters, focusing the viewer's attention, and boosting emotions. He has the unenviable job of finishing the sound within budget, on time, and balancing the needs of the sound crew (who must remain loyal to him), the director (with whom all film birthing pains are shared), and the producer (who pays the bills and is often unimpressed with excuses for cost overruns or delays). Since so much of the job is administrative, the supervising sound editor must be as nimble with Excel as with Pro Tools.

Sound Designer

This one is tricky. Not long ago, in the days before hair designers, lifestyle designers, and food designers, this term was used to describe specialists subordinate to the supervising sound editor who were called in to make the sound for extraordinary scenes or to create specific moods—like the mood of a spaceship passing a black hole—beyond the scope of the normal sound team. These days, there is a blurring between sound designers and supervising sound editors. For some reason, the term "designer" carries a swagger lacking in the clerklike "supervisor."

Assistant Sound Editor

Essential in the sprocketed world, the first assistant sound editor is increasingly hard to find in budget sound cutting rooms. Her role, far less defined than in the past, ranges from obtaining and preparing all necessary material from the picture department (a hugely important task) to setting up and managing the cutting room, locating alternate takes, and fending off the world. A good assistant is worth her weight in gold, but it's ever harder to convince an independent producer to spring for the extra salary. Fight to have an assistant, even if only part time.

Apprentice

In nonunion work you'll almost certainly have to do without an apprentice —nowadays often called "intern," perhaps to avoid payment. Apprentices are there to learn—cutting room techniques, protocol, and discipline—and to erase lots of fantasies about sound postproduction. They help the sound editors by loading and archiving sound materials, transcribing scenes, and performing similar tasks.

Sound Effects Editors

On action films it's easy to understand what the sound effects (SFX) editors do. A helicopter crash, or a motorcycle chase, or the USS *Enterprise* zooming away from an exploding star are obvious examples of sound effects editing, and are usually the kind that win awards. But most of the miracles performed by SFX editors go unnoticed by the public. Every scene, even the quietest middle-of-the-night conversation between two people, will be populated with small "background" sound effects that aid the dialogue, influence the mood, create a rhythm, and motivate characters' actions. Sound effects editors often specialize in certain types of action (cars, fights, gunfire, etc.) and may be called to a project for specific scenes. On smaller films, it's common for the supervising sound editor or sound designer to do at least some of the sound effects editing. On miniscule films, the supervising sound editor *is* the sound effects editor.

Dialogue Supervisor or Dialogue Editor

The dialogue supervisor (big films) or dialogue editor (small films) is responsible for all production sound editing (i.e., if it was recorded during the shoot, it's the dialogue editor's responsibility). Whether removing noises, replacing bits of dialogue from alternate takes, organizing and smoothing tracks, or preparing the track for ADR editing, the dialogue editor must create a seamless track in preparation for the dialogue premix. On large projects, a dialogue supervisor oversees a team of editors.

ADR Supervisor or ADR Editor

Inevitably, certain lines will need to be rerecorded after the shoot. Technical problems, impossible recording conditions, new lines for story enhancement, and a director's yearning to "improve" an actor's lines are but a few of the reasons for bringing the talent into a studio to rerecord lines. The ADR supervisor works with the director and picture editor, as well as the dialogue editor and supervising sound editor, to create a list of lines in need of rerecording. The ADR supervisor directs the actors in the recording session and creates a plan for the ADR editor. It's the ADR editor who matches the thousands of takes of **loop** lines to the dialogue track, finessing for sync, delivery, pitch, and attitude. On smaller films, one person will usually be both supervisor and editor. On microscopic films, the dialogue editor wears all of these hats.

ADR Engineer

ADR, or "postsync," is recorded in a studio, but must perfectly match dialogue that was recorded in a limitless number of locations. The ADR engineer selects and places the microphones, manipulates the electronics, and positions the actors for the best match to the original recording. He's usually an employee of the recording studio where the postsynchronization recordings are made, but "ringers" are not unheard of.

Foley Supervisor

Every film needs some help from Foley, which at the very least is used to cover holes caused by ADR and fix a few disastrous omissions of action. As budgets increase, Foley can take on an ever escalating narrative role, adding color, texture, and character. Any film destined to be dubbed into foreign languages requires Foley wall to wall. The Foley supervisor collects requests from all of the sound editors as well as the supervising sound editor and the director and picture editor, and then compiles the complex list of sounds and props needed. He supervises the Foley recording sessions as well as the editing, often carried out by an army of Foley editors.

Foley Walker and Foley Recording Engineer

Together these Foley artists bring you the actual sounds that liven up the track, enhance the drama, and cover gaps. The Foley walker must figure out which prop or shoe/surface combination will produce the right sound, and the Foley engineer is responsible from all technical considerations, from microphone placement to track layout.

Foley Editors

Whether footsteps or key jangles, most Foley has to be edited after the recording session. Foley editors must, of course, get everything into sync, but that's the most superficial aspect of their work. Rearranging a series of footsteps for maximum dramatic effect or structuring the elements of a body fall to suggest more than meets the eye is their job. Dedicated Foley editors won't be found on smaller films. Instead, other editors will handle this responsibility.

Music Editor

Few people understand the music department. For one thing, the music editor often reports directly to the director, not to the supervising sound editor, and so usually is a bit of an outsider. She must work closely with the film's composer to "fit" the score onto the film and seduce acquired music into the film's structure.

Rerecording Mixer

Sooner or later the film gets mixed. The mixer has to make sense of the scores of tracks generated by the sound guys. Somehow, it usually works. The rerecording mixer almost always works for the studio that mixes the film. He's the ultimate source of answers to the question: Can you fix this in the mix?

In many ways a sound postproduction crew is hierarchical. There are apprentices, assistants, editors, and a supervisor. This may ruffle some egalitarian feathers, but the system is designed to constantly train the next wave of editors. Study all you want, but editing is still largely learned on the job, and nothing beats working under an experienced craftsperson.

CHAPTER 5

Getting Sound from the Picture Department to the Sound Department

Much of your success as a dialogue editor hinges on your relationship with the picture department, particularly the assistant picture editor. Simply put, you need materials from them that aren't always convenient to come up with. Your understanding, charm, and decency in dealing with the folks in picture can make the difference between an easy start or several days of begging, deal making, or strong-arming—never knowing if it will get you the elements you need to do your job.

It's not uncommon to encounter some friction with the picture department. Despite your best negotiated attempts to keep changes to a minimum, changes will happen. Your multipage memos about items you must receive in order to get the job done will be mislaid and you'll be happy to receive half of what you asked for. You'll discover that the editor forgot to tell you about a new scene yet to be shot, and throughout the gig you'll be disappointed with "unnecessary" changes or sloppy paperwork. Lighten up; the picture guys have at least as many pressures and problems as you do, and they're not out to get you. We're all on the same side.

It's in your interest to quickly identify and overcome any problems with the picture team. Separate structural frictions from personal ones and remember that the film is what counts. However you go about this, get over it and move on with your job. At the same time, don't forget the power carried by the picture editor. In most film cultures, she's the pinnacle of the postproduction tower, so don't throw your frustrations in that direction.

The Picture Cutting Room

At the start of preproduction, the supervising sound editor will be in contact with the production office. Depending on the type of film and its budget, as well as his relationship with the director, he may become involved at the script level or may simply show up a few times during the shoot to carry the sound department's flag. During picture editing, the supervising sound editor will become increasingly involved with the picture department. His crew will provide temporary sound effects for the picture edit and prepare tracks for temp mixes for studio screenings and focus groups. By the time the picture is locked, the supervising sound editor and a small sound crew will be very intimate with the mechanics of the film and the dynamics of the picture department.

As the dialogue editor, you probably won't become officially involved with the film until a few days before picture lock, unless you're called in to assist with temp mix tracks. But don't wait until picture editing is completed to establish contact with the picture staff and with the film. Your sanity and success will depend in part on having a good relationship with the picture people.

Often on very low-budget films, the picture editor and assistant leave the film as soon as the picture is locked. This means there's no one around to answer questions, find paperwork, or help you read those illegible sound reports. The Avid has already been rented to another client, so you can no longer easily look into how a problem scene was put together. If you didn't get what you need while the picture department was on the payroll, you're out of luck; or you have to contact an editor who's already on another job and barely remembers your film.

On a film with a decent budget, the job of moving the film from picture to sound rests on the shoulders of the assistant sound editor, so you may never need to do any of this. However, to be prepared for the job where you have no assistant, read on.

The Dialogue Editor's Relationship with the Picture Department

Your most valuable contact in the picture editing room is the first (and likely only) assistant editor. This is the person who will (or won't) save your neck. The picture editor is important, of course, but may not be your most useful contact, since she'll be focused on other matters during audio postproduction. When you first introduce yourself in the cutting room, be nice to the picture editor because she can help you get your next job and can provide needed insight into the film, but spend your time with the assistant because that's where all the information is.

Today many small films don't employ a full-time assistant picture editor, but instead use an assistant as needed to digitize materials at the beginning of the project, to periodically maintain the database, and to "get the project out of the Avid" when the maestro finishes. If there is an assistant picture editor, meet with him to clarify your needed materials and confer on protocol. Watch the (still unfinished) film and note sections where you're sure to need alternate takes. Although you'll always need to rifle through the original tapes in search of alternate material, in any cases where the picture assistant can line up alternate takes on the timeline and include them on your OMF, you'll save immeasurable time and it won't cost him much in the way of added work. Make sure you agree with the assistant on matters of OMF formats, EDLs, paperwork, and the like.

Run a series of tests with the assistant picture editor to confirm that the OMF you get meets your needs and that the material is complete and in sync. It's especially important to coordinate tests with the picture cutting room when dealing with unusual production problems or recording systems you're not familiar with (such as hard-disk field recorders). These tests can fend off problems down the line, and they help to create a relationship between you and the picture assistant, whose value can't be underestimated.

Finally, a couple of words about cutting room etiquette. Remember that a picture editor(s) is a very important member of the film crew. Treat her accordingly. On a practical front, be aware of a few traps you can encounter while visiting the cutting room. First, there'll undoubtedly be lines in the film that are noisy, bumpy, off-mic, and so forth, and the picture editor may inquire, "Can you fix this, or do we have to loop it?" Before you answer, take a breath and count to ten. The correct answer is almost always, "I can't tell you here and now, but give me the track and I'll do some tests with the supervising sound editor and the mixer." Seems pretty obvious, but let's run down the reasons:

- You don't know the answer, since you can't hear well in a picture cutting room.
- You haven't had a chance to look for alternate takes or "fakes" such as close-up (CU) sound on wide-shot (WS) pictures.
- You won't be forgiven if you're wrong.

The only reason to rush to an answer, positive or negative, is to look smart and please the editor. It's not a good way to operate.

The other socially uncomfortable bind you may find yourself in is at the end of the editing room screening when the editor or director turns to you to ask what you think of the film. If you're bowled over by the screening, your response will be one of natural enthusiasm. But if you're still scratching your head when the lights come up, you can always hide behind, "I was so involved in listening for dialogue issues that I can't really give you a fair answer." Armed with this reply, you don't waste precious screening time trying to think of something clever to say about the film.

Essentials for Dialogue Editing

Picture editing is finished—well, *almost* finished—and there's enormous pressure on you to get moving. The film is inevitably behind schedule, and somehow you're expected to take up the slack. However, if you start too soon you run the risk of having to make too many unnecessary **conformations**— adjusting your already manicured scenes to a new picture cut—which wastes your time, wrecks your budget, and shatters your mood far too early in the project. At the same time, no one wants to be a jerk and single-handedly delay the production on principle.

What Is Needed?

So, just what are the rules about what you absolutely must have before starting to edit the dialogue on a film? The following paragraphs will tell you. Keep in mind that they contain some terms not discussed yet. If you're unfamiliar with an acronym or expression, check the glossary.

Locked Picture You need a locked picture, split into reels. There's locked and then there's *locked*. Assume that even the most organized director/editor team will make a few picture changes after declaring the film locked. Conformations—that list of changes awaiting you on your desk each morning—are just part of the game. On the other hand, beginning to cut the dialogue on a film whose direction is unclear or that must still undergo focus group testing is crazy. You may spend more time making changes than editing. Even so, you don't have to wait for the entire film to lock. Often, the interior reels stabilize before the first and last reels. After all, the first reel carries the burden of exposition and character introduction, while the final reel resolves the story and sends the viewers on their merry way. So when time is of the essence and everyone is on your back, you may be able to start on a "safe" interior reel.

If the production provides a digital picture, such as a QuickTime movie, make sure to obtain a "hard" copy on videotape. You can use the tape to redigitize the video if needed, and the tape can serve as the arbiter of sync problems.

OMF to Match Final Picture You'll need a complete OMF of all edited tracks and any bonus audio material you expect to receive from the picture department. Make sure the OMF version (the cut of the film) matches the version of the picture you'll be working with. Label both the video and OMF with the same version name.

Audio and Video EDLs The audio EDLs will be essential for finding alternate takes. The video EDLs will be useful for confirming changes, for making perspective cuts, and for general housekeeping.

Original Recordings and Associated Sound Reports More and more films are recorded on hard-disk recorders. If such is the case with yours, you'll receive a hard drive (probably the same drive holding the OMF and EDLs) with all of the original recordings. There may be DVD backups, too. If your film sound was recorded on DAT, you'll receive a large box of tapes. However the sound was recorded, you must receive the **sound reports**, the paperwork that describes what's on each tape (or in each day's recording folder in the case of hard-disk recording). You'll use this paperwork to locate alternate takes and **wild sound**.

List of Shooting Dates for Each Scene If your film was recorded on a hard-disk recorder, the soundfiles are likely stored in folders identified by the shoot date. A table correlating scene numbers with shooting dates will save many headaches.

Lined Script The lined script from the shoot is used for locating material and revealing **coverage** within each scene. It gets its name from the vertical lines drawn over the text, indicating which takes cover each part of the script.

That's it for the essentials. You absolutely must have them before starting. Missing any at this point spells trouble down the line, and a production that can't provide these key elements is going to cause you heartache. Other elements, although not life or death in importance, are nonetheless worth asking for.

- *A list of characters and actors.* Sooner or later you'll learn the character names and the actors playing those roles, but with this list in hand you can start naming regions and making ADR calls without too many phone calls to the production office.

- *A contact list* including the director, picture editor, producer, associate producer, postproduction supervisor, and production office. You never know when you'll need to contact someone.

Splitting Reels

Back when all films were cut on upright Moviolas or console editors, sync was a physical truth rather than a metaphysical goal, and editors' work habits were much more standardized. Picture editors and sound editors alike cut on 1000-ft reels. Now most films are picture-edited on one continuous time-line because any decent video workstation will allow for such massive sessions.

However, you can't mix a continuous soundtrack that runs the length of a film, then send it to the lab and not expect to be laughed (or yelled) at. Films are still printed in reels of no more than 2050 feet, so that sets the limit of how you mix. And since films are mixed in reels, so too are they edited for sound, which means that before you accept a film from the picture department, it must be broken in to reels. This isn't the dialogue editor's responsibility, but if your picture editor is inexperienced it's in the interest of the sound department to police the reel-splitting process. Here are some rules to observe in order to have sound-friendly reel splits:

- Avoid splitting within a musical cue or in a place likely to have one later. Even if the mixer and sound supervisor manage to pull off this feat (which isn't assured), the music cue will be at the mercy of projectionists and their ability to properly splice together the reels.
- Don't allow any significant sound within the first second of a new reel. This sound will fall within the **changeover** and could cause trouble.
- It's usually easier to break a reel between scenes rather than in the middle of a scene, where this transition will be very exposed. If timing demands a reel change within a scene, pick a picture cut with a bit of "air" on either side. Both traditional changeovers (two-projector) and splicing reels into platters can result in eating into the first and last frames.

Protect yourself by refusing to begin work on a project whose reels aren't yet split. Such a premature start can come back to haunt you in the form of complicated rearranging of scenes (work often not included in your deal with the producer). Plus, a client who insists on beginning dialogue editing on an unsplit film is a client with other dangerous surprises lurking in the wings. Make them split the reels. Properly. Period.

The OMF and a Brief History of Nonlinear Editing

When picture and sound were edited on film, elements were completely transportable from one cutting room to another, from a Steenbeck in Paris to a Moviola in Los Angeles. Your plan for sound didn't depend on the technology used by the picture editor or the sound facility. As long as the rules were followed, everything was interchangeable. Yes, there were a lot of rules to know, but they rarely changed.

Like all technological advances, from the cotton gin to the robotic assembly line, digital picture and audio workstations came about partly to reduce labor costs and extract more efficiency from the remaining workers. The initial equipment costs were numbingly high and the trailblazers paid dearly for their new toys. But once the technology was proven and the economies of scale began reducing costs, there was real potential to get more for less. Edit room staff was progressively whittled away until today it's not uncommon to find a small film with no assistants. On the other hand, it's now possible to edit with brain-numbing accuracy and produce multiple versions of a scene in a snap. You can work efficiently and quickly, and with more technological horsepower in your lowly workstation than took man to the moon, you can perform miraculous sound processing feats.

CMX-600 and Montage

The first digital audio and video editors were freestanding pieces of hardware with rooms full of processors and storage devices. The CMX-600 that was released in 1971 (yes, 1971) is considered the first nonlinear video editor; it was the result of a partnership between CBS and Memorex that produced this editor years ahead of its time. Video was recorded as an analogue FM signal, while audio was recorded as a pulse amplitude signal and stored in the video's horizontal blanking.

The six IBM drives held a whopping 30 minutes of half-resolution black-and-white picture and sound, plus an address language that would later develop into SMPTE timecode. If you wanted to edit onto an audio track, you had to dedicate one precious hard drive to audio. Edit information was stored on 1-inch punch tape, which was loaded into a CMX-200 online editor for assembly.[1] By today's standards the CMX-600 was crude, but the six units manufactured forever changed the way we look at electronic editing.[2]

---

[1] A good history of the CMX-600 can be found in "A Reflection/Eulogy" by Bob Turner (*SMPTE/New England Newsletter*, January 1998).

[2] Technical details on the CMX-600 were graciously provided Jack L. Calaway.

In 1984, the Montage Picture Processor was introduced. It was a surreal array of 17 or more Super BetaMax players shuttling, winding, playing, and coughing out commitment-free scene previews. Preparing for an editing project was a huge task, but the actual editing worked pretty well. The same year, Lukasfilm announced EditDroid,[3] a laser disk-based random access editor, whose sound cousin was SoundDroid. The technology behind EditDroid and SoundDroid was acquired by Avid in 1993, and many of the key developers of SoundDroid went on to form Sonic Solutions.

Nonlinear Workstations

The late 1980s witnessed the births, and often the deaths, of countless nonlinear sound editing systems for the sound-for-picture market. Overwhelmingly, these tools were hardware-based proprietary systems that often settled into a market niche. Most of the sound workstations were offshoots of music editors, while others were spawned from restoration and mastering, coinciding with the introduction of the compact disc. Some were built from the ground up for audio postproduction. All of these workstations were closed systems, so neither code nor file formats were easily exchanged between different manufacturers' products. Still, as long as you kept your job with one studio, life really was getting better.

This "Brave New World" fell apart when jobs had to move from one facility to another. Worse, there was no sane way to take a finished picture cut and begin working on the production sound. Typically, a **reconform**, often done by hand and ear, was the only way to get the picture editor's cut to the sound department. This cumbersome and time-consuming chore took much of the fun out of random-access production sound editing.

Auto-Assembly and OMF

It wasn't long before a method was devised to automatically conform the original takes based on the picture editor's choices, assuming that the original production sound came with timecode. Auto-assembly was invented. Using an EDL for source name and address information and the RS-232 or RS-422 protocol to control the source machine (initially ¼-inch tape with timecode and later DAT), manufacturers offered a way, however clumsy, of moving from picture to sound. But the resulting soundfiles were based on proprietary platforms and weren't the least bit interchangeable. You still couldn't mount

---

[3] For a riveting personal history of electronic picture editing, see *In the Blink of an Eye, Second Edition*, by Walter Murch (Los Angeles: Silman-James Press, 2001, pp. 75–146).

a picture editor's drive onto a digital audio workstation and start editing. Nor was it possible to do part of a project on one type of machine and then move to another.

It's not that no one was paying attention. Standards setting groups—Society of Motion Picture and Television Engineers (SMPTE), Audio Engineering Society (AES), and European Broadcasting Union (EBU)—were looking for ways to normalize the exchange of this rich and diverse picture and sound data. Since such organizations are notorious for moving slowly, it was the industry that made the first meaningful foray into file transfer protocol. In 1992 Avid Technology, not yet in the audio business, introduced its Open Media Framework Interchange (OMFI, commonly shortened to OMF), designed specifically to allow Avid files and EDLs to be opened directly on any number of audio workstations.

For a few years in the early 1990s, OMF was promising to be the Esperanto in which all machines would seamlessly communicate, allowing transparent postproduction. Once it became a standard, like SMPTE timecode or any digital audio format, equipment choices would be based solely on desired features and price rather than on embedded architecture, since it would be painless to move between makes and models. Of course, reality eventually reared its head.

Between manufacturers' reluctance to expose their proprietary codes to competitors' eavesdropping and Apple's unwillingness to release into the public domain the underlying container code, OMF never attained real "standard" status.[4] Instead, it continued to be a product of Avid and later Avid/Digidesign. This accidental ownership did nothing to make other manufacturers either comfortable or cooperative beyond what was needed to make their workstations accept an Avid project. The utopia of open exchange would have to wait, although OMF did become the de facto standard for moving files between workstations.

OMF-1 and OMF-2 Because OMF was complicated and its implementation for each manufacturer required complex code-writing somersaults, Avid did its best to keep the protocol available to developers. However, within a few years, it was clear—given so many changes, bug fixes, improvements, and the culling of initial mistakes—that OMF needed to change, so OMF-2 was released in 1996. OMF-1 and OMF-2 are not compatible formats.

---

[4] A brief but outstanding history of OMFI is "Workstation File-Format Interchange" by Ron Franklin, in *Mix Magazine* (vol. 1, October 2002).

For most audio workstations, it doesn't matter which OMF format you receive from the picture department, as long as you have the necessary software on your computer to translate that format into your machine's language. You can't convert an OMF-2 file using an OMF-1 translator. This is yet another reason to talk with the picture department long before the picture is locked.

AAF and MXF

Building on the successes of OMF, and learning from its failings, two new file exchange tools were created. One was the **Advanced Authoring Format** (AAF), created by the AAF Association, a consortium founded by Avid and Microsoft. Avid donated the core OMF model, and Microsoft provided a container code to replace the Apple proprietary container that had long haunted OMF. AAF offers more rugged and bug-free file interchange than did either OMF version. Moreover, the software development kits given to manufacturers for implementation have been more extensively tested than were Avid's OMF development kits, so industry implementation should be easier. AAF stands a good chance of becoming a real, rather than de facto, standard, unlike unlucky OMF.

Media Exchange Format (MXF) is a **media wrapper** that standardizes the way different media are revealed to applications, thus facilitating file exchange for very different types of material. Working in conjunction, AAF and MXF allow a far more efficient vehicle than OMF for file exchange than did OMF.[5]

Exporting the OMF from the Avid

When the picture editor (or assistant) creates the OMF from which you'll create your initial session, she has the choice to keep separate the soundfiles (the "media") and the session instruction set (in essence, the EDL plus other control and naming information) or to embed all of this into one giant file. You shouldn't have trouble with either format, but there are a few things to think about.

---

[5] For a more detailed discussion of AAF and MXF, see "Advanced Authoring Format and Media Exchange Format" by Brooks Harris, in *The Editors' Guild Magazine* (vol. 24, no. 3, May/June 2003).

To Embed or Not to Embed

A single embedded file is less cumbersome to move around, so it behaves better when sent via an FTP site or with Digidelivery.[6] There's but one file to keep up with rather than thousands. The primary downside of an embedded file is that you can't access the individual soundfiles within it. If you get an embedded OMF of a reel but need only one or two files from the session, you must convert the entire reel to get them. Of course, unless you're using a very slow computer or are frighteningly low on disk space, opening a new OMF isn't all that taxing.

Preparing the OMF in the FCP/Avid

Securing an OMF from Final Cut Pro (FCP) or Avid is a pretty run-of-the-mill exercise, but if you're new to this picture team, run a short test a few days before final delivery. It's frustrating to receive an OMF file that either doesn't open or opens incorrectly. For some reason, the sound department often gets the OMF just as the picture people go home for the day, typically on a Friday or right before that three-day holiday that you were planning to use to make up for lost time. A tiny amount of coordination with the editor can help avoid lost time or lost tempers.

Most major sound facilities supply clients with "OMF cookbooks" that walk picture editors through the process of delivering an OMF that will fit with the facility's equipment and way of working. One example is shown in Figure 5-1. Remember, OMF isn't a real standard but rather a proprietary translator, so small changes in equipment or methodology can result in huge problems. Find out what your editing facility requires and make a document for the picture people describing what they need to do.

When you open the OMF, make sure that the regions are named as they were in the Avid. Normally region names will include scene/shot/take information and perhaps a note from the director. Expect to see something like this:

32B-4 Bob eats spinach

or at least

32B-4

---

[6] Digidelivery is a proprietary file exchange service marketed by Digidesign.

Archer City Sound Productions

**INSTRUCTIONS FOR CREATING AN OMF DOCUMENT
ON AVID FOR USE WITH PRO TOOLS**

Create a new bin for the Avid sequence.
Create a copy of the Avid sequence to be used for OMF export.
Select whether you want to export audio or video or both.
Remove grouped clips and locators before consolidating the session.
In the Timeline Display enable *Media Names* or *Media File Names*.
- To find offline media, type *CMD+F* (*CTL+F* on PC systems).
- Type *Media Offline* (note that this is case sensitive); select the *Timeline Text* checkbox.
- Correct or delete all references to the located offline media. Even a one frame-long offline clip could crash the OMF.

Remove all audio effects (except fades).
- Enable all audio tracks on the sequence.
- Use the EQ tool to globally remove all the EQ effects in the sequence.
- Use the *AutoGain* tool to globally remove all automatic gain settings from the sequence.
- Use the *AudioSuite* plug-in window to globally remove all audio effects.
- Mark the entire sequence (IN-OUT) and render all effects.

Copy the sequence to the new bin and save the bin.

Creating an OMF on Avid Media Composer ABVB (before version 10):
Consolidate the sequence directly to the drive being delivered to the sound department.
- Before beginning the consolidation, be sure that the drive partition is empty.
- Choose handles of at least 150 frames.

Avid will write the files to a new *Media Files* folder.
- Choose *OMF 2.0* file format, check *Audio Only,* and select *Standard-AIFC.*

It is advisable to also check *With Media*. This option will embed all media files into the OMF file, creating one massive file.

To check the OMF composition you've exported, use OMF Tool (preferably version 2.0.8).
This free tool for Mac platforms will create a Pro Tools project and verify that all your data is intact. There is currently no known free utility that provides the same check for PCs.

Creating an OMF on Avid Media Composer Meridian/Adrenaline/Nitris (version 10 and above) and Avid Express Pro:
Select the sequence.
On the *File* menu, click *Export.*
- In the *Options* section, select *OMF 2.0.*
- Select a partition free of media files and supply handles of at least 150 frames.
- Convert all the media to AIFF format, and project sample rate and bit depth.

If there are wild sounds/ambiences/room tones recorded for the project, be sure to create separate sequences and export OMFs for them as well. Normally, these will already be organized in independent bins.

Figure 5-1 Example of an OMF "cookbook" for the picture department. Large sound facilities often provide such standardized guidelines.

If you don't see sensible information as your region names, but rather a serial list number or gibberish, go back to the picture folks and sort out the problem. Without valid scene/shot/take information, your job isn't just a little harder but worlds more difficult. Don't start editing until you get the region names right, no matter how high the pressure or how strong the urge to get moving.

The Edit Decision List

As a dialogue editor you can't get away from **edit decision lists** (EDLs). When you auto-assemble, recreating the picture editor's cuts from DAT or other linear sources, you have to understand and be able to manipulate EDLs. The same goes if you're using file-linking programs such as Titan to access all recorded channels of a track that was edited in the Avid using only a mono mixdown. Even the most basic dialogue editing skills—finding and using alternate takes to lose noises, improve acting, or resurrect wide, off-microphone shots from their watery graves—require that you know your way around an EDL.

Dissecting an EDL

The industry-standard CMX3600 EDL (see Figure 5-2) isn't the least bit difficult to learn, it's just humorless and terribly monotonous. Plus, as a means of describing edit information so that one machine can understand another, it couldn't be more ill-suited: It's very data frugal, and parts of its information, such as channel mapping, are amusingly cryptic. Fortunately, the CMX3600 won't be around much longer, as the AAF Association is developing a new format. For now, though, you can't escape it.

Even though picture editors regularly cut to eight or more audio tracks, the CMX3600 format can describe only four at a time. Films edited with more than that require multiple EDLs, each representing a 4-track group. The EDL in Figure 5-2 reflects tracks 1 through 4 of a 12-track edit on a Final Cut Pro.

An EDL Event Let's look at one event from an EDL. Learn one line and you've got the whole thing.

```
003    DVD09    AA    C    13:38:11:02 13:38:12:23 02:00:24:06 02:00:26:02
*  TO CLIP NAME:  24-07 OF 7 ANNOUNCED 6 JORDAN BORDER T131 MERGED
*  COMMENT: 08-02-04
```

The top line describes the source of the audio (it could just as easily be video) and its original timecode, plus its location in the edited film. The comment lines (indicated by asterisks) give the scene and take as well as other notes from the picture department. Table 5-1 provides details on these and other fields in this event.

In Figure 5-2 the title of the project is on the top header line. Beneath the title, you may see FCM ("frame count mode," meaning the way the EDL counts the number of frames in a second) followed by NON DROP FRAME or DROP FRAME

```
TITLE:   Lost in Jordan Reel 2 A1-4


001   GEN      AA    C           00:00:56:05 00:00:56:06 01:59:58:02 01:59:58:03
AUD    3      4
* FROM CLIP NAME:  BARS AND TONE (PAL)
002    BL     NONE  C           00:00:00:00 00:00:00:00 02:00:20:16 02:00:20:16
002    DVD09  NONE  D    016 13:38:29:24 13:38:33:14 02:00:20:16 02:00:24:06
AUD    3      4
* TO CLIP NAME:   24-07 OF 7 ANNOUNCED 6 JORDAN BORDER T131 MERGED
* COMMENT: 08-02-04
003    BL     AA    C           00:00:00:00 00:00:00:00 02:00:24:06 02:00:24:06
003    DVD09  AA    D    008 13:38:11:02 13:38:12:23 02:00:24:06 02:00:26:02
* TO CLIP NAME:   24-07 OF 7 ANNOUNCED 6 JORDAN BORDER T131 MERGED
* COMMENT: 08-02-04
004    DVD09  NONE  C       13:38:33:14 13:38:33:14 02:00:24:06 02:00:24:06
004    BL     NONE  D    008 00:00:00:00 00:00:00:08 02:00:24:06 02:00:24:14
AUD    3      4
* FROM CLIP NAME:  24-07 OF 7 ANNOUNCED 6 JORDAN BORDER T131 MERGED
* COMMENT: 08-02-04
005    DVD09  AA    C       13:38:12:23 13:38:12:23 02:00:26:02 02:00:26:02
005    BL     AA    D    001 00:00:00:00 00:00:00:01 02:00:26:02 02:00:26:03
* FROM CLIP NAME:  24-07 OF 7 ANNOUNCED 6 JORDAN BORDER T131 MERGED
* COMMENT: 08-02-04
006    BL     NONE  C           00:00:00:00 00:00:00:00 02:00:26:02 02:00:26:02
006    DVD09  NONE  D    001 13:38:30:08 13:38:33:14 02:00:26:02 02:00:29:08
AUD    3      4
* TO CLIP NAME:   24-07 OF 7 ANNOUNCED 6 JORDAN BORDER T131 MERGED
* COMMENT: 08-02-04
```

Figure 5-2 Excerpt from a CMX3600 edit decision list. The title line indicates the project name and reel number and the audio channels included in this EDL. On NTSC edit decision lists, the type of timecode will also be indicated on the title line.

or 24 FPS or 25 FPS. As you would expect, this flag refers to the timecode type for the edited tape or session, that is, the timecode flavor of the edit master, not necessarily that of the source material. Often on PAL EDLs you won't see an FCM listing, since there are no expected FCM variables in the PAL universe; PAL editing systems default to 25 fps. It's unlikely that this flag will be incorrect, but anything can happen. If you're absolutely sure that the FCM indication is wrong, you can correct it when you clean the EDL (to be discussed soon).

The two "comment lines" beneath the event line begin with an asterisk. This is a signal to most postconform programs that the line is not an event,

Table 5-1 Fields in a CMX3600 EDL Event Line

Column	Field	Description
1	003	**Event number**. A series number that makes it easier to refer to specific edits.
2	DVD09	**Source**. The originating media—the source roll, in this case a DVD made from a Cantar hard disk.
3	AA	**Record channels**. The channels in the session on which the sound was recorded (or edited), *not* the source channels.
4	C	**Transition type**: cut (C), dissolve (D), wipe (W), key (K), etc.
5	13:38:11:02	**Source start time**. Where on the original field recording, the event begin.
6	13:38:12:23	**Source end time**. Where on the original field recording the event ends.
7	02:00:24:06	**Record start time**. Beginning of the event in the edited program.
8	02:00:26:02	**Record end time**. End of the event in the edited program.

but is instead a comment that can be used to name the region in your session.

```
003  DVD09     AA    C 13:38:11:02 13:38:12:23 02:00:24:06 02:00:26:02
*  TO CLIP NAME:  24-07 OF 7 ANNOUNCED 6 JORDAN BORDER T131 MERGED
*  COMMENT: 08-02-04
```

In this event, the text line

```
*  TO CLIP NAME:  24-07 OF 7 ANNOUNCED 6 JORDAN BORDER T131 MERGED
```

identifies the scene and take (and notes that the voice slate on the recording was incorrectly identified as take 6 instead of take 7). This is the line you'll import for the region name. More on that later. The next text line:

```
*  COMMENT: 08-02-04
```

is included by the picture editor to aid in file matching from the original Cantar BWF files. Cantar, like most hard-disk recorders, includes all of the takes from one shooting day in a folder whose name is the date of the recording. This information won't be imported into the postconform, since it's of no interest to you once you're editing and because you can import only one text line per event.

For the most part, that's it. There are, however, a few quirks worth looking at. For example, the EDL event below includes a fade from black.

```
006     BL  NONE   C        00:00:00:00 00:00:00:00 02:00:26:02 02:00:26:02
006   DVD09 NONE   D   004  13:38:30:08 13:38:33:14 02:00:26:02 02:00:29:08
AUD  3    4
* TO CLIP NAME:  24-07 OF 7 ANNOUNCED 6 JORDAN BORDER T131 MERGED
* COMMENT: 08-02-04
```

Notice that event 006 occupies two lines. The source of the first line is BL, which stands for "black." Notice too that this part of the event has no duration. Now look at the next line. Rather than the usual C, for cut transition, there's a D followed by 004. This double-line event represents a 4-frame dissolve ("fade" in audio terms) from black (silence in the case of sound) to the material on DVD09.

The fact that the first line of the event has no duration is a vestige of how dissolves were made in the days of linear videotape editing. If you wanted to dissolve from tape 32 to tape 67, for example, the CMX editor would make an edit precisely at the beginning of the transition. This "zero cut" was the splice point between normal footage and the transition effect. At the end of the dissolve, there would be another splice to return to normal footage. Pro Tools handles fades and dissolves in more or less the same way, although the process is invisible to the operator.

In truth, by the time you get an EDL it should be stripped of dissolves since an auto-assembly program can't generate fades for your session. Ask the assistant film editor to convert fades to cuts before generating the EDLs. If he can't, you can easily do it yourself with EDL Manager.

The other common source symbol in an event is AX, or AUXILLARY, which specifies a video switcher or signal generator. You'll commonly see AX at the head of a reel, signifying PAL or NTSC color bars that coincide with the 1 kHz reference tone. It's unlikely that you'll encounter AX pointing to meaningful dialogue information.

There's something else odd about event 006: the record channel. Rather than A for audio channel 1, A2 for audio channel 2, or AA for both 1 and 2, the word NONE appears.

```
006   DVD09  NONE   D   004  13:38:30:08 13:38:33:14 02:00:26:02 02:00:29:08
AUD  3    4
```

What's the point of an audio recording with no record track enabled? But wait, on the line below you see AUD 3 4, which means that event 006 is edited to channels 3 and 4 in the Avid session. Remember, the CMX3600 EDL is a very old means of expressing video edit decisions. Its ancestors were controllers for VTRs with only two channels. In the glory days of linear videotape editing, there were many flavors of EDL, any of which could have made for a better way of expressing multichannel edit data. As is often the case with standards, however, the weakest of possibilities became the norm. AAF and especially the AES31 audio decision list (ADL) will solve all of these problems, as they are designed to handle real-world data transfer issues and are delightfully sample-accurate.

Finding the End of a Shot

Ask a film editor to identify the last frame of a shot and you'll be shown the last image connected to the shot in question. The sync block counter will read that shot's ending footage. This is clear, and it reflects the way we relate to physical objects. Consider that the last step in France before entering Belgium is on the French side of the border; the last word on a page in a book is, in fact, the last word before you turn to the next page. So, if the last frame of a shot is 231 feet, 12 frames, the next shot will begin at 231 feet, 13 frames. Seems pretty obvious.

But video, being a constantly evolving, ever scanning illusion, doesn't work this way. By design and necessity, the last frame of a shot in video isn't the last frame we see but rather the beginning of the next frame. Look at this EDL excerpt.

```
003   DVD09    AA     D       13:38:11:02  13:38:12:23  02:00:24:06  02:00:26:02
004   DVD09    AA     C       13:29:30:08  13:29:33:14  02:00:26:02  02:00:29:08
```

Here line 003 ends at 2:00:26:02. The next event, 004, begins at 2:00:26:02, and not a frame later, as you would expect from the commonsense film model. (See Figure 5-3.)

Printing the EDL

To conveniently find alternate takes when you edit, you'll need to print the EDLs. To easily troubleshoot conform problems, you'll need to print the EDLs. Recycle paper and you won't feel so bad about the amount of paper you're using, but to make for a manageable editing experience, you have to print the EDLs.

To make your life easier, put a header on each EDL page. Include the project name, page number, reel number, and the set of tracks represented in the list

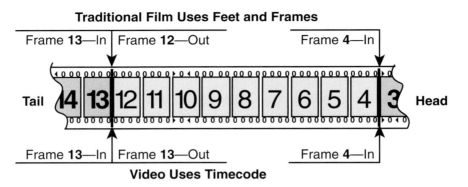

Figure 5-3 The *out* point of a shot is measured differently in video than in film. In film, the last frame physically within a shot is considered the out frame; the next shot begins with the next frame. In video, out is considered to be the frame *after* the end of the shot, and the next *in* frame will have the same timecode value.

(audio 1–4, audio 5–8, audio 9–12, video, etc.), as shown in Figure 5-4. These lists all look alike, and when you're hurriedly searching for an alternate take, it's useful to know which is which.

Print with a fixed-width font such as `Courier 10`. If you have someone do the printing, check the first few pages. It's not uncommon for an EDL illiterate to improperly wrap the lines, making the lists all but impossible to use.

Cleaning an EDL

If you're going to auto-assemble[7] from tape or link files from original 24-bit BWF files, you'll almost certainly have to do some preparatory work on the EDL. It's important that the list is **clean**, containing no illegal situations in which edits end before they start or where column widths aren't standardized. You must also confirm that naming conventions are respected and that notations are consistent.

---

[7] By now it should be pretty clear that I'm using the term "auto-assembly" or "autoconform" to generically describe using an EDL and original recordings to recreate the picture editor's audio cuts. PostConform is a commonly used term, but since it's a Digidesign trademark, I try to avoid it. Most DAW manufacturers provide such a utility, either within their DAW program or as a freestanding application.

```
LOST IN JORDAN, ver 7                    Page 1                    R2 A1-4
TITLE:    LOST IN JORDAN R2 A1-4
001   GEN      AA    C         00:00:56:05 00:00:56:06 01:59:58:02 01:59:58:03
AUD   3      4
* FROM CLIP NAME:  BARS AND TONE (PAL)
* FROM CLIP IS A STILL
002        BL   NONE  C         00:00:00:00 00:00:00:00 02:00:20:16 02:00:20:16
002   DVD09   NONE  D     016 13:38:29:24 13:38:33:14 02:00:20:16 02:00:24:06
AUD   3      4
* EFFECT NAME: CROSS FADE (+3DB)
* TO CLIP NAME:   24-07 OF 7 ANNOUNCED 6 JORDAN BORDER T131 MERGED
* COMMENT: 08-02-04
003        BL   AA    C         00:00:00:00 00:00:00:00 02:00:24:06 02:00:24:06
003   DVD09   AA    D     008 13:38:11:02 13:38:12:23 02:00:24:06 02:00:26:02
* EFFECT NAME: CROSS FADE (+3DB)
* TO CLIP NAME:   24-07 OF 7 ANNOUNCED 6 JORDAN BORDER T131 MERGED
* COMMENT: 08-02-04
004   DVD09   NONE  C         13:38:33:14 13:38:33:14 02:00:24:06 02:00:24:06
004        BL   NONE  D     008 00:00:00:00 00:00:00:08 02:00:24:06 02:00:24:14
AUD   3      4
* EFFECT NAME: CROSS FADE (+3DB)
* FROM CLIP NAME:   24-07 OF 7 ANNOUNCED 6 JORDAN BORDER T131 MERGED
* COMMENT: 08-02-04
```

Figure 5-4 Excerpt from a CMX3600 EDL printout. Note the prominent header, which will appear on each page. Since each reel may have three or four EDLs, easy-to-spot identification will save you time when you need to quickly find a shot or investigate problems.

EDL Manager The easiest way to clean an EDL is with a list manager program such as Avid's EDL Manager, which can be downloaded from the Digidesign web site. With EDL Manager, you can instantly clean the list or convert it between SMPTE or EBU timecode formats or either of Avid's "PAL-film" formats. Figure 5-5 shows EDL Manager's Options page.

The Options page is your chance to decide which elements of the Avid session are saved to an EDL and in what format. Beginning in the upper left corner, select *CMX_3600* as the EDL format. Many choices are available, but CMX3600 is the standard and the only one that will work without trouble. If, while looking at your EDL printout, you see only two audio channels displayed, chances are you've chosen another EDL type. *CMX_340*, for example, is a 2-track standard. Make sure the list begins at event 1, and choose *LTC* as the list master Timecode Type.

The DupeList/Preread section concerns tape-based video assembly and doesn't influence sound post. When using linear videotape for the final

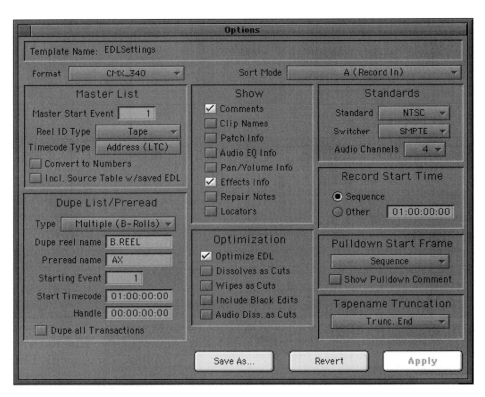

Figure 5-5 Options page of Avid's EDL Manager.

assembly (online), you can't dissolve from a source videotape to itself (since you can be at only one location on a tape at a time), so you have to copy specific sections onto a work tape, or "dupe reel."

The Show section determines which information is displayed in the final EDL. Choose between *Comments* and *Clip Names* depending on the auto-assembly program you're using.

Standards refers to the type of timecode serving as the basis of the list, in other words, the record timecode. In the NTSC universe, it's possible to have an assortment of non-drop-frame and drop-frame *source* material, but you can have only one *record* timecode. This should be set to the timecode format of the program automatically. If not, change it to NTSC, PAL video, or one of the two PAL film settings. Check several edits in the EDL against the realities of the Avid session or the videotape to make sure you've done nothing stupid with the timecode.

The *Switcher* setting in the Standards section concerns the protocol with which the editor controller communicates with the video switcher ("vision mixer"). You needn't bother with this. Do, however, set Audio Channels to 4. The oh-so-exciting option of 16 channels isn't valid for CMX3600 EDLs.

Record Start Time is set to *Sequence* and left alone. Don't mess with this one unless you're prepared to offset all of your regions once the new sessions are conformed.

Pulldown Start Frame has to do with the correlation between the video color framing sequence and the 4-frame 2:3:2 telecine pulldown sequence. Normally default to *Sequence*, which uses the parameters embedded in the original list. Good news for PAL editors—this isn't your problem!

Tapename Truncation controls how overlong tape (source) names are shortened into CMX3600 legal names. The choices are obvious.

Finally, the big moment: Optimization. This determines how events will be modified in the new EDL and therefore how your auto-assembly will interpret transitions like dissolves, wipes, and, most important, audio dissolves. You're not interested in keeping the picture editor's transitions—besides, the OMF gives you a perfect reference of what the editor was up to when he made them. Why muddy up the EDL with all these unnecessary dissolve commands? Check all of the options except *Include Black Edits*, which is unnecessary.

Click *Apply* and you'll see the cleaned EDL in the EDL Manager window. Save it into an appropriately named folder, using a hierarchy something like this:

```
Lost in Jordan (film title)/
        EDLs (all EDL files)/
                EDLs postcleaning (as opposed to raw EDLs or print-ready EDLs)/
```

Repeat for each EDL. Remember, there'll be a lot of EDLs per reel. Each reel could easily have three or four audio EDLs and a video EDL, so on a 6-A/B-reel film you may have 30 EDLs per "layer" (raw EDLs, postclean, print-ready, etc.). It pays to be obsessively organized.

Optimizing an edit list does more than enforce the changes you've chosen. An EDL cleaning program will format the list in a manner acceptable to most auto-assembly utilities. Some picture workstations generate EDLs not completely within SMPTE norms. Using such lists without first cleaning them may result in unpleasant surprises. If you regularly prepare EDLs and you need more flexibility than the free utilities can offer, consider a more serious EDL management tool such as EDLMax.[8]

Getting Clip Names into Your Regions

It's important that your session region names reflect the scene/shot/take information from the Avid and, ultimately, from the original recordings. You can in fact cut dialogue without this information in the region names, but you'll expend so much energy figuring out camera angles and digging about for clues to sources that you'll be exhausted before you've even begun.

Comment or Clip Names As we saw previously, shot information is carried below the main edit line in an EDL, either as a comment or as part of a clip names line. If you don't have comments in your EDL, send the list back to the picture department and ask for a version that includes scene/shot/take information in the COMMENT field. In most auto-assembly programs you can choose which line to import: comment or clip names. There'll also be an option to drop certain recurring text that you don't want in your region names. For example, you don't want all of your regions looking like

```
*COMMENT:  21B/4
```

It's pretty obvious that you'd prefer to work with just

```
21B/4
```

It's much easier to get good, consistent results if the picture editor provides the shot information on the comment line rather than as a clip name. The reason is that *COMMENT: is always *COMMENT:, whereas CLIP NAME can begin with *FROM CLIP NAME: or *TO CLIP NAME: or a few other variants. If shot information is carried on the comment line, all you need to do is tell your auto-assembly to delete the string COMMENT: *{space}{space}* and region names will be correctly labeled. If, however, you inherit a list that uses the more troublesome clip name line for passing along shot information, you must delete these long prefixes or you'll end up with unusable region names.

---

[8] EDLMax is a multipurpose EDL management tool made by Brooks Harris Film & Tape, Inc. (*http://www.edlmax.com*).

An easy way to remove these strings is to import each EDL into a word processor such as Microsoft Word. (See Figure 5-6.) Note the assorted strings that precede the scene/shot/take information in the clip name line. One string at a time, perform global replaces to rid the line of the prefix.

So *TO CLIP NAME: 24-07 becomes 24-07. *Don't delete the asterisk (*) at the beginning of the string* because many auto-assembly programs use this to dis-

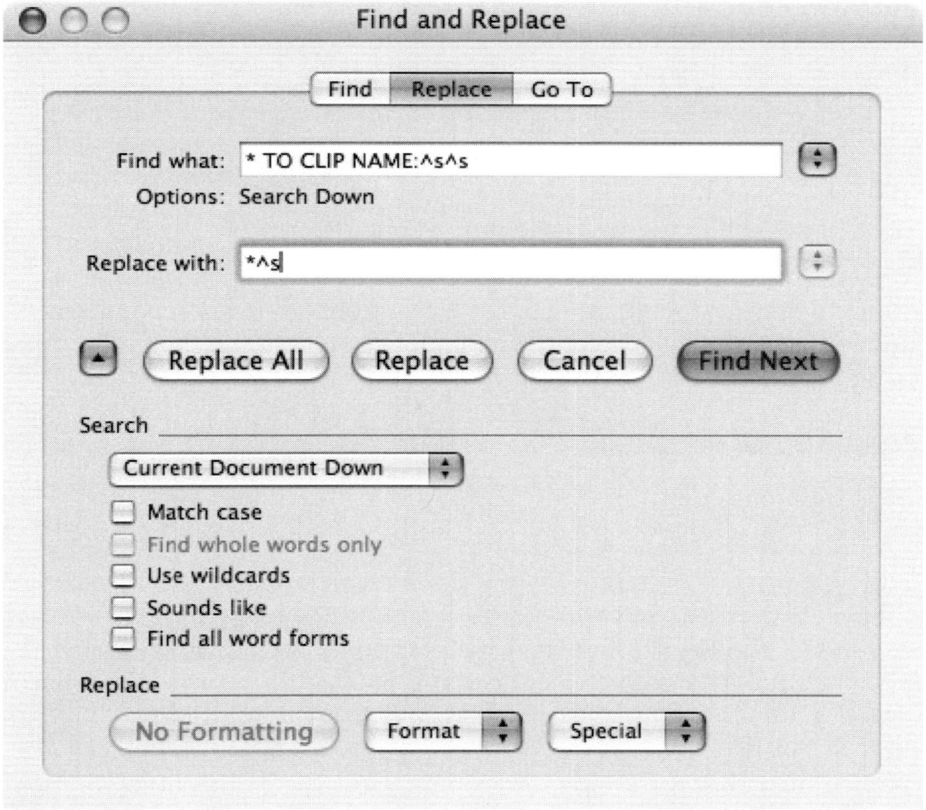

Figure 5-6 Screenshot of Microsoft Word global replace. In this example, all occurrences of *TO CLIP NAME: {space}{space} are replaced with *. Repeat this procedure for each of the strings preceding scene and take information in the EDL. This isn't necessary if the comment line carries the scene and take information, since most auto-assembly programs can delete one variable from the string and COMMENT never varies.

tinguish a comment line from an event line. Lose the * and you won't see your shot information. Repeat the global replace for each of the text string variations preceding the shot information in the CLIP NAME line.

Saving the EDL

When you finish this round of cleaning, save the EDL with a new name, *as a text-only file*. Auto-assembly programs can't read Word (.doc) files, so your hard work will go unrecognized. Just to keep all these EDLs straight (there's still one more set of files to go!), you might want to add another folder to your existing EDL hierarchy:

```
Lost in Jordan (film title)/
    EDLs (all EDL files)/
        EDLs post cleaning (as opposed to raw EDLs or print-ready EDLs)/
        EDLs for printing (these have headers and other formatting to
          ease reading)/
        EDLs for post conform (that's what we just created)/
```

The Auto-Assembly

Nothing's worse than perfecting a bad idea, so once you've prepared one EDL for auto-assembly, do a test conform of a few events to see that everything is working properly.

Auto-Assembly Setup

Connect the timecode from the TC DAT, video, or HD player to the synchronizer. Don't rely on the 9-pin timecode. Pulling the timecode from the RS-422 will likely work, but the results can be inconsistent, and it's difficult to see the advantages of inconsistent timecode.

Next, connect the RS-422 between the computer (or synchronizer) and the source machine. Alternatively, you can use a TimeLine Lynx as the machine controller, or the computer's serial port and V-LAN translators. Whichever method of machine control you choose, try manipulating the player via the auto-assembly program's transport panel to test the connections. Figure 5-7 shows the PostConform transport panel.

Being able to PLAY, FF, REW, and so on, from the transport panel doesn't guarantee auto-assembly success, but if you can't at this point manually control the player from the computer, it's certain that the computer won't be able to automatically find the needed source sounds.

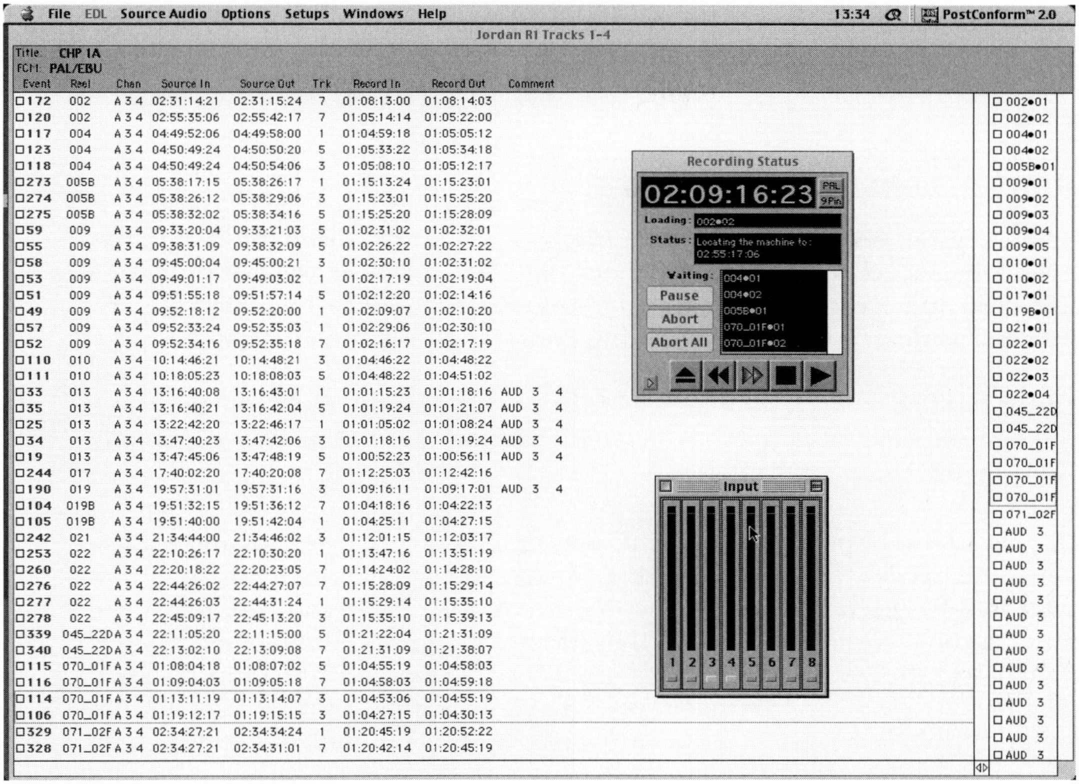

Figure 5-7 Even though it has no OS-X version, PostConform is still a favorite application for autoloading and conforming tape-based field recordings to create Pro Tools sessions.

The player, the audio interface, and the synchronizer must receive the same video reference. Certain audio devices can't directly accept reference video, so use word clock—derived from the master video source—to synchronize them. A quality TC DAT recorder or a freestanding analogue-to-digital-to-analogue (A/D/A) converter can generally be used to create word clock from video reference.

Don't get cheap on video reference. Although you can actually do a manageable postconform without taking it seriously, you're building your dialogue house on sand, which is never a good idea. Working without proper video reference risks sync problems, and a poorly clocked system imposes jitter on the digital audio stream, lessening "crispness" and robbing the dialogue of much needed punch and depth.

Auto-Assembly Step by Step

Some digital audio workstations, such as Pyramix, have built-in auto-assembly and conform utilities. Others, like Pro Tools, use external programs to record and conform original material to match an EDL. In either case, the process, as described in the following paragraphs, remains the same.

Clean the EDL Check for errors, clarify COMMENT fields, and confirm source roll names. Make sure that the information in the COMMENT fields is consistent. Print the EDLs for later reference.

Import EDLs Import your EDL into the auto-assembly program and choose your preferences. Once it's imported, you'll see your EDL or something that resembles it. Each line represents one event, for which you can adjust the input audio record channels and the **channel mapping**. Channel mapping is a matrix that correlates the EDL's "Track" instruction with the input source channels to create appropriately placed events in the completed session. In general, leave this setting alone. Run a test, and if you don't like the channel mapping results, start making changes.

When you import an EDL into an auto-assembly program, it will create record blocks, which may include only one event or several depending on your recording preferences and the manner in which the film was edited. Typically you're asked about **handle length**, which refers to how much extra material is recorded before and after the edit event, and **load spacing**, which combines several neighboring source events into one soundfile depending on your preferences.

You'll also be asked to choose which comment prefixes (such as *COMMENT: or *FROM CLIP NAME:) will signal scene and take names for import as region names.

Load the Sound Normally you choose to let the auto-assembly program automatically load the necessary sounds by controlling the DAT, DA-88, HD player, or whatever tape source holds your original recordings. After all, the joy of using an auto-assembly program is witnessing the player screaming back and forth, with your pristine sounds being recorded automatically while you read *Mad* magazine. All auto-assembly programs load by source roll, beginning with the lowest. It would be crazy to load in program order because you'd be constantly changing source rolls.

Periodically, you'll be asked to change tapes. If there's a timecode problem and the machine can't properly cue, you'll have to set the player to "local" and manually cue the tape past the timecode irregularity.

There are times when you don't want to use the auto-load feature. In such cases, you load the sounds manually and conform later. You may, for example, want to load *all* of the dailies, then link the files to the EDL for auto-assembly. This will place all of the recorded takes at your disposal, although not in a very well-managed format. (To make all takes available on your workstation, you're far better off loading the original tapes directly into the DAW, dividing them into takes, and then creating files from these regions.) If your movie was recorded on a hard-disk recorder, you can copy all of the soundfiles onto the workstation drive, later linking the files to an EDL.

Conform the Session Once the auto-assembly program finishes recording the required sounds from the original tapes, you're ready to conform the sound material to match the EDL. In truth, what you're doing is linking the EDL events to the recorded soundfiles. If the sounds were autoloaded by the program, these links have been established without your intervention. If, however, you're conforming previously recorded files or the original field recording files, you must manually link the EDL with the sounds.

If you receive a new (changed) EDL of a reel *before you've begun to edit*, you can once again conform the session with the existing soundfiles. However, since the new EDL wasn't the basis for the autoloading, it won't automatically link to the old soundfiles and you have to manually reestablish the link. If you've already done considerable editing on a reel, a new session is of little use. You could import the session reflecting the new EDL into your Pro Tools session, but then you have to redo your edits. You're usually better off performing a conformation of your Pro Tools session to match picture department changes (see Chapter 14). Only if there's new raw material in the revised picture cut (not just new edits of old material) should you go to the trouble of making a new postconform.

Test before Autoload Before spending all night loading tapes only to discover in the morning that the FCM was set incorrectly or that your audio 3 and 4 edits are mute, run a test. To make certain that the EDL is correctly formatted for the auto-assembly, select about ten contiguous events that include sounds from at least three sound rolls (DATs) and perform a test load and conform.

If, despite a few sync problems, the conform works, you can continue with the rest of the reel. If the conform is missing many regions, investigate naming problems. Events designated as audio 3 and/or 4 that result in empty regions indicate a channel-mapping problem. Some auto-assembly programs expect audio destined for channels 3 and 4 to originate only on inputs 3 and 4. That's pretty hard to do when your source audio is a DAT! In such cases you must remap the audio for all audio 3 and 4 edits to enter via inputs 1 and 2 on the interface. Usually you do this by individually opening each event within the auto-assembly program and changing the input from 3 and 4 to 1 and 2.

Now you know that the edits are in the right place and that you're recording the correct channels from the original recordings. However, you don't know yet if the DAT sound is playing at the right speed. Before (finally!) embarking on an hours-long postconform, find the longest uninterrupted take in the reel and perform an auto-assembly of that region. Play the conformed event against the guide track and check for sync. If the conformed sound drifts against the guide, check the video reference on the player as well as the sample rate on the synchronizer. Once the conformed long take plays back in sync with the guide track, you're ready to begin the auto-assembly.

Autoconform Files from a Hard-Disk Recorder

It's possible to use PostConform to auto-assemble projects originating on hard disk, although there are programs better suited for this task. Titan,[9] for example, enables you to create Pro Tools sessions from one or more EDLs, combined with the location recorder's original SDII or BWF files. (See Figure 5-8.) It also facilitates conforming edited Pro Tools sessions based on EDL-formatted Avid change lists.

- When you load an EDL into Titan on a computer with access to the soundfiles—either locally or across a network—Titan will automatically correlate files with EDL events based on certain arguments you present. The program first looks for a source roll number, which in the case of a hard-disk recording is a folder whose name is usually the date of the shoot.
- Having found a candidate folder, Titan will seek the appropriate timecode and automatically extract the event. Any failures, whether

---

[9] Titan is a product of Synchro Arts Limited (*www.synchroarts.com*).

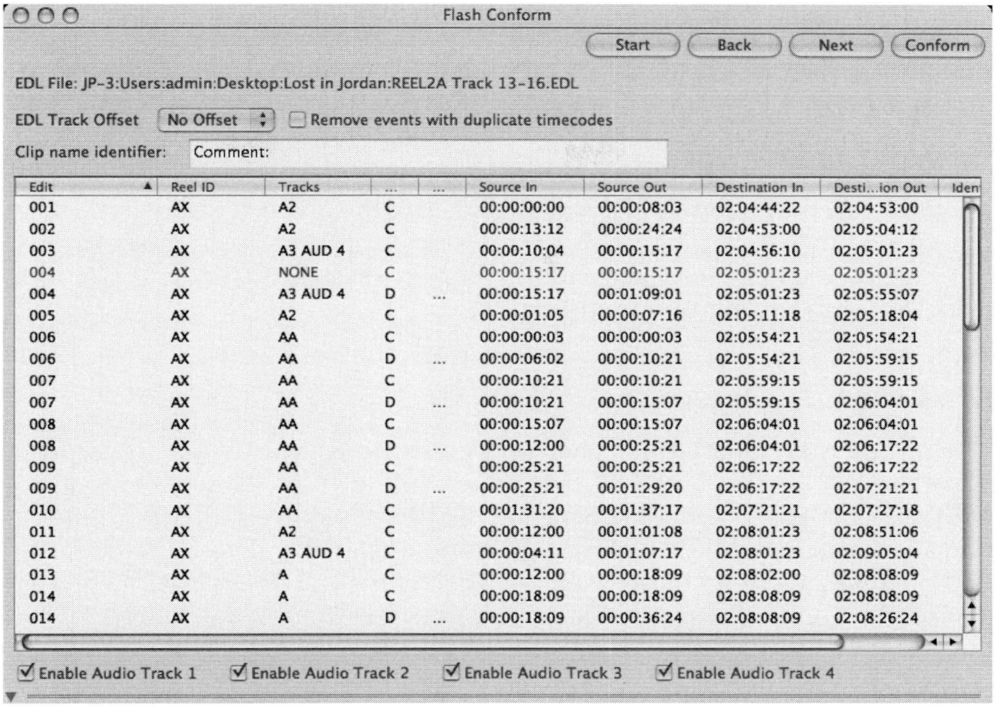

Figure 5-8 Titan's Flash Conform is a convenient way to conform (file-link) file-based edit lists to create editing sessions for digital audio workstations.

due to incorrect folder names, timecode (timestamp) errors, or missing media, will be reported in an error log.

- You must answer questions about the naming scheme for the sound-files, file type, and timecode format. As expected, you're asked to locate the folders containing the soundfiles and to name the soon-to-be-born Pro Tools session.

As with other auto-assembly processes, you must choose which comment text string the program will use as a trigger for naming the resulting Pro Tools regions.

Auto-assembly from files is massively easier than it is from tape, since there's no loading to do. The only caveat is that file-based auto-assembly programs like Titan can be very finicky about EDL formatting, COMMENT field structure, and naming schemes. Some of the time you save by not having to load sounds from tape may be squandered in playing with EDLs. Yet another reason to become skilled at EDL list management.

Merge All Channels

When you've conformed all of the EDLs for a reel, you'll need to merge them into one large session per reel. Open the new sessions one by one and set the start time for each to the correct value for that reel; then save the sessions. Begin this process with the highest track number (e.g., channels 13 through 16) and work down so that the last session for which you set the correct start time is channels 1 through 4. Into this session import the tracks from the other auto-assembly sessions. Finally, import the OMF tracks. You're now ready to begin setting up for editing.

Metadata Demystified

When you deal with multitrack hard-disk recordings, you inevitably confront metadata. Although devised to streamline workflows and automate repetitive processes, file-based metadata occasionally turns into to a source of intimidation and insecurity. You've been dealing with metadata all your life, probably without realizing it, yet the sudden intrusion of the word *metadata* into normal postproduction conversations leaves even confident editors wondering what they're not grasping.

Simply put, metadata is data about data. A classic example is a library card catalogue (the metadata), where you'll find pertinent information about books (the data). Since it's far easier to search a card catalogue than to wander aimlessly through the stacks, it's not difficult to see metadata's value. When you comb the Web with a search engine, you're querying metadata about billions of web sites—certainly easier than randomly typing URLs.

In audio postproduction there are many day-to-day brushes with metadata. Look through the directory of a sound effects library and you're dealing with metadata. Pour over the log sheets from a narration recording session and you're using the stuff. Search for an alternate take of dialogue using an EDL and sound reports and you're working with two levels of metadata to locate the sounds you want.

The surge in multitrack hard-disk field recordings is the reason that metadata is such a popular topic of water cooler conversations at post facilities. Behind this are three realities: (1) with more channels of information, there's more to keep up with; (2) most picture editors don't want to drag around six or more tracks of sound for each shot, so there must be a way for them to cut with a mono production mix and then for the sound department to painlessly access the isolated tracks; (3) there's always been a lot of metadata in the pipeline, but now it's largely computerized, which makes it much scarier. (And, of course, there are fewer people on the payroll to sort out the information so there's more pressure on the survivors.)

Broadcast Wave Format

Making all of this data management possible are rich soundfile formats, such as the increasingly standard **Broadcast Wave Format** (BWF) files, which carry more than just sound, including timestamps and scene/shot/take and all sorts of other information. BWF, an enhancement of the familiar WAVE (.wav) file, has quickly become an industry favorite. Since the prime reasons for creating it were interchangeability between platforms and ease in managing multichannel recordings, BWF has been widely adopted in audio production and post.

Microsoft WAVE files are made up of components called *chunks*, that is, blocks of data containing specific types of information with the largest chunk containing the audio data. Each chunk has an identification field and a size indicator so that any number of machines can read the file, address what they can cope with, and disregard the rest. This helps to make this format more universal than those that aren't compartmentalized because it allows numerous manufacturers to develop applications for similar tasks without having to completely rewrite their source code.

Start with a linear PCM WAVE file (not all WAVE files are linear PCM), add a **broadcast extension chunk**, and you have a BWF file,[10] as shown in Table 5-2. The information in the broadcast extension chunk is standardized enough to be readable on many platforms, yet flexible enough to be useful in film and television production, TV and radio broadcasting, multimedia and games, and other applications.

The Impact of Disk-Recorded Files

Many vintage Avids can't accept files with word lengths greater than 16 bits, so once the picture is edited there must be a way to replace the edited 16-bit soundfiles with their 24-bit parents. By using a metadata management

---

[10] A thorough description of the BWF format can be found in "The Broadcast Wave Format—An Introduction" by Richard Chalmers of the EBU Technical Department, in *EBU Technical Review* (Fall 1997). Also see "BWF—A Format for Audio Data Files in Broadcasting," *EBU Technical Specification* (June 2001); and "Broadcast Wave Format (BWF) User Guide," a publication of the European Broadcasting Union (*http://www.ebu.ch/en/technical/ publications/userguides/bwf_user_guide.php*).

Table 5-2 Major Components of the BWF Broadcast Extension Chunk

Field	Contents
Description	256 characters worth of shot description, mic types, etc.; *not* the file name
Originator	Sound recordist or project
Reference	Unambiguous identifier for locating the file; *not* the file name
Origination date	Date of recording
Origination time	Time of recording
Time references	Time reference since midnight, in samples
Version	BWF format version
UMID	Unique Material Identifier—helps track the history of the file
Coding history	Coding type (e.g., linear PCM, MPEG, etc.)

program such as MetaFlow or Majix,[11] you can load 16-bit mixdowns into the Avid and keep track of all of the original 24-bit tracks. At the end of the picture editing, you can use a file-linking program like Titan to conform multitrack, 24-bit files to the decisions made in the 16-bit Avid. Because the metadata houses information about each track of each shot, metadata management programs also serve as databases of alternate takes and additional tracks, often supplanting traditional sound reports.

After a day of shooting, the sound recordist provides the assistant film editor with a DVD or hard disk of the field recordings (which can even arrive at the cutting room on a keychain flash disk). Rather than load the recordings as digital audio, the assistant will merely copy the BWF files into the Avid. At the same time, the files are copied to the dialogue editor's drive. All metadata concerning the takes (scene/shot/take, timecode, number of tracks, etc.) is automatically logged with the files. There's a huge amount of information available within these metadata files, and once you have it in your system you can do all sorts of things with it. The Excel spreadsheet shown in Figure 5-9 is from a production recorded to BWF files with an Aaton Cantar, transferred to QuickTime via Sebsky Tools,[12] and picture-edited with Final Cut Pro.

With the metadata as the starting point, the dialogue editor can set up a database in Excel or FileMaker Pro. Making this database available to

---

[11] MetaFlow was a product of Gallery Software, but is now out of production. Majix is manufactured by Aaton to work exclusively with its Cantar hard-disk recorder.

[12] Sebsky Tools was manufactured by Dharma Film but has been discontinued and replaced by Dharma's other BWF-to-QuickTime product, *bfw2qt*. Dharma makes other products to aid the transfer of projects from Avid to FCP.

	A	B	C	D	E	F	I	K	N	P	X	A
1	File Name	Master Comment 1	Shoot Date	Sound Roll	Media Start	Media End	Dur	SR	Tracks	Log Notes	Aud Format	Last M
2	VB9437_1	WILD LUGGAGE CLAIM	30/1/05	DVD01	07:11:34:00	07:12:59:14	01:25:15	48K	1	rehearsal	16-bit Integer	Tue, Feb 22, 2(
3	VB9438_1	WILD GUITARRE 1	30/1/05	DVD01	07:38:10:00	07:39:31:06	01:21:07	48K	1		16-bit Integer	Tue, Feb 22, 2(
4	VB9439_1	WILD GUITARRE 2	30/1/05	DVD01	07:41:07:00	07:43:13:20	02:06:21	48K	1	Full Take	16-bit Integer	Tue, Feb 22, 2(
5	VB9440_1	WILD GUITARRE 3	30/1/05	DVD01	07:43:41:00	07:47:07:01	03:26:02	48K	1	Full Take	16-bit Integer	Tue, Feb 22, 2(
6	VB9441_1	WILD GUITARRE 4	30/1/05	DVD01	07:47:50:00	07:50:16:11	02:26:12	48K	1	Full Take	16-bit Integer	Tue, Feb 22, 2(
7	VB9442_1	test	30/1/05	DVD01	08:57:02:00	08:57:34:03	00:32:04	48K	1	FS	16-bit Integer	Tue, Feb 22, 2(
8	VB9442_2	test	30/1/05	DVD01	08:57:02:00	08:57:34:03	00:32:04	48K	1	FS	16-bit Integer	Tue, Feb 22, 2(
9	VB9443_1		30/1/05	DVD01	09:00:05:00	09:00:10:14	00:05:15	48K	1	FS	16-bit Integer	Tue, Feb 22, 2(
10	VB9443_2		30/1/05	DVD01	09:00:05:00	09:00:10:14	00:05:15	48K	1	FS	16-bit Integer	Tue, Feb 22, 2(
11	VB9444_1		30/1/05	DVD01	10:05:35:00	10:06:01:03	00:26:04	48K	1	FS	16-bit Integer	Tue, Feb 22, 2(
12	VB9444_2		30/1/05	DVD01	10:05:35:00	10:06:01:03	00:26:04	48K	1	FS	16-bit Integer	Tue, Feb 22, 2(
13	VB9445_1	01A-1 second clap	30/1/05	DVD01	10:06:06:00	10:09:03:04	02:48:23	48K	1	Full Take	16-bit Integer	Tue, Feb 22, 2(
14	VB9445_2	01A-1 second clap	30/1/05	DVD01	10:06:06:00	10:09:03:04	02:48:23	48K	1	Full Take	16-bit Integer	Tue, Feb 22, 2(
15	VB9446_1		30/1/05	DVD01	10:14:16:00	10:14:20:00	00:04:01	48K	1	FS	16-bit Integer	Tue, Feb 22, 2(
16	VB9446_2		30/1/05	DVD01	10:14:16:00	10:14:20:00	00:04:01	48K	1	FS	16-bit Integer	Tue, Feb 22, 2(
17	VB9447_1	01A-2	30/1/05	DVD01	10:17:25:00	10:20:46:04	03:08:04	48K	1	Full Take	16-bit Integer	Tue, Feb 22, 2(
18	VB9447_2	01A-2	30/1/05	DVD01	10:17:25:00	10:20:46:04	03:08:04	48K	1	Full Take	16-bit Integer	Tue, Feb 22, 2(
19	VB9448_1		30/1/05	DVD01	10:21:08:00	10:21:13:02	00:05:03	48K	1	FS	16-bit Integer	Tue, Feb 22, 2(
20	VB9448_2		30/1/05	DVD01	10:21:08:00	10:21:13:02	00:05:03	48K	1	FS	16-bit Integer	Tue, Feb 22, 2(
21	VB9449_1	WILD CHARIOTS AIRPORT	30/1/05	DVD01	10:21:20:00	10:23:24:06	02:04:07	48K	1	wild	16-bit Integer	Tue, Feb 22, 2(
22	VB9449_2	WILD CHARIOTS AIRPORT	30/1/05	DVD01	10:21:20:00	10:23:24:06	02:04:07	48K	1	wild	16-bit Integer	Tue, Feb 22, 2(
23	VB9450_1		30/1/05	DVD01	10:41:55:00	10:42:06:13	00:11:14	48K	1	FS	16-bit Integer	Tue, Feb 22, 2(
24	VB9450_2		30/1/05	DVD01	10:41:55:00	10:42:06:13	00:11:14	48K	1	FS	16-bit Integer	Tue, Feb 22, 2(
25	VB9451_1	01A-3	30/1/05	DVD01	10:42:11:00	10:45:35:07	03:13:19	48K	1	Full Take	16-bit Integer	Tue, Feb 22, 2(

Lost in Jordan FCP batch files #1

Sheet1 Sheet2 Sheet3

Figure 5-9 Once you've imported the metadata from the location mixer's hard-disk recorder, you can set up a very powerful tool for finding, comparing, and commenting on your soundfiles.

everyone on the sound team greatly increases efficiency. And if you add comments, it will point other editors to fruitful soundfiles and keep you—and them—from repeatedly exploring blind alleys. Remember, though, you're a sound editor, not an IT manager. These lists and databases are here to help you to edit more efficiently. They're a means rather than an end, so don't be overly obsessed with spectacular spreadsheets.

Each workstation has its own way of dealing with the vagaries of metadata, 24-bit sound, and multitrack soundfiles. To complicate matters, the brand of hard-disk recorder used in production will influence the route you and the assistant picture editor will take to manage the project. This needn't be overwhelming; you just have to discover early in the production, long before you start editing, how the film is being shot and recorded. Talk with the assistant picture editor as soon as shooting begins; she's after all the one who will be syncing the dailies and organizing the paperwork, and who'll catch the potential pitfalls of the system. At the very least, learn the following:

- Which hard-disk recorder was used? What's the sample rate and bit depth? What's the file format (hopefully BWF)?

- Which picture workstation was used? Which model and software version? The version number is vital information, since two different software versions of the same picture workstation may have wildly different capabilities. Can the workstation accommodate the original 24-bit soundfiles?
- Will the editor cut with all of the recorded audio tracks or use a mixdown?

Armed with this information, approach colleagues who have faced similar jobs and seek their advice. Visit the web site of the manufacturer of the hard-disk recorder used on the film. Go to the Avid or FCP web site. Spend some time in Internet forums to look for pertinent advice.

You're not the first person to face this hurdle. The key to successfully negotiating the overwhelming set of possibilities is to first gather the information just listed and categorize the problems you'll face. Once you know what you're looking for, it's not hard to find the answers.

- As soon as you have access to a sound editing room, arrange a very short test with the assistant picture editor. Ask for a 10-event Avid session that represents the issues you'll encounter once the picture is locked.
- Ask about mono tracks representing multiple tracks, 16-bit soundfiles linked to 24-bit originals, shooting days whose timecode crossed midnight[13]—these issues can trip you up when you conform the film.
- Request picture as well as sound so that you can check sync.
- Get an OMF as well as an EDL so that you can easily test the accuracy of the edits as well as the OMF sound quality compared to the original recordings.

It's much better to learn of a trap now than to wait until the picture is locked and the weight of the production is on your shoulders. Now you have time to go back to the books to learn what you did wrong and to get the picture department to change some habits.

---

[13] *Crossing midnight* refers to recordings with timestamps that begin before 23:59:59:00 and continue into the next timecode day. A take that "ends before it begins" is disastrous when using linear editing systems but merely an inconvenience when working with file-based recordings.

CHAPTER 6

Burn-Ins, File Names, and Backups

There are many quality-of-life matters you can address as you set up your editing realm, some that will make editing easier and others that will protect you from disaster. Developing a sensible file-naming system will make for happier editing—and your colleagues will know which of your sessions to use when you're not available. A smart backup system will avert the worst of disasters and help you to sleep at night. And intelligently preparing your videotapes will reduce errors and save time.

Some of the processes described in this chapter will be handled by an assistant, if you have any luck at all, but there will be times you need to handle them on your own. Plus, it doesn't hurt to know what your assistant is up to.

Make a Timecode Burn-In

Whether your picture is on videotape or in a digital video file, try to make a copy of it and insert a timecode burn-in. Using tapes without a burned-in timecode window, relying instead on the VTR's character inserter, is at times unreliable and inconsistent. If your tape contains only LTC (longitudinal timecode[1]),or if that's all your VTR can interpret, timecode is valid only at

---

[1] Timecode can be placed on a tape in a number of ways. The oldest method involves converting the 80-bit timecode data stream into an analogue signal and recording it onto a dedicated channel (the timecode track). In olden days, before VTRs had dedicated timecode heads, an analogue timecode signal would be recorded onto an audio channel. This caused all sorts of problems, including nasty crosstalk. Called LTC (longitudinal timecode), it worked very well at play speeds but wasn't accurate at very slow speeds. LTC is worthless when the VTR is stopped. To get around this problem, a timecode was developed that can be read at nonplay speeds. VITC (vertical interval timecode) is placed in the vertical blanking of the video, just above the picture area. If you reduce the picture size or roll the picture down, you can see it in the form of dancing white dots and dashes. Most VTRs read both LTC and VITC and know how to switch between the two as the play speed changes. Finally, there's BITC (burnt-in timecode), also known as "window dub" or "timecode window." This is a graphic, human-readable display of the current timecode address inserted into the video. The fact that your videotape has a burn-in is no guarantee that the tape has machine-readable timecode.

Figure 6-1 Place the timecode burn-in at the top of the frame, taking care not to cover other windows. The other information on the screen is largely for the picture department, but it occasionally comes in handy. In this frame from *Jellyfish*, by Shira Geffen and Etgar Keret, the original windows are (clockwise from upper left): lab roll, videotape number, dailies timecode, Keykode. (Reproduced by permission of Lama Films.)

play speed. Without VITC (vertical interval timecode), neither the VTR's timecode character inserter nor your workstation's timecode interpreter can accurately define addresses as you "scrub," making reliably defining scene changes and perspective cuts impossible. Even with VITC there are pitfalls.

When you have a timecode burnt in on the tape (see Figure 6-1), the noise bar[2] of the video will wipe over the timecode window and you'll see the frame change. It's more like working on film.

---

[2] The noise bar is the "frame line" that wipes over the video as you slowly scrub from one frame to the next. Since there are two fields in a frame, two noise bars must pass over the screen to advance one frame. If your VTR has a timebase corrector or dynamic tracking, you likely won't see the noise bar.

Most Avid cutting rooms are incapable of burning the timecode directly onto the video image, so the burn-in becomes a two-step process. First obtain a regular videotape "digital dump" from the Avid or Final Cut Pro. Next send the tape to a video facility for dubbing with a burn-in or, if so equipped, do it yourself. Making a dub with a timecode burn-in isn't rocket science, but you should pay attention to a few details whether you're making the copy yourself or writing the instructions for the dubbing facility.

- Place the timecode window at the very top of the frame, outside the image if possible. Smaller is better. Try not to cover up any of the other information fields, but since this tape is just for you and not for negative cutting, only the source sound timecode window is truly important. If the timecode window is at the very top of the frame, it will be the first information updated by the noise bar as you scrub the VTR. As small a matter as it may seem, this actually saves considerable time over the course of the film if your picture is on tape.[3]
- Be certain that the play and record VTRs, the timecode generator, and the timecode inserter are all locked to the same video reference.
- Confirm that both channels of audio are transferred, not mixed together. Also, the LTC and VITC timecode must be copied with the dub. You're much better off passing the timecode through a TC generator and "jam-syncing" the code than you are just patching the timecode as though it were an audio signal (it *is* an audio signal, but a very special one).
- Clearly label the tape with title, date, reel number, and version name or number, along with any technical details.

When editing to a QuickTime movie or other disk-based video player, I prefer to make a timecode burn-in before digitizing the picture so that I'll have a permanent "hard-copy" timecode display. Establishing sync with a nonlinear player is much like voodoo, and throughout the editing process the question of gooey sync looms. By physically stamping the timecode onto the video, it's simple to sync picture to sound and quite easy to confirm sync when you're in doubt.

---

[3] There are arguments, at times passionate, about where to place the timecode burn-in— at the top or at the bottom of the frame. You've heard my reasons for the top. There are, however, times when it's best to place the burn-in at the bottom of the frame. If you use the character inserter in the Betacam or DV player to create your burn-in, rather than using an external timecode inserter, you're better off placing the burn-in at the bottom. With the timecode window at the top, the built-in inserters may "print" the timecode into the video before updating the time. You end up with BITC that's one field late.

Digital Picture Pitfalls

There are many ways that nonlinear video players can lead your sync astray. If, for example, you're working with Pro Tools on a Mac, onboard QuickTime picture playback without an extra video card will inevitably result in unreliable sync. Forget what the manufacturers tell you. As your session gets heavier, sync becomes more erratic—sometimes spot-on, other times quite loose. To achieve worry-free sync when working to digital picture, use a separate video device as a picture player. This could be a video disk recorder, such as the Pixys video recorder/player from Fairlight[4] or the V-Cube from Merging Technologies.[5] Or turn last year's computer into a virtual video player with Virtual VTR.[6] You can also achieve excellent results using a separate high-quality video card that provides reference-locked video playback.

Postproduction facilities may jump at the opportunity to trade in an expensive, maintenance-heavy Betacam player for an extra FireWire drive and an inexpensive video interface box. But editors pay the price of this cheapness, always wondering about sync. If you have any influence over the purchasing choices of the facility where you work, encourage the use of proper external video recorder/players. Life's too short to constantly worry about sync.

Use Smart File Names

The ease with which you can produce and compare endless variations of a cut is one of the greatest blessings—and curses—of digital audio workstations. There are countless reasons for different versions of an edit, and by the end of the project you could easily have created hundreds, each represented by its own session file.

- The picture editor makes some changes after picture lock, and you have a new version.
- You decide to pursue a new creative path on a scene, so you create a new version.
- You put together a dialogue cut for a temp mix or for a special screening, and a new version exists.
- A couple of times a day you "save as" under a new name so that you have a way to backtrack in case of file corruption and to protect yourself from your mistakes and misjudgments. These files get new names.

---

[4] See *www.fairlightau.com.*
[5] See *www.merging.com.*
[6] See *www.virtualvtr.com.*

Table 6-1 Fields in a Dialogue Session File Name

shortname	Abbreviated film name used by all editors. Probably the name the lab uses on files relating to the film.
Dial	Indicator that the session is about dialogue and not SFX, BG, etc.
R	Reel number.
ver	Picture version the session applies to. Could be the date when the video was modified or the picture version name or number. Could also refer to special attributes of the session (director's version, screening version, merged-session version, etc.).
edit	Dialogue edit in this picture version. Might be a series number (1, 2, 3, . . .) or date of the edit.

Of course, each version is a new session. You have to name these files something, so you might as well give them names that illuminate. With all of this in mind, here's a suggestion for dialogue session file names:

```
shortname Dial Rx ver x, edit x
```

which translates into what's shown in Table 6-1.

Barring other reasons for creating new versions, I'll do a save as twice daily, once at lunch and once at the end of the day. If my starting file for the day was Jordan Dial R5 ver4 edit 3, my midday save will be Jordan Dial R5 ver4 edit 4, and my end-of-the-day save will be Jordan Dial R5 ver4 edit 5.

If I come in the next morning only to realize that the double cheeseburger at yesterday's lunch so clouded my judgment as to render the entire afternoon's work unusable, I can always revert to edit 4, not tell anyone of my disaster, and swear off heavy food for the rest of the gig. If I'm going to try an editorial path I consider likely to fail, I'll make a new edit (possibly Jordan Dial R5 ver4 edit 5a) that differentiates this experimental version from the "straight" work I've done. If edit 5a fails to be brilliant, I can easily revert to edit 5.

Perform a normal save, in which the session file is overwritten, as often as you can remember. You can also use your workstation's auto-save feature to make overwrite saves of your sessions at regular intervals.

Back up Your Files

Needless to say, you must have a plan for backing up your soundfiles and sessions. Unlike SFX editing, where your bank of soundfiles is constantly growing, dialogue doesn't generate a lot of new files after the OMF import and/or auto-assembly, so you can do one big backup at the beginning of the project and most of the work is done. Still, you have to back up daily the handful of new files you inevitably generate: the bounces, consolidations, and processed regions. Open your session without them and you'll face embarrassing holes. Also, any **destructive** process, such as Pro Tool's pencil tool, alters your originals. Such modifications aren't stored with the session, but rather exist as changes in the underlying soundfile, which must be backed up once again or the changes won't show up in reconstituted projects.

Finally, don't forget to back up your ADR files. Say you record an ADR session from a remote location via ISDN and then trip on the drive's power cable, smashing the drive and its contents to pieces. Who's going to look stupid? Back it up.

By far the easiest way to back up a session's new soundfiles and keep them up to date is with a backup utility such as Mezzo or Retrospect.[7] Whether you back up to a FireWire drive, a DVD, a tape drive, or across a network, backup programs keep track of changes to your drive since the last backup session and incrementally copy only what's necessary.

Without special software you can still manage your backups with confidence; it's just a bit more work. After the OMF and autoconform are opened and you've created your master sessions (one per reel), copy the entire project to a large FireWire backup drive. On your work drive, label (color code) all of the files that have been copied.

- As you edit, pay attention to where you put new soundfiles. Fewer target folders mean fewer places to look for them.
- At the end of each work day, open all of the folders to which you've been adding soundfiles. Sort by modification date, and the new, unprotected files will come to the top. These new files won't carry a color label since they haven't been copied to the backup drive. Copy them (from every applicable folder) to the backup drive now. Previously copied soundfiles that have undergone destructive changes—such as with Pro Tools' pencil—will sort near the top of the list because they were recently modified, but they'll carry a color label from previous backups, making them a bit harder to find.
- Don't forget to copy your session files.
- Finally, color label the newly copied files to indicate that they've been backed up.

---

[7] Mezzo is a product of Grey Matter Response. Retrospect is made by EMC Dantz.

CHAPTER 7

Screening the OMF/PostConform— The Spotting Session

All films have directors, and we must listen to them and honor their wishes, even though any honest sound editor can recall times when he thought the director was off the mark. "If only he'd listen to me, Rome would be saved." Get a grip. It's not your film, and you may not be seeing the big picture. Plus, drawing blood over a breath or a chair squeak isn't a sign of maturity. Besides, the director just may be right.

On a typical small film, you'll meet with the director two or three times: just after the OMF or autoconform is opened and checked for accuracy, near the end of your editing, and perhaps again just before the dialogue premix. Depending on the dynamics of the sound department and the film's budget, you may see the director more often or you may have no meetings at all with her, turning instead to the supervising sound editor for guidance.

Spotting Session Basics

The initial spotting session with the director is the most comprehensive meeting, as it involves the entire sound crew along with people from the film you may never see again. In many ways, though, it's one of the easiest because there's no baggage yet and expectations and spirits are often high. Most of the burden in this meeting falls on the supervising sound editor. Still, there are things you have to pay attention to.

- Note problems that may result in unexpected work on your part and report them to the supervising sound editor during the meeting. It's best to put these on the table now.
- Discuss whatever *general* ADR issues you observe in the first screening (if there's an ADR supervisor and/or editor, you're pretty much off the hook on this one). Most ADR calls can be made only after detailed study of the tracks, yet it's all but certain that the producer will want a ballpark idea of the film's ADR load *during* the meeting.

- Get a list of the director's ADR wishes, as this not only will tell you which lines must be replaced but will also give you some insight into the director's aesthetics and hobby horses.
- Make sure you have all the materials you need. This is a rare time when you have the attention of the director and others from the production. If you're having a problem getting materials from the production office, now's your chance to lean on someone with authority.
- Make sure you understand the schedule—screenings, ADR recording dates, rough dialogue mixes for the SFX department, dialogue premixes, and so on—before the meeting is over. This initial screening should make you feel more informed and confident, not the opposite.

It's All about Listening

If this is your first time seeing the film, you'll have to work doubly hard during the screening. You need to listen for dialogue issues (off-mic recordings, noisy settings, radio mic problems, dolly noise, etc.), and at the same time pay attention to the narrative so that you know what's going on and can start to think about the dialogue's contribution. Following the narrative is never really the problem—that part comes naturally. The hardest aspect of a screening is suspending the story enough so that you can notice the problems. Left to our own devices, we tend to "veg out" with the movie and fail to notice all but the most obnoxious dialogue errors.

Staying in contact with a film you're screening and looking beyond the story are largely matters of brute-force discipline. You just have to make yourself focus. A few tricks may help.

- Take the best seat in the room, front row center if you're screening on a workstation. You, more than anyone, need to hear the tracks.
- Be relaxed. Find a good chair and get comfortable.
- Use a form like the one in the Figure 7-1 to remember what questions to ask and what to listen for.
- As each scene begins, immediately identify the **room tone**, the noise level, and the quality of the dialogue. Take notes if necessary. By gathering this information at the beginning of each scene, you needn't worry if your mind wanders a bit. As soon as the scene ends, be alert for the next scene's troubles.
- Watch for moving cameras. When the camera moves there's likely to be dolly noise or perhaps unwanted footsteps. When the camera moves up or down, there's a good chance of camera pedestal or crane

Job Bid Form

Client and Contact Information

Client:	Phone:	Fax:
Producer:	Phone:	Fax:
Director:	Phone:	Fax:
Editor:	Phone:	Fax:

Project Information

Title:		
Projected length:	Current Length:	# reels:
Lab:	Post-production supervisor:	
Sound Recordist:	Format:	Sample rate:
Was room tone recorded?	What % of locations have tone?	
Mono/Split/Stereo	How split:	Mics:
Camera:	Format:	DP:
Editing machine:	Where?	
Type of film:		Quality of Edit Room Paperwork:
Are editor and director experienced filmmakers?	Are they "technical?" Is there a sound book?	Have they worked abroad?

Screening Report

Where screened:	How:	Date:
Version seen:	Format screened:	
Brief description of film:		
% of film is Dialogue:	Action:	Music montage:
Describe quality of dialogue:		
Status of tracks:	Atmo noise:	
	Off mic dial:	
	Camera Noise:	
	Dolly noise:	
	Distortion:	
	Wind/clothing:	
	Other (describe)	
Other comments:		

Figure 7-1 An evaluation form for preliminary screenings. Use it to compile information about the client and the film, the expectations of the client, and technical details from the screening. It serves as a useful reminder of what you need to listen for during the screening.

noise. It's very easy to miss even the most scandalous dolly noise when the movie is good. Just remember: A moving camera spells trouble.

• After a reel or so, pinch yourself. You may be drifting or have become waylaid by the story. It's actually easier to screen a mediocre film than a masterpiece, since you're less likely to be kidnapped by the plot. Films in a foreign language are even easier to study.

CHAPTER 8

Managing Your Time

Unlike many kinds of film work, dialogue editing is amazingly unsupervised. If you're editing the music or effects for a television special, or perhaps a documentary, you'll usually be working with a client or a supervisor. But if you're cutting dialogue on a feature film, you're mostly left to your own devices. A dialogue job with a lot of work and only a deadline to guide you requires planning and discipline.

Screen First

I like to screen a film before I actually begin working on it, even before the initial spotting session. And I prefer to do this any place but the picture editing room, the worst imaginable listening environment. The ideal spot is the dubbing stage where the film will be mixed, ideally with the rerecording mixer and someone from the production. This offers several advantages.

- You—and everyone else—will hear the dialogue tracks in all their naked glory, not masked by the buzz of the Avid's drives or disguised by the small speakers of your editing room. The raw tracks almost always sound their worst in the full-spectrum mix room, so the client can no longer say, "Hey, it sounded great in the Avid."
- You and the mixer can discuss ADR, hopeless scenes, and other technical issues.
- There are few distractions in a mix room or screening room, so you can better assess the dialogue as it relates to story and character.
- Screening in a mix room is expensive, so the producer probably won't let the meeting last all night.

The purpose of the initial screening is not to solve the innumerable problems of the film's dialogue but for you to decide these issues.

- Do you want to do this gig?
- How long will the dialogue take?

- What are the unusual problems?
- Ballpark, how much ADR is necessary?

That's all. But that's a lot.

Use an Evaluation Form and Past Project Timesheets

When I screen a film for the first time, I bring a form for evaluating it (refer to Figure 7-1). I use it to remind me to ask the right questions and to make it as easy as possible to compare this film with past projects. This helps me come up with a schedule and a budget, and it's also handy for recording my impressions of what to expect from the director and picture editor.

After the screening, I use my report to see how the film stacks up against previous projects. Of course, this only works because of another piece of data: my project timesheets, where I record my working hours and what I do each day on a project. I use them to make sure I'm on target with my hours and that I'm being paid fairly, and as an archive to use in budgeting future projects. (See Figure 8-1.)

When I see a film for the first time, I ask myself which of my former projects it reminds me of. Once I can limit it to a few choices, I check the timesheets and have a pretty good idea where I stand. Of course, it often matters little what I think about the needs of the dialogue. What ultimately sets the rules is the (often seemingly arbitrary) budget the producer has assembled. If a producer has etched into his mind what your budget will be—your fee and your allotted hours—then there isn't much you can do about it. If you think it's doable, take the gig. If not, walk away.

Set Daily Goals

You've negotiated the number of studio hours available to you and settled on a schedule. You know the deadline, and you know when the film will arrive. Aside from a screening here and there, no one cares how you organize yourself. Still, to make sure you finish on time and that the project doesn't turn into the film from hell, you must plan your days.

Because dialogue editing is a predictable, methodical operation, it's relatively easy to break it into parts and develop a plan. I normally organize dialogue work into three passes, with the first one being the most demanding and each successive pass more general and flowing. A typical plan breakdown is shown in Table 8-1.

"Lost in Jordan" timesheet

Date	Day	Start	Stop	Hours	Comments
05/01/03	1	10:00	19:15	09:15	screen w/ Alex; organize; help Tomer
06/01/03	2	07:30	17:30	10:00	finish synching; R5 pass 1
08/01/03	3	07:30	17:45	10:15	load WS (5 hours downtime!)
08/01/03	3	18:00	19:00	01:00	organize WS
12/01/03	4	10:00	19:15	09:15	R5 dialogue
13/01/03	5	07:30	18:00	10:30	R1 dialogue; work with Alex
14/01/03	6	07:45	17:30	09:45	R1 dialogue
15/01/03	7	09:00	11:30	02:30	screen film
15/01/03	7	12:30	16:15	03:45	R2 dialogue
16/01/03	8	07:45	18:00	10:15	R2 dialogue, screen for ADR with Alex
19/01/03	9	10:00	19:00	09:00	Conformation Ver A->Ver B
20/01/03	10	07:15	18:30	11:15	screen w/Amos; R3 dialogue
21/01/03	11	07:30	16:30	09:00	R3 dialogue, guide tracks
22/01/03	12	08:00	18:15	10:15	R6 dialogue
23/01/03	13	07:45	18:00	10:15	R4 dialogue
26/01/03	14	09:45	17:45	08:00	R4 dialogue
27/01/03	15	07:45	18:00	10:15	R4 dialogue, R7 dialogue
28/01/03	16	08:00	16:00	08:00	chceck AP#1, begin pass #2
29/01/03	17	07:45	18:00	10:15	Pass #2
30/01/03	18	08:15	16:00	07:45	Pass #2, screen with Amos and Alex
02/02/03	19	10:00	18:00	08:00	ADR edit
03/02/03	20	08:15	18:30	10:15	ADR edit
04/02/03	21	07:45	17:45	10:00	ADR edit; re-sync to 2nd AP
05/02/03	22	09:30	17:00	07:30	screen w/ Alex; package film; cuesheets
06/02/03	23	09:45	20:15	10:30	screen w/ Alex; package film; cuesheets
10/02/03	24	07:45	18:15	10:30	TV: edit new material, day 1
11/02/03	25	08:00	17:30	09:30	TV: edit new material, day 2
12/02/03	26	08:30	16:30	08:00	TV: edit new material, day 3
13/02/03	27	07:45	18:15	10:30	TV: edit new material, day 4
16/02/03	28	10:15	18:15	08:00	TV: edit new material, day 5
05/03/03	29	15:45	18:45	03:00	TV: screen with Alex
10/03/03	30	18:00	20:15	02:15	TV: final fixes
				00:00	
				00:00	
				268:30:00	

Figure 8-1 A timesheet for tracking editing hours. Recording time spent for each part of a project makes future estimates more accurate.

The schedule shown in the table is front loaded, with the overwhelming majority of my editing time devoted to getting started and completing the first pass. Why?

- Much of dialogue editing is about finding the truth amid so many shouting tracks. Allocating so much of your time to structure, organization, and correctness pays off in the end.

Table 8-1 Dialogue Editing Passes

Step	Time	Process
Preparation	Two to three reels per day	Prepare OMF and postconform, confirm sync, organize and label tracks, remove unnecessary channels, add sync pops and reference tones, mark scene boundaries, set up archive system.
Pass 1	Approximately 60% of schedule	Organize tracks, balance shot transitions, replace problems with alternate takes. Do basic level balancing, make scene transitions, remove some noises, screen dialogue edit first time for director.
Pass 2	Approximately 25% of schedule	Edit ADR into scenes (assuming ADR editor has chosen and synchronized the ADR lines; if not, do this, too), remove remaining noises, watch complete scenes and correct "flow" problems, screen second time for director.
Pass 3	Approximately 15% of schedule	Do director's changes and fixes, remove more noises, watch entire film (several times) and solve "flow" and logic problems, revisit outtakes for problem scenes, prepare session for dialogue premix, print cue sheets, prepare final project archive.

- Many problems don't rear their heads until you've cleaned up a scene. You need to expend enormous effort balancing tracks, replacing horrors, responsibly splitting, and getting rid of noises before you can find out what's *really* going on in the scene. Once you turn the sow's ear into a respectable silk purse, it can be easy to sort out the other issues.
- Pass 1 is simply time consuming. Here's where you hunt through alternate takes to fix diction or remove a noise. That takes time. Also, you have to take detailed notes of what you can't fix so that the ADR supervisor (who could be you) will know what to spot for ADR recording.
- Pass 1 is when you discover the structure and character of the film. Sometime near the end of it you realize that you actually *will* finish the project.
- For me, pass 1 is the "get run over by a bus" pass (some call it the "heart attack" pass). Although there's much work to be done in passes 2 and 3, those can be picked up and done by any competent editor if I make it through pass 1 and then drop dead on the way home.
- It's a personal thing. I like to work very intensely at the beginning of a project so that I can quickly overcome the "how will I ever finish this?" jitters. Plus, it makes the end of the job deliciously relaxed. I never do an all-nighter at the end of a project.

Schedule Your Time

Make up a schedule that marks the important landmarks of your film. These landmarks aren't yet your steps in the process but rather the important dates for it.

- Picture lock
- More realistic picture lock
- OMF and other materials delivered to you
- Character A leaves the country; character A returns (and is available for ADR)
- Director not available from _____ to _____
- Holidays and personal commitments
- Studio rented out for another job on these days _____
- First screening with director and picture editor
- Final screening with director and picture editor
- Dialogue premix
- Anything else useful

Put these dates on your calendar. They're the realities you have to deal with. Of course, everything will change, but you have to start somewhere.

See how many days remain for actual editing. If you originally had 30 days for dialogue editing but 4 will be taken up with ADR spotting, director meetings, and the like, assume you have 26 actual working days. Using the percentages from Table 8-1, determine how many days you have for each step in the process. Your 26-day schedule for a 6-double-reel film might look like what's shown in Table 8-2.

Before plugging these days into your calendar, remove one or two from pass 1 and one from pass 2. Unfair? Perhaps, but this is your contingency if something surprising comes up. Something surprising *always* comes up. The computer breaks, your child gets sick, the director wants to screen *again*, you get stuck in an unanticipated ADR recording session. It's limitless. Stealing from yourself about 10 percent of your editing budget will save you when you need it.

Now you can create a schedule that might look like Figure 8-2.

As a last step, I calculate how much film time, on average, I must complete during each shift. Our imaginary 6-reel film is 105 minutes long and we've budgeted 15 days for the first pass. This means we have to average 7 minutes of film dialogue each day to stay on schedule. Of course, some days are good, others are bad. There are times you're the smartest, most creative editor ever seen and times when you wonder how you got the job. That's why the

Table 8-2 Breakdown of 26-day Schedule

Step	Time	Process
Preparation	2 days	Prepare OMF and postconform, confirm sync, organize and label tracks, remove unnecessary channels, add sync pops and reference tones, mark scene boundaries, set up archive system.
Pass 1	15 days	Organize tracks, balance shot transitions, replace problems with alternate takes, basic level balancing, scene transitions, remove some noises.
Pass 2	6 days	Cut ADR into scenes (assuming an ADR editor has chosen and synchronized the ADR lines; if not, do this, too), remove remaining noises, watch complete scenes and correct "flow" problems.
Pass 3	3 days	Make director's changes and fixes, remove remaining noises, watch entire film (several times) and solve "flow" and logic problems, revisit outtakes for problem scenes, prepare session for dialogue premix, print cue sheets, prepare final archive of project.

7-minute average is just that—a benchmark for this film—but it's a useful tool for knowing where you stand.

Occasionally you'll find yourself editing smaller projects with very quick turnarounds. Say you have a 90-minute documentary for which you have to edit (or rather salvage) the production sound in three days. That's 30 minutes of film per day! Now, if you work a 10-hour shift, which means about 9 useful hours, you have to average about 3½ minutes of film per hour of work. The first day will be slow because you have to set up your session, label the tracks, and get to know the film. So day 2 will have to be extra aggressive (as though you could be more aggressive!) to make up for lost time from day 1. Some people find this kind of micro-organization stressful and neurotic. Others find it comforting. Your choice.

Estimate How Long the Editing Will Take

Even if you're an ace estimator and you have an impressive database of previous jobs to use for budgeting your new job, you'll quickly realize that the dialogue budget—and hence the amount of time you'll have to work on the film—is largely out of your hands. It's common for a producer to ask you how long you think it will take to make a masterpiece out of her muck. After a good deal of detailed analysis, phone calls to colleagues, and educated guesses, you decide on seven weeks. Don't be offended when your thoughtful response is met with "Seven weeks, you think? That's nice, but we're going to do it in three weeks." You wonder why she asked.

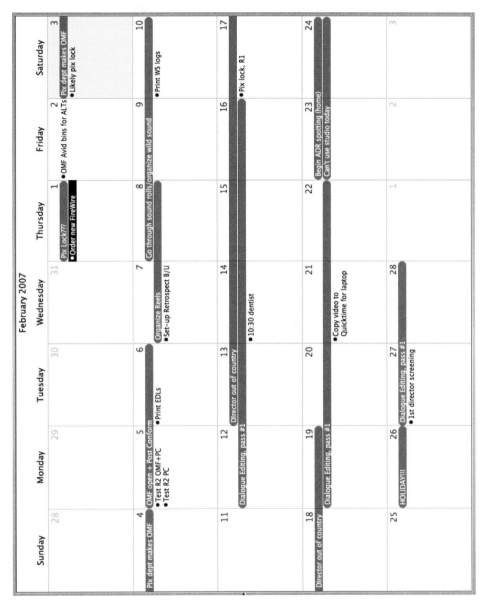

Figure 8-2 One month of a dialogue editor's life.

Although it's not really up to you to decide how much time and money the film's dialogue will get, it's still important to have a grasp of the possibilities. At the very least, you need to know if it's worth your while to take the job. Use the timesheets from previous projects as a guide for estimating how long the job *ought to* take. If your estimate is reasonably close to the producer's mandate, then you can likely scrimp a bit here, give up a few free hours there, cut a corner or two in places, and pull it off. But if the schedule you're being "offered" is wildly out of line with any comparable project you've done under similar circumstances, reconsider the offer.

What's "reasonable"? In general, two weeks per reel of dialogue (without ADR) is very comfortable. It depends, of course, on the problems you'll inherit with the tracks, as well as the expectations and temperament of the director. With two weeks per reel, however, you really have nothing to complain about. On low-budget films, a week a reel is more common, and even this is doable if the gods are with you. But when the schedule creeps below a week a reel, beware of problems. It's by no means impossible to cut a film in less time, but there'll be the inevitable compromises. I've cut dialogue at a reel a day, but such jobs are more embalming than editing. And if you're the least bit conscientious, very tight schedules result in far greater stress than more reasonable gigs do. You work harder only to be paid less.

Negotiate

When negotiating your time and fee, try to keep the dialogue and ADR as separate items. First of all, they *are* separate. Dialogue editors edit, ADR supervisors plan and direct the ADR, and ADR editors cut the tracks. On small films, though, it's common for the dialogue editor to have some (or all) of the ADR responsibilities. Since small films often have "just a little" ADR, there may be no ADR supervisor and the dialogue editor is expected to fill in the gap. Before you shake hands on the deal, clarify your ADR responsibilities: spotting, planning, directing, recording, and editing.

ADR supervision is a full-time job. Properly spotting the calls and preparing the paperwork aren't minor tasks. Be certain that you know the range of your responsibilities before you settle on a fee and schedule. If the supervising sound editor is covering the ADR spotting, planning, and recording, or if there's an ADR supervisor, you may be left with just the ADR editing. Once the supervising sound editor comes up with a count of the lines to be recorded, you can calculate how long it will take to cut those lines into the film. There's no need to get petty or paranoid or greedy about the extra work. Just take this into account when you're making your deal.

Negotiating the amount of time you'll have to work on a film is one of your most important responsibilities. It's not just about money. If you can get an extra week, or even a few more days, to spend with the film, your tracks will be more than happy to show their appreciation.

Work Out of Sequence

As you organize your tracks and figure out how scenes were constructed, you'll begin to crack the code of the film's dialogue. You'd think that cutting dialogue would be very similar on all films, but it's just not true. Beyond the obvious technical differences, each film's dialogue tracks have personalities of their own. It's up to you to figure out what they are. The more time you spend with a film's dialogue, the closer you'll come to understanding how to edit it. Too bad for the first reel you cut, because that's where you know the least, where you're stabbing in the dark for inspiration. As you work more on the film, you get better at knowing what to do to make the tracks happy.

The first and last reels of any film are its most important. During the first few minutes of a film, viewers—listeners—pass judgment on the soundtrack. "Is this a competent soundtrack? Is the dialogue well edited? Can I relax and enjoy the movie, or do I have to be on the alert for sound silliness?" Like meeting prospective in-laws, you only get one chance to make a good first impression. Don't blow it.

Similarly, there's no room for sloppiness or insecurity in the last reel's dialogue, since the "sound memory" that a viewer will go home with comes from the end of the film. Run a perfect 3½ laps of a 1600-meter race but choke on the last turn and you'll be remembered only for your fizzle. The last reel is no place to learn how to cut the film.

Combining all of these factors, I don't edit dialogue in film order. I always start with an interior reel and then work my way outward. I also never save the final reel for last, since I can count on being tired and stressed at that point. A typical 6-reel editing sequence might be 3,2,1,6,4,5. I don't eliminate editorial teething pains by beginning with an interior reel, but I bury them in a less critical location, in the film's "soft underbelly."

There's another practical reason to forgo the first and last reels when you begin editing the dialogue. You did everything in your power to make sure that the picture department locked the film before handing it over to you. In truth, though, there's nothing you can do to prevent an avalanche of changes. The problems of the film really are bigger than you, but this doesn't mean that you have to be stupid about changes. Beginning your edit in the middle of the film may buy you a bit of peace. Of course, you can't predict where postlock picture changes will occur, but it's reasonable to assume that the first and last reels are more vulnerable than the interior reels to change. Story setup problems occur largely at the beginning; resolution issues, at the end. If the film is still having birthing pains after picture lock, the odds are good that the first and last reels are most at risk. Start with an interior reel, and hopefully by the time you're ready for the exterior reels the dust will have settled.

Expect Changes

Despite your 3-color cross-indexed schedules (or perhaps because of them), things will change. The film will be recut, a key actor will be away during ADR, the director will need a special scratch mix to show at her daughter's birthday party. That's filmmaking. Take a breath, pull out a fresh calendar, and redo your schedule. You'll survive.

CHAPTER 9

Getting Started on Dialogue Editing

You have all the materials you need, or at least everything you'll ever get. Now you have to organize your workspace. There's a huge temptation to dive in and get to work, but dialogue editing is a process that benefits handsomely from good preparation. A little time spent now will pay off manifold. I promise.

Different jobs require their own approaches, but here is a pretty reliable list of what you need to do to prepare each reel's session for editing. Each task will be discussed in detail later.

- Sync the OMF[1] and the auto-assembly (postconform) to the guide track.
- Copy the auto-assembly tracks. Disable and hide the OMF and the auto-assembly copies.
- Remove redundant dual mono regions.
- Set up your tracks (this is easier with a template session).
- Add reference tones.
- Add sync pops to match your head and tail leaders.
- Mark the boundaries of the scenes on each reel.

The Monitor Chain

To make wise decisions, you have to be able to hear properly and you have to trust both your monitors and your room. This means setting up and maintaining the cleanest, shortest, and most consistent monitor chain possible. Using the best amplifier and speakers you can manage, and avoiding unnecessary electronics in the signal path, will help you far more than you realize. Don't underestimate the impact of the room size, shape, and sound isolation.

---

[1] The OMF will almost certainly be in sync with the edited guide track, but it's worth checking. An auto-assembly (auto-conform) will more likely exhibit region-by-region sync problems.

"It's only dialogue so the listening environment isn't critical" is an argument bound to blow up in your face.

Within reason, always work at the same listening level and start each day aligning your monitoring equipment. If you're monitoring through a mixing console, make sure your signal is aligned throughout the entire path. Just because your −18 dB reference reads "0 VU" on the output side of the console, you aren't necessarily avoiding overlevel distortion within the console. If you don't know how to align the console you're working with, ask someone.

Forgo the Filter

Despite temptation, don't monitor your dialogue through a filter. Some editors listen through a high-pass filter in order to eliminate the low-frequency mess that causes shot mismatches. Their argument is that since low frequency is usually reduced in the dialogue premix—across all dialogue tracks—there's no harm in doing so. You're not going to hear those low frequencies anyway, right? Well, maybe. Unless you edit dialogue in a film mix room, you don't have the bass response necessary to make good bass-related room tone decisions. If you filter your monitor chain, you're going to encounter surprises in the mix.

Moreover, dialogue editing is about resolving problems through editing. It's not about filtering. This sounds pedantic and inflexible, but it's the only way to look at it if you want good results. If you can get a scene to work despite unsteady bass in the room tone, you stand a far better chance of getting good results in the dialogue premix. Cutting through a filter is akin to washing dishes without your much-needed eyeglasses. Of course it goes easier; you just can't see the spots you're missing.[2]

Sync Now!

Before you begin editing or organizing your material, make certain that every region of your session is in sync with the guide track. Normal human laziness will tell you that since there's ample opportunity to check sync why bother now. Here are some reasons you should bother now rather than later:

- Your session is now as simple as it will ever be. As you work, it will become more complicated, heavier, and more difficult to manipulate.

---

[2] There are times when you have to filter a soundfile before you can edit it. A *very* low-frequency tone (say less than 40 Hz) may make glitch-free editing all but impossible, so removing it with an AudioSuite high-pass filter may be necessary before proceeding.

- Syncing the OMF and the postconform (if it exists) to the guide track before you make a safety copy means that you'll always be able to use the safety copy as an absolute sync reference.
- Doubts about sync will make you crazy. If you *know* your tracks are in sync, you never need to worry. This leaves you free to edit, to create, and to think about things more important than the silly sync Schnauzer gnawing at your ankles.
- You're just starting the film and you have yet to get a feel for it. Going through the film a shot at a time is a good way to familiarize yourself with how it's structured.

It's a joy to edit knowing that the film is *really* in sync.

Know What You're Syncing To

If you're working to a digital picture, you'll sync to the audio track of the imported movie. Import the movie's audio onto a new track, lock it, and use it as your sync reference. Syncing to the guide track doesn't necessarily mean that the sound is in sync with the picture—it's only as tight as the assistant picture editor made it. However, you need to start *somewhere*, and the film's guide track is a comforting place to begin.

If your picture is on videotape, you have two options. If you're monitoring your sound through an external mixer, mix the VTR's audio with the output of the workstation to compare sync. If you don't have an external mixer, open an aux track and run the VTR audio through this input. Syncing against a guide track on videotape means you have to recue the tape and wait for the workstation to lock each time you want to check sync. This is time consuming.

You're much better off recording the audio from the videotape into your session on a new track, called a "guide track" or GT. Recording is in real time, of course, but this is another opportunity to study the film. Besides, this is what assistants are for. Use the guide track's timestamp to automatically sync it to the session. Then **lock** the track so that in a moment of passion you don't lose its sync. A reference out of sync is of little use.

You probably won't be able to determine the *real* sync of the film—the actual relationship between picture and sound—until you receive a telecine of the first answer print (discussed in Chapter 16). This high-quality transfer reflects the negative cut of the film and is the final arbiter of sync. For now, sync to the guide track and readjust the sync on only the most criminally out-of-sync shots.

Syncing the OMF

Normally, the OMF won't have any local sync variations. You can usually select the entire OMF and move it back and forth until it phases with the reference. Here's how you do it:

- Make an edit group of all tracks holding the OMF.
- Set the **nudge** value to ¼ frame.
- Mute all tracks other than the OMF group and the guide track.
- If, as a gift, the picture department included pan automation in the OMF, delete it and pan all tracks center.
- Select the entire OMF and play the session.
- Since you usually don't have grave problems with the OMF sync, you'll likely hear either perfect "whistling" phasing or a very short "slap." If the sync between the guide track and the OMF is good but not perfect, stop playback and press *Nudge* twice (the direction is arbitrary). Play again. If things got worse, nudge in the other direction; if it's getting better, keep it up until you hear perfect phasing. This isn't brain surgery.
- When syncing an OMF, there's rarely a need to set the nudge value less than ¼-frame, as most sync problems will be in increments of ½-frame.

Syncing an Auto-Assembly

Depending on the method of auto-assembly, you may encounter weird, unpredictable sync offsets for each region of your auto-assembly session. Resyncing this sort of mess is slow and ugly. However, there are software solutions for such problems.

Titan was the software package we used in Chapter 5 to conform a file-based project. The original sound was recorded on a hard-disk recorder, and we used Titan to recreate the picture editor's project, using the original BWF files. Titan has several other utilities up its sleeve. One of them is *Fix Sync*, which automatically aligns an auto-assembly to a guide track. The process is sample-accurate, whether or not you used Titan for the conform.

If you don't have Titan or another auto-sync program, you'll have to do this by hand and ear. When you have varying offsets and you don't know in which direction each region will vary from the reference, you're probably better trying a sync plan like this:

- Make an edit group of all tracks of the auto-assembly.
- Output the auto-assembly to one side of a stereo output. Output the guide track to the other side. It doesn't matter if you put the auto-

assembly on the right or left, but always do it the same way so that you don't have to think about it. I always put the reference on the left.

- Play one auto-assembly region and the guide track together. Adjust the volumes so that left and right are equal. If the sync offset is big, it will be pretty clear if the auto-assembly region is late or early. Sometimes small sync differences are hard to hear when played in a "panned-out" manner. In this case, listen to the stereo image. If the auto-assembly is on the right and the stereo image is "pulling" to the right, then the auto-assembly region is early. When sync differences are very slight, you tend to favor the earlier signal, perceiving it as louder.[3] Nudge the auto-assembly region until the sound is centered in the stereo field and you hear the phasing sound that indicates sync.
- If you're using an external mixer to monitor, pan the two channels to center and listen for absolute phasing.
- Repeat this process for all regions.

Setting Up Your Editing Workspace

Once you have an in-sync OMF and auto-assembly, choose the one you want to use for your edit. Odds are you'll pick the auto-assembly as it will probably sound a bit better. If so, make the OMF tracks inactive and hide them; then copy the auto-assembly tracks, and make them inactive and hide them. (See Figure 9-1.)

Why go to such trouble? What will these copies buy you? The OMF copy, even if you don't use its sounds, is a useful reference. Fades, temporary sound effects and music, and volume automation are all intact and will help you understand what the picture editor was trying to accomplish. Plus, non-timecoded material, such as "edit room ADR," will be in the OMF but probably won't show up in the auto-assembly. When you start editing a scene, listen to the OMF tracks to get into the editor's head. Then you can go back to the virgin auto-assembly tracks with a good idea of the editor's artistic and storytelling hopes for the scene.

The copy of the auto-assembly will come in handy if you inadvertently offset or delete a region. Just unhide the track and copy the missing region into your dialogue tracks in sync. You can also use these unaltered regions as guides if you need to conform your edit to a new picture version. Unlike your elegantly overlapping edited sounds, these virgin regions have the same start

---

[3] This phenomenon is called the "Haas effect" or "precedence effect" and is used in many psychoacoustic processors and algorithms.

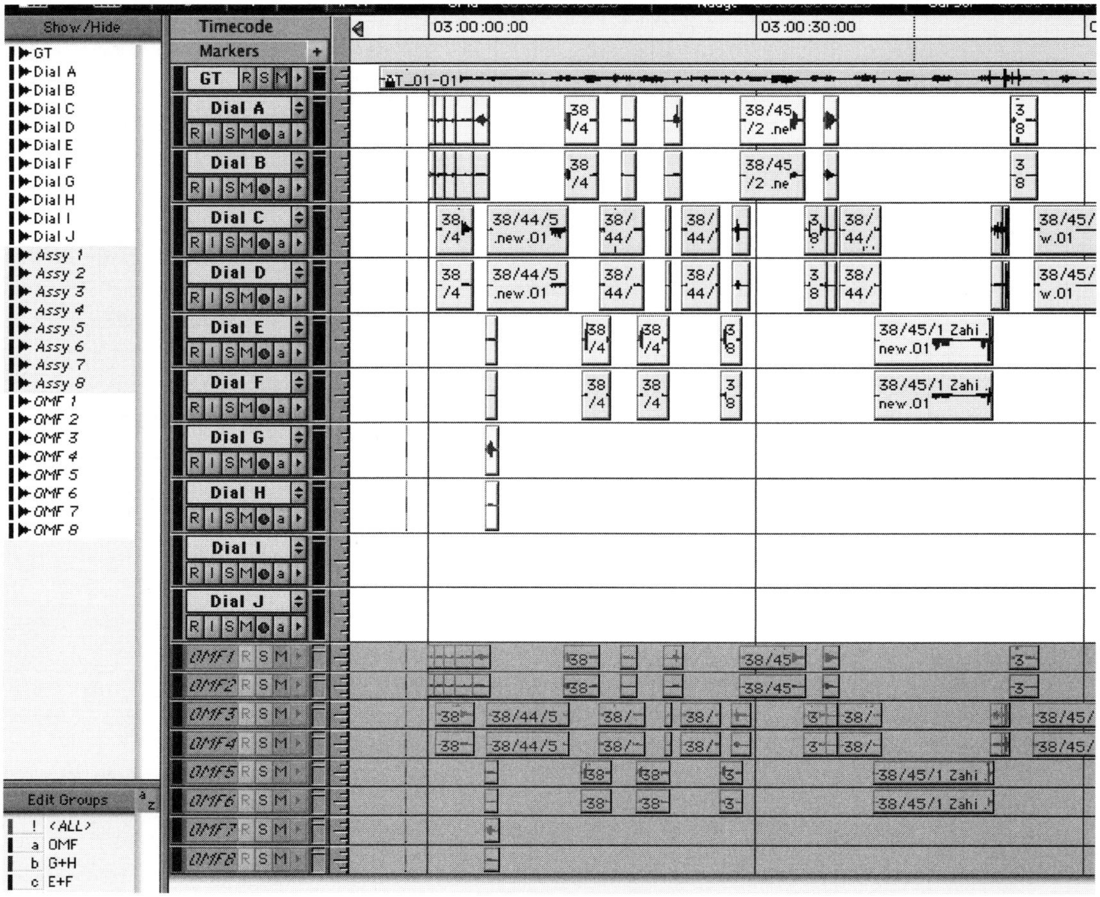

Figure 9-1 Auto-assembly regions appear on the dialogue tracks; copies are disabled and hidden (Assy 1, Assy 2, . . . , Assy 8). OMF tracks are disabled and soon to be hidden. They contain the picture editor's level automation and temporary SFX, music. Note that the top track contains a locked mono guide track from the Avid digital dump.

and stop times as the EDL, so you can use them to calculate offsets and figure out what the picture editor did to make the change.

Working with Just an OMF

Often you won't have an auto-assembly, just an OMF. If that's the case, make a copy of the OMF (after you've confirmed its sync) and then make the copied tracks inactive and hide them. Delete the picture editor's volume and pan automation, as they make room tone editing next to impossible. Keep all picture cutting automation in the hidden copy of the OMF, and you'll have a convenient reference when you can't figure out what the picture editor was thinking.

If you're on an insanely quick job, say a 45-minute documentary with only two days for production sound editing, you may choose to keep the picture editor's automation and just "make it nice." I never do this because I still find it faster to start from scratch, but all's fair in love and war and guerilla sound editing. It's up to you.

Labeling Your Tracks

Each track must be named. This ought to be pretty obvious, but even the most obvious things in life often need to be said a few times. Of course, labeling your tracks means deciding how you want to organize your work, and this involves understanding the complexity of the film, the capacity of the rerecording mixing desk and rerecording mixer's preferences, and the habits of your supervising sound editor. Busy films or films with lots of perspective cuts need more tracks; action films need extra PFX tracks; poorly organized OMFs mandate more "junk" tracks. Table 9-1 shows the standard dialogue template for small films.

Some people like to use letters to name tracks. Others prefer numbers. I like letters for tracks that will make it to the dialogue premix (e.g., dialogue, ADR, PFX, X) and numbers for tracks I created just for my convenience (junk, work, etc.). As long as your rerecording mixer is content, it really doesn't matter which you use.

Work and Junk Tracks

Some workstations, like the SonicStudio, allow you to work on several time-lines at once and to have numerous open sessions. Most DAWs, however, present all of your work on one timeline, as though you're working on a piece of multitrack recording tape. One of the downsides of a single timeline, as in Pro Tools, is that you don't have a "safe" area to work in without worrying about damaging your session. That's why I always create several extra tracks where nothing of value lives.

It's here, on the "work" tracks that I open long files with no worry that I'll cover up another region well offscreen. (The danger is not that you'll delete a region that you can see—after all, if you're paying attention, you'll see it.

Table 9-1 A Typical Dialogue Track Layout for Small- to Medium-Length Films

Tracks	Source	Audio Format	Comments
Dial A → L	Mono from original field recordings	Usually mono	Use Dial 1 → 12 or Dial A → L. Let the supervising sound editors and mixers decide.
Work tracks 1, 2, 3, and up	Blank	Mono and/or stereo	Use as "safe" places to open files, make complex edits, and use shuffle mode.
Junk 1 → 6	Blank	Usually mono	Use to file away anything you don't want in your active tracks but don't want to delete.
PFX A → D	Blank for now	Mono	Use for production effects you want to separate from the dialogue either to use in the international version mix or for better mix control.
ADR A → D	Mono (or wider) files that will originate in your ADR recording sessions	Mono	Don't place ADR lines onto dialogue tracks.
Dial X, Y, Z	Blank for now	Mono	"X tracks," use to hold lines you removed from the dialogue tracks and replaced with matching tone fill. The rerecording mixer uses the X tracks to compare the original line and the ADR line.

The risk lies outside your screen, where you can cause all sorts of unseen damage.) The work tracks are also where I record new sounds into the workstation and where I perform any editing operation that calls for **rippling** the track, as in Pro Tools's *shuffle* mode, which is very convenient but famous for knocking tracks out of sync.

I also open several new tracks, inelegantly entitled "junk." Any sound I don't want in the mix but still want to have around just for safety I put on a junk track. As you work your way through a film, there are some regions you can delete with total confidence. For example, when you use phase cancellation to discover dual mono regions, you can throw away one side of the dual mono pair with a clean conscience. You'll never need it again.

On the other hand, if you're editing a scene with a boom on one channel and a radio microphone mix on the other, you may decide to use only the boom but you probably aren't cavalier enough to toss the radio mic. Junk tracks are great places to store—in sync—these unwanted regions without clogging up your sessions. I also use them to store alternate takes as I reconstruct a shot. Plus, they're a convenient place to keep room tone for a scene.

Neither "work" nor "junk" is a standard industry name or concept. Too bad. To my way of thinking and working, this model serves well. Use it or find something else that works for you.

Templates

If you edit a lot of films, or if you're embarking on a 12-reel feature, you'd do well to make a master template session that you can open, offset, and use as the basis of each reel's session. If you're a master typist, this isn't necessary, but if you get tired of typing "Dial A," "Dial B," and so on, over and over again for each track in each session, make a template and be done with it.

A template, shown in Figure 9-2, is a generic session containing the named tracks as well as the head beeps and the reference tones. For each reel you make slight modifications to the template before importing your audio tracks. It beats rebuilding from scratch, and it helps ensure that each reel has the same track sequence, which is something rerecording mixers appreciate. Here are some tips on making templates:

- Properly set the sample rate and bit depth to match the film.
- Build your template for reel 1. Session start: 00:57:00:00. Reference tone: 00:59:00:00–00:59:30:00. Head sync pop: 00:59:58:00 (if the picture timecode "hour" rolls over at FFOA. If the hour is at "picture start," the sync pop will fall at 01:00:06:00). On reels 2 and on, reset the session start (R2 = 01:57:00:00; R3 = 02:57:00:00; etc.). Also move the reference tone and sync pop to the appropriate timecode locations for each reel.
- Open about 20 mono tracks and label them accordingly. Include the work and junk tracks.
- Save a copy of your template on the internal hard drive of the computer (or on a CD or USB Flash drive), since your next film will probably need a very similar template.
- Import both the OMF and the auto-assembly of each reel into a *copy* of this session.

One Giant Session or Several Smaller Ones?

Some editors like to combine all of the dialogue reel sessions into one giant timeline so that they can have the entire film before them without having to

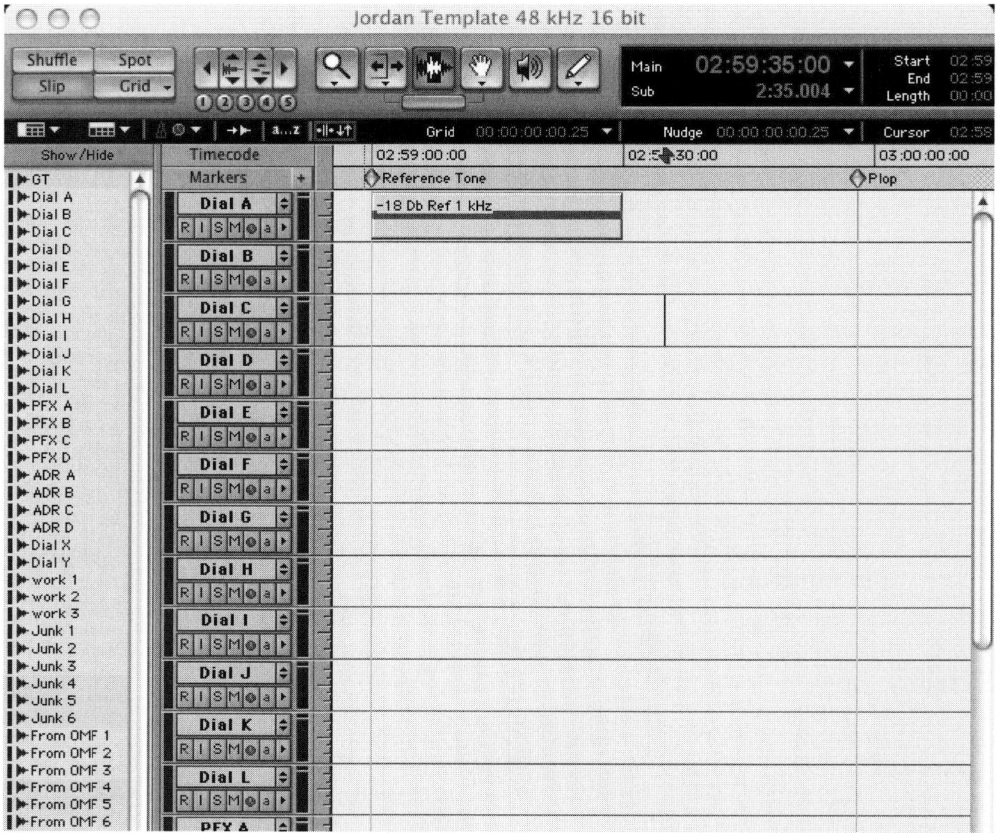

Figure 9-2 A dialogue layout template.

quit one reel's session to access another. I think this is a bad idea. For background or SFX editors, there are some worthwhile reasons to work this way. After all, if you're building the backgrounds for a scene that takes place at a location visited many times throughout the film, it's nice to be able to cut and paste between reels. Effects editors, too, can benefit from having the timeline of the entire film before them.

But dialogue editing issues are local, not global across the whole film. There's rarely a need to steal sounds from another scene, and even when you do it's not hard to find the file and import it. I organize my work into one session per reel. Here are some reasons:

• Short sessions are quicker to work with, they load faster, and they make the computer happier.

- If a 1-reel session is damaged or corrupted, it's less catastrophic than when a 6-reeler is wrecked.
- The horizontal scroll bar has much better resolution in short sessions.
- A version change in one reel is easier to deal with than it would be in a composite session. You can modify the affected reel, change its name to reflect the version number change, and nothing else is affected.
- Some workstations give you a limited number of memory locater markers, useful tools for marking scene boundaries, perspective cuts, and the like. Older Pro Tools, for example, give you 200 memory markers per session, which is seldom enough for an entire film but typically adequate for a reel of dialogue.

Eliminating Unnecessary Mono Regions

When recording to tape, many location mixers will print onto two channels, whether mono shots recorded with one boom microphone or split tracks (such as a boom on one channel and a radio microphone mix on the other). (See Figure 9-3.) The result: Almost all of your sound from the OMF or auto-assembly will come to you in the form of pairs. Sometimes a pair contains two different signals, but often it contains two identical tracks.

Before you start editing, find these **dual mono** tracks and delete one side of the pair. The duplicate does you no good whatsoever and can cause all sorts of trouble, including the following.

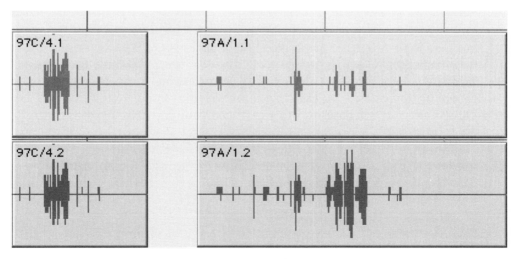

Figure 9-3 A dual mono event (left) and a split track event.

- Processing differences between the two tracks could result in unequal latencies and hence phasing.
- Two identical tracks mean twice the work, twice the fades, double the click removal, and more tracks consumed.
- It is much harder to organize your scene when lugging around these useless tracks, and it's difficult to glance at the scene's layout and know what's going on when you have unnecessary material.
- The extra regions make your session bigger and more unwieldy.

And remember, there's *nothing* to gain from having two tracks with the same sound.

You could, of course, rely on your ears to compare the two sides of each region, or on your eyes to evaluate the waveform of one side of a pair against the other. You could also paint your house with a toothbrush. There are a few thousand regions in a film, and I think life is too short to wear myself out on such foolishness. Somewhere in your studio you have the tools to help you hunt down these annoying dual mono files.

Using an external console, pan to center the two tracks making up the pair in question. Set the output of your DAW to discrete channels rather than summed stereo. Invert the phase of *one* channel strip on your console to see if the tracks are the same or are different.

If you're using a DAW and no external console, insert a simple plug-in into every other dialogue track and use it to inverse its phase. (See Figure 9-4.)

- Pick a zero-latency plug-in. I like to use a 1-band equalizer (EQ) because it sits near the top of the list of options (so it's easy to get to), its interface is charmingly low-tech, and it's free of latency. Pro Tools's Trim plug-in is also useful. Every workstation has a mechanism for reversing the phase of a track; you just have to look.
- Open the inserted plug-in, flip the phase, and copy the plug-in onto every odd track.
- Temporarily disable volume automation for all tracks so you can make volume adjustments to the track without "fighting" the automation.
- Solo the two tracks you want to check. If they're identical, you should hear almost complete phase cancellation. Adjust the volume on either of the sides of the pair to perfect it.
- If you're unsure if the two tracks are phase-canceling, mute one. If the sound suddenly becomes much louder, with more low frequency and fuller fidelity, you have a match. You can delete either side of the

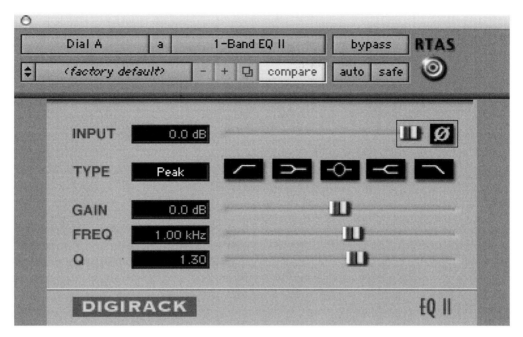

Figure 9-4 Locate dual mono pairs by inserting a zero-latency plug-in into *every other track*. In this example, a Pro Tools 1-Band EQ RTAS plug-in is used to reverse the track's phase. Note the phase reversal button.

pair—they're similar enough to phase, so it doesn't really matter which one.

- If the sound doesn't get louder (or even gets quieter) when you mute one side of the pair, then it's not a dual mono pair. Leave it alone. At this point, don't try to choose which track to use. (See Figure 9-5.)
- Repeat this for each paired region.
- Don't forget to turn on your automation and remove the phase reverse insert when you finish.

Scenes

Film editing is based on scenes. A scene usually tells a freestanding mini-story and is limited by time, location, or story issues. Each mini-story has a life of its own, with its own rules, quirks, and personality. Together, the scenes tell the greater story of the film. Unless your project is *Rope* or *Timecode* or

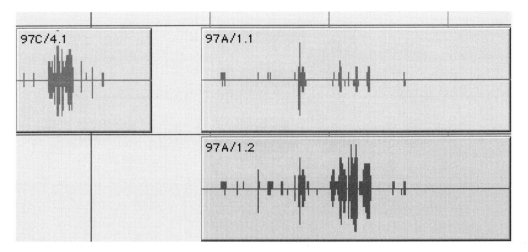

Figure 9-5 Delete one side of the dual mono pairs. At this point leave both channels of the split track pair intact, even if one side is unacceptable.

Russian Ark, you'll know the boundaries of a scene when you see them. If you're not sure when a scene changes, talk to the director or the supervising sound editor (you may think it impossible *not* to know when a scene changes, but some transitions are ambiguous and need to be addressed).

Dialogue editors have a special relationship with scenes, for within their confines we try to make everything seem continuous, smooth, and believable. At their edges, however, we usually want to slap the viewers a bit to tell them that something new is happening. As a result, scene changes are almost always quick and at times brutal. Mark scene boundaries before you begin editing and your work will be much simpler.

- Breaking the film into scenes helps to organize the work and it gives all of the editors a standard vocabulary when discussing the film.
- Mark scenes before you begin editing and you needn't hunt around for the right frame of the scene boundary while you're passionately editing. You can keep up a good creative pace.
- Before you begin editing, the scene changes in your OMF will probably be hard cuts, centered on the transition and easy to spot. But as you edit and create crossfades, you'll lose the location of the original edit unless you marked it with a memory marker.
- Markers make it easier to apply standard scene transition durations (1 frame, 2 frames, etc.), since you have a reference around which to build your crossfades.

- Markers make it easier to easier to prepare for the mix.
- If you establish the scene breaks and place markers, the rest of the editing crew will be able to use your marks. This saves time and ensures that all scene transitions will be sharp and even and on the correct frame, not staggered messes that lack energy.

Apply short, sensible names to the scene markers, and you can use the markers list to instantly navigate to a scene; for example, (1) Sc33 INT car Sarah, (2) Sc17 EXT Bob runs, and (3) Sc45 INT kitchen fight. Make up your own naming system as long as you can pack all the information you need into a small name cell.

Marking Scene Changes

Once your editing team has agreed on the scene boundaries, it's easy to mark them. (See Figure 9-6.) Here are the Pro Tools instructions. Other workstations have comparable routines.

- Locate to the first frame of a new scene and press *Enter* on the numeric keypad. You'll see the New Memory Location dialogue box.
- Type the name of the new scene.
- To see a list of all markers, press *CMD+5* (numeric). Use this list to navigate through your film. If you're using digital picture, this feature is extremely valuable because you can use the list to jump instantly from one scene to the next.

Beeps, Tones, and Leaders

In the days of analogue recording, every piece of tape, magnetic film, or optical track carried a series of alignment tones at its head. With these tones—usually 1 kHz, 10 kHz, and 100 Hz—as references, a tape could be played back properly on any well-maintained machine, anywhere in the world. A set of standard (and very expensive) alignment tapes were used to ensure that the machines were set up for proper recording and playback. Every assistant in the industry spent more time than he cares to remember aligning analogue machines. The system was amazingly simple, and it worked.

Today analogue machines are all but unheard of and machine alignment is a lost art. With digital, there's little to align. Unfortunately, the myth that there is *nothing* to align has resulted in some problems. Analogue-to-digital-to-analogue (A/D/A) converters do need periodic adjustment, something small studios rarely get around to. Plus, the fact that a maintenance engineer once had to regularly align analogue recorders kept him in touch with the

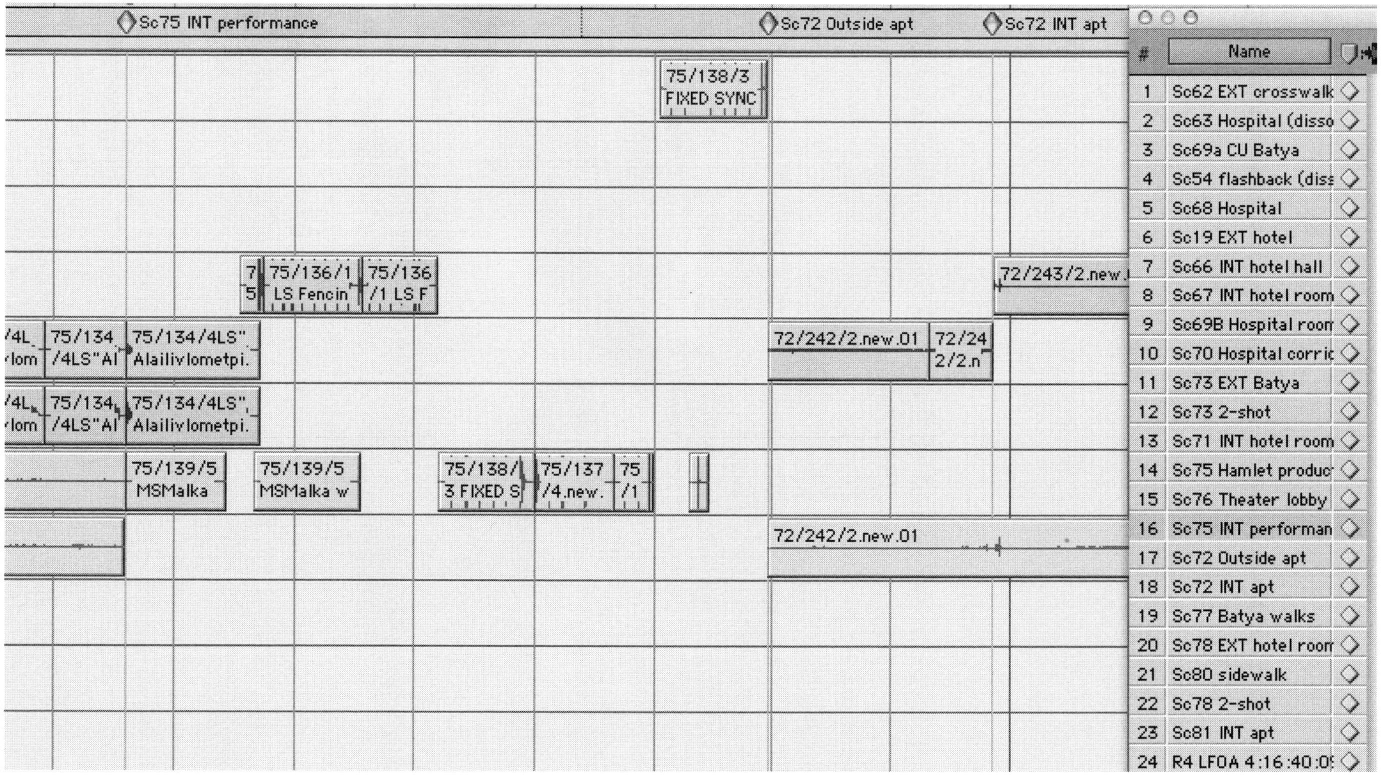

Figure 9.6 Markers (*top*) are added to indicate scene changes. Most workstations provide a list of markers or locator points (*right*) that can be used to navigate through your session.

machines. That daily or weekly interaction was an opportunity to learn of other looming problems.

Even though you're working in digital, you still have to place alignment tones (often called "reference tones") on your tracks. Why?

- You have to have a reference tone to daily align the monitor chain in your edit room.
- If you make a rough mix, or "bounce," of your work as a guide track for the effects, backgrounds, Foley, or music editors, it must have a reference tone attached so that other editors can use it at its proper level.
- When you bring the tracks to the mix, each track's reference tone ensures that you've routed and patched the sound correctly. You can also see if you have a bad connection (a −6 dB tone level indicates a missing leg on a balanced connection). If a particular track is not going to be used on a reel, a missing tone on it will tell the mixer to ignore it during that reel.

Making a Reference Tone

A large studio probably has a ready collection of reference, or calibration, tones, either on the internal drive of each computer or on the network. Ask. A studio's "Tones Folder" will likely have an assortment of options such as these:

Sync pop 44.1 KHz, 16 bit	Sync pop 44.1 KHz, 24 bit
Sync pop 48 KHz, 16 bit	Sync pop 48 KHz, 24 bit
1 K reference @ −18 dB, 44.1 KHz, 16 bit	1 K reference @ −18 dB, 44.1 KHz, 24 bit
1 K reference @ −18 dB, 48 KHz, 16 bit	1 K reference @ −18 dB, 48 KHz, 24 bit
1 K reference @ −20 dB, 44.1 KHz, 16 bit	1 K reference @ −20 dB, 44.1 KHz, 24 bit
1 K reference @ −20 dB, 48 KHz, 16 bit	1 K reference @ −20 dB, 48 KHz, 24 bit

Make sure to pick the reference tone and sync plop to match the sample rate and word size of your session, as well as the reference level of the studio and the local film community. Nowadays, most facilities use a reference like this:

$$-18\,dBFS = 0\,VU = +4\,dBu$$

or

$$-20\,dBFS = 0\,VU = +4\,dBu$$

This means that, in a properly set-up audio chain, a digital reference of −18 dBFS (full scale, the standard digital scale with 0 as the absolute highest value) equals 0 on an analogue VU meter, which equals 4 dBu, which is 1.23-volt RMS.

There are many excellent discussions of level, headroom, and the like.[4] Debates over the "right" reference level are longstanding, passionate, and often personal, so this is not the place to get into it. Bottom line: Before you begin your project, determine the reference level of the original field recordings, talk to your studio engineer to learn the local reference level, and have a chat with the rerecording mixer. Together, you can come up with a reference level. Odds are it will be –18 or –20 dBFS. If your studio doesn't provide reference tones, the best place to find them is on a commercial alignment CD. If this isn't an option, you can download calibration test files.[5]

Most workstations provide a way to make a reference tone. It's not the best choice, but it will do in a pinch. In Pro Tools, for example:

- Click on *Dial A*.
- In the session *Start* and *End* windows at the top of the interface, enter a start time of 00:59:00:00 and a duration of 30 seconds. (This example is for reel 1.) You'll see this area highlighted in your session.
- Choose the Signal Generator *AudioSuite* plug-in. Select a 1000 Hz frequency, –18 dB level, and sine wave. Then press *Enter*. You'll see a new tone created on the track.
- Label the tone "1 K reference @ –18 dB." You can reuse it for other sessions; just remember where it's stored. Better yet, put a copy in your personal folder on the computer's internal hard drive or on your USB Flash drive.
- Copy the tone onto every "real" track (not a work or junk track). *Mute every tone except the tone on track 1*; otherwise, you'll go deaf and give your speakers an unnecessary workout.

Using Your Reference Tone for Daily Alignment

Each editing day should begin with a quick alignment of your monitor chain. Running a tone through your monitor mixer and external meters will ensure that you're always working at the same monitor level and that your meters can be trusted. Sending a known reference through your system will also tell you if you have a technical problem. If the reference tone doesn't behave as

---

[4] For a thorough explanation of the mysteries of exchanging signals between analogue and digital domains, see "The Ins and Outs of Interfacing Analogue and Digital Equipment" by Hugh Robjohns, in *Sound on Sound* (May 2000).

[5] One source of quality calibration test files is Blue Sky International (*www.abluesky.com*).

you expect, you'll know to look for problems. This is especially true when you're sharing a studio with other people rather than working in your own basement. There's no telling what goes on when you're not there.

If there's a minor inconsistency between the two stereo channels, trim your monitor console accordingly. But if you notice a disparity of 3 or 6 dB, there's a problem in the chain. Talk to the studio tech rather than compensate with the trim pots.

The Sync Pop

The importance of the **sync pop** (which is also called "plop" or "beep" depending on where you live) can't be overstated when you're working on a film project. Even if the "film" was shot on video or HD to be blown-up to 35 mm, sync pops are vital. Filmmaking is technically a very sophisticated industry, filled with extraordinary computers at every turn, and timecode is used to synchronize each step of the postproduction process. Until the very end, that is. When the final film negative is joined with the finished sound-track, the visible sync pop on the optical negative is manually aligned with a known location on the film. This hasn't changed in 75 years.

But why bother placing sync pops on the session from the very beginning of the job? Why not wait until you're packaging the job for the dialogue premix?

- If you knock your session out of sync, you can use the pops (head or tail) to resync it.
- You'll periodically make guide track "bounces" for the other editors. If one of these editors isn't working with a file format that includes timecode (say, regular WAVE files), she has to use the pop for sync reference.
- Everyone assumes that the dialogue editor is on top of issues like sync, paperwork, and film versions. People trust your pops, so get them right.
- It's just the way it is. Reels must have reference tones plus head and tail pops. If you don't do them, you'll come across as a video/MIDI geek and the film people won't take you seriously.

The head sync pop is one frame long and it begins 2 seconds before the start of each reel. So if your **first frame of action** (FFOA) on reel 2 is 2:00:00:00, the sync pop will fall at 1:59:58:00. Many film editors place the "hour mark" (1:00:00:00, 2:00:00:00, etc.) at the **picture start** of the leader (see section on page 121 for more about leaders). The picture start is 12 feet, or 8 seconds (at 24 fps), before the FFOA. If it's at 2:00:00:00, place the sync pop at 2:00:06:00; the FFOA will then be at 2:00:08:00. If the leader was correctly placed by the picture department, the final "flashed" number of the countdown will coincide with your pop.

The placement of the tail sync pop is a bit more enigmatic. It depends on the kind of tail leaders you're using. If the videotape or video file doesn't have a tail leader, put a pop exactly 2 seconds (48 film frames or 50 PAL video or 60 NTSC video frames) after the **last frame of action** (LFOA). Talk to the sound supervisor or picture editor on the project about the rules for tail pops on your project.

Head Plops for 25 fps Projects

Most films are shot at 24 fps, since that's the speed at which they're usually shown. However, for those editing in PAL, films will occasionally be shot at 25 fps. If you're making a made-for-PAL TV movie with no plans for a theatrical release, you might shoot at 25 fps to

- Avoid the ugly treatment of motion that comes from 24 → 25 fps telecine transfers.
- Allow you to work on *any* video editing system, not just "film smart" systems like Film Composer.
- Easily and cheaply avoid flicker and rolling when filming scenes that include television screens in the shot.

On films shot and edited at 25 fps destined to be shown *only on PAL television* (at 25 fps), the head pop is placed at the normal spot: 2 seconds, or 50 frames, before FFOA. As far as you're concerned it's a video project.

Some theatrical films are shot at 25 fps, edited at 25 fps, sound-edited and mixed at 25 fps, and *then* projected at 24 fps, for more or less the same reasons described earlier. Such a project will have a head sync pop 48 *film* frames before FFOA, which in this unusual case is also 48 video frames. So you place reel 1's head sync pop at 00:59:58:02 (or 01:00:06:02 if the timecode hour falls at picture start rather than FFOA). Thankfully, you won't have to deal with this very often, and if you live in North America you'll never see such silliness.

Similarly, if the picture originated in a 25 fps tape format, whether SD or HD, and will be scanned to film for 24 fps projection, place the head pop 48 frames before FFOA, as though it had been shot on film running at 25 fps. Remember, the film will be slowed down once the mix is finished.

SMPTE Leader versus Academy Leader

There are two kinds of head leader: SMPTE and Academy. Both allow the sound and picture to remain synchronous throughout the postproduction process. Each has a "picture start" mark 12 feet before the FFOA and is used by projectionists to crossover from one projector to the other as the reels change.[6] The head leader is also used to line up a film projector with mag recorders and players for mixing, and you'll need it if you ever want to look at your mix on a Steenbeck or other film editing table.

So, what's the difference between the two leaders? Nothing, except that the SMPTE counts in seconds whereas the Academy counts in feet. The Academy will pop on the number 3; the SMPTE will pop on 2. As long as you placed your sync pop 2 seconds before the FFOA (48 film frames, 50 PAL frames, 60 NTSC frames), it will fall at the right place no matter which leader your picture editor used; that is because at 24 fps, 35 mm film travels 90 ft/min and 90 ft/min equals 1.5 ft/sec, so 3 feet equals 2 seconds.

When you work on a "normal" film—shot at 24 fps, transferred to video (PAL or NTSC), and edited with Avid Film Composer or FCP's Cinema Tools—the effective film speed on videotape will remain 24 fps (23.976 fps in NTSC). A scene that was 100 seconds long when shot will be 100 seconds when you watch it in the Avid[7] and 100 seconds long when shown in a theater. Hence, the start mark will always be 12 feet, or 8 seconds, before LFOA on a reel.

When you get a reel, whether a digital dump from the picture editor or a telecine of the answer print, measure how many seconds lie between picture start and FFOA. If it's not 8 seconds, there's a speed problem or the film was shot at 25 fps. Talk to the supervising sound editor or picture editor. Just don't ignore the problem.

---

[6] Modern theaters rarely screen films from two crossover projectors. Instead, when a film arrives at the cinema, the projectionist strips the film of its leaders and splices together the reels. The reels are combined onto one huge horizontal platter for continuous projection, so the projectionist needn't babysit the projector so closely and instead can control several room's screenings simultaneously. This is much more cost effective for the cinema owners. The bad news is that there's no longer a skilled projectionist keeping close tabs on focus, framing, and sound.

[7] Actually, when the 100-second clip is viewed in an NTSC video environment (whether on videotape or on a picture workstation), the scene will run 0.1 percent slower than 100 seconds because of NTSC's 29.97 fps frame rate. However, back in a film environment, the clip will again be 100 seconds long.

Wild Sound

Most of the audio from the shoot is sync sound, recorded while the camera was rolling. However, a decent sound recordist will take the extra time to record additional sounds that may have been missed, botched, or unavailable while shooting the scene. You can't rely solely on sync recordings to put together a proper scene, so these extra sounds are lifesavers. Here are just a few of the reasons to record wild sound:

- For dialogue that couldn't be recorded during the shoot; for example, Butch Cassidy and the Sundance Kid jumping off a cliff and screaming.
- For a long shot of two characters talking to each other. In the rain. Under umbrellas.
- For shots in which there is simply *no* place for a microphone. A long shot of a couple of nudists is a good example.
- For shots ruined during the filming. A plane flies over, a train goes by. Perhaps the location mixer couldn't call for another take, but had the good sense to call the actors aside and record the scene wild.
- For specialty sounds difficult to recreate with sound effects. If there's an unusual car or motorcycle in a scene, a good location mixer will record its sounds, knowing that the production may never find them elsewhere. It's true that a well-heeled sound effects department will hire a custom recording specialist to record effects, backgrounds, and vehicles. But anything you can get on the set is (1) free, (2) available to all editors from the outset, and (3) certain to match the dialogue recordings.
- For room tone. The location mixer, if at all possible, will record room tone for each scene—the sound of a scene without talking, footsteps, phone rings, and the like; in other words, *silence.*
- For location-specific sounds. If the scene takes place in a jail cell, for example, the sound recordist may capture special details such as the door, the springs on the bed, or the toilet, all within the special acoustics of the jail cell.

"But," you may ask, "aren't all of these sounds replaced by ADR or Foley later?" Often yes. However, at times a bit of wild dialogue will save a scene from the pain and suffering (and save the production the expense) of ADR. A "save" created from alternate takes and wild sound will almost always be more effective and believable than an ADR line helped along with Foley.

As you organize the wild tracks from the shoot, copy the nondialogue recordings and give them to the sound effects editor. There's nothing like the real thing when it comes to building realistic-sounding scenes.

Finding Wild Sound

Wild sound is captured whenever the opportunity arises, so it's not neatly organized in one section of the recordings. To find wild sound, you first have to learn to read a **sound report**, the log of sounds recorded during the shoot. There are many kinds of sound reports, depending on the recording format, the source of the paperwork, and the temperament of the location mixer. Some are still small enough to fit inside the box of a ¼-inch Nagra tape. Historically, these were in triplicate: one copy for the sound transfer lab, one for the production office, and one that would live in the box. Nowadays the forms are bigger because few people record on Nagras. (There's no way you can get enough meaningful information onto a form that will fit into a DAT case.)

Figure 9-7 is a classic example of a report for small 2-track recordings. It's pretty simple, yet it provides all the vital information. The location mixer fills in scene, take, and DAT ID number for each shot, along with useful mic information in the COMMENT field. "Left: boom, right: radio mic mix" would be a typical statement. Assume the information is the same on subsequent shots until another statement supersedes it. There may also be notes such as "plane over last half" or GT (*guide track*, which means that the recording isn't good enough for use in the final track but can be used when you loop the shot or replace it with wild dialogue). Figure 9-8 shows another kind of sound report designed for use with 4-track hard-disk recorders.

When you begin a project, you don't know anything about the sounds you'll be working with. Collecting wild sound before you start to edit will save you grief later, and it's an efficient way to get to know the raw material of the film. As you dig through the tapes, you'll inevitably learn things about the shoot, the location mixer, the director, and the issues facing the film's sound.

Since at this point you won't have the time or the patience to listen to every take on each tape, use the sound reports to locate material that interests you. Be on the lookout for notes or abbreviations that point you to wild sound. (See Table 9-2.)

Look carefully at your sound reports and locate any notes like those in the table. With the exception of guide tracks, all of these wild sounds should be recorded into a workstation session called "Wild Sound." Make sure you name each recorded wild sound, using a logical, consistent, searchable naming scheme. You should include the scene name associated with the recording.

Jane Doe, sound recordist
23, rue Robert Giraudineau
Vincennes, France 94200
+33-1-41-74-62-91

Sound Report

Sound roll#_____

Camera roll#_____

Date _____

Production:		Episode:	
Producer:	Phone:		Cell:
Director:	Phone:		Cell:

Sound report for two-track recordings made on DAT
or hard-disk recorder.

Timecode 25 fps EBU unless otherwise indicated.

Scene	Shot	Take	DAT ID	Timecode Start	Notes
				: : :	
				: : :	
				: : :	
				: : :	
				: : :	
				: : :	
				: : :	
				: : :	
				: : :	
				: : :	
				: : :	
				: : :	
				: : :	
				: : :	

Figure 9-7 Typical sound report for a 2-channel recording.

Your name		Your contact information DATE:_____
		PAGE:_____of_____

Production:	Contact phone number:
Director:	Producer:

Sound Report for Four-Channel Digital Disk Recorders

Shooting Date:	Time of 1st recording:	Time of last recording:
Location Mixer:	1st cameraroll:	Last camera roll:
Boom Operator:	Type of recorder:	Whose recorder?:
DP:	Camera:	Film speed:
Audio sample rate:	Bit depth:	Reference tone:
TC type:	Time of day?	File format:
Recording media:	Back-up media:	

Folder name (date):_____   **Use one set of reports per shooting day.**

#	File Name	Shot	Scene	Take	TC Start	Channel assignments			
1						1	2	3	4
notes:									

#	File Name	Shot	Scene	Take	TC Start	Channel assignments			
2						1	2	3	4
notes:									

#	File Name	Shot	Scene	Take	TC Start	Channel assignments			
3						1	2	3	4
notes:									

#	File Name	Shot	Scene	Take	TC Start	Channel assignments			
4						1	2	3	4
notes:									

#	File Name	Shot	Scene	Take	TC Start	Channel assignments			
5						1	2	3	4
notes:									

#	File Name	Shot	Scene	Take	TC Start	Channel assignments			
6						1	2	3	4
notes:									

Please note any take which crosses midnight.

Figure 9-8 Typical sound report for a 4-channel hard-disk recording.

Table 9-2 Common Abbreviations in Sound Reports

Abbreviation	Term	Description
WS	Wild sound	Any nonsync recording, including location sound effects, room tone, and atmospheres. It also includes dialogue retakes from shots where the sync sound was botched or impossible to record and lines not recorded with the original sync recording such as extra breathing and off-camera voices of principal actors.
WT	Wild track	Also wild sound. I prefer WT for dialogue and WS for nonvocal sounds such as location sound effects. Use WT if WS might be mistaken for "wide shot."
Wild	Wild recording	Also wild sound. "Wild" is the broadest description of non-sync recordings.
RT	Room tone	Used to fill holes in the track, aid in shot transitions, and prepare tracks for ADR; *not* the same as a background/atmosphere.
Atmo or BG	Atmosphere or background	A recording (usually stereo) made at or near the shooting location that the effects or background editors use to build a "soup" of tracks to describe the time, place, or season, and to affect the mood of the scene. Don't confuse with room tone.
GT	Guide track	A track for reference only, not for actual use because of unwanted background noise or other problems. Also used on music "playback" scenes, where a mic was open on the set to record stage sounds that may be useful when syncing the music.
PFX	Production sound effect	On-set sound effects recordings.

Making a Printout of Wild Sound

Most workstations allow you to make a text file of the contents of a session, which can be very useful for quickly creating a list of your project's wild sounds. The process varies by workstation, but once you create a text file you'll almost certainly have to do some editing to remove unwanted details and organize the information in a manner that makes sense for you. You can use a spreadsheet or word-processing program for this clean-up process. Figure 9-9 is an example of a wild sound list for a very simple film. Keep something like it handy while editing.

By now you may be wondering, "Why go to all the trouble of loading the wild sound and creating a list before you know if you'll need it?" After all, you may well get through a scene not using it at all. You'll fix the bad lines

EVENT	REGION NAME	DURATION
	all sounds BFW mono	
1	01 RT, ver 1 INT bedroom night	00:00:54:20
2	01 RT, ver 2	00:00:47:14
3	02 RT park night, some WT footsteps	00:00:39:23
4	03-06 RT Shula's house	00:00:30:21
5	12-15 wild Sam + Dana together	00:00:21:03
6	12-15 wild text , good rustle @ 01:01:01:01	00:00:46:01
7	12-16 wild Dana lines, take 1	00:01:01:12
8	12-16 wild Dana lines, take 2	00:00:25:00
9	12-19 wild Sam lines	00:00:33:12
10	12+20-22 wild car in and out	00:03:31:17
11	12 wild Jeweler lines	00:01:07:15
12	22 RT hospital room	00:00:55:23
13	24 wild Rebecca lines 01	00:00:46:14
14	24 wild Rebecca lines 02	00:00:50:08
15	55-57 wild text 01	00:00:37:03
16	55-57 wild text 02	00:00:41:14
17	55-57 wild text 03 with mask	00:00:39:12
18	58 wild Debby lines	00:00:21:00
19	66 + 03-06 RT Shula's house	00:00:30:21
20	66 wild Goldi "Shoot him" + breaths	00:00:23:14
21	71 wild steps	00:00:54:09
22	71 wild text Rebecca	00:00:56:01
23	71+72 RT	00:01:10:12
24	73+74 wild "no coincidence" take 1	00:00:39:15
25	73+74 wild "no coincidence" take 2	00:00:22:10
26	73+74 wild "no coincidence" take 3	00:00:45:15
27	73+74 wild "no coincidence" take 4	00:00:44:11
28	81 RT hospital waiting room	00:01:08:13
29	82 RT Goldi apartment	00:01:20:06
30	86 RT studio	00:00:25:20
31	86 wild rustle	00:01:19:18
32	90+91+92 wild Rebecca	00:00:32:24
33	90+91+92 RT apartment day	00:01:12:16
34	96 wild start of scene	00:00:30:21
35	96a wild Debby	00:00:18:17
36	97a RT park w/birds	00:01:01:12
37	97a wild Dana shouting 01	00:00:47:04
38	97a wild Dana shouting 02	00:00:47:08
39	99+100 wild Sam	00:00:22:24
40	110 wild Taxi in and out	00:01:20:06

Figure 9-9 A wild sound list created from original recordings.

from alternate takes, piece together some missing rustle from a later section of the scene, and replace off-mic wide-shot dialogue with close-up sound. Fine. However, if you look at the list of wild sounds as you start editing a scene, you'll better understand the problems encountered when the scene was shot.

I keep the wild sound list taped next to the monitor so that I have no excuse but to check it before I begin each scene. There's probably a reason the wild recordings were made, so being familiar with them may be useful. It could alter the way I look at the scene, although it may not make any difference in my scene-cutting battle plan.

CHAPTER 10

Now, the Actual Editing

At last, it's time to edit. No more setup to be done, no more preparation work. As you begin, keep the following two main purposes of the dialogue editing process in mind so that you can be efficient and focused.

- *To serve the film* by creating clean, focused tracks, free of anything that gets in the way. This is how you can help move the story along and create minute details that enhance plot, character development, and drama.
- *To prepare tracks* that can be mixed easily and productively. No matter how creative, clean, or detail-rich your tracks, if the mixer can't quickly make sense of them, all of your work is in vain. You'll never have enough time in a dialogue premix to give your tracks the time they deserve, so you have to edit with an eye to the mix, presenting your tracks in such a way that the mixer spends her time creatively, bringing out the best in them rather than trying to figure out your system.

Respect these two goals—craftsmanship and procedure—and the rest will work out.

Splitting Tracks

The first real step in editing is to split the tracks within a scene so that each camera angle (shot) has its own track. This will make it easier for you to understand the scene and allow the scene to "talk" to you. It will also make for a sensible mix when the time comes. Give the rerecording mixer a beautifully edited but badly organized scene and your work will be wasted (plus, you'll hear some well-deserved harsh words). If you've done any popular music production, you know that you organize the recording, editing, and mixing of each song by instrument. (See Figure 10-1.) You might have a track for the lead guitar, one for the bass, one for the synth, a few for the drums, and of course one for the singer. In your mix, you'll want a specific

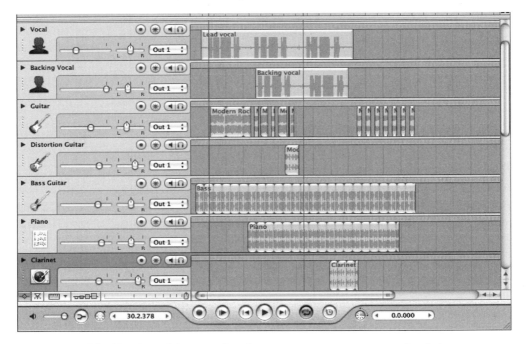

Figure 10-1 Idealized tracking session for a pop song as seen on Apple's Soundtrack Pro. Each instrument occupies one track on a song. On another song, the track geography may be totally different, depending on the song's needs.

combination of EQ, dynamics, and effects for each instrument and voice throughout the song.

If the guitar lives on the same track throughout the song, you can easily apply its required processing without interfering with the other instruments and without any undue automation acrobatics. If you record a few bars of guitar on a certain track and then drop in some drums followed by a few lines of vocals, you can imagine how difficult it becomes to control the music. You'll spend all your time executing exotic processing automation and lose focus on the real issue—telling a story through music.

In many ways you face the same issues in dialogue editing. *Within a scene*, each camera angle, each perspective, every character behaves like an instrument in a pop song. By properly organizing the scene, you gain the same control you achieve in music mixing. Each shot will have its unique characteristics, and by putting each one on its own track—within that scene—you're making life much easier for yourself and for the mixer.

Be careful not to take this music analogy too far. The "rules" of a scene—who's on which track—are true only within the one scene you're working on. Just because Bill's close-up is on Dial C in scene 76, he doesn't have to appear on Dial C throughout the film. Nor do you need to create hundreds of tracks to accommodate all the people/angle combinations you'll encounter. On a film of average complexity, you should be able to elegantly edit the dialogue using no more than 16 tracks, still providing the order and logic needed to wrangle the tracks within each scene. This is possible only because you recycle the tracks on entering a new scene. Unlike music production, where a track takes on the name of its "inhabitant," dialogue tracks steadfastly hold onto their names: Dial A, Dial B, and so on.

Fortunately, the key to organizing your session by shot presents itself as soon as you open the session. Unless you're especially unlucky, the scene, shot, and take information (or the slate and take number if the production used a sequential slate-numbering system) will appear on the region names. (See Figure 10-2.)

An Example of Scene Organization by Shot

Before the shoot, a scene must be broken into shots. At its most basic level, a scene will contain a master shot, close-ups for each speaking character, perhaps a two-shot or a dolly shot, and whatever other angles are needed to move the story along. Let's imagine a simple two-person interior scene and see how it can be broken into shots. In the drawing room, Fanny and Edmund

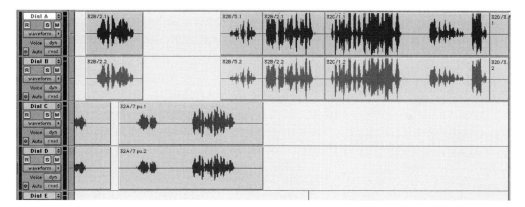

Figure 10-2 Use the information in the region names to identify scene, shot, and take.

are engaged in a bit of courtship (the dialogue is transcribed from Jane Austen's *Mansfield Park*, first published in 1814).[1]

Edmund

Now I must look at you Fanny, and tell you how I like you; and as well as I can judge by this light, you look very nicely indeed. What have you got on?

Fanny

The new dress that my uncle was so good as to give me on my cousin's marriage. I hope it is not too fine; but I thought I ought to wear it as soon as I could, and that I might not have such another opportunity all the winter. I hope you do not think me too fine.

Edmund

A woman can never be too fine when she is all in white.

That's the script. The director will visualize it into shots, and the assistant director will organize a sensible shooting order based on locations, availability of actors, and weird production demands. You'll end up with a script breakdown like this:

Scene 32, INT day drawing room, Edmund and Fanny

Shots:

32	MWS	Establishment shot, Edmund + Fanny left of frame, large clock on right
32A	MCU	Fanny
32B	CU	Edmund
32C	WS	through window

When the scene is shot, the script supervisor keeps track of which parts of the scene were successfully filmed from each angle. This **lined script** will enable the film editor, and later you, to see which text was covered during each shot and take. In the real world, the script report will include **coverage** details for each take so you can easily know what you have to work with and where your pitfalls lie. It's rare that all shots, or angles, will cover the entire scene. Usually, a scene is blocked so that certain sections are covered by specific angles. Otherwise, you end up wasting film and shooting time, both of which are expensive.

The lined script in Figure 10-3 is hideously oversimplified, but you see how the picture editor can use the script notes to learn what sort of coverage exists.[2] He'll pick from this treasure trove of shots, selecting the best moments

---

[1] From the edition published by Penguin Classics (London, 1994, p. 224).

[2] Rather than identify shots as "scene/shot (letter)/take," some productions use a "scene/shot (slate)/take" naming system. *Slate* identifies the shot in the sequence in which the movie is being shot, whereas the scene-based name reflects the script order. Our close-up of Edmund could have been identified as 32/193/4, meaning "scene 32, shot 193, take 4."

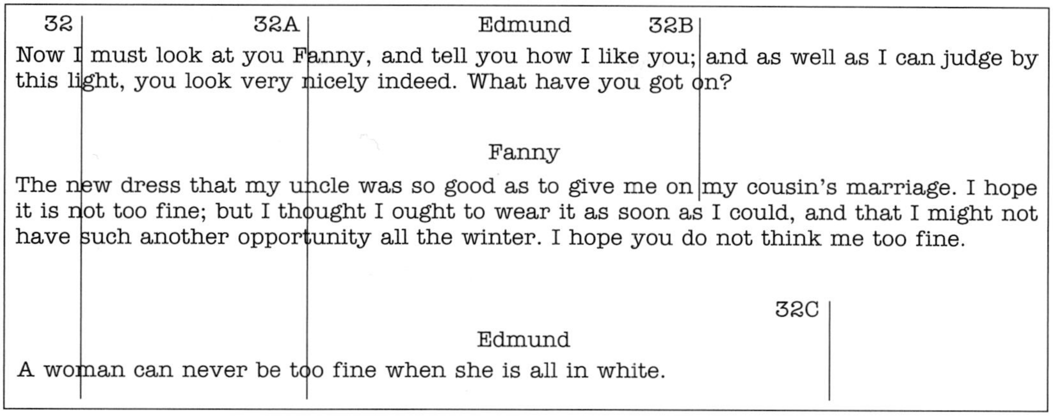

| 32 | 32A | Edmund | 32B | |

```
32 |              32A |            Edmund        32B|
Now I must look at you Fanny, and tell you how I like you; and as well as I can judge by
this light, you look very nicely indeed. What have you got on?


                                         Fanny
The new dress that my uncle was so good as to give me on my cousin's marriage. I hope
it is not too fine; but I thought I ought to wear it as soon as I could, and that I might not
have such another opportunity all the winter. I hope you do not think me too fine.


                                                              32C |
                                        Edmund
A woman can never be too fine when she is all in white.
```

Figure 10-3 Much simplified example of a lined script.

and the greatest performances, and piece together a believable, emotional scene that pulls the viewer through the action and into the next scene.

Split by Sound Edits, Not Picture Edits

In the scene shown in Figure 10-3, begin by placing every appearance of shot 32 (the master shot) on Dial A, all 32A regions on Dial B, and so forth. (See Figure 10-4.) Later you might decide to further split the regions, but this is a good start—and it's very easy. Remember that even though you're splitting the dialogue regions by shot, you're not (or you are but very rarely) cutting with the picture. You're splitting by "microphone angle" and your splits will be based on sound, not picture, edits. If picture editors always cut picture and sound at the same moment, films would be awfully boring, so sound and picture edits are often staggered.

In the scene with Edmund and Fanny, the editor might have cut to Fanny's close-up (CU) before Edmund completed his first speech. Although we were seeing Fanny's appreciative face, we would hear the end of Edmund's track. Still holding onto Fanny's CU, we would hear her lines, now in sync with her picture. At the end of Fanny's lines, the picture editor may choose to hang on to her CU for a few moments, even while we hear Edmund's retort. In all such cases, split the dialogue based on sound edits only.

At this point, you don't know anything about the tracks, but you can make certain blind assumptions. By organizing the scene by shot, you can better understand its sound issues. Plus, this configuration will make the mix sensible and logical.

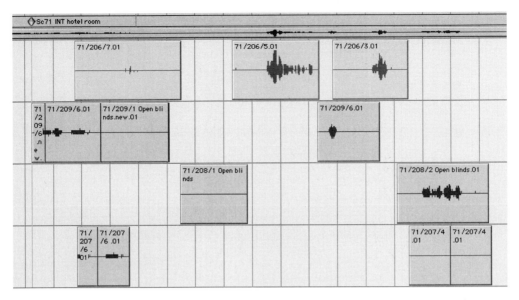

Figure 10-4 As you begin to split a scene, the most sensible place to start is by shot. In this example, scene 71, all of the regions from shot (or "slate") 206 go to Dial A, regions from shot 209 go to Dial B, and so forth. The sequence is a matter of taste, but many editors place the first shot to appear in a scene onto the first track used in that scene.

Additional Splits

At times you'll want to split your tracks beyond the basic shot-of-origin mode. Perspective cuts, telephone conversations, problematic noises, or places where you want extra focus are just a few of the reasons to do this. If, for example, the picture editor used three different takes of Edmund's close-up, two of which have the same room tone and another that suffers from a low-frequency rumble, you should split the rumble-infested take onto its own track. After all, it will unquestionably need special processing because of the noise, and it will likely benefit from longer room tone transitions.

Don't be shy about splitting; tracks are cheap. In general, splitting is better than not splitting, but thoughtless or unnecessary splitting creates more problems than it solves. Talk to your rerecording mixer about how many tracks you can use, and how detailed he wants the splits to be.

Unnecessary Inserts

Just because the picture editor gives you a shot, you don't have to use it. If, while talking to Fanny, Edmund (32B) takes a thoughtful pause and the picture cuts to Fanny silently nodding her approval, the picture editor will probably cut both picture and sound to Fanny's shot (32A). When the lecture continues, the editor will cut back to Edmund's track. What you're left with is a change of room tone when we cut to Fanny and another when we return to Edmund. (See Figure 10-5.)

Clearly, if Fanny says something or makes an audible sigh or movement, you'll need her insert to maintain a sense of reality. However, if the sound from her insert offers no useful information, you'll end up moving back and forth between room tones for no reason. Not only does this make you work harder than necessary, but it subjects the viewer to yet another room tone transition. If the inserted room tone doesn't help the story, get rid of it and cover the inserted shot with room tone from Edmund's track. (See Figure 10-6.) The result: A smoother track that's easier to cut and easier to mix. Everyone wins.

How Many Tracks?

In general, you want enough principal dialogue tracks to be able to cut two consecutive scenes of average complexity without reusing tracks. So if, on average, you use 6 tracks per scene, you'll want 12 to 14 primary dialogue tracks. Sometimes things get out of control and a long or madly complex scene uses ten or more tracks, so the next scene will necessarily reuse some. Don't worry.

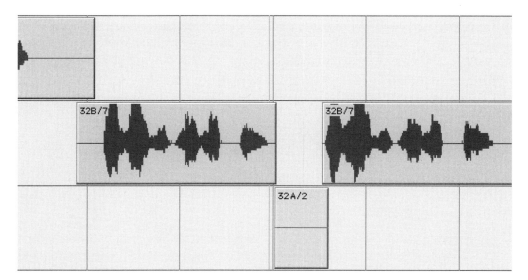

Figure 10-5 When you cut from 32B to the silent cutaway of Fanny, 32A, you may introduce unnecessary room tone changes and gain nothing in exchange.

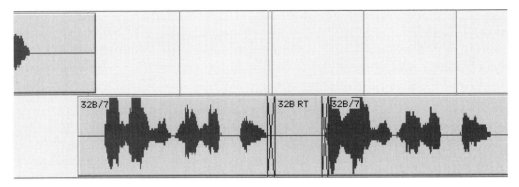

Figure 10-6 If there's absolutely no interesting information in Fanny's short cutaway, remove it and fill with Edmund's room tone. Also, if Fanny's cutaway has useful information but is unacceptably noisy, remove it and fill with tone from 32B. Later, Foley may be added to liven up the gap.

On small films I typically use about 14 main dialogue tracks. By the time I get to the dialogue premix, I've added a few ADR tracks, some production effects, and X, Y, and Z tracks, ending up with about 30 altogether. Any mixer can handle 30 tracks, but if I'm working with a mixer or dubbing stage I don't know, I'll e-mail a list of my tracks and ask if this arrangement is reasonable.

No matter how many tracks you end up with, be sure to have the same number on each reel, in the same order. Even if you don't use every track on each reel, go to the mix with every track in its proper place, muted if unused. This way, the tracks will always come up on the correct channels of the mixing desk. Repatching is a nuisance and always leads to mistakes.

Splitting Scenes

Just as you split your tracks within a scene, you can split one scene against the next, making for easier mixing. Most rerecording mixers prefer to "checkerboard" their dialogue premixes (or predubs) onto different premix record tracks so they have greater control over scene transitions or additional processing during the final mix.

If your mixer wants to work this way, try not to recycle tracks on adjacent scenes. Say that one scene uses eight tracks (Dials A → H); try to start the next scene on track 9 (Dial I). The third scene will then begin again on Dial A. (See Figure 10-7.) If you have a very long or complicated scene that won't

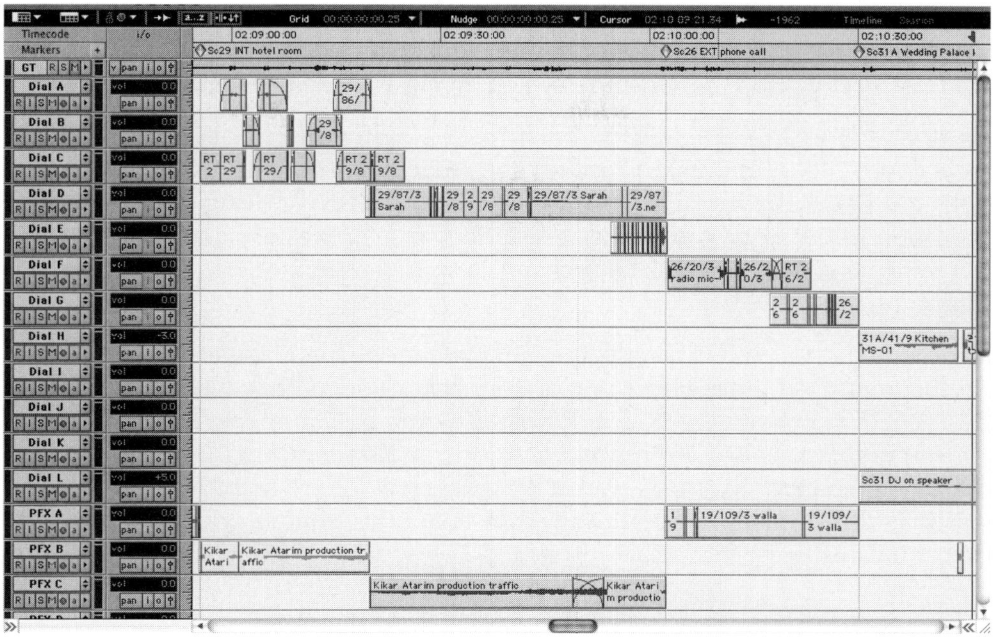

Figure 10-7 Try not to put adjacent scenes on the same tracks. Here scene 29 is on Dials A, B, C, and D, plus PFX B and C. Scene 26 (including its split, which begins during scene 29) is on Dials E, F, and G plus PFX A. The beginnings of scene 31A can be seen on Dials H and L.

allow checkerboarding, just make sure that its first couple of shots start on tracks that weren't used at the very end of the outgoing scene. (See Chapter 16, Preparing for the Mix, for more on this topic.)

Shot Balancing and the Rules of Thumb

Dialogue editing's most important sleight of hand is taking the elements of a scene, often shot at different times or under dissimilar conditions, and nursing them into a living scene that viewers will truly believe to be *real*. Matching the voice qualities, the degree of "on-mic" sound, and the level and quality of the room tone and creating narrative-enhancing perspective are what make a scene shine. Shot balancing removes the *mechanics* of filmmaking, but exploits the *language* of film to allow the sound of the dialogue to be more than just the carrier of the text.

Remember, films are shot with one camera, not in script order. Between each shot or setup (not each take), the camera relocates, the lights are reset, and all sorts of other things change. This results in a new sound for each angle. Sometimes the difference between shots is hardly noticeable; other times the contrast is shocking, leaving the edited scene all but unlistenable.

Compare cinema's single-camera approach with video studio production techniques. Soap operas and many TV comedies are shot multicamera (i.e., with multiple cameras), either in front of an audience or designed to give you the impression that an audience exists. Because scenes are shot more or less in real time, there's little difference in the sound characteristics from one shot to another.

There's usually no change in set or lighting between shots (since they're shot multicamera), so there's little reason for each angle to have a different sound. Besides, these productions are almost always shot on a sound stage, so the overall noise and the differences from one angle to another are under much better control. Finally, the sound source doesn't change with the picture—the sound is captured from a common studio boom or a battery of radio mics—so there's no resulting change in room tone or sound color. (See Figure 10-8.)

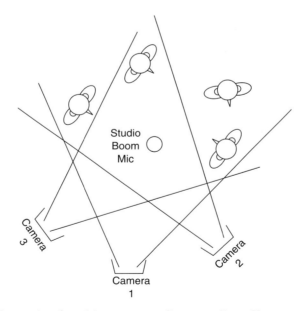

Figure 10-8 A schematic of multicamera studio recording. Shown are the characters, the boom microphone, and three video cameras. Sound is captured from studio boom microphones or from several wireless microphones. The character of the sound doesn't change from shot to shot.

Now, back to film production. Imagine an interior restaurant scene (we'll call it scene 45) in which three people—Bob, Betty, and Blanche—are talking. Betty's back is to the kitchen, so her room tone includes refrigerator rumble in a large, hard space as well as some shuffling about. Bob's back is against a soft banquette, so his room tone is comparatively quiet. Behind Blanche is the rest of the restaurant—goodness knows what her shot sounds like, but it's probably full of air conditioner noise. (These shots have far more similarities than differences, but in this example we'll exaggerate things for the sake of clarity.)

The scene consists of several shots (see Figure 10-9):

1. Wide establishment shot of everyone at the table, scene 45.
2. Medium close-up of each of the three characters:
   a. Betty CU, scene 45A
   b. Bob CU, scene 45B
   c. Blanche CU, scene 45C
3. Medium shot, POV from the kitchen, scene 45D.

Now piece together an imaginary scene from the shots just given. The picture editor will analyze each one and fashion a scene that exploits the strengths

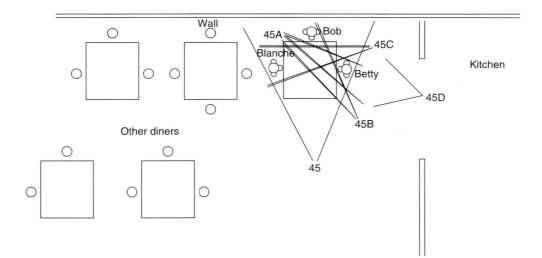

Figure 10-9 A schematic of scene 45. Note the different camera setups for each shot. Also note the landmarks in the room and their relationships with the characters and the camera. The geography of the room helps define the room tone for each shot.

of the footage (and conceals its weaknesses) to best tell a story. Chances are, the resulting sound bumps aren't the editor's highest priority. The picture people tell the story; we try to make it work. Besides, "It all sounded pretty good in the Avid!"

Once you open the OMF, the scene is immediately annoying. Cuts between Betty and Bob result in two mismatched kinds of kitchen noise, while moving to Blanche you lose the hum of the kitchen only to hear the din of the restaurant. And neither of the wider shots cuts well against the close-ups. Even if the scene is interesting and dramatically effective, it won't sound like a movie because of the bumps. How can this happen? How can the picture editor do this to you? Easy.

- Picture editors have things on their minds other than the sound of shot transitions, so what to you seems an unforgivable lapse of judgment makes perfect sense to them. They're right. The story is what counts. Let the sound department deal with the bodies.
- Between the hard drives, the computers, and the lousy speakers, you simply can't hear in a modern picture editing room. Nothing masks bad cuts like computer and air conditioner noise.
- Picture cutting rooms are rarely equipped with adequate mixers, amplifiers, or loudspeakers.

Scene 45 is sitting on your desk and, for whatever the reason, it doesn't work.

Every time there's a change in sound sources, room tone, voice characteristics, or level, you're temporarily knocked out of the scene—reminded that this is a movie. Since every ounce of your film-literate brain wants to think of scene 45 as real life, you get back into the scene quickly enough. But the magic is temporarily violated with each cut. Before you can effectively attack the other issues (noises, overlaps, replacements, perspective, etc.), you must make the scene reasonably smooth. Otherwise, the irregularities caused by room tone mismatches will make it all but impossible to listen for the more subtle problems. (See Figure 10-10.)

You soon discover, however, that smoothing scenes is a constant tradeoff between total noise and evenness, and many novice editors err on the side of noise. "Lay down a wall of room tone," the logic goes, "and you can mask the differences between shots." Or you can mask the differences between the shots by running a vacuum cleaner in your cutting room while listening to the scene, but that's hardly a solution. (See Figure 10-11.)

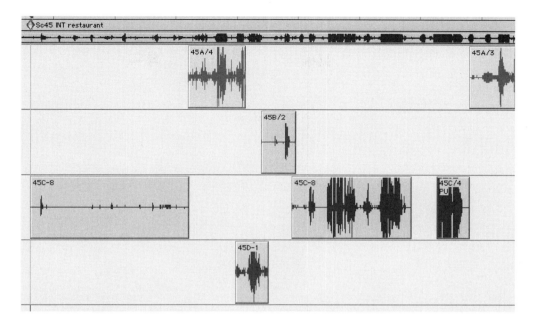

Figure 10-10 Detail from scene 45 after you've organized the tracks but before editing. Each shot has different room tone, so the scene is bumpy. Note that Blanche (45A) and the shot from the kitchen (45D) have much heavier room tone than the other shots have.

Although there are (rare) occasions when you want to include a wall-to-wall carpet of room tone in a scene, you shouldn't count on this as a solution to shot mismatches. But because this ill-conceived practice is so common, it's worth looking at why you shouldn't work like this. Look again at Figure 10-11. We've done nothing to ease the transitions. True, the bumps are less audible, since the problematic transitions are hiding behind the room tone track. During the dialogue premix, however, you'll undoubtedly remove some of the ambient noise and the mask will lose its cloaking ability. The cleaner you make the tracks sound, the more this editing technique will betray you.

Aside from being ineffective, this technique makes for noisy tracks. Throughout the scene, at least two tracks of room tone are playing. Twice the room tone, double the noise floor. The original problem wasn't within the shots but only at the transitions, so why should we add unnecessary noise to the middle of perfectly respectable shots? This brings us to the first fundamental rule of thumb for dialogue editors.

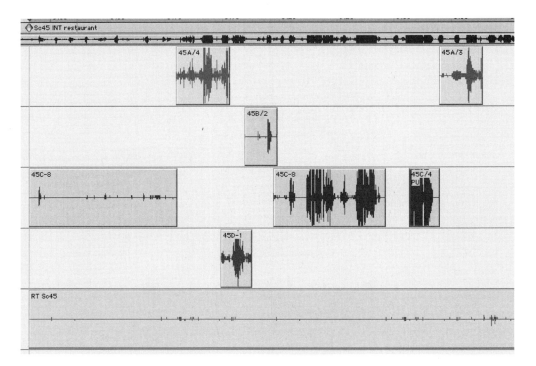

Figure 10-11 Room tone was applied for the entire duration of scene 45 in an attempt to mask shot mismatches. The underlying problem has not been solved, and the scene will now be much noisier.

Rule One: *Whenever Possible, Play Only One Source of Room Tone at a Time*

Let each shot speak for itself, overlapping room tones only at transitions. It's true that there must be constant room tone running the length of a scene. After all, it's the air that a scene breathes. However, in most circumstances the room tone comes from the regions themselves. Only when there's a hole in the production track do you add a steady track of tone.

In Figure 10-12, each shot **crossfades** into the next. Here we were lucky because there was sufficient clean room tone within the handles of each shot to allow for easy crossfade creation. There's no added, steady room tone track; instead, the room tone comes uniquely from the shots that make up the scene so it rarely has more than one source. "But," you ask, "what about the cross-

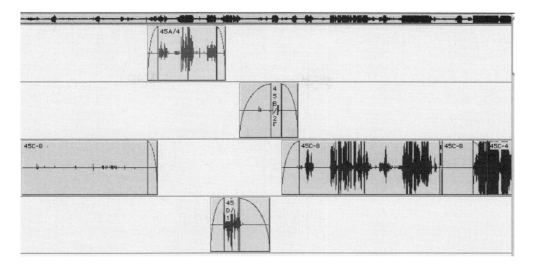

Figure 10-12 Detail of preliminary edit of scene 45. Regions overlap more or less symmetrically and there's no supplemental room tone track. The room tone for the scene is carried by the shots themselves.

fades? During these transitions two room tones are playing at once." Yes, but as one shot fades in its partner fades out, so the sum of the two is never more than 100 percent of the average level of the shots. You haven't broken the rule about avoiding more than one simultaneous tone.

Creating crossfades between regions doesn't eliminate sound differences between shots. It merely lengthens the transition so that you don't notice the changes. Human "hearing memory" is surprisingly short, so it doesn't take much to fool the ear into thinking that a transition is smooth. Just spread the transition over a bit of time and most listeners won't hear a thing.

Once you construct smoothing crossfades between shots, the scene will almost certainly sound quieter, as though you equalized or otherwise cleaned it. There will likely remain "swells" as you move back and forth between shots. When the room tone characteristics of two adjacent shots are very different, there'll be peaks and troughs in the overall noise level as well as changes in the sound itself. During the dialogue premix you'll process these crossfaded shots to further minimize the mismatches. This brings us to the next basic rule of dialogue editing.

Rule Two: *Evenness Is a Trade-off between Noise and Smoothness*

When two shots don't match well, you'll inevitably hear their transitions despite crossfades. By lengthening a crossfade, you'll smooth the transition and give the impression of evenness. At the same time, this will increase the total noise since there'll be a longer period during which two room tones are playing. What's the "right" length? Of course, there's no answer to that. It's a choice, so use your judgment. Don't be afraid to experiment with fade lengths; a tiny change in overlap can make a huge difference in balance, noise, and smoothness of the crossover.

Why Bother? Since you're going to equalize and noise-reduce the shots during the mix, why go to such editorial trouble to smooth the transitions? Won't the processing during the dialogue premix mitigate the differences between the shots? Yes . . . but. Imagine you're painting a badly damaged window frame. The goal is a smooth, evenly covered surface that you can achieve either by slathering on a couple of thick coats of paint or by carefully scraping and sanding and filling, then applying a primer and sanding again—only then applying several thin coats of finishing paint. Either way the window gets painted. But in the lazy example you lose the details of the carpentry. The surface may be covered but it's not "articulate." It may be relatively smooth, but it's covered with a thick crust of paint that masks the sharp lines, bevels, and joints of the underlying wood. In short, the craftsmanship is lost. Because in the careful example you took the time to fix the holes, mend the transitions, and smooth the surface, you need to apply only as much covering as is absolutely necessary. The paint finish is smooth, yet the personality of the underlying woodwork is maintained.

Such is the case with dialogue editing and mixing. Whereas it's true that you can smooth almost any shot transition if you throw enough EQ and noise reduction at it, you have to ask yourself, "At what cost?" Scenes not properly prepared prior to the mix require much more processing to achieve an acceptable amount of smoothness. Because of the excessive filtering they may lack life, or sound thin and metallic, or at worst like a cell phone. This leads us to the third rule of thumb.

Rule Three: *Design Scenes That Require the Least Amount of Processing*

When your transitions are smooth, they're less objectionable to the ear. Hence, they require less shot matching. Of course, certain shots will need to be "helped along" and the entire scene will need noise reduction, but since your dialogue transitions largely take care of themselves, you don't need to overcook it. This allows the rerecording mixer to put more energy into making the shots sound nice—robust, full, warm, articulate. The dialogue hasn't been stripped of its character, so there's more to play with.

Ironically, the noisier the location of the scene, the bumpier you can leave your dialogue edit. If you're cutting a scene with lots of traffic noise, rest assured that the sound effects editor can sort out a problematic dialogue transition with a well-placed car-by or other background motion effect. No one will notice one more car-by amid a noisy scene, and the tiny added motion energy will bridge the gap.

On the other hand, no scene is harder to cut than an intimate conversation in a dead quiet bedroom at three in the morning. There's nothing to hide behind, and if the shots aren't naturally well matched, it's a nightmare to cut back and forth. If there's camera noise on one shot but not on the other, you have very few smoothing resources and you can't count on the SFX guys to save you. There are few appropriate atmospheric sound effects that can be used to mask the bumps, so you're on your own.

Transition When There's No Handle

In our restaurant scene with Bob, Betty, and Blanche, the editing gods indeed smiled on us. We were able to create clean room tone bridges merely by opening each shot's handles. As we pulled out the handles, we didn't encounter any footsteps, breaths, or words to ruin the room tone. Finding good "free" room tone like this isn't unusual, but to find it for a whole scene is unheard of. Count your blessings.

What do you do when the handles don't provide the room tone you need for transitions, as shown in Figure 10-13? You must create room tone, attach it to the region, and then make your crossfade. The next section deals in depth with room tone—what it is, how to make it, how to manage it. But first let's look at an example of bridging shot transitions using room tone you've found or created. (See Figure 10-14.)

Often when the handle's room tone is of no use, you'll find enough elsewhere in the same shot. Since the character of most room tones varies over time, looking nearby has two advantages: It's easy and it's likely to match. (See Figure 10-15.)

Remember, the room tone you're attaching to a shot must come from that shot (but not necessarily from the same take). Doing otherwise defeats the point

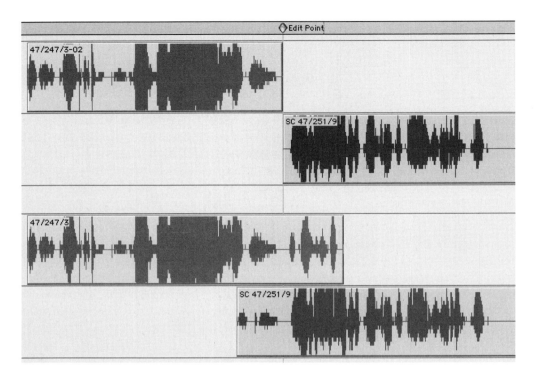

Figure 10-13 Just because you have a handle doesn't mean it's useful. Here you see the OMF edit (*above*) and after opening handles (*below*). The marker indicates the location of the original cut. Note that there's no useful room tone in either handle. Always listen for words, breaths, and motion sounds when opening handles for tone bridges.

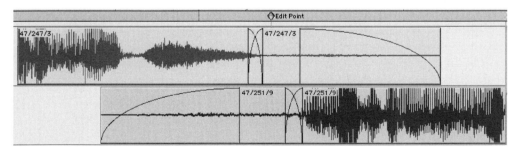

Figure 10-14 Create room tone "bridges" from nearby sections of the same shot. Here the two regions from Figure 10-12, which had no usable handles of their own, are linked using copies of adjacent room tone from the same shot.

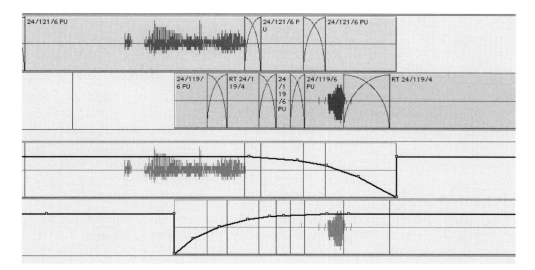

Figure 10-15 Room tone bridges are constructed from small segments of appropriate room tone from the same take as the main regions (*above*). Note that crossfades are used between the room tone segments. *Below* is the volume automation showing the crossfade between shots 121 and 119. Many workstations allow you to fade across several faded regions rather than having to resort to level automation.

of splitting tracks and organizing your scenes by shot of origin. If you can't find appropriate room tone elsewhere in the shot, try copying the region to a work track and fishing through the entire take. This technique is described in the next section.

You've now smoothed shot transitions in two ways: the lucky way, where you find usable room tone in the shots' handles, and the more common method, where you copy or construct a tone transition. Although each set of regions poses unique transition problems that require their own solutions, all shot transition puzzles are solved with some variation of these techniques.

Using Room Tone When Editing Dialogue

Room tone is the single most important tool of dialogue editing. Just as woodwind players are obsessive about their reeds, or fly fishermen have a mystical relationship with their flies, so too are dialogue editors fanatical about room tone. Without it, you can't edit.

At the same time, the term "room tone" is grossly misunderstood and misapplied. To many, it means "an interior atmosphere." To some, it's any atmosphere. Wrong on both counts. *Room tone* is the "silence" in any location recording, what's left from a take when you remove the words, the footsteps, and the rustle. It describes the location (interior or exterior) at which a scene was shot, and it helps define the essence of a shot.

Room tone's lofty position is due both to the trouble it causes and to the way it conveniently rushes to the rescue. Bumps in an edited scene are usually caused not by differences between characters' voices but rather by differences between their room tone. It's room tone that sets the shots apart, interfering with the magic of cinema continuity. And it's room tone that enables you to create a smooth and believable scene. Dialogue editors use room tone in every stage of editing. These are some of the most obvious examples:

- To bridge between different shots within a scene, lending the impression that the scene is a continuous action rather than a collection of shots.
- If added judiciously, to ease the transition between quiet close-ups and boomy wide shots.
- To remove noises from dollies, denture smacks, lip flaps, offscreen talking, and so on.
- To replace the environmental sound when dialogue must be rerecorded (**ADR**). Any missing body action sounds are replaced with **Foley**.
- To enhance international versions of films (**M&E**) when original room tone is added to atmospheres so that the international version resembles the original-language version.

Room Tone versus Backgrounds or Atmospheres

Simply put, room tone belongs to the dialogue department, whereas atmospheres (also called "backgrounds" or "ambiances" depending on where you live) are the domain of the sound effects/background department. Dialogue recordings are mono (perhaps multitrack, but not stereo), and so is room tone. Atmosphere recordings are usually stereo, although some are mono. Good room tone will have all of the characteristics of the shot that it's fixing. Level, color, pitch, "action"—all of these attributes must match the shot at the moment in the scene when they're used. Even if the location mixer records a stereo atmosphere of the set, this is not the same as a room tone and its uses are different.

Finding Room Tone

A location recordist will try to record room tone for each scene filmed. This will solve some of your problems, but it's not necessarily the answer to your

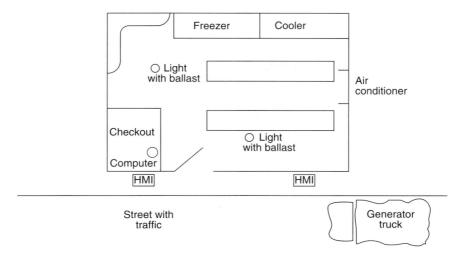

Figure 10-16 Shooting on location means mismatched room tones. In this convenience store, there are several sources of steady noise, many of which can't be turned off. Add to that the traffic outside and the noises created by the shoot itself—ballasts and the generator—and you see how it's hard to depend on a "general" room tone recording intended to cover the whole scene.

prayers. If there are four shots for a given scene, for example, each one will have its own distinct sound. Maybe the lights have moved; perhaps there's a noisy highway behind a character in one angle but not in others; or the camera may be closer to the actor (and microphone) in one shot than in the others so the camera noise is discernibly louder in that shot. The reasons for mismatched room tone are endless. (See Figure 10-16.) When the location mixer records 30 seconds of room tone for the scene, whose tone is he recording? The shot with the camera? The shot with the highway noise? The shot with more lighting ballast noise? Or perhaps an "average" room tone for the scene?

To make matters worse, it's often very difficult for the location mixer to enforce a few seconds of *real* silence on the set while she records. Her call for "Total silence!" doesn't mean "Whisper softly into your cell phone" or "Slowly open your lunch." "Absolute quiet!!" doesn't mean that the continuity person can complete her notes or that the grip can play with his pliers. Bottom line: You'll rarely be able to find good room tone within the wild room tone recordings from the set. You have to make it yourself.

Creating Room Tone

A common myth is that you need to locate only a small snippet of decent tone and then you can loop it to cover any duration. Wrong. Unless you've created a room tone so sterile that it totally lacks texture, any loop you attempt will be heard as just that: a loop. Reasonably long stretches of room tone can be looped, but even these usually require some tricks to avoid sounding repetitive. (See Figure 10-17.)

Another myth is that you can successfully create loads of room tone in a sampler. It can be done, but the result is rarely natural, alive, or believable. For the most part, if you want good room tone for a shot you must collect bits and pieces of it from within the shot and then piece together a convincing construction. (See Figure 10-18.)

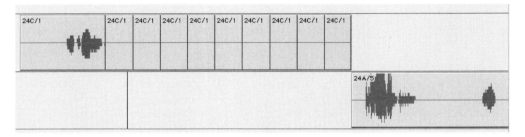

Figure 10-17 A room tone loop fills the hole between two shots. A string of regions that looks like this will sound like a loop. Anything this symmetrical means that the editor didn't listen while filling the gap.

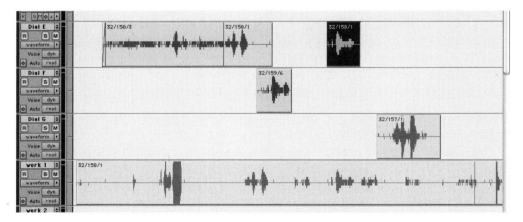

Figure 10-18 More room tone is needed for the highlighted section on Dial E. If a region's natural handles aren't useful, copy the region to a work track and completely open the region's handles. There'll be many possibilities for finding good room tone.

The new room tone must come from within the same shot as the material it's supporting. Using another shot's tone won't solve your problems. What do you do?

1. Make of copy of the region for which you're trying to create room tone. Paste it onto one of your work tracks.

2. Open the handles of this region all the way to its boundaries.

3. If you're working on a Pro Tools, enter **Shuffle** mode. On other DAWs, use a mode that allows you to **ripple** tracks while editing. (Take note: One of the main reasons you created work tracks was to have a safe place for ripple editing. If you use Shuffle mode on a "real" track, you'll lose sync on all of the track's downstream regions.) Remove all dialogue and noises from this region. The region will become increasingly shorter and you'll be left with room tone only. You can actually remove most of the words and noises without listening to the track; let the graphic display and your gut be your guide.

4. Make a couple of fine passes, each time removing more and more unwanted noises, breaths, and rustle. You should end up with a very smooth chunk of room tone, devoid of recognizable landmarks. The process is much like making a reduced sauce—you cook it for hours and hours until it becomes a small, perfect concentrate.

5. You can automate the process of isolating room tone with Pro Tools' Strip Silence function. (See Figure 10-19.) This feature, equivalents of

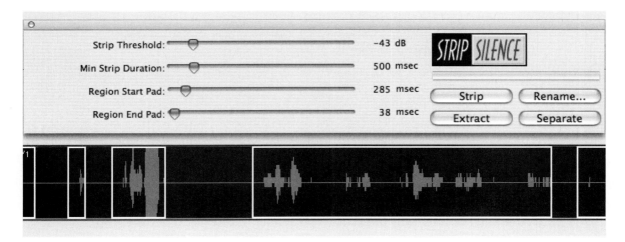

Figure 10-19 Pro Tools' Strip Silence dialogue box.

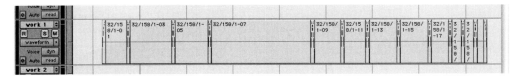

Figure 10-20 Even out room tone with crossfades.

which are found on most workstations, asks for a threshold volume and a duration, which it uses to define "analogue black." If you dial in −35 dB and 500 ms, for example, it will create a new region wherever the peak level doesn't exceed −35 dB for at least a half a second. Once this criterion is met, it will create a new region. Some people like to work with Strip Silence; I prefer to create room tone manually.

6. When your room tone is smooth and without transient sounds, perform crossfades at each of the edits you created. This will smooth the cuts and prevent clicks (especially important if your room tone carries lots of low-frequency information). (See Figure 10-20.)

7. You'll want to create a consolidated region from your jumble of crossfaded clips. One complete region is easier to edit, fade, and automate. Plus, you'll have a properly named room tone region that will appear in your regions list and can be imported into other reels of the film. Before consolidating this string of edits, be certain that you're happy with the edits and the crossfades, since once consolidated the edits can't be fixed. Consolidating creates a new soundfile, which you must subsequently name.

8. Name the new file using a sensible, systematic, easily sorted naming scheme—for example, "RT Sc32 Bill WS (quiet version)." This provides all the information you need to find the right room tone without scratching your head. You don't want to end up with hundreds of room tone soundfiles named "Aud_1-1." Begin the soundfile name with "RT" and all of your room tones will sort together. Begin with the scene name and it will live among the other regions from the scene. How you name your room tone creations is not important as long as you're consistent. Later in the scene, or perhaps when you edit the ADR, you'll need the room tone files you painstakingly created. Make it easy on yourself by giving them consistent, logical names.

Figure 10-21 Consolidate the tone into one manageable region. Trim off the region's outer edges (seen here beyond the highlighting) before copying to leave "wiggle room" for crossfades and edit point positioning.

9. If you're working on a Pro Tools, return to the Slip mode. If you are using another workstation, leave the ripple enable mode and return to normal editing.

10. If you're going to immediately edit with your new room tone (which is usually the case), trim away the beginning and end of the sound-file before copying it to a track adjacent to the one you're editing, from which you'll cut and paste as necessary. Trimming the top and tail of the soundfile provides a handle you can use to fade or trim any new edit. (See Figure 10-21.)

Using All Takes to Create Room Tone

If, after you cull the words, noises, and other unwanted irregularities from your expanded take, there's not enough room tone to work with, you can extract what you need from *all* of the takes of the shot.

- Find all of the alternate takes of the shot in question, including the one used in the film. (See Chapter 12 to learn how to do this.) String the takes together, one after another, onto the work track.
- Follow the procedure described earlier for extracting quality room tone from the takes. When finished, consolidate and name the new room tone file.

Dealing with Changes in Room Tone Pitch or Volume

Small, recognizable sounds—that tiny click, the miniscule footstep, the quiet lip smack—will betray you when you repeat a section of room tone. Plus, it's not likely that the click, step, or smack riding along with room tone will happen to fall in an appropriate spot in the scene. Get rid of such signatures.

However, sometimes it's not enough to remove the telltale noises. Say you're looping a piece of room tone that rises in pitch over the course of its 5-second

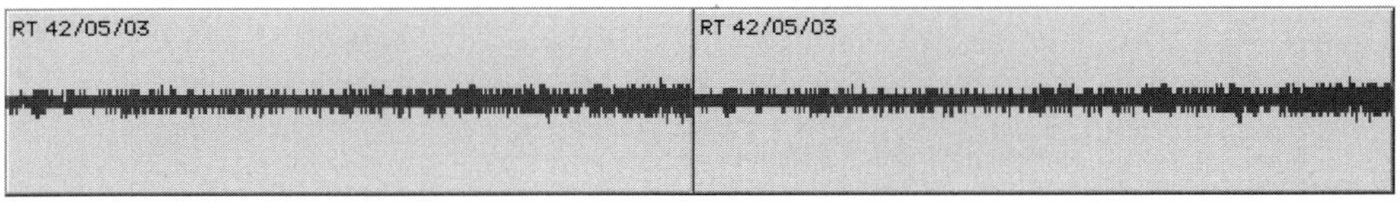

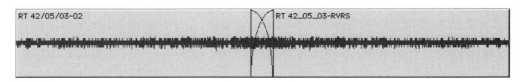

Figure 10-22 This room tone region tends to get louder with time, so looping it will result in a sudden drop in level followed by a slow rise. The same problem can arise when the level is even throughout the region but there's a steady change in pitch. Either way, there'll be a bump at the edit.

Figure 10-23 Assuming there are no sounds with patterns (voices, birds, car horns, etc.) or with a clear attack and decay, you may be able to loop a room tone with a pitch or level pattern by reversing the soundfile.

life (nondescript background traffic rumble is an example). Merely repeating the cue will result in a "reset" of the pitch at each loop edit. Even though you carefully removed the noises, your loop still sounds like a loop. (See Figure 10-22.)

You can often create a good loop from a pitch-periodic room tone file by copying and reversing the room tone. (See Figure 10-23.)

- Make a copy of your clean room tone region. Make sure there are no acoustic sounds such as footsteps, birds, or voices in the clip.
- Use your DAW to create a new, reversed region.
- Trim a small amount from the end of the original file and the beginning of the reversed file. Edit these shortened soundfiles together and crossfade as necessary.
- Consolidate and name the resulting soundfile.

The room tone will still have a cyclical pattern, but it will be smooth and complete rather than cut off in mid-period. In a pinch, it will work fine as long as you don't overuse it.

Matching Room Tone and Dialogue

Go to great lengths to avoid applying EQ or other processing to a room tone during editing. If you have to change the room tone to match a shot, there's probably something wrong with it. Try again to find a better match, since "fake" room tone will come back to haunt you. Remember, it's unlikely that you can hear as well in your cutting room as on the mixing stage, so bold processing of room tone clips will likely backfire.

If all honest attempts at finding acceptable room tone fail, then all is fair game. Equalize if you must, but listen to your work in a mix room—before the premix—to make sure you haven't fooled yourself into believing that the edit works. It's horribly embarrassing to play these tracks in the dialogue premix—tracks you're so proud of because of the nerdy manipulations you've subjected them to—only to hear that they sound nothing like the dialogue you're trying to match.

Using Room Tone to Remove Noises in Dialogue

Location recordings are filled with small noises that often go unnoticed on first listening. The causes of these short nuisances are limitless, but the most common are static discharge, cable problems, lip smacks and dentures clacks, dolly track, and crew noises. Individually, these tiny sounds don't amount to much, but collectively they steal focus from the dialogue and leave the impression that the set is much noisier than it really is. Thankfully, these transient noises are easy to remove as long as they occur between words.

Small ticks and pops can usually be replaced with room tone, but first you have to find them. The easiest way is by **scrubbing** until you pinpoint the click. Then zoom in to the offending noise. Find a tiny piece of adjacent room tone, copy it and paste over the click, and add short crossfades. (See Figures 10-24 and 10-25.) If you're removing several clicks within a small region, use a different piece of room tone for each replacement so it doesn't sound like a loop.

Techniques for removing such noises are discussed in more detail in Chapter 12, Damage Repair.

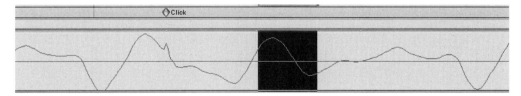

Figure 10-24 Often clicks are very hard to spot visually. The click here, indicated by the marker, can be fixed by replacing it with adjacent material. The selected sound will be pasted over the matching part of the region containing the click. Line up the sine curves to avoid making new clicks.

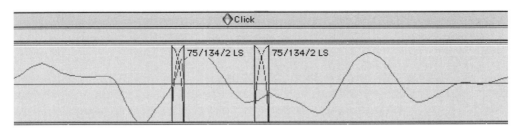

Figure 10-25 The copied material covers the click, and short crossfades prevent introducing other problems. Note that the line of the waveform follows a more or less predictable path even after the new material is inserted.

Figure 10-26 Room tone copied from a pause in dialogue. Don't copy the entire available room tone. Omit a bit on either side of the selection so you can easily adjust the edit point and make crossfades.

Copying Less Room Tone Than You Need

When copying room tone from a pause, take *less* than what's available. Leave some clean tone in the handle beyond what you select so that when you edit it into your track you'll have some extra room tone to play with and use for crossfades. (See Figure 10-26.) Remember, if there's motion or clothing rustle in the area you're repairing, your "fill" room tone must contain matching action. Don't go to the trouble of adding clean room tone to a rustle-filled shot when the resulting quiet will be distracting.

Working with More Than One Channel of Dialogue

When mono Nagra was the industry standard, most location recordings came to the dialogue editor on single-channel 35 mm mag stripe. For better or worse, you were at the mercy of the location mixer, whose job it was (and still is) to combine all of the on-set microphones into a single mixed track. Then along came stereo Nagra and later DAT, which enabled location mixers to provide two separate mixes or two solo tracks, depending on the complexity and needs of a shot. There were pioneers like Robert Altman, who was recording on multitrack tape as early as 1975 with *Nashville*, but two-track location recordings remained the norm until very recently.

As hard-disk recorders become the standard, multitrack field recordings are changing the way everyone works, not just the pioneers. Now when you get an OMF or EDL from the picture department, it's not at all unusual to be confronted with four, six, or more tracks per take, plus a mono track or split-track mixdown of the solo tracks. Given enough time, you can exercise great control over the tracks, bringing them to the mix well planned and highly focused. But how often do you have the time to sort through so many options?

When you're facing a scene in which every shot has several channels of original audio, it's easy to lose your perspective and choke on the abundance of sounds. Do you pick one track or play them all? Do you play two tracks at the same time? The answer, of course, is "it depends."

Many shots—a close-up of a talking head, a two-shot of seated characters, even a group of people—can be recorded perfectly well onto one channel using a boom, a directional microphone, and a skilled boom operator. Any of these scenes can sound great on one track if the recording team is nimble. Assuming that this single track is well recorded, nothing could be easier for you. Just fix the head and tail of the shot, remove any unwanted noises, and you're done.

On the other hand, it's really satisfying to have at your disposal every microphone—radio mic and boom—so that you can choose exactly where you want to focus. You have fewer overlap problems and no worries about the location mixer or boom operator missing his cue. Again, the problem is having the time to sift through the material.

Deciding Which Track to Use

Despite the recent proliferation of hard-disk recorders, most low-budget films are still recorded on two tracks, whether on DAT or another media. Typically, you'll find a boom on the left channel and a radio microphone or a mix of radio microphones on the right, but this will vary by location mixer, and it will all be written down in the sound reports. (Throughout this section, let's assume you're using the OMF. However, the same rules apply when working with tracks generated from an auto-assembly.)

No offense to our friends in the picture department, but the last thing you want is for the picture editor to decide for you which track to use for each shot. As long as you don't lecture her on montage, she can stay out of your microphone decisions. Early in the picture editing process, ask the editor to use both DAT audio tracks throughout the editing. Failing this, ask the assistant picture editor to include both audio tracks before creating the OMF regardless of the tracks chosen by the editor. This way you'll have easy access to all DAT tracks.

When you first open the OMF, you probably see two channels for every event. As you learned in Chapter 9, you first have to decide which of these two-track events are dual mono. Even though many shots are still mono (Why should they be otherwise?), you'll eventually run into multitrack shots. What you do with these extra channels is largely guided by common sense, but it will also depend on the wishes of the film's rerecording mixer. If you've never prepared tracks for the person who'll be mixing your dialogue, have a little talk. Find out how he likes to receive multimicrophone, multitrack elements. Does he want all decent tracks to be available (and prepared) for the mix, or does he prefer that you make the call? How should you present the main choice? The other channels? Muted? Unmuted? Find out. The rest is up to you.

Deciding which channel to use is extraordinarily situation-specific, so the best I can do for you in a book like this is to set some basic rules, which, once having learned, you can forget and then trust your gut. For example, earlier we learned the first rule of thumb of dialogue editing: *Whenever possible, play only one source of room tone at a time.* A simple, even crossfade often works well when crosscutting from one boom shot to another. (See Figure 10-27.) It also

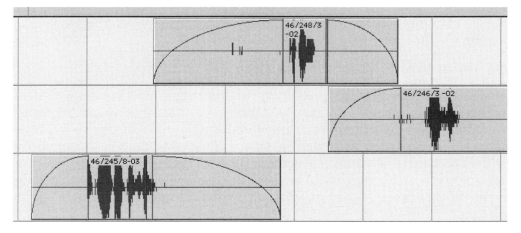

Figure 10-27 Boom shots crossfading against each other. This is the most straightforward and easiest of all shot transitions.

works with two radio mics in one shot. As long as the shots are reasonably similar, then symmetrical crossfades almost always give you good results.

One Shot, Two Mics, Similar Room Tone—No Dialogue Overlaps Imagine a long shot in which two people walk toward the camera. There's no **headroom** for a boom, so both actors are wired with radio microphones. (See Figure 10-28.) Each carries her own room tone, but the tones aren't overwhelmingly different from each other. This doesn't sound altogether bad, and you may be tempted to do nothing at all, leaving both tracks. However, there are a few pitfalls in leaving both running simultaneously.

- You're unnecessarily playing two tracks, even though only one person is speaking at a time. This doubles the room tone noise.
- Since both tracks are always open, you increase the chances of radio microphone distortion, clothing rustle, and other nasties coming from the nonspeaking character's mic.
- Whenever one of the characters speaks, you hear her voice twice— once close and on-mic and again through her partner's microphone, muffled, off-axis, and slightly delayed. The resulting dialogue is less punchy because you now have two wavefronts: one tight and crisp; the other gooey and late. If you remove the off-mic track, you'll usually get better articulation and a sense of reduced ambient noise.

Contrary to general opinion, mixing two radio mics separated by a reasonable distance won't often result in phasing. In fact, you'll hear phasing only when

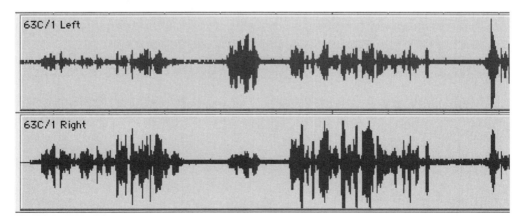

Figure 10-28 A typical pair of radio microphone tracks. The characters are each wearing a wireless, and their room tones are similar. Normally, you won't want to let both tracks play at the same time, as all sorts of problems may arise.

the two characters are very close—kissing, hugging, or passing near each other. Cutting this shot is actually quite simple. Assuming that there's a pause between each character's lines, you can crosscut as though the sounds came from separate shots. (See Figure 10-29.)

Never fade during a line of dialogue. Put another way, there should never be any dialogue inside a fade. If there's no room to crossfade between characters, you can likely cut in places where strong modulation will mask the edit. (See Figure 10-30.)

Removing the off-mic information will make your shot sound crisper and more articulate. If you hear one character's room tone coming and going with

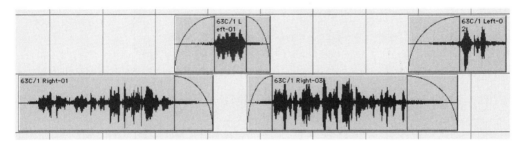

Figure 10-29 When two radio mic tracks carry similar room tone, you can usually crosscut between them. Listen to all of your fades (in solo) to make sure you're not including any of the "other" side of the conversation in your track.

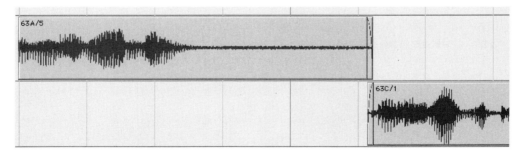

Figure 10-30 If the region you're fading to (in this case, 63C/1) doesn't have a usable handle, or if attempted crossfades result in audible changes in room tone, hide the shot transition in the strong initial modulation of 63C/1's beginning. Often you can mask moderate changes in room tone behind such a heavy attack. Listen carefully to the transition—with plenty of **preroll**—to make sure you're not fooling yourself.

her lines, first extend the room tone bridges. If this doesn't work, it's likely that the room tones are too dissimilar, either in volume or in texture, and you'll have to try a different approach. Read on.

One Shot, Two Mics, Similar Room Tone—Dialogue Overlaps In the real world, people often interrupt each other. Sometimes it's an aggressive or excited attempt to make a point, but more often it's just part of the rhythm of speech. As if by some mandate from above, movie dialogue is much more serial—one person speaks, the other responds. It certainly makes for easier dialogue editing. When one character does interrupt another in a film, it's called an **overlap**. Usually, but not always, it's a problem.

When a character's track is corrupted by the sound of her conversation mate's voice, you'll likely have to replace the end of the on-mic line as well as the beginning of the incoming line. At least that's the rule. However, when you're cutting back and forth between reasonably well-balanced and isolated microphones, overlaps don't always cause you grief. If there's very little crosstalk between mics, you can play both tracks for the duration of the overlap and hope for the best. The power of the interruption's attack will often mask the doubling of tone, so you won't notice a noise increase. If both sides are clean and on-mic, you can probably get away with playing both tracks for a few words.

Sometimes playing both tracks during a two-microphone overlap doesn't work. The increase in ambient noise due to room tone doubling may be audible. You may encounter strange coloring of the voices from the interaction of the two mics. Or you may hear a doubling of words if the two characters are far enough apart to create a timing difference but not so far as to keep them off of each other's tracks. In such cases, you must reconstruct from outtakes both the end of the corrupted line and the beginning of the interruption. (See Figure 10-31.) Chapter 12 discusses techniques for locating the alternate take material needed to salvage these overlaps.

Boom on Track 1, Radios on Track 2—Similar Sound Occasionally a boom and a radio microphone will crosscut surprisingly well despite common sense telling you otherwise. Try using the cross-cutting technique shown in Figure 10-32. Odds are good it will work. If not, continue reading.

One Shot, Two Microphones—Dissimilar Room Tone Sometimes it's not possible to crossfade back and forth between the two microphones of a shot. At each crossfade you hear a wave of changing room tone energy and the

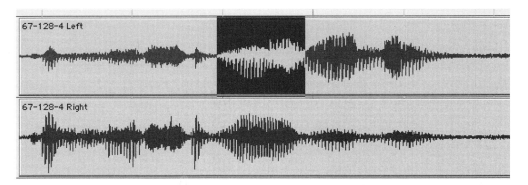

Figure 10-31 A typical two-radio microphone overlap. In the highlighted section, the top (*left*) track interrupts the bottom track. Outside the highlight, only one track is "on-mic" and the other can be eliminated. During the overlap, both characters are talking, which means that their lines are contaminated during the overlap and probably have to replaced.

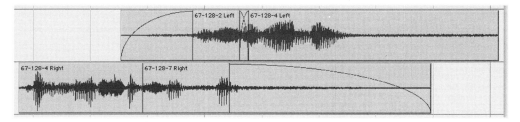

Figure 10-32 Both sides of the overlap have been repaired. A new beginning (67-128-2, *left*) replaced the damaged attack on the top track, and a clean ending (67-128-7, *right*) replaced the corrupted end of the bottom track.

scene loses its footing. Matters are made worse in "cutty" scenes, since the frequent cuts are constantly reminding the ear of tone mismatches. This is a common situation when editing a scene with a boom and one or more radio mics, but two radio mics can also result in the same problem.

Figure 10-33 shows a classic scheme for cutting between strongly mismatched shots. Room tone fills are edited for each angle and kept separate from the shots. This gives great flexibility, but may prove to be too much work. When one shot's room tone is much louder than the other's, try first filling the heavier track (usually the boom) with room tone and fading in and out on the quieter track.

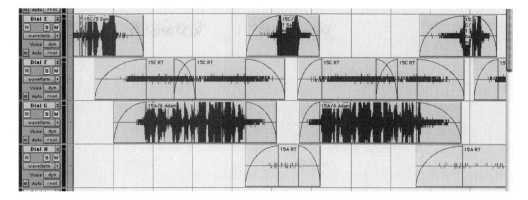

Figure 10-33 What's left of the original pair is on Dial E and Dial G after cutting the scene. The tracks have dissimilar room tone, so a simple back-and-forth edit plan won't work. Here, all off-mic signal was replaced by the matching room tone and placed on the track beneath. This four-track plan is a bit cumbersome, but it gives the rerecording mixer the most flexibility in balancing smoothness versus noise.

- Eliminate all off-mic dialogue on the boom track (i.e., when the dialogue of the other person is heard on the boom channel, replace it with good boom room tone).
- If the radio microphone room tone isn't too loud, you can either create short tone bridges leading up to the dialogue or cut from silence to radio mic with no tone bridge, assuming that the dialogue attack is loud enough to mask the change in room tone level. Figure 10-34 shows how to construct such a shot.
- Use volume automation to slightly reduce the boom channel's level while there's dialogue on the radio microphone channel. Match the timing and curve of the automation with the fades on the radio track. How much can you lower the level of the channel that carries the dominant room tone? Probably not more than 3 dB, but it depends on the two tracks. (See Figure 10-35.)

You may encounter scenes largely covered by a boom microphone that also include a few inserts from radio mics. (See Figure 10-36.) Often, the radio microphones will carry less room tone than the boom, so the inserts will stand out. An easy way to match these shots without increasing overall noise is to run a track of the boom's room tone parallel to the room tone segments. The mixer can easily control the amount of room tone with respect to the shot. There are many other applications for this parallel tone technique, such as production effects (PFX) editing and ADR editing.

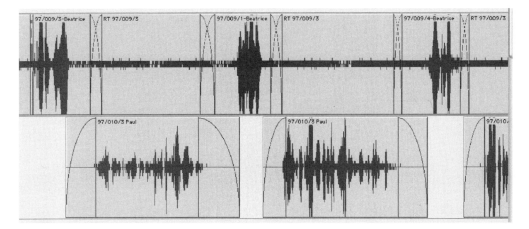

Figure 10-34 The top track is a boom and the bottom track is a radio microphone with much less room tone. In this case, Paul's mic can probably fade in and out without continuous tone, since the noise of the boom microphone masks any swells in his room tone.

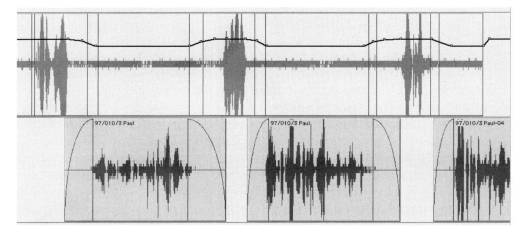

Figure 10-35 Even though Paul's radio microphone track carries little tone compared to Beatrice's boom, its room tone will contribute to the overall noise level. Slightly reducing the level of the boom track while the radio mic is playing will help smooth the scene and make it quieter.

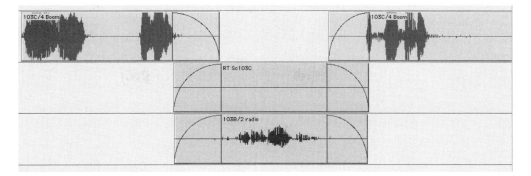

Figure 10-36 Occasional quiet radio microphone inserts can be balanced and controlled by providing a parallel track of the boom's room tone.

One Microphone per Channel—Dissimilar (and Loud) Room Tone In the last example, one channel overpowered the other so you only had to create one track of continuous room tone. The other, quieter track could effectively "hide" behind the noise of the dominant track. Now you're facing two noisy tracks, each carrying its own room tone. This poses an unsettling choice between smoothness and noise. Certainly, the smoothest option would be to run both tracks all the time so there's no energy or tone change between the two. But this causes two problems.

First, as in any of the examples shown, the off-mic track, with its slightly out-of-sync, muddy sound, will compromise the clarity of the speaking character. Adding this inarticulate muck to an otherwise decent bit of dialogue will weaken attacks and add an unwanted "halo" around the words. Even with a noisy room tone problem, the normal rules of cutting still apply. The other problem is that running two tones all the time makes your edit awfully noisy. No getting around that.

Once you've tried other, less draconian solutions, you're left with the option of creating two fully toned tracks and then minimizing the double room tone noise as best you can with volume automation.

- On each track, remove the off-mic dialogue and replace it with appropriate room tone.
- Once you've finished the editing, use volume automation to reduce redundant room tone as much as possible. (See Figure 10-37.) When, for example, the character on Dial B is speaking, lower the level of the added room tone on Dial A until you reach a point where you can

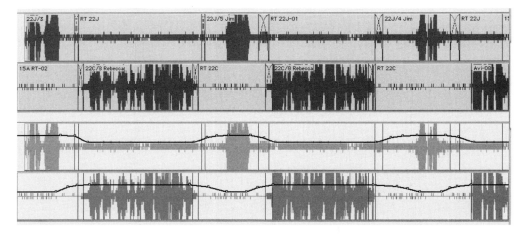

Figure 10-37 Complete tone fill for two noisy, nonmatching tracks (*top*). Filling off-mic sections will clean room tone and help with articulation, but it results in a noisy scene. Volume automation (*bottom*) reduces noise buildup.

hear the room tone changes. At that point, back off a bit with the level reduction.

- Before all these automation gymnastics, talk to the rerecording mixer. There's a chance he won't want you to automate the tracks in this way but to do just the editing. Usually the mixer appreciates all this work—if it's done well. Sometimes, your efforts are met in the mix with "Get rid of all this silly automation!" Find out what to do.

Two Acceptable Tracks—Which to Use?

Rarely in life are you saddled with too many good choices, but this dilemma does occasionally appear in dialogue editing: You encounter a scene recorded with a radio microphone and a boom and, amazingly, both sound pretty good. Which one to use depends on your access to the rerecording mixer. If you can play the scene to the mixer (or, barring that, to the supervising sound editor), you can get an opinion as to which way to go. Some mixers will ask you to fully prepare both tracks so that the choice can be made in the mix. Others will leave the choice to you.

On zero-budget films, I prefer to make the decision myself. If I'm familiar with the way the mixer works, I'll move the unused track—unedited—to a junk track. If I don't know the mixer, I'll prepare the unused track (up to a point) and then move it to junk. I remove the unused source from the active dialogue tracks since I don't want it brought into play unless we encounter a problem mixing my selection. Of course, I could edit both tracks side by side and mute the unused side of the pair. But this ties up a lot of track real estate and takes too much time, so I avoid it.

Bottom Line: Common Sense and Luck

We've looked at several archetypal two-track situations, each with its own specific set of problems. And we saw lots of rules. Yet most editorial messes fall into grey areas, so rarely will stridently following the rules bring the *truth*. Instead, you have to analyze each problem, try the most appropriate solution, and then wing it. These are the main points to remember:

- Two-microphone editing is always a tradeoff between smoothness and total noise level. Keep enough mics open and you can make anything smooth. But at what cost? Crosscut as much as you can without causing unacceptable changes in room tone.
- Talk to the mixer if possible to see if your edited scene can be mixed or if you need to rethink your plan. And remember: Many scenes don't need to be perfectly void of room tone changes. A skilled sound effects editor, upon hearing your edited guide track, will add a quiet car-by here, a discreet child's cry there, and no one will notice the occasional foible in the dialogue track.
- Except when both characters are speaking simultaneously or when it's otherwise impracticable, get rid of all off-mic dialogue. It only muddies up the track.
- When you must run simultaneous room tones because of mismatched levels or color, try to automate the tracks in a way that reduces the total volume of the room tone.

There'll be times when you simply must use both channels. If there's continuous action on both tracks, there's no way to cut back and forth. In such cases, remove all the unwanted noises you can from each track and present both to the mixer. There's nothing more you can do.

Multitrack Recordings

It's more and more common to encounter multitrack dialogue recordings because there are many advantages to having lots of tracks. A clever location mixer will provide a good mix as always, recorded onto one or two tracks, but he can also provide prefader, unmixed microphone tracks. The picture editor, and later you, will still get a production mix that, quite honestly, is acceptable most of the time. After all, the production mixer has studied the script and is on location with the actors and the boom operator, so his mix carries the magic and energy of the shoot.

Still, sometimes you need to get back to the original tracks because something didn't work out so well. For example:

- The production mixer missed a cue, so the beginnings of an actor's lines are off-mic. You hear the correct microphone fading in too late.
- The boom operator missed the cue, so the speaker is off microphone until the microphone pans into focus. You can try to resurrect the line from a nearby radio microphone. Success is unlikely, but the attempt is noble.
- The location mix is good, but you want to change the focus of the scene. Since you have all of the elements of the shot, it's easy to reconstruct the shot and alter its balance.
- A nonspeaking character touched her radio microphone. That channel was open at the time, so the mix was corrupted with mic noise. Go back to the solo track and pull what you need, without the noise.
- There's an overlap problem. You may be able to solve it with other tracks of the same take. In the end you may have to go to alternate takes but this is certainly the easiest place to start.

Simple two-microphone scenes can benefit from multitrack recording. Say you have an interior wide-shot urban scene with two characters far enough apart to warrant two microphones. The close-ups are covered with one boom. Since we're in the city, the dialogue recordings are punctuated with bus-bys and car-bys and the occasional siren. If there's a siren-by over a wide shot, how do you deal with the continuation of this background sound when the picture cuts to a close-up? Place another microphone away from the action, distant enough to avoid picking up the dialogue in the recording but close enough for it to capture the same noises the set mics do. Record this on the third track. When the picture editor cuts away, you'll find the conclusion of the siren-by on track 3.

Unfortunately, this flexibility isn't free. More tracks means more editing, and with so many options you can choke on the bounty. Unless you have an unlimited budget (unheard of), try to stick to the location recorder's mix if it's good. When you accept a job with multitrack recordings, have a long, hard talk with the supervising sound editor about her expectations regarding time and methodology.

Planning for Multitrack Editing

There are many ways to organize a production/postproduction workflow to suit the needs of the picture and sound post departments as well as the resources of the location mixer.[3] Long before shooting begins, the location mixer must meet with the supervising sound editor, the picture editor, and the postproduction manager or producer. (A quick get-together in the hotel bar the night before the shoot doesn't count.) The result of this meeting will be a flowchart that everyone has agreed on, understands, and signed off on. Done well, a multitrack project recorded on hard disk, picture-edited with a mono mix, and sound-edited with all available tracks will pass without a hitch. Mess up the communications along the way and you'll have a nightmare on your hands. And you, the dialogue editor, will likely to be the one to bear the brunt.

Once you have all of the tracks—whether by file-matching the original BWF files or by opening an OMF from an appropriately endowed picture workstation—you have innumerable choices before you. However, the actual editing is no different from any other job. And as with all editing, you must make choices first. Even if you have six tracks to choose from, odds are that at any given moment only one character is speaking. Lose the other tracks, but don't delete what you don't need. Instead, move it to a junk track, in sync. If you have a hunch that an unused track may be wanted in the mix, prepare it and move it to an easily accessible track. Choose wisely when selecting which track to use, and the rest of the process will go amazingly well.

Making Sense of a Scene

Dialogue editing is the last line of defense against a scene that doesn't make sense. Granted, there's not much you can do if the narrative itself is falling apart, but you can prevent the soundtrack from adding to or even creating the folly. For example, when a scene is supposed to be exciting or busy, a picture editor may stack up production sounds, feeling that "more is more." This works when the sounds in the sonic soup—each and every one—make sense and have specific roles to play. But when sounds are dolloped indiscriminately, whether by a picture editor or a sound editor, the result isn't excitement. It's a mess.

Here are some examples of poorly thought out, faux-exciting scenes:

> Three ten-year-old girls are playing in a bedroom. They begin to dance and spin. As they become more vivacious, they start to giggle and

---

[3] There are several good articles about managing the workflow of multitrack film projects. To learn more, see the Suggested Readings at the end of this chapter.

laugh, and the laughter builds until they're interrupted by their humorless father. Since the girls are partly hidden by a doorframe in the master long shot, the picture editor layers several takes of the girls' squealing. No major lip-sync problems, he reasoned, so why not make the scene "beefier" this way? On an initial screening of the film, this trick might go unnoticed. You'll play along with the intensifying frolicking and likely not realize that rather than just three voices—one for each girl—you're hearing six or nine or more. The catch: This doesn't make sense. Even if most viewers can't initially identify the problem with the scene, they'll feel the scene is clogged, undisciplined, and without dynamics.

You're editing the production sound of a car chase. What in the Avid screening seemed like a reasonably exciting collage of revving and squealing and shifting just doesn't hold up to scrutiny. The engines aren't consistent, the points of view aren't well planned, and more often than not a car "speaks" with two or more voices at once. This isn't believable, and it doesn't develop. It lacks dynamics and seems to have no sound plot. Of course, in a car chase scene most of the work will fall into the lap of the sound effects editor. Still, you'll find yourself in situations like this, where the picture editor considered ever escalating noise a substitute for exciting sound editing. Analyze each shot to decide what's important, then develop a plot to the car chase's sound. In action scenes, each shot is usually about one thing and one thing only, so press your point on that single detail.

You're editing a documentary, and the picture editor has created a voiceover from a character's interview footage. In one case, he placed the attack of a new line under the ringout[4] of the previous one to keep a correct rhythm and prevent an unnatural pause in the sentence. The result, however, is a double-voicing. We simultaneously hear two elements of the character's voice, a vocal technique you'll find only in Tibetan monasteries. Never allow more than one element of any character's voice—words, breaths, nonverbal vocalizations—to play together. There are very few ironclad rules in this book, but this is one of them: *People can make only one vocal sound at a time.*

---

[4] In this context, *attack* refers to the leading edge of a sound—the first modulation of a phrase. When discussing dynamic processors, *attack* means the speed with which the processor responds to an input signal. *Ringout* is the acoustic residue (echo, reverb, diffusion) left at the end of a phrase.

These messes come in all shapes and sizes, and it's up to you to sort them out. If you inherit such an unfocused scene from the picture department, don't start polishing it right off the bat. Solo each shot, one by one, and figure out what the editor had in mind with it. If you can make this sound work, do it. But if the shot is better served by replacing the sound with another take, go through the alternates to find a shot more focused.

Nothing is sacred, and as long as you honor the intentions of the editor and director you're on safe ground. Remember, they were trying to enhance the scene using the available resources, often for a temp mix or just to figure out where the heart of the scene lies. This sonic collision wasn't intended to stand the test of time but rather to give direction. It's up to you to make something permanent.

Start by thinning and simplifying. Analyze each sound, keeping the ones that contribute to the scene and stowing away the ones that are superfluous, confusing, or useless. Make the scene work at its most basic. Get the levels right. Fix the transitions. Make it behave. Then you'll know the scene better and be in a position to make sense of it. In the case of our giddy little girls, first make the scene work with no frills. Make it accurate and believable and then see how you can toss in a single girl's voice from time to time to add to the fun. Repeat this with each of the girls, taking care never to allow any of the three to talk "on top" of herself.

Excitement is not about constant yelling or car revving or crying. It's about well-timed dynamics. Screams and shouts and laughs lack excitement when there's no point of reference, just as a rock-and-roll concert at a constant "eleven" is boring. What draws us into the girls' ecstatic laughing isn't its brute-force volume but the swells and ebbs, the story told by their sounds. Find a way to create a dynamic within their voices and you're on your way to drawing the viewer's attention closer to the scene.

You can accentuate a loud sound by "clearing" a quieter space just before the crescendo. An 85 dB slap to the face isn't terribly impressive when sitting on an 84 dB noise floor, but a naturally created quiet section just before the slap—built through believable swells and holes in the underlying dialogue elements—will make the insult seem much louder. The increased dynamic range will tell your ears as much. The drop in the surrounding noise just prior to the slap gives the viewer the impression that the gods themselves made room for the ensuing whack. Making space for a loud noise is mostly a mix issue, but it's also your concern because sounds that end naturally are more effective than quiet created with fader moves.

When you finish a complicated layered scene, ask yourself if there really is a narrative thread to the sounds you've compiled. Also ask yourself if you have a plan for mixing the scene. If the honest answer is that you don't have a clue how this scene will be mixed or that you're "stabbing in the dark," you owe it to the scene to have another look. However, if you can honestly claim that each sound has a role to play and that you'll know how to navigate through the sequence come mixing time, you're on your way to creating a focused, tight, exciting scene.

Suggested Readings

Aaton. *Aaton Audio: Post Chain v10, www.aaton.com.* (Specific to the Aaton Cantar.)

Argy, Stephanie. "Roll, Cut, Print: A Conversation Between Sound Professionals from the Set, the Edit Room and the Mixing Stage." *The Editors Guild Magazine* 1(25), January/February 2004.

Munro, Chris. "Multi-Track Production Recording: Using Digital Disk Recorders to Improve Quality and Simplify Post Production." *The Editors Guild Magazine* 1(25), January/February 2004.

Stratmann, Erich, and Benson, Phil. "Metadata & Metaflow." *The Editors Guild Magazine* 24(3), May/June 2003.

CHAPTER 11

Image, Depth, and Perspective

So far we've concerned ourselves with making scenes smooth and believable. We've looked at ways to even out ugly shot transitions and examined what to do when faced with many tracks from which to choose. Unfortunately, these are the very procedures that some editors point to when claiming that dialogue editing is boring and wanting of soul. "Sound effects editing is filled with opportunities for artistic expression, but not so dialogue!" Rubbish.

You have to do your basic scene balancing before you can get to the fun stuff. It's very difficult to manipulate subtle changes in the focus of a scene if you can't hear past the room tone explosions at each edit. In the same way, you can't paint your walls until you fix the falling plaster. Once your scenes run smoothly, however, and there are no serious problems with noises or off-microphone sound, you're ready to begin adding some life to the dialogue.

In this chapter we'll begin to turn flat dialogue into something with depth, focus, and story.

Dialogue in the Soundscape

Film dialogue is overwhelmingly mono, usually coming exclusively from the center speaker.[1] As shockingly retro as this may seem, there are good reasons for it. Logic tells us that the apparent sound source of a line of dialogue should mimic its visual source. Given the ever growing number of channels on a big-league film print, you'd think we'd take advantage of some of those channels and move the dialogue around the screen. See it on the left; hear it on the left. Same goes for the right. Moving character? No problem, automate a pan from left to center to right and into the audience. Simple? Yes, but set

---

[1] Such generalizations are always dangerous. There are, of course, stereo dialogue films and there are giant gee-whiz films that place dialogue all around the screen because, well, they can. And there are artistic films that play with stereo images for reasons beyond those of traditional narrative.

up such a dialogue scene on your workstation and you'll sense the lunacy of your "logical" plan right away.

Panning

People interact differently with dialogue than with music, sound effects, backgrounds, or Foley. We're both more critical and more imaginative with dialogue, and when it's panned, we're not the least bit forgiving. Rather than enhancing the film experience, panned dialogue (other than an occasional offscreen line or **group loop**) often takes the viewer out of the scene—the last thing you want. Problems crop up when you place dialogue anywhere but in the center loudspeaker behind the screen.

Here are some of the factors that go into dialogue placement within the sound image:

- To create a versatile stereo field for the dialogue, you can produce a phantom center image between the left and right loudspeakers and your dialogue will be dead center when you want it there. With a simple left/right pan you can put the words wherever you want; since it's stereo, this isn't as complicated as a multichannel pan. A great idea for the handful of viewers sitting in the sweet spot of the theater, for whom phantom center is indeed center and the pans behave properly. For the rest, the center pulls to one side and the pans don't move linearly. Everyone's experience of the dialogue is different, and the dialogue is generally gooey. With a center loudspeaker, the dialogue is grounded in the middle of the screen and most viewers will experience the movie as planned. Center channel dialogue keeps the viewer focused on the screen rather than wandering off toward the exit lights.

- You rarely need to pan the dialogue. Watch a movie, almost any movie, and you'll realize that the dialogue isn't moving around, although your brain "pans" the sound in the direction of its visual source. Without trying, you connect source and voice. Now try the opposite. Pan your dialogue to match the placement of the characters. After the initial thrill of this hyperrealism, you'll likely admit that it's not working. It may be "accurate," but it's annoying. Worse yet are moving pans. Few sound gimmicks take you out of the film more resolutely than dialogue moving around the screen.

- You're determined to pan some dialogue. What will you do when you encounter a cut in which your character's screen placement suddenly changes? If you want to lose your audience very quickly, try sending a character's voice all the way from one side of the screen to the other.

- You can place or pan a production effect, such as a car-by, but you have to be careful to follow some rules. If the effect is carrying the room tone of the shot, panning it will result in the shot's room tone panning—a very unsettling effect. Properly toning out the track and preparing the PFX element will keep the scene believable. (See Chapter 13 for more on production effects editing.)

The bottom line on dialogue imaging is that you can, in fact, do a bit of panning but you must be terribly sober about it. Normally, however, the dialogue comes out of the center speaker and none other.

Depth

Just because film dialogue is mono doesn't mean it's flat. In a flat scene, the dialogue sticks to the screen. Everything is given equal weight, so there's no focus. To "manage" levels, the scene is compressed too much so it presents itself as a wall of sound. There's no air in the sound, and the scene is fatiguing to watch. In short it lacks depth.

When a scene has depth, there's a feeling of space around the words. There's a focus, however subtle, that not only guides the viewer but adds commentary. And even though all of the dialogue is coming from one speaker, there's a feeling of layers, as though some sounds stay near the screen while others move progressively away from the speakers.

Achieving Depth

First of all, it certainly doesn't hurt to start with excellent recordings. When the dialogue is well recorded and on-axis without too much ambient noise, you don't have to overcook the tracks in the premix, so you can hold onto the natural roundness of the voices. The reflections in the room, undamaged by aggressive noise reduction, contribute to a sense of space.

But depth control is mostly about well-planned, well-mixed tracks. When you receive an OMF, the narrative is there but there's no discipline in the tracks and it's impossible to find the personality of each region. As you reassemble the shots, rid them of noises, and smooth the transitions, you develop an understanding of how the regions work and how they fit together. You begin to understand them in a way that you couldn't when they were all jumbled together. Each scene, and in fact each shot, you discover, contains a "moment." This moment is the focus of the action. Make sure that it isn't compromised by a footstep, door close, or other natural but ill-placed sound. Give the featured moment a bit of space in which to breathe, thus putting it on stage.

Split off the regions you want to separate from the rest of the scene. You'll manipulate these separated regions later, in the premix. A tiny bit more volume here, a little less there, wetter, sharper, duller.[2] If you want to push a shot further back toward the screen, split it off so that the mixer can change the EQ to darken the sound, reduce the level a bit to make it less prominent, or create a little reverb.[3] Even a tiny amount of trickery will create distance between foreground dialogue and a manipulated background element, and the process can be used to imply physical, emotional, or social separation.

Depth and the Mixer

Ultimately, most of the depth in a scene comes from the countless tiny fader moves that the mixer executes while predubbing. "Microdynamic control," you might say. The finesse of the mixing process pulls one shot from the screen and pushes another back, so plan the tracks so that you and the mixer can take advantage of your editing fantasies. Prepare tracks that seduce the mixer into playing with depth.

If, on the other hand, you don't dissect your tracks enough to let them talk to you, or if you merely "process" your tracks in a workstation rather than giving them the time they need in a proper dialogue premix, you probably won't achieve the separation and depth you're seeking. If you limit and compress as a substitute for manual fader moves, you clog the air within the tracks and the light in the conversation will darken. There's a reason that dialogue is premixed on a dubbing stage.

I don't mean that you can't achieve a decent dialogue premix with a workstation. It can be done, but you need time and a decent interface that encourages you to constantly interact with your tracks. You have to work with a controller whose latency is small enough and whose fader resolution is high enough to allow for instant, fine adjustments. Even with the right tools, however, you'll probably spend as much money—and a lot more time—doing a competent dialogue premix in a workstation as you'd spend on a budget board mix. Unfortunately, mixing "in the box" is usually associated with low-budget

---

[2] The English language is not "rich" when it comes to describing sound qualities. Often the most efficient way to discuss sound is through metaphor. Hence, descriptions such as "wet" (reverberant), "dry" (little or no reverb), "sharp" (rich in high frequency, when describing nonmusical sounds; high in pitch when describing musical sounds), and "dull" (poor in high-frequency elements; the opposite of "bright").

[3] Under normal circumstances it's nuts to add reverb to a track while you're working in a cutting room. When I say "add reverb" I mean organize your tracks in such a way that the mixer can easily add reverb (or EQ or dynamics or delay) to the shot.

productions, so you're expected to "box-mix" the tracks in less time, not more, than you'd get for a mix on a mixing stage. Still, by planning your tracks well and knowing what's important in each shot, you can develop rich, deep scenes that will survive even in-the-box mixes.

Focusing on One Character in a Group

Imagine a choir singing with our protagonist standing on the second riser. The scene begins with a wide shot, and we hear the whole choir singing. As the camera slowly dollies toward our herione, we want to call attention to her voice. We may do this purely for "realism"—to sense more of her voice as we approach, providing another layer to the sound. Or we may want to psychologically focus on her, to reflect on what we learned of her in the last scene or to telegraph something soon to happen. In the mix we might subtly lower the choir's tracks to lend her an unnatural aura of isolation.

Achieving Focus in Common Situations

Whatever your objectives, you'll need to create a clean sync track with nothing but the character's voice that you can mix with the track from the wide shot. Normally, this is done with postsync (ADR), where you prepare the actress's lines and then rerecord her singing, sync to picture. Rerecording singing is in many ways easier than rerecording spoken dialogue, since most music carries a predictable rhythm. The actress need but learn the "quirks" in her onscreen performance to make a good match. (Chapter 15, ADR, discusses how to spot the shots, prepare the paperwork, and record and edit the lines.)

A similar situation is a dolly shot that moves down a line of football players attempting to sing the national anthem. As we approach an athlete we hear his voice strengthen, hold and fade away as we pass, only to be overtaken by the next one entering the frame. In this case, you'll record ADR for each of the featured characters, panning (maybe) and fading (certainly) the lines as the camera moves down the line. If, when approaching individual players, you can hear their voices on the original recording, you'll need to replace the take with a less specific version. Otherwise, you run the risk of hearing someone singing with himself.

Perspective

In a scene with two characters, the sound level of each character often remains the same regardless of who's on screen, as though we're sitting somewhere between the two, listening. However, there are questions of perspective that must be asked. Cut to a wide shot and we may or may not change the sound to match the change in picture perspective. On a very close shot, we may or may not accentuate this physical closeness with a bit more volume. Even if we cut to a long shot—a point of view that would in the real world certainly affect our sound perception—we may stick with a close-up sound. Or we may completely muffle the dialogue to reflect the frustration of trying to eavesdrop from across the yard. These are choices about sound perspective.

Simply put, perspective in sound reflects decisions we make concerning our relationship with the screen action as well as the relationships—physical and emotional—between the characters within the scene. In the conversation scene from the last paragraph, we kept the same perspective when cutting from one close-up to the other, and hence kept the same volume, EQ, and reverb for the two characters regardless of who was on screen.

This wasn't only because they were seated relatively close together but also because they were communicating with each other, carrying on a conversation, so there was some sort of emotional contact. There was no reason to honor the "fact" that during a cutaway to the nonspeaking character there would logically be a sense of sound separation. Respecting reality—pulling back the dialogue a bit as we cut to the listener's face—would emotionally separate the two. However, when we cut to a wider shot, we must decide what we're trying to accomplish.

Are we, the viewers, being shut out? If so, a strong perspective cut that reminds us of *our* outsider status would make a point. If, on the other hand, we keep the scene steady, ignoring the change in picture perspective, we keep the focus on the conversation rather than on the physical world. It's as though the conversation transcends changes in our viewpoint.

Perspective to Achieve Emotional Separation

I recently edited the dialogue on a film about a mother coming to terms with her adult son's impending death. The film deals with a mother and son struggling with the pains and mistakes of their past. Much of the film takes place in the son's bedroom, so there's not a lot of action. At the beginning of the film, the two characters don't know how to connect, since they'd never learned how to talk to each other. During these early scenes, Mom aimlessly cleans Son's room as they talk *at* each other.

Since there's no real chemistry between the two at this point in the film, I forced a bit of perspective on all off-camera dialogue. As we watched Mom clean nervously while "listening" to her son's harpings, the son's dialogue was very slightly attenuated and made a tiny bit wetter, as though Mom was hearing but not listening. When Mom was talking and we lingered on a cutaway of Son, her voice, too, was made slightly distant.

The film progressed, and after the inevitable row there was some real, though painful, connection between the two. As they battled and reconciled, the perspective difference between them vanished. They weren't exactly getting along, but they were communicating. The rest of their conversations in the bedroom were mixed at equal volume, keeping the characters connected.

Perspective to Achieve Physical Distance

The most recognizable perspective cuts are about physical rather than emotional or psychological distance. For example, Mom and Dad are arguing in the kitchen. We cut to the other end of the house where we see a frightened child listening, along with us, to the muted shouts of the parents. This is a classic perspective cut that tells us something about the size of the house, the parents' ability to keep their problems from the child, and about the way the child perceives the argument.

Another example from *Hamlet*, Act 3: In Scene IV Hamlet and Gertrude are arguing in her chamber; the action might cut from one close-up to another and be sprinkled with medium and wide shots. More than likely we'd keep this conversation rather level, to constrain the energy of their argument and to hold the focus on the fight. But when cutting to a behind-the-curtain scene to see all of this from Polonius's point of view, it's his breathing and body motion that comes to the forefront whereas the fight between Hamlet and Gertrude sounds lower and a bit darker.

This perspective split not only accentuates the spatial separation between the two sides of the scene but also calls on a film language convention used to describe eavesdropping. By pushing the main part of the scene (for example, Hamlet and Gertrude's brutal argument) to the background, we make Polonius the focus of the shot. His fear, his anger, and his humanity are what counts. This sort of perspective cut is a common way to identify the outsider as well as to give some depth to a scene.

Perspective to Achieve Social Isolation

Sometimes there's no real physical separation, yet you use perspective to separate one member of a group from the rest. Imagine a circle of schoolgirls, giggling and gossiping, largely at the expense of one of them—let's call her New Girl. All dialogue between the girls in the circle is prepared and mixed in a normal way, so nothing initially seems wrong to an outsider. But the teasing intensifies, and New Girl becomes increasingly frustrated. To make a point, we force perspective on the sounds of the other girls when the camera cuts to New Girl. We begin to experience the badgering from her point of view.

The sounds of the provokers become wetter, lower in level, and maybe a bit darker, all to show the increasing separation between New Girl and the group. When we cut back to the other girls, the sound is normal again, further stressing the frustration of the victim. Not only is she subjected to the other girls' taunts but, worse, she's separated from the society she so wants to be a part of. By the end of the scene, we may have lost all sound when we share New Girl's viewpoint. She gives up and tunes out. Most of the emotional message of the scene is delivered through sound manipulation.

Perspective cuts to emphasize emotional separation need not be delivered with a hammer blow. The ones I used to divide Mom and dying Son aren't severe—just a 2 dB level drop, a little EQ, and a tiny bit of reverb. Few people will notice, but this subterfuge makes a difference. Other times, when you want to stress distance, separation, or fear, you can apply aggressive perspective.

Remember, leave the equalization, dynamics processing, and reverb for the mix. Plan the subtle storytelling, then organize your tracks so that it's easy to develop your ideas with the rerecording mixer.

The Telephone Split

If you stand beside someone who's talking on the phone, you hear only one side of the conversation. Of the person at the other end you hear, at most, occasional squawks and clicks. You won't be able to follow the exchange. Often this is what happens in a film. If the filmmaker doesn't want the viewer to know what's up on the other end of the line or wants a realistic feeling, you'll get a straight, realistic scene like this.

However, another convention in film language allows us to hear both sides of the conversation, as though we were listening in. This trick, unrealistic as it is, can be useful as an efficient way to kill off exposition and other essential information, and it serves to electronically bring together two characters, all the while keeping them physically separate.

Editing the Telephone Split Like it or not, the telephone split is part of the language of film, so you'd best know how to do it. Here's how:

- *Mark each location change cut* in the scene. Remember, these marks are based on picture, not sound, edits.
- Split the tracks at the picture cuts. You'll edit onto four tracks:
  - Character A "live." We're with this character, so we hear his voice in a natural way. We hear this track only when seeing character A.
  - Character A "phone." This is the phone voice of character A as heard by character B. We hear this track only when character B is on the screen.
  - Character B "live." We're with this character, so we hear her voice in a natural way. We hear this track only when seeing character B.
  - Character B "phone." This is the phone voice of character B as heard by character A. We hear this track only when character A is on the screen.
- From the moment the phones are picked up, *edit two sets of room tone:* one for the live voice and another for the disembodied voice coming over the phone. Phone noise doesn't come and go with speech, like a walkie-talkie. Instead, there's a constant noise floor coming over the phone.
- Once you edit the tracks, removing all unnecessary noises, fixing articulations, and doing all of the things you normally do with dialogue, soften (*lengthen*) the perspective cuts a bit. Usually, two to three frames of crossfade will do, but it depends on the effect you're after as well as the relative noisiness of the tracks. (See Figure 11-1.)

Using the Right Edit

During a crossfade, two sounds are of course playing at once. Ideally, there's neither a "bump" from excess energy nor a "hole" from a loss of energy. Most of the time you don't pay much attention to this. If you set up your preferences correctly (and you're not sharing the machine with another editor who changes your preferences while you sleep), everything ought to work well. But what if you try a perspective cut and something goes terribly wrong— your edits bump. What happened?

Crossfades

Normally you're cutting or crossfading between two different sounds. (See Figure 11-2.) Even when you're crossfading between different parts of the

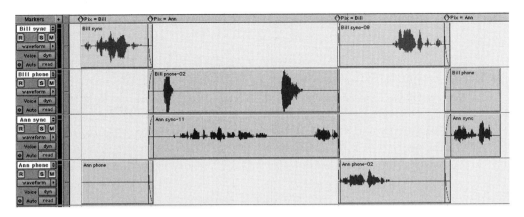

Figure 11-1 Example of a finished phone split. The markers indicate which character is onscreen. Continuous room tone for each character prevents the phone from "keying in and out" like a walkie-talkie and maintains a steady room presence when a character stops speaking. The tracks have been renamed for this demonstration. Only if the film has an extraordinary number of phone conversations do you create dedicated phone tracks.

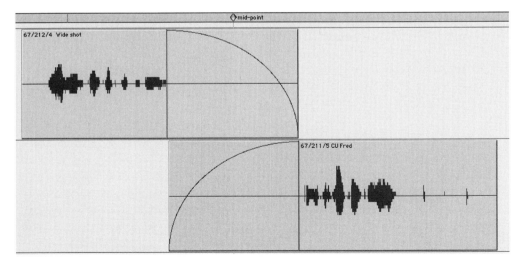

Figure 11-2 A "normal" crossfade between two shots. Note the symmetrical fades that provide 3 dB of midpoint attenuation.

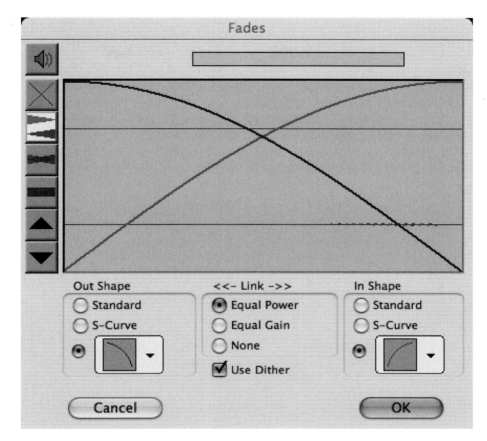

Figure 11-3 The Pro Tools fade control window showing a 3 dB attenuation at crossfade midpoint. This is the fade you'll use under normal circumstances. Pro Tools calls this "Equal Power" crossfade linking. Most DAWs offer a similar dialogue box.

same soundfile the material is usually not from the exact same moment, so you aren't crossfading across phase-aligned material. One side fades out and the other fades in, and the 3 dB attenuation at the fade's midpoint is perfect to prevent a rise or drop in level during the transition. (See Figure 11-3.)

Crossfades for Perspective Cuts

With any type of perspective cut, including a phone split, you have to pay attention to the type of edit linking you use. (See Figure 11-4.) To create a

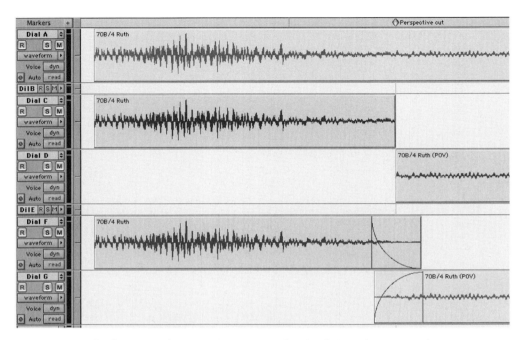

Figure 11-4 The history of a perspective cut. On Dial A is the original region, crossing a perspective cut marker; the cut is seen on Dials C and D. The faded perspective cut is on Dials F and G. Note the very steep fadeout on Dial F. This provides a 6 dB midpoint attenuation, sufficient to compensate for the "bump" normally caused by playing two phase-coherent sounds simultaneously.

perspective cut, you first begin with one continuous region. You perform an edit, likely at a picture-motivated location, and then split the region on to two tracks.

Once split onto two tracks, the regions are overlapped and then crossfaded. The amount of overlap depends on the "rules" of the film you're working on and the transition softness or harshness you're trying to achieve. Now begins the problem. Use the same –3 dB crossfade that you normally use and you'll hear a rise during the crossfade.

Because the material being played during the crossfade is precisely the same on both tracks, it plays together twice as loudly as a during a "normal" crossfade. Whereas 3 dB was enough attenuation to quell a rise in our first example (refer to Figure 11-2), during a perspective crossfade we need 6 dB of midpoint attenuation to achieve unity. (See Figure 11.5.)

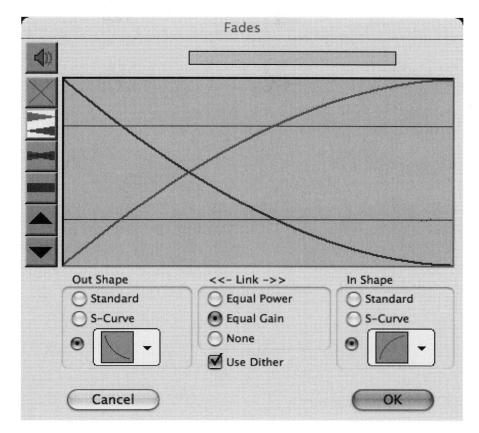

Figure 11-5 The Pro Tools fade control window showing a 6 dB midfade attenuation, which is what Pro Tools refers to as "Equal Gain" fade linking. It's used only for perspective edits, where both sides of the crossfade are exactly the same.

Using the wrong amount of attenuation is a very common mistake, and it shamelessly foils attempts at smoothness. Get into the habit of listening to all crossfades. If something sounds strange, don't start moving the fade right away. First double-check the fade and make sure the fade linking is set correctly.

CHAPTER 12

Damage Repair

You've smoothed your scenes, and your dialogue tracks, although still unmixed, sound quieter and more pleasant. Your control over perspective has added new depth to the scenes, and it's possible to hear nuance in your massaged tracks. What you probably don't notice are the endless noises populating the recordings. Your brain wants to hear content, so it filters out most noises and leaves you with the relatively "low-baud" information: the words. So what's the problem? After all, you understand everything.

You can hold a conversation at a loud dinner party or even in a dance club. Under such taxing conditions you lose nuance and perhaps a bit of information, but you usually figure out the missing words thanks to context. Still, you'll inevitably find such a conversation exhausting and at some point give up and zone out. It's just too much work. So, too, with motion picture dialogue. Any dialogue that's "polluted" with even small noises wears down the viewer and diminishes the movie experience. Background noises lessen dialogue's punch and give a false impression of greater overall room tone level. And since most background noises afflicting dialogue tracks come not from something within the story but rather from sounds on the set or in the environment, the viewer is constantly reminded, "This is a movie!" The magic is broken, even if most viewers are unaware of it.

What Are Noises?

The world is a noisy place. Even the most vigilant location mixer can't do much about airplanes, traffic, and other exterior sounds other than to beg for additional takes.

Usually, you solve such steady-state noise problems (severe traffic, air conditioning and compressors, birds) and momentary background noises (car-bys, horns, neighbors yelling) by replacing words, sentences, or entire scenes with alternate takes or wild sound or looping. There are also many borderline cases, where noise is a nuisance but doesn't interfere with the dialogue. A scene shot next to a busy street, for example, can be justifiably noisy. The fact that you have to labor to hear a few words might help the viewer to sympathize with the character, who also must strain to understand and be understood. Remember, though, that a noisy dialogue track saddles you with a noisy scene. The scene will never be quieter than the dialogue premix, and you won't be able to isolate the dialogue.

Whereas a reasonably noisy dialogue track might be acceptable in such a logically loud setting, even the slightest amount of inappropriate background noise can kill a quiet, intimate scene. A scene where a couple sits in their living room in the middle of the night discussing their troubled relationship loses its intimacy and edge if we hear traffic, airplanes, the neighbor's TV, or a crewmember walking around the set. It has to begin with dead quiet dialogue. The supervising sound editor may choose to color the scene with quiet spot effects, an interesting and mood-evoking background, or music. But the dialogue editor must be able to deliver a track with no disturbances to create a world of two people in a very quiet room—alone with all their problems.

When a scene is downright noisy, you'll probably have to call the entire scene for ADR, forcing the supervising sound editor to create a sound space from scratch. On the other hand, there are steady-state noises that the rerecording mixer can clean in the mix. In either case, you should consult the rerecording mixer or the supervising sound editor.

There are, however, many more tiny noises that you won't repair by ADR line replacement or through equalization or electronic noise control. Transient noises, the not-so-silent warriors in the conspiracy to screw up your tracks, have several sources for which you must be on the lookout. For example:

Actors
- Unusual or inappropriate vocal sounds: unsavory, off-camera, or loud lip smacks
- Dentures, bridges, and other dental work (always a delicate subject)
- Stomach gurgling (you can always tell when a take or ADR line was recorded just before lunch)
- Footsteps that interfere with the dialogue or introduce an unwanted accent
- Body mic clothing noise or other rustle interference
- Other clothing interference (jangling earrings, clothing "swooshes")
- Unusual diction that results in clicks or pops

Electronics

- Brief but loud clicks caused by electrical disturbances or static discharge
- Clicks caused by bad mic cable connections (usually louder and longer than static discharge clicks)
- Radio mic breakup (usually a long-duration problem that most often requires replacement of the shot)

Crew

- Dolly pings
- Camera pedestal hydraulic/pneumatics
- Crew footsteps
- Crew talking(!)
- Continuity stopwatch(!)
- Grip tool rattles

Another common source of damaged dialogue is sounds that don't come from the set, but we'll deal with them later.

Finding Noises

Before you can fix the noises in your dialogue, you have to find them. In most cases, eliminating noises isn't difficult, but noticing them is daunting. It sounds easy, but it's a skill that separates experienced dialogue editors from novices. Even if you pride yourself on your superhuman listening skills and canine hearing, you have to learn how to listen for the annoying ticks, pops, and screeches that besiege every dialogue track. They're in there, coyly taunting you to find them.

First, you must discover as many noises as you have time, patience, and budget for. Then, before blindly eliminating every one, you have to ask yourself, "What is this noise? Does it help or hurt the story?" Period. It's actually as simple as that; you just have to stay awake and aware.

Focusing on Noises

Every step in the process of filmmaking is sorcery. It's all about getting the viewer to believe that this story *really happened* as shown in the final print. As a film professional you like to think that you're immune to this seduction. You know *it's not real*. Yet when you screen the offline picture cut or watch a scene over and over, the most obnoxious noises might slip right past you. Just like the average movie fan, you're sucked in.

How do you learn to spot noises before someone else does? After all, it's pretty embarrassing to screen your seemingly perfect tracks—that you lovingly massaged for weeks—only to have a friend of the assistant picture editor comment, "What about those dolly sounds?" Sure enough, three scenes with flagrant dolly noises. No professional heard them because they were captivated by the story, but someone who walked in off the street noticed immediately. It's your job to hear and correct these sounds, so you must find ways not to fall victim to the story's siren song.

Evaluating Noises

Question every noise you hear. Don't fall into the trap of "Well, it was part of the location recording, so it must be legitimate." Obviously, if the gaffer dropped a wrench during a take, you replace the damaged word. However, when an actor's footstep falls on a delicate phrase, you might be reluctant to make the repair, thinking it's a "natural" sound.

Remember, there's nothing natural in the movies. To see if it's a good decision to lose the errant footstep, fix it. Either you'll miss it, finding the rhythm of the scene suddenly damaged and unnatural, or you'll see a new clarity and focus. If removing the footstep results in a rhythmic hole but greatly improves articulation, you can call for Foley at that point so that the necessary footstep is in place but controllable. Better yet, find another, quieter production footstep to replace the offender.

The most rewarding part of careful listening is that once you've heard a noise or had it pointed out to you, you'll never again *not* hear it. It's just like the "Young Maiden/Old Woman" illusion, where if you look at it one way you see an old woman but when you look at it another way, you see a beautiful maiden. For some it takes a long time to see the maiden as well as the hag, but once your brain has identified both, you will always be able to quickly separate the two. Just so, you can listen to a track many times and never hear the truth. But once your brain wakes up to it, you'll hear that click in the middle of a word and wonder how you missed it the first few times around. Ignoring the meaning of the dialogue and focusing on the sounds is a useful tool when searching for unwanted noises. Listening at a reduced monitor level can help you hear beyond the words.

The following sections describe the most common origins of the noises you'll encounter. Use them to learn how to locate unexpected infiltrators.

Dollies and Cranes

Dolly noise is easy to spot since dollies and cranes don't make noise when they're not moving. It's simple: When the camera moves, listen for weird sounds—for example:

- Gentle rolling, often accompanied by light creaking and groaning.
- One or more pairs of feet pushing the dolly.
- Quiet metallic popping or ringing, indicating flexing dolly track rails as the heavy dolly/camera/camera operator combination crosses over them. The tracks are made of metal, so this flexing resembles the sound of an aluminum baseball bat striking a ball. Occasionally you'll hear this bat sound even when the dolly isn't moving. It might come from the track settling after the dolly passes over it or from a crew member lightly bumping the track.

Too Many Feet

Unnecessary footsteps are easy to hear but hard to notice. When you first listen to a scene involving two characters walking on a gravel driveway, all seems normal. You hear dialogue and some footsteps. But something inside tells you to study this shot more closely and check for problems. Ask yourself how many pairs of feet you hear. If it's more than two (which is likely), you have a problem. Picture how the shot was made and you'll understand where all the noise comes from. How many people were involved? Let's see: two actors, one camera operator, one assistant camera operator, one boom operator, one location mixer (probably), one cable runner (probably), one continuity person, one director. That's a lot of feet. But because you expect to hear *some* feet in the moving shot, you initially overlook the problem.

As with dolly noise, be on the lookout for a moving camera—in this case handheld; that's where so many noise problems breed. Find out how the footsteps interfere with the scene by replacing a section of dialogue from alternate takes or wild sound (discussed in later sections), noting any improvement. It's likely that the scene will be more intimate and have a greater impact after you remove the rest of the crew's feet from the track.

Fortunately, a good location recordist will spot the trouble in the field and provide you with workable wild lines, and perhaps even wild footsteps, to fill in the gaps. Otherwise, you'll have to loop the shot.

Crew

Remember, there are a lot of people on a set all of whom move, breathe, and make noise, so be on the lookout for these noises:

- Footsteps that have nothing to do with the actors.
- "Quiet" background whispers. (There's no such thing while sound is rolling.)
- Pings from tools inadvertently touching light stands, the dolly, the track, and so on.
- The continuity person's stopwatch when she times the take. It's got to be done, but unfortunately most modern stopwatches beep. Dumb. You'll rarely hear beeps during the action part of a take (although they can sneak in), but they'll make you crazy while searching for room tone. And they can really wreck a period scene.

Sound Recording

Sadly, many unwelcome noises can and will get into the tracks as by-products of the recording process. The boom operator, sound recordist, and cable puller are all very busy capturing manageable dialogue, and sometimes bad things happen.

- *Small, short clicks.* These may be from small static discharges or cables. Once you learn to listen, they're very easy to spot, and far more common than you'd think.
- *Longer electrical clicks*, possibly associated with brief signal interruptions.
- *Clothing rustle* caused by a body mic rubbing against clothing or against the protective "tent" built to protect it. These scratches usually last longer than static discharge clicks and are therefore much harder to fix.
- *Fish pole noises.* A conscientious boom operator will have removed his rings and jewelry before the shoot, but at times you may hear something scratching on the boom.
- *Shock mount noises.* If the mic isn't well seated in the shock mount, you may hear low-frequency "thuds" in the track. This is the mic absorbing energy from the boom that should have been absorbed by the shock mount.
- *Dropouts.* When a digital tape recorder's error correction circuitry gives up, you're left with a dropout, a short piece of silence often with a nasty, ragged edge. There are other reasons for dropouts, such dodgy connectors, but the end result is the same. Fortunately, they're much

less common with hard-disk-recorded files, so you'll be seeing less of them.

- *Poor digital tracking.* This is a combination of small ticks with a "cell phone" artifact imposed on the dialogue. Unfortunately, you can't fix this one once it's in the workstation. Instead, you must reload the original material onto a machine that will play the material properly. Often, the original recording machine is the best bet, but sometimes you'll need to have a technician tweak the recorder to match the bogus specifications of the tape. Not a pretty spectacle.

- *Wind distortion.* A nasty problem that can be long-lasting and cover a wide frequency range. A director or picture editor might become so used to a scene with wind distortion that he'll fight you when you insist on removing it. "But the sound is so authentic, so exciting," he'll argue. Rubbish. Fight him. Wind distortion is as ugly as any other distortion, and if it's on your dialogue track you can do nothing to remove, enhance, or shape it. Have the effects editor replace it with something just as exciting but pretty. Result: good, clean dialogue with controllable, pristine stereo wind.

Actors

With so much attention paid to getting the best sound from actors' voices, it's no surprise that you're occasionally faced with all sorts of sounds coming from an actor that you'd just as soon not hear. We all make noises that aren't directly part of speech. Someone you're talking to may be producing an array of snorts, clicks, pops, and gurgles, yet you'll rarely notice.

Comparatively normal human noises often sneak under the radar when we're in the heat of a conversation because our brains simply dismiss them as non-information of no consequence. Yet when you record this conversation, the body sounds lose their second-class status and take their rightful place as equal partners with the dialogue.

What sorts of vocal and body noises should you be on the lookout for?

Dental Work Dentures, plates, bridges, and the like can make loud clicking noises. They're easy to spot because the clicks almost always coincide with speech. Unfortunately, denture clicks usually get louder in the dialogue premix, where dialogue tends to pick up some brightness. At that point, they become impossible to ignore.

Most people with fake teeth aren't thrilled about advertising the fact, so a serious round of click removal is usually welcome. Also, relentless dental noise is almost certain to get in the way of story and character development. There's a chance that the character's persona calls for such unenviable dental problems. If that's the case, the supervising sound editor may elect to remove all dental details from the dialogue and have the effects or Foley department provide something more stylized, personalized, and controllable.

Mouth Smacks and Clicks People make lots of nonverbal sounds with their mouths. Sometimes these sounds have meaning that would be difficult to express in words: a sigh or a long, dramatic breath can say worlds; a contemplative wetting of the lips can imply a moment of reflection before words of wisdom; a clicking of the teeth or tongue may suggest thought or nervousness. An actor's clicking, chomping, snorting, and sighing may be just what the scene calls for, or it may be just more commotion that comes between the scene and the audience.

Your job is to spot each nonverbal sound and decide if it conveys the mood and information you want for the scene or if you need to thin out or replace or eliminate it. Things to think about when listening for smacks:

- *Is it off-screen? Probably lose it.* Here taste and style are more important than rules of thumb, but in general if you don't see the lip smack there's probably no real reason to keep it. All those unseen noises are just that: more noise to get in the way of the story and mood.
- *Is it appropriate? If not, replace it.* Just because the actor made a vulgar, slippery onscreen smack immediately before tenderly saying "I love you" doesn't mean you have to use it. Yes, it's on-camera, so you must have something in order to avoid **lip flap**, but need it be so ugly? Did that phlegm-soaked snort really make the scene more effective? What does it do for your emotional reaction to the lines? Wouldn't a nice, moist lip opening sound better than the original slurp? Also, if any mouth noise attacks sharply, sounding more like a click, replace it.
- *Is it missing? Sometimes the problem is a missing mouth noise.* When you see a character open her lips, you may need to reinforce the action with some sort of smack, small though it may be. Otherwise the viewer senses lip flap, the annoying movie sensation when you see mouth action but don't hear any corresponding vocalization to make it real.

The sounds a character makes between sentences or words can be as important as the information contained in the text. Get it right and you'll dramatically increase the drama and emotion of the scene.

Clothing We've seen how clothes rustling against a body mic can be a nuisance. Many other common clothing noises are just as bad and require a sharp mind and a keen ear.

- Inappropriate or annoying shoe sounds, whether footsteps or squeaks
- Corduroy pants or jackets, which often make a rustle when moving
- Anything made of plastic
- Coins and keys
- Large earrings and bangles

Actors and Microphones You'll inevitably encounter places in the track where the actor sounds a plosive consonant, such as a *P* or *B* or the equivalent, in whatever language you're working in. There's no point getting into why this happens; your job is to fix it. Usually, you'll have to replace that section of the contaminated word, but there are some filtering tricks that may work.

Fixing Noises

Once you've trained yourself to listen for the countless rattles, pops, clicks, and snorts squatting in your tracks, the next step is to decide what to do with them. There are two basic editorial tools for removing unwanted noises: room tone fill and replacement. Noises falling between words or action can almost always be removed by filling with appropriate room tone, whereas noises falling on top of words or actions, or even just before or after dialogue, require searching through alternate material to find appropriate replacements.

Let's look at these two techniques, remembering that there are many ways of fixing noises and as many opinions as there are editors. With time you'll settle into your own way of working, synthesizing all of the techniques and creating your own private stockpile.

Room Tone Fill

Small electrical clicks, individual clothing–mic collisions, lip smacks, and the like, are easily removed with room tone, but only between words, not within them (or only rarely within them). (See Figure 12-1.) Here's what you do to remove these tiny noises:

- When you hear the unwanted noise, stop and note its whereabouts on the timeline.
- Use a scrub tool to localize the noise. Set your workstation preferences so that the insertion point will "drop" wherever you stop scrubbing, so

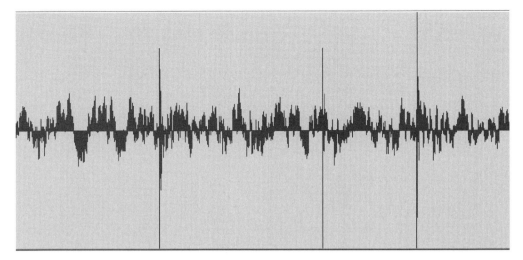

Figure 12-1 Small clicks typical of radio microphone trouble.

that you can easily zoom in to the click. On Pro Tools this is called "Edit Insertion Follows Scrub/Shuttle." You'll be surprised how difficult it can be to see a click. Common sense would say that a relatively loud one would proudly display itself in the waveform, but the nastiest of clicks can hide amid ambient noise and are found only with a combination of scrubbing and enough experience to know the telltale signs.

- Zoom in closely enough to identify exactly what you're removing. There's no point fixing an area wider than needed. If the click is hard to spot, you might want to place a comment or a temporary sync mark at the location so you don't lose it.
- Find the room tone you'll use to eliminate the noise. If the noise occurs in a relatively boring stretch of tone, without rapid changes in pitch, level, or texture, you can usually copy a small piece of tone immediately adjacent to it and blast over the problem area. Make the patch just a bit wider than the noise you're covering to leave room for crossfades and adjustments. If you're copying a section of room tone between two noises, leave a bit of extra, unused tone outside your selection to provide a handle area and some "fudge space" after you make the edit. (See Figure 12-2.)
- If removing more than one closely spaced noise, don't use the same piece of room tone to repair both problems, as it may create a looplike sound.

Selection copied for room tone

Figure 12-2 Good room tone can usually be found nearby. Note that the selection is smaller than it could be. Leaving a bit of usable room tone outside the selection creates a handle that gives you maneuvering room when removing the noise. The handles also allow more flexibility with crossfades.

- If you can't copy a short piece of room tone adjacent to the offending noise, find a piece from another portion of the take. (See the section on room tone in Chapter 10.)
- Usually, you'll make a small crossfade at the head and tail of the insert to avoid a click and to help smooth the transition. This is especially true when the underlying room tone is very quiet or if it contains substantial low-frequency information.

A couple additional tips and tricks will come in handy:

- If you smooth your edit with a crossfade, don't allow your fades to enter the area of the noise you're covering. If you do, you'll hear vestiges of the noise and you won't be any better off than when you started. As a rule, listen separately to *all* fades you create—fade-ins, fade-outs, and crossfades—to ensure that you haven't left behind a little gift.
- Pay attention to the waveform cycle when inserting room tone. Most workstations can perform a decent, click-free edit despite wave cycle interruptions, but if there are a lot of low-frequency components in the room tone it's hard to avoid a click. Help your workstation do its job by lining up the waveforms as best you can, then make crossfades to smooth the leftover bump.

Removing Short Clicks with the Pro Tools Pencil

Very short, nonacoustic sounds such as static discharges and very brief cable clicks can be removed with the Pro Tools Pencil. (Most workstations have similar tools that enable you to redraw the soundfile's waveform.) When used on an appropriate noise, the pencil and its counterparts can be miraculous. However, there are a couple of very important things to remember when using them. First, unlike almost every other process, the pencil modifies the parent soundfile. Second, it's inappropriate for all but the shortest problems and if there's a significant acoustic element—such as a long ringout—it just won't work and you'll be stuck with a low-frequency "thud" where once you had only a tiny click.

Using the Pencil Using the scrub tool and waveform display, find the click in question. (See Figure 12-3.) The waveform usually isn't very helpful until you've zoomed in close. More often than not, the click will appear as a jagged edge along an otherwise smooth curve. It could also appear as a very small sawtooth pattern along the line of the curve. Although small, a glitch like this can cause a lot of trouble.

Remember that the pencil is a destructive process, which is rare in nonlinear editing. Any change you make with it will affect the original file as well as every occurrence of this part of the soundfile. A mixed blessing. If the click occurs in the middle of a line repeated many times in the film, the modification will present itself in every recurrence of that line.

Say the film begins on the deathbed of a family patriarch, who at the moment of his demise manages to murmur, "Don't forget the peanut butter!" On several later occasions we hear Dad's ghost say, "Don't forget the peanut butter." It's the same clip. The film ends and we still don't know what it means. Bad film, what can I say?

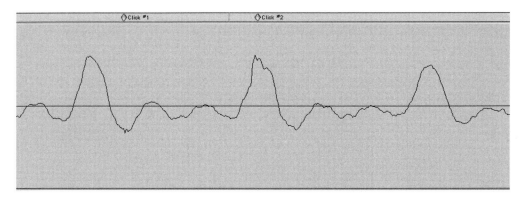

Figure 12-3 Compare the three troughs and note the small irregularity on the left (click 1). Note the rough edge on the center peak (click 2). These tiny irregularities caused a crackling noise.

If there's a short electrical click in the middle of the word "peanut," you fix it once with the pencil and you've fixed every occurrence. This is an unusual case, however. Normally, you want to protect the soundfile from any stupidities you might cause with the pencil, so remember this rule of thumb: *Before using the pencil tool*, make a copy of the section you intend to repair. To make a safety copy of the region you're about to operate on:

- Highlight a section of the region, a bit wider than the damaged area.
- Make a copy of the sound in the region. It's not enough to copy the region itself, as this doesn't create a new soundfile. Instead, consolidate or bounce the selected region, creating a new soundfile and leaving the original audio safe from the destructive pencil. (See Figure 12-4.)
- Zoom in very close to the click. Filling the screen with one sound cycle is a good view. Select the pencil tool and draw over the damaged area. Take care to create a curved line that mimics the trajectory of the underlying (damaged) curve, or what that curve "should have been."
- Redraw the smallest possible portion of the waveform. Otherwise, you run the risk of creating a low-frequency artifact.
- Move the boundaries of the now fixed consolidation until there's no click on the edit. Fade if necessary to avoid clicks (it's generally better to move the edit location than to fade).

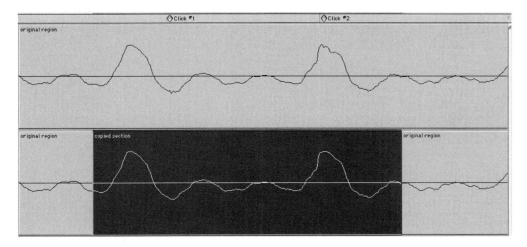

Figure 12-4 *Top:* The segment from Figure 12-3 with two clicks (labeled with markers). *Bottom:* The area to be repaired was consolidated (highlighted in black) to create a new, tiny soundfile. The pencil was used to redraw the waveform. Compare the smooth curves below with the jagged originals.

Reducing Clothing Rustle and Body Mic Crackle

When clothing rubs against a lavaliere microphone you hear a nasty grinding. This can often be avoided with careful mic placement, but by the time the problem gets to you, elegant mic positioning isn't really the first thing on your mind. You can't filter out the noise, as it covers a very broad, mostly high, frequency range. Normally, the only way to rid yourself of this sound is to collect the alternate takes of the shot and piece together an alternate assembly (see the upcoming section on alternate takes). You should also add this line to your ADR wish list.

However, if you've exhausted the alternate lines and the actor is no longer on speaking terms with the director and refuses to be looped, you can try one cheap trick that occasionally works. Many workstations offer a plug-in designed to reduce surface noise on 78-rpm recordings. Called "de-clickers" and "de-cracklers," they're usually found in restoration suites used in cleaning and remastering old recordings. Two examples among many are Waves' X-Crackle and X-Click and Sonic Solutions' DeCrackle and DeClick offered as part of its NoNOISE® suite.[1]

When closely compared, the waveform of a transcription from an old vinyl record and that of a dialogue recording contaminated with mild clothing rustle have many similarities. In each case, what should be a smooth curve is instead serrated stubble. De-cracklers and de-clickers use interpolation to smooth out local irregularities. Maybe, just maybe, you can use them to smooth out your curve, reducing the clothing rustle to a manageable distortion. Before you start, make a copy of the region so that you have a listening reference and can return to normal should this noise-removal plan prove ill conceived.

As with all interpolation processes, you're better off making several small, low-power passes than one powerful pass. Compare this to the window-painting analogy I use in Chapter 11: You'll get far better results with several finishing coats than with one thickly slathered soaking. All in all, don't develop great expectations for this method of cleaning up clothing rustle. Its results are often mediocre. Still, when you have no other choice, a bit of de-crackle may be an acceptable fix. Besides, what are your options?

---

[1] X-Crackle and X-Click are trademarks of Waves Audio Ltd. DeCrackle and DeClick are trademarks of Sonic Solutions.

Repairing Distortion with De-Crackling

Distortion can't be removed. Really, it can't, and your only recourse is to replace the distorted words with alternate material. However, when your back is against the wall and there's no choice, de-click and de-crackle may help. Why? Look closely at the waveform of a distorted track and you'll see two main problems. First, the waveform is truncated, like sawed-off pyramids. That gives you the ugly compression of a distorted sound. Second, the plateaus are jagged and rough, not unlike the waveform of a 78-rpm record. As with removing clothing rustle, repeated passes of a de-click utility followed by de-crackling may smooth the rough edges and even rebuild some of the waveform's natural contours.

- Make a copy of the section of the waveform you're repairing to get back to the original soundfile if necessary. Processes like de-click and de-crackle often add a bit of level to a region, so make sure that there's at least 3 dB of headroom in the original soundfile when you start this operation.[2] It's not good enough to lower the level through volume automation. You have to lower the level of the original file before making the copy. Or you can make a copy with the "Gain" AudioSuite processor, which will result in a new soundfile with enough headroom to accommodate the peaks that will likely result from the de-click and de-crackle processes.
- Start with the de-clicker on a very high threshold setting. One of the few good things to say for distortion is that most of the damage is confined to the loudest material. That's why you start with a very high threshold, leaving the undamaged majority of the signal unaffected. In essence, what you're doing is aggressive processing on the topmost part of the waveform.
- After one very powerful pass, apply five or six additional passes, each one less aggressive than its predecessor. Remember to keep the threshold high to avoid harming the undamaged, lower-level material. Repeat the same process with the de-crackler. Begin very aggressively and then progressively back off.

Many restoration tools allow you to monitor the removed noises, switching between the dregs you're removing and the cleaned results. This is handy for determining if you're overprocessing. If you can hear components of the

---

[2] If you're working with 24-bit soundfiles, you can afford to drop your level by 6 dB since you have such a huge dynamic range available.

program material (that is, the dialogue) while monitoring the removed noises, you're damaging the original track and should back off. If you don't have this monitoring option, you can listen to what you've removed by placing the de-clicked/de-crackled soundfile on a track adjacent to the original region, syncing the two, and listening with one of the regions out of phase. If your sync and level are precisely aligned, you'll hear only the removed sounds or distortion harmonics.

De-crackling isn't the first line of defense against distortion or removing clothing rustle. You stand a much better chance of making a proper fix if you go back to the original recordings and find an alternate take, or just give up and loop the line. Even so, it's good to have a bag of tricks to help you out of impossible situations. The result may not be glorious, but at times mediocre is better than nothing.

Solving Dolly and Crane Noise Problems

Dollies and cranes are a particularly ugly source of noises, which tend to go on much longer than run-of-the-mill ticks, clicks, and pops. A moving dolly can spread its evil across several lines of dialogue, so doing something to fix such noises is much more complicated. Before giving up and calling the scene for ADR, try to reconstruct the damaged part of the scene from alternate takes, hoping that the noises don't always fall on the same lines.

Fixing a line ruined by dolly noise is no different from other fixes that call on alternate takes. First find valid alternates, then line them up under the damaged shot and finally piece together the outtakes to create a viable line. You have to know how to quickly and painlessly locate the other takes from that shot in order to find alternate lines, more room tone options, and the comfort of knowing you've checked all possibilities.

Alternate Takes

Because life isn't always fair, sooner or later you'll run into noises within words. Then you'll have to look through the dailies for alternate takes that convey the same energy and character as the original but without the unfortunate noise. At first, going back for alternate takes seems a monumental task, so you invent all sorts of excuses not to do it. Once you realize that it's a not lot of work, though, you'll discover a huge new world of possibilities that make your editing not only more professional and effective but much more fun and rewarding.

Before you begin the quest for alternate takes, check your list of wild dialogue cues to see whether you have wild coverage for the scene. You never know, and it could save you some grief.

Finding Alternate Takes

The process of finding alternate takes starts at the beginning of the project. It hangs on getting from the production the items you absolutely must have to safely start any dialogue-editing project. (See Chapter 5.) Let's review:

- *All original recordings.* These may consist of a box of DAT or Nagra tapes, a Firewire drive with all the disk-originated BWF files, a DVD with the same files, or even a DA-88 tape or a hard disk from an MX-2424 if the original recordings were made in a multitrack format. However the sound was recorded, you have to have all of the original sound elements.
- *Safety copies.* You don't need to have the safety copies with you. In fact, it's not a good idea for the master and the safety copy of *anything* to be stored in the same space. Just make sure that the production went to the trouble (and expense) of making safety copies before beginning postproduction. They're comparatively inexpensive, and the potential consequences of not having them are appalling. Few things cause that heart-sinking feeling like the sight of a master cassette coming out of your studio DAT player followed by a trail of crinkled, ruined tape. If there's no copy there's no hope.
- *Sound reports.* It's pretty hard to hold a DAT tape to the light, squint, and divine what sounds reside there. You need help to find the scene and take you're looking for. When the location mixer records sound, she makes logs of the scenes, shots, and takes on each tape, as well as room tone, wild lines, and wild SFX. Her logs are essential for you to determine the options you have for solving problems on your tracks.
- *Lined script.* If possible, get the lined script; it contains notes on each scene's coverage. You can never have too much information.
- *EDLs.* You need one video EDL for each reel of film, as well as one audio EDL for each set of four audio tracks in the Avid or FCP edit for each reel. (See Chapter 5 for an explanation of EDLs.) The EDL is one of your most important tools. You can't get by without it, especially if your original sound is on tape.
- *List of scenes and their shooting dates*, if the location sounds originated on hard disk. It's much easier to find alternate takes on disk-originated recordings because you don't have to wade through tapes. However, you need to know in which folder the scene is hiding.

It's useful to have the continuity and camera reports and whatever relevant notes you can get your hands on. Some dialogue editors think this is too much information, a waste of space, and an indulgence. Let them. When it's three in the morning and you *must* find an alternate take and all of your normal paper trails have failed you, the script continuity or camera reports may be just what it takes to fix the shot and get home to bed.

Finding Alternate Takes

If the original location sound was recorded on tape, whether DAT, TC Nagra, or DA-88, for the most part you can use the procedure in the following sections to find all the alternate takes. However, experience and desperation may lead you to explore other routes too.

Highlight the Damaged Region If you're using Pro Tools, the start and end timecodes of the highlighted region are displayed at the top of the screen as Start, End, and Length. (See Figure 12-5.) Other workstations have similar displays. At this point, the length of the segment isn't interesting, so ignore that cell. Use the Start and End timecode values to find this take in the EDL.

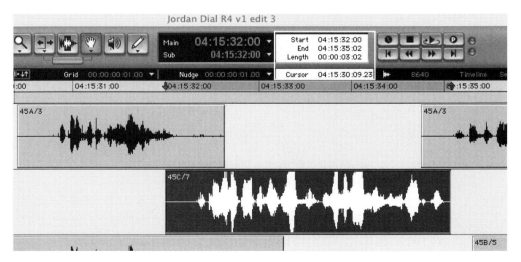

Figure 12-5 If the original recordings are on tape, begin your hunt for alternate takes by selecting the region and noting the start and end times. Find these times in the appropriate EDL to determine the source DAT and timecode.

Find the Correct EDL When you printed the EDLs for each reel, you added the header "Title, Reel __, Audio CH 1-4 [or 5-8, or 9-12, and so on], page __." Perhaps this seemed unnecessary when you made the printouts, but now it pays off. The secret of success at this point is to find the material as quickly and painlessly as possible so you don't lose your excitement and creative spirit. When you made the printouts, you were still clueless about the film and were hardly in the heat of creative passion, so you could afford the time. Now you don't want to slow down for anything.

If your EDLs span 9 or 12 tracks, you don't know in which one you're going to find your shot. However, most film editors edit with the production sound on the first four tracks, using the rest for temporary sound effects, music, temporary mixes, and the like. Odds are good that you'll find your problematic production sound in the list "CH 1-4."

Find the Event Always follow the same sequence of EDL columns to track down your alternates:

- *Record In and Record Out,* the two rightmost columns. Unless something is terribly wrong, your EDL will be printed "A-mode," sorted in ascending Record In time. The easiest way to locate an event is to look through the Record In times until you find a timecode that matches or is near the region you're looking for. Next, look at the Record Out time for the same event and make sure that your highlighted region falls between Record In and Record Out. Be careful—it's not unusual to find two events with the same Record In time, so make sure that the event you've marked in the EDL is the most likely candidate.
- *Confirm scene and take.* To make certain you've found the EDL event describing the region you're trying to replace, look at the Comment field immediately under the event line. A decent picture department will insert Comment fields that contain scene and take information. Confirm that the event listed in the Comment field is indeed the same as the name in your session region.
- *Determine the source tape.* Look on the source tape column to see which DAT or other source the recording came from.

Find the Correct Tape Go to the pile and find the tape in question.

Check the Sound Reports In the sound report that comes with each sound roll, you'll find a list of the tape's contents. Usually it won't include timecode, but this is no real loss. There are many useful items in a sound report, but at

Table 12-1 Common Abbreviations for Shot Types

Code	Meaning	Explanation
FT	Full take	Complete take of scene from beginning to end, or the complete text blocked for this shot.
FS	False start	Scene was stopped immediately after beginning because of acting mistake or technical problem. Action can restart within the same take after a false start.
INC	Incomplete	Scene was stopped midway because of a problem or because the director needed only a portion of it.
PU	Pickup	Take doesn't begin at the top of the scene but at a later point because of midscene mistake or because the director wants just one section of the shot.
WT	Wild track (wild sound)	Sound was recorded without picture because there was no practicable way to record sound or because the location mixer found sound problems.
MOS	Picture without sound	Scene shot without sound. This could be a silent cutaway or an action shot. All slow-motion or speeded-up shots are filmed MOS.

this point the most interesting are the sequence of shots and the presence of any wild sound. Location recordists commonly use abbreviations to describe takes. (See Table 12-1.)

How Many Takes Are Available? If your damaged take is 12C/4, you can be reasonably sure that there are at least three other attempts at a good take. Of course, takes 1, 2, and 3 could be false starts or simply no good, but they'll probably still give you a chance for replacement sound. There could easily be takes later than 4, so check the sound reports before winding to the location on the DAT just to see what you're up against.

Cue the DAT to the Correct Take If your sounds were recorded on a DAT, you'll most likely have a start ID at the beginning of each take. Most useful. To find your initial cue, fast-wind the tape to the approximate *source* timecode of your damaged take. Once safely within the original take, press "Backwards Index" on the DAT player to find where it begins. Listen to the voice slate to confirm that you're within the correct take. If your damaged take is take 4, press Backwards Index four times (you're already in take 4, so you have to subtract for that take, too). You'll be cued to the beginning of take 1. Use the sound report as your map through the sound roll and use the index function to navigate to the available takes.

Find Applicable Takes and Record Them Cue to the applicable sections of each alternate take and copy into the workstation. Check each one.

- *Is the offending noise on this take too?* If so, it means that the noise is rhythmically tied to the action. It could be an annoyingly accurate dolly operator or an actor who always plants her feet on the same line. Discovering these consistencies is a setback but by no means a fatal one. You just have to listen to every take and hope for a slip in the machinelike regularity of the noise source.
- *Does actor use exactly the same language?* Remember, you're not replacing an entire take, just a word or two, so it, as a whole, can vary from the take the director chose. The relevant section must be exactly the same, however, unless the noise-damaged line is off-camera. Even then, be careful not to undermine the choices of the director.
- *Does actor speak with approximately the same speed and pitch as in the original?* Once you choose a replacement take and import it into your session, you'll have some control over the length, speed, and pitch of the line, although less than hoped for. Try to get it right as you select.
- *Are the tone and attitude of actor the same as in the original?* You're replacing a line for technical reasons, but what's most important is maintaining the spirit of the line chosen by the director. Ask yourself why the director chose this one over another. Find that special quality that sets this read apart. Honestly ask yourself if the replacement serves the film as well as the original line did.

Plan B: Check Other Angles Obviously, you want to find an alternate take from the same shot (or angle) as the original to increase your chances of a decent sound match. However, sometimes you can't find useable alternate takes from the same angle. When that happens, first make a note in your ADR spotting calls but don't give up on the sound rolls just yet. Perhaps you can find the replacement lines within a compatible shot. This is where the sound reports really pay off.

An Example of Locating an Alternate Take from Another Angle

Say you're working on scene 88, an interior scene with two characters, Alfred and Elizabeth. The scene is made up of these shots:

- 88—master shot (wide) with both characters
- 88A—single shot of Alfred
- 88B—single shot of Elizabeth
- 88C—medium two-shot of both characters
- 88D—dolly shot for part of the scene

You need to fix Alfred's close-up lines, but you've already exhausted all takes for shot 88A, the angle used in the film. Where else should you look for material that will save Alfred from looping?

- Shot 88B isn't likely to help, as Alfred will either be off-mic or nonexistent, with the continuity person or director reading his lines. Still, it's worth checking the sound reports to see if your actor is present and was given a mic. Unlikely, but possible.
- You probably won't find joy in the master shot (shot 88) either. Because it's a wide shot, the sound will be either very wide or on radio mics, both of which can make for a difficult match. However, desperate dialogue editors do desperate things, so if all else fails give it a try.
- The dolly shot (shot 88D), depending on what it is, could be of help, but don't make it your first choice as it may introduce new problems. Since this is a pickup (a take including only a part of the scene), you can use the shooting script to find out if it includes the parts of the shot you want. Do this before you start looking to save yourself some unnecessary wading through takes.
- Head straight for 88C, the medium two-shot. It's the most likely place to find Alfred with a microphone in the right place.

Once you find some qualifying alternate takes, record them into your work-station, making sure that the filenames reflect the scene and take numbers. A collection of files named "Audio 1" isn't particularly helpful, especially when it's time to import the files into a session.

Finding Alternate Takes on Hard-Disk-Recorded Projects

More and more location mixers are recording field tracks on portable hard-disk recorders. These recorders run the gamut in price and quality, but in general they deliver good tracks, naturally better suited to the needs of post-production. There are many advantages to recording on hard disk versus on a DAT.

- *Lot of tracks.* With four to eight tracks, plus mixdown tracks, hard-disk recorders offer powerful possibilities in field recording. A location mixer can provide both solo radio mic tracks and a boom track and mixes of the two. This allows the picture editor to work with a mono or two-track guide track mixed from all of the original channels. The dialogue editor will later relink the original solo tracks to the guide track to have better control. Multiple tracks can, of course, be a curse as well as a blessing. You're much better off with a quality old-fashioned field mix than with an undisciplined collection of solo tracks.

- *Durability.* Although not wildly robust, hard-disk recorders are likely to hold up better than DATs in the field under adverse conditions (of course, you could say that all field recordings are made under adverse conditions).
- *No tape to buy.*
- *Backups are easier.* The location mixer will provide a backup of all recorded material, either on DVD or hard disk. No more making time-consuming DAT backups.
- *Automatic naming of takes.* Any decent hard-disk recorder will automatically name each take following a variety of naming conventions.
- *Having 24-bit field recordings.* Don't let anyone tell you that there's no advantage to 24 bit over 16 bit. Listen: Improved dynamic range means more headroom, greater clarity, and more depth. It's better, it's better, it's better.
- *Much better bookkeeping.* Because BWF files allocate part of the file for metadata, you can store a great deal of shot information with each recording. The metadata is part of the file, so it can't be easily lost. This greatly reduces human error down the line and is essential for managing multiplexed files in postproduction.
- *Making video dailies is much easier.* When a film's sound is recorded on DAT, loading the dailies into the video editing workstation begins with two time-consuming tasks: digitizing the picture and digitizing the sound, both of which must occur in real time. Sound recorded on hard disk arrives in the picture cutting room on a hard disk, CD, DVD, or flash card. No sound digitizing is necessary, just copying onto the DAW's sound drives.

Editing sounds originating on hard disk rather than tape makes life easier in two ways. First, you have every take available on your workstation all the time. Second, you can organize your database any way you choose, making it conform to your way of thinking or even your mood.

For a dialogue editor, the true beauty of jobs recorded on a nonlinear system isn't the technical considerations or even the vastly improved sound. It's that you'll edit better because you'll lose any excuse not to check the alternate takes. When you work with DAT-based projects, there's always a tiny (or not so tiny) voice in your head telling you all the perfectly good reasons not to go back to the dailies. You eventually convince yourself that there probably aren't any decent alternates or at least nothing that compares to the original. "Besides," you tell yourself, "this noise isn't really all that bad." Human nature maybe, but not a formula for great dialogue editing. Having everything at your fingertips strips you of most excuses for laziness.

There are any number of ways to organize the database of your original recordings. Some editors prefer Excel-style spreadsheets. Others like to create a database in a program such as FileMaker Pro, which enables complex searches and endless report formats. You can view in creation order (like a DAT) or by scene, shot, comment, or whatever else you like. I find it useful to make comments in the database as it helps me find other takes. At the very least, my notes warn me that I've already visited a take only to discover it was no good. You feel pretty stupid checking out the same take more than twice.

Choose the Right Parts

You've imported the likely alternates into your session. Now you have to find out which one will make the best fix and then cut it into your track. I find it easiest to move my work tracks directly beneath the track with the damaged region. (See Figure 12-6.)

To select the best alternate take, try the following procedure. You'll develop your own technique with time, but this isn't a bad way to start.

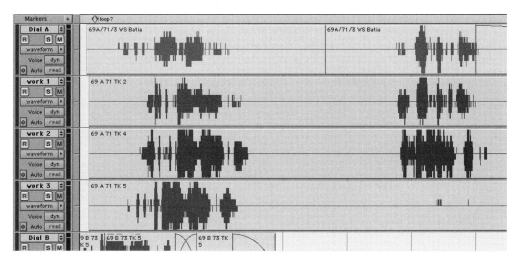

Figure 12-6 Move several work tracks directly beneath the track with the damaged line. This way you can easily and safely compare and edit your alternate takes. In this example, the original line is on Dial A (*top*) and three alternates are lined up on the work tracks.

- Place a marker at the location of the noise you want to eliminate so you can navigate back to your target location after scrolling through long soundfiles.
- Import the alternate take soundfiles into your session.
- Drag alternate take regions onto work tracks, more or less lined up with your original region (refer to Figure 12-6).
- On each alternate take region, remove all but the desired material.
- Line up the beginning of each alternate take region with the beginning of the original damaged region.
- Listen to the original take and then each of the alternates. Pay attention to cadence, tone, and attitude and how they match up with the originals.
- Put aside the takes that patently differ from the original, but don't remove them from the session as they might hold hidden secrets. Just get them out of the way. Now you'll have only the best takes, lined up roughly in sync under the original line.

On rare occasions, an alternate take will have all the right attributes—the speed, mood, and linguistic "music" (cadance, timbre, energy, spirit) of the original. You need only sync it to the original and edit it into the track. However, you usually have to work a bit harder. Often, one part of the line will work well but another will be wrong. There are a number of things you can do to create the perfect replacement.

Combine Parts of Several Takes Listen to the original line—beginning, middle, and end. Describe to yourself its spirit. I often invent a nonsense rhyme to describe the music and energy of each part of a line. Then I play back the nonsense tune in my head as I listen to parts of each potential replacement. By taking the language out of the dialogue, I can better focus on its music. It's not uncommon to combine pieces of two or three or more takes to make a good alternate line.

Get the Sync Right Tricks and tips for syncing are akin to fishing hints—everyone has the perfect secret, certain to give you great results in the shortest time. In truth, it's a matter of time, experience, and a knack for pattern recognition. Try a few of these pointers and develop them into a technique of your own.

- *Break the line into short, easily managed sections.* If you start off with too much material, your attempts at sync will be compromised from the outset. Try rhythmic blocks of no more than three or four words.

- *Find a landmark consonant in the phrase.* Consonants are easy to spot. The plosives (*P*, *B*, etc.) or the stops (*T*, *D*, etc.) usually rise above the plain of the rest of the word's waveform. They're also important because their short durations serve as clapper boards, revealing to the audience if a shot is in sync or not. Start syncing by lining up a landmark consonant with the same sound in the original. Do this to all your alternates because you don't yet know which takes you'll be using.
- *Check the length.* Compare the length of the original take with the semi-synced alternates. Unless the actor is a machine (in which case your job will be very easy), each take will have its own internal rhythm even if the overall lengths don't vary too much. Look for a shot whose internal rhythm most closely replicates that of the original.

After you've completed these steps, it's time to listen again. It's easy to get caught up in the graphics and begin slipping here, nipping and tucking there, with little regard for content. Remember, we're performing a very delicate operation here, replacing words while respecting the character, mood, focus, and drama of the original line and at the same time worrying about sync. Listen to the original. Close your eyes so that you can visualize the flow of the phrase. Sometimes I see a phrase as colors with varying intensities, modulating with the line. This lava lamp of transposed information helps me categorize the line's technical as well as emotional attributes.

If you're allergic to touchy-feely notions like "visualize the phrase," please indulge me. First, I find closing my eyes very valuable. It removes the stimulus of the computer monitor so I'm not influenced by visual cues. Second, I find it useful to assign shapes and/or colors to the elements of a phrase or word, as this rich shorthand is often easier to code and remember than the raw sound. As I said, sometimes I reduce the phrase to nonsense sayings to provide a sort of mental MIDI map for interpreting it. Finally, imagining the phrase as colors or shapes is very visceral and helps me quantify its *real* workings. Of course, you're free to think of all of this as hogwash and use your own tricks.

Saving the Original Line Once you find the replacements for each section of the line, you're ready to construct the fake. First, however, you need to copy the original line to a safety track. I use my junk tracks for this.

There are two kinds of lines you never want to throw away: those you replace with alternates and those you replace with ADR. The reasons are pretty obvious.

- The director hates your replacement line and would rather put up with the problem noise than give up the special characteristic of the original.
- You misunderstood the point of the line when you made the replacement, so its emotional key is now missing or incorrect.
- The replacement line doesn't match well either in sound quality or acting energy.
- The editor is very territorial and can't stand it that you replaced a line.
- A week after you replaced a line, you realize that your month without sleep really *did* cloud your judgment.

All of the preceding is true for ADR as well as alternate take replacements.

Changing the Speed

Most workstations have plug-ins for "fitting" replacement lines, whether ADR or alternates, to match your original, but you need to know how they operate before you can make them work for you. It's not uncommon to hear the telltale artifacts that these voice fitters create when used irresponsibly. The trick is to prepare the track before you use the fitter, never to ask the processor to do more than is reasonable, and to honestly listen after its every use. If it sounds weird, it will never get better.

Time Expansion/Compression Tools Time-stretch tools ("word-fitting" tools like VocAlign fall into this category) change the duration of an event without changing its pitch. Unlike pitch-shift tools, which behave like variable-speed analogue tape machines by changing the sample rates and then resampling, time stretchers add or subtract samples as needed. If a phrase is too long, they'll remove enough samples to get to the right length. If the phrase is too short, they'll duplicate samples to lengthen the selection.

You have to know where to make the splices. If you tell it that you can't tolerate any glitches, the time-stretch tool will make all of its splices in the pauses between words or in other very safe places. After all, who's going to hear the splice where nothing is said? Or sung? Or played? What you end up with are essentially unchanged words with dramatically shortened pauses as well as truncated vowels and sibilants. Thus, if you order a 10 percent length reduction, the line will indeed be 10 percent shorter but the speed change won't be consistent. This is especially noticeable with music, where time compression/expansion can result in a "rambling" rhythm section.

If you want better local sync, choose a more "accurate" time shift. You're now telling the tool that local sync is more important, even at the risk of glitching.

In extreme cases, you'll have perfect local rhythm because the tool is splicing at mathematically ideal locations, ignoring content. But the glitches resulting from this "damn the torpedoes" approach are often unacceptable.

Here you have to make informed compromises. All time expansion/compression tools provide a way to control the delicate balance between "perfect audio" and "perfect rhythmic consistency." You just have to figure out what it's called. Usually there's a slider called something like "Quality" that indicates how glitch-tolerant the tool should be. The less glitch tolerance (that is, higher "quality"), the worse the rhythmic consistency. The more you force the rhythm to be right (lower "quality"), the greater your chances of running into a glitch. As expected, the default Average setting will generally serve you well.

Before you process a region with a time expansion/compression algorithm (see Figure 12-7), make an in-sync copy of it. Here's how this will help you:

- If you need different time expansion/compression ratios for separate parts of the line, you'll find it helpful to have the original version handy. Given that time expansion/compression routines are far from transparent, the last thing you want is to process an already altered file.
- As you construct the phrase, you'll find sections that need time flex and others that don't. With a copy of the unprocessed region standing by, it's easy to access the original for editing.
- If you process the original without making a copy first, and then decide your entire syncing logic was wrong, you'll have to re-edit the line.

Word-Fitting Tools As you'll see in Chapter 14, many tools are available for locally time-stretching a line; that is, comparing the waveform of the original with that of the alternate and manipulating the speed of the alternate to match the reference. Word fitters use, more or less, the technology of time expansion/compression, but they're largely automatic—able to look at small units of time and make very tight adjustments. Still, they have the same real-world limitations that time expansion/compression has: quality versus sync. All of these tools offer some sort of control to enable you to make that choice. Play with them and get used to how they work.

Time expansion/compression and word-fitting tools create new files. You'll have to name these. Do it, and be smart about it. I'll name a section of a shot that I stretched something like "79/04/03 part 1, +6.7%." A word-fit cue I might name "79/04/03 part1, VOC" (for VocAlign). If you don't sensibly name your new files, you'll eventually regret it.

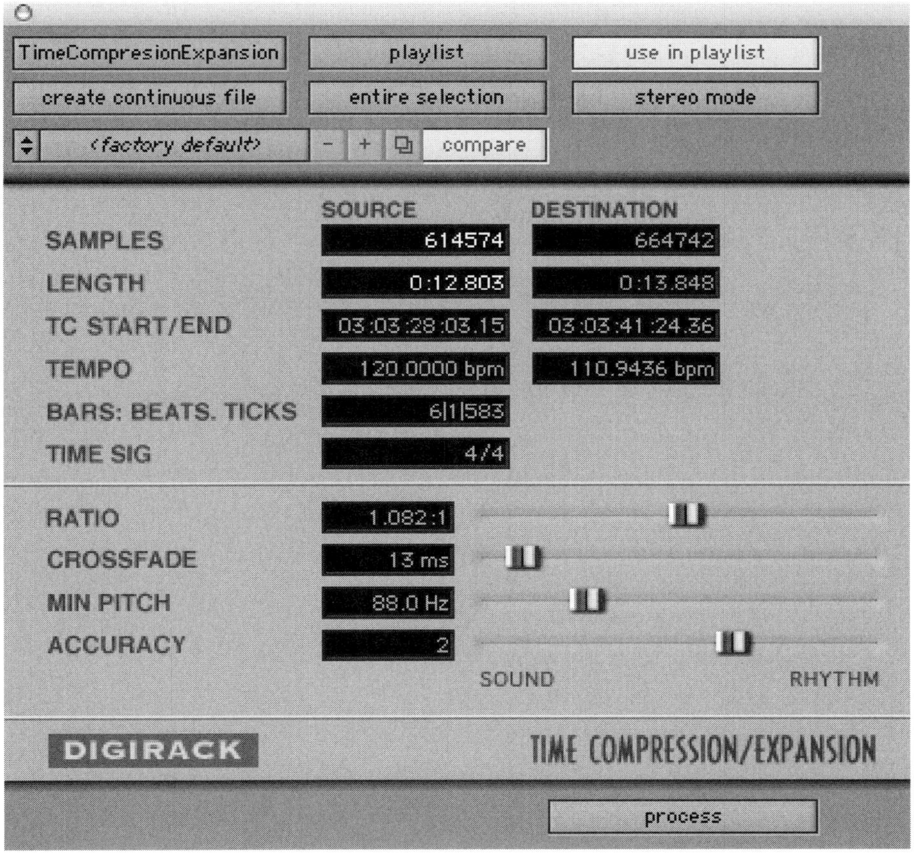

Figure 12-7 Digidesign's Time Compression/Expansion AudioSuite processor. Many manufacturers offer such products, and they all work in more or less the same way.

Syncing the Alternate Line

You'll find a full treatment of syncing and editing alternate lines and ADR in Chapter 15. Here I'll just briefly outline the steps.

- *Place* one empty work track directly beneath the original line. Your alternate lines will be just below it. It's on this blank track that you'll build your new line.

- *Copy* the original to a junk track.

- *Find* the most suitable replacement from the alternates you lined up below it for each section of the original line.

- *Cut and paste* the appropriate sections from the alternate takes onto the blank track, more or less in sync with the original.
- *Start syncing* each subsection with your rough assembly of the new line.
  - Get the length right. The best way is to try editorial nips and tucks to adjust the pauses. Do this before you begin any VocAlign or time-stretch processing. You can shorten and lengthen during pauses, but if you lengthen a bit of "silence," make sure you don't introduce a loop by repeating a tick, click, smack, or other recognizable noise.
  - Don't be afraid of cutting in the middle of a word. Contrary to common sense, you can actually trim in the middle of the certain word sounds. Your two greatest friends when syncing alternate takes are hard consonants, such as *T* and *P* and *B*, and sibilants, such as *S*, *Sh*, *F*, and *Ch*. Use the hard consonants as visual benchmarks to tell you where you stand. Use the sibilants as convenient cutting locations within words. You can almost always cut within a sibilant sound—to shorten or lengthen—and get away with it.
  - Do as much manual editing as you can before resorting to the length-changing tools. The easier you make life for the processor, the better results you'll achieve.
- *Listen* to what you've constructed. Watch the alternate line in sync with the picture, then compare it with the original. Although it's great to be able to match waveforms, you can easily forget what this is all about: convincing dialogue, solid sound, and language a normal person (as opposed to a computer) would believe.
- *Do* your time-stretching work. Use a word-fitting tool or just a time expansion/compression plug-in, whichever you have and whatever makes sense to you. Be sure to logically label the resulting regions.
- *Slide* it over the original when you finish the line. Fix the fades and move on to the next fix.

Overlaps

People interrupt each other all the time. Sometimes out of excitement, sometimes out of anger or arrogance, actors are always stepping on each other's lines, and such "overlaps" cause ceaseless headaches. Let's return to our friends Alfred and Elizabeth and see what can happen to movie sound when people step on each other. Here, again, is the list of shots for scene 88:

- 88—master shot (wide) with both characters
- 88A—single shot of Alfred

- 88B—single shot of Elizabeth
- 88C—medium two-shot of both characters
- 88D—dolly shot for part of the scene

Odds are pretty good that the master shot has both characters either on a boom or on two radio mics. Same goes for 88D, the dolly shot. 88C was probably recorded with a boom; the two single shots, 88A and 88B, almost certainly. During shot 88A the boom was focused on Alfred; anything Elizabeth said was hopelessly off-mic.

In an otherwise outstanding take of 88A, in which Alfred is complaining to Elizabeth about the cost of hockey pucks in Brazil, Elizabeth interrupts the end of Alfred's sentence to tell him that he's an idiot. Back in the picture editing room, the editor and director piece together a back-slapping row between our two characters. The picture editor includes Elizabeth's interruption on Alfred's track, cutting to Elizabeth at the first rhythmic pause. No one but you notices that Elizabeth's first four words are off-mic, having come from Alfred's track. What do you do? You announce that it must be fixed, either with ADR or alternate lines.

Overlaps put you in a bad position. Often the director and the editor won't notice them while editing because they're so used to hearing the cut. You're the only one who notices, so you'll be stuck trying to justify the extra ADR lines or the time spent rooting around in the originals to find the replacement material. Still, if you ever want to show your face at the sound editors' sports bar, you can't let it go. Overlaps with off-mic dialogue aren't acceptable.

When Elizabeth (off-mic) interrupted Alfred (on-mic), she ruined both of their lines. The end of Alfred's line is now corrupted by an ill-defined mess, so it must be replaced from alternates. Let's hope that Elizabeth won't jump the gun in other 88A takes. We also have to replace the head of Elizabeth's line (88B) so that she'll have a clean, steady attack. Again, we have to rub our lucky rabbit's foot in the hope that there'll be a well-acted alternate 88B from which we can steal Lizzy's first few words. If alternates don't help, you'll have to call both characters for ADR on the lines in question. But since you'll face the problem of matching the ADR into the production lines, it's in everyone's interest to use alternates to fix the problem.

When shooting a fast-paced comedy in which the characters regularly step on each other's lines, a location mixer may use a single boom plus a radio mic on each actor. If this is recorded on a multichannel hard-disk recorder, you stand a better chance of sorting out the overlap transitions. However, even if you have nice, tight radio mic tracks of each character, you'll have to be careful of the off-mic contamination from one of them. There's no free lunch.

Fixing the Acting

It's not unusual for actors to slip in their diction, slur a word, or swallow a syllable. Often you can fix these problems the same way you remove noises— go back to the alternate takes and find a better word or phrase. Of course, you'll copy and put aside the original since that little "slip" may turn out to be the reason the director chose the shot. Also, when replacing a line because of an actor's problems, you'll keep it to the bare minimum so that the spirit of the line is unaltered.

The hardest part of "actor cleaning" is remembering that you have the resources to improve the line and then overcoming your natural laziness, which keeps telling you, "What's the big deal? That's the way she said it."

Removing Wind Distortion

Location recordists go to great lengths to avoid wind distortion. They protect the mic from the wind using shock mounts and screens with all sorts of lovely names (including "zeppelin," "wind jammer," "wooly," and "dead cat"). Regardless, it's a certainty that sooner or later you'll curse the location mixer for "not noticing" the wind buffeting the mic on the Siberian blizzard wide shot.

You can often remove this very low-frequency distortion in the mix with a high-pass filter set to something like 60 Hz. As with all filtering issues, you should talk with the rerecording mixer or the supervising sound editor about how to proceed. If you're really lucky, the mix room will be available and you can listen to the scene in the proper environment. You can also do a poor man's test by running the track through a high-pass filter in your editing room and playing with cut-off frequencies between 60 and 100 Hz. Keep in mind that wind distortion will always sound less severe in your cutting room than on the dubbing stage, so don't get too excited by the results.

If, God forbid, you decide to filter the tracks yourself in the cutting room, you *must* make a copy of the fully edited track before filtering and put the original on a junk track. Many a time I thought I was doing my mixer a favor by "helping" the track a bit with a high-pass filter, only to have the mixer stop, turn to me, and ask, "What were you thinking?" What sounded like a vast improvement in my little room was now thin and cheap. Plus, the energy from the wind noise was still evident. The mixer gently reminded me of the division of labor. "You cut," he said, "I make it sound good." Thankfully, I had stashed the original (completely cleaned and edited) onto a junk track and with no effort the Empire was saved. Still, who needs the humiliation?

So what should you do about wind distortion? I suggest you build two parallel tracks: the original—fully edited and faded and cleaned of nonwind noises, but still containing the wind buffeting; and an alternate version assembled from other takes, free of the wind noises. Mute your least favorite version. This way you're prepared for anything that might happen in the mix. If the mixer can remove the wind noise from the original take without causing undue damage to the natural low frequency, great. If not, you're prepared with a wind-free alternate. Either way you don't get yelled at.

Removing Shock Mount Noises

Like wind noises, shock mount noises appear as unwanted low-frequency sounds. But unlike wind, which usually lasts a long time, they're almost always very brief. Like dolly noise, which occurs with camera motion, shock mount noise is usually tied to a moving fishpole. This makes it easier to spot.

You can often succeed in removing shock mount noise with very localized high-pass filtering, usually up to 80 Hz or so. As with any filtering you perform in the cutting room, *save a copy of the original*. You usually won't want to filter the entire region but just the small sections corrupted by the low-frequency noise. If possible, listen to the results of your filtering in the mix room, with the mixer. Here you'll learn if you under- or overfiltered, and you'll hear any artifacts you couldn't hear in the edit room.

Of course, the *right* way to fix shock mount noise is, yes, to find replacements for the damaged word in the outtakes. This way you don't risk any surprises in the mix.

Getting Rid of Dolly Noises

It was dolly noise over dialogue that started the discussion on using alternate takes to repair damaged lines. By now it should be clear how to piece together a new sentence from fragments of other lines. What makes dolly-related damage interesting is the fact that the noise source is always changing, so you usually must line up all reasonable alternates and hope that the annoying cry of the dolly occurs at slightly different places on each one. You end up constructing an entirely new line from the best moments of all the takes. If this doesn't work, you'll have to rerecord the line.

Reducing Ambient Noises

Background noise is the bane of dialogue tracks. Location recordings are noisy, suffering from traffic, air conditioning, generator and camera noises, and assorted rumbles. You've smoothed each scene so that shot transitions are bearable, but there's still an overall unacceptable noise level. What can be done?

Traditionally, noise reduction is done in the dialogue premix. You edit, the mixer mixes. Simple. However, as technology improves, plug-ins get cheaper and better, budgets degenerate, and mixes get shorter, you may find yourself doing some noise reduction in your cutting room. It's not necessarily a positive trend, but you should know how to deal with it.

Noise reduction can miraculously save a scene. Or it can make your tracks sound like a cell phone. Here are the secrets to nursing your tracks through noise reduction:

- Talk to your supervising sound editor and mixer to come up with a plan. Stick to noise reduction processing, leaving normal EQ and dynamics for the dialogue premix.
- Make fully edited safety copies of all regions you're going to process.
- Understand what each processor does.
- Get to know your noise problem so that you can intelligently attack it.
- Know when to stop.

Getting Answers from the Supervising Sound Editor and Mixer

Select representative samples of the noises throughout the film. String them together so that your presentation will be as efficient as possible, and note the timecodes of the original scenes in case you need to return to them for context. Discuss each noise problem with the mixer and supervising sound editor, *and* remember to ask the following questions:

- Can this problem be fixed, or will the lines be rerecorded (ADR)?
- Who'll fix each line? For each problem, determine if the editor or the mixer will do the processing.
- What sorts of processing will be used?
- If you plan to use inserted plug-ins, what ones are available in the mix room and what DSP limitations and latencies will be encountered?

Even an abbreviated version of a meeting like this will make for an enormously more productive mix. And you'll avoid those damning looks from the mixer during the dialogue premix that say, "I can't believe you did that!"

Preparing for Noise Reduction

Broadband noise reduction plug-ins often have enormous **latencies**, so you usually can't use them as real-time processors amid your other tracks. If you did, your processed tracks would be miserably out of sync. Instead, you have to process the tracks and create new soundfiles. However, before processing you have to make a copy of the original region. I place this safety copy on one of the junk tracks, in sync, of course. Some people put it on the X, Y, Z tracks, but I like to reserve those for ADR-related regions. Truthfully, this is between you and the mixer.

Since any AudioSuite operation will create a new soundfile, you may want to open up the beginning and ending handles of the region first. (See Figures 12-8 and 12-9.) Just because the edit works well before noise reduction doesn't mean that the transition will be effective once the tracks are cleaned. Previously unheard background sounds (such as "Cut!") may emerge after cleaning. Similarly, track cleaning may alter the balance between adjacent shots, necessitating a longer handle. Pulling out an extra bit of handle—if available—means you'll have to redo the fade after noise reduction is complete, but you'll be left with a better set of options to play with.

Noise Reduction Tools

One reason noise reduction so often turns out miserably is that editors don't understand the tools. This is one of the key arguments that mixers have

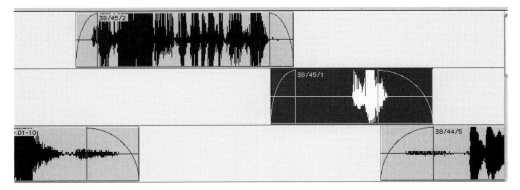

Figure 12-8 The highlighted region of this soundfile needs to be processed. Any AudioSuite operation will create a new region without handles.

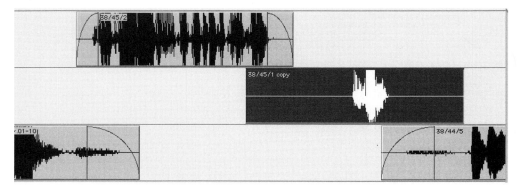

Figure 12-9 Before processing, delete the fades and open the handles. This will give you greater editing and fade options when working with the soon-to-be-created region.

against editors reducing noise in the editing room rather than in the mix. You may have an impressive selection of tools at your disposal but use them incorrectly and you'll inflict damage. Typically, there are three types of tools for managing background noise:

- *Filters.* These equalizers, notches, buzz eliminators, and so on, are best suited for **harmonic** noises.
- *Interpolation processors.* These tools remove clicks and pops on vinyl, but can also be used for lavaliere microphone rustle and even mild distortion. (The de-crackle and de-click plug-ins for reducing radio microphone rustle and mitigating distortion, described earlier, are examples.)
- *Broadband processors.* Originally designed to eliminate hiss on archival recordings, these multiband expanders have become more and more common for general-purpose noise reduction.

Most botched, artifact-laden noise reduction jobs happen during broadband processing. Because processors that remove broadband noises (de-noisers) often have names like "Z-Noise"[3] or "DeNoise"[4] or "BNR"[5] (broadband noise reduction), it's not irrational to think that this is the place to head with all your noise problems. The result: Having failed to use filters or interpolation

---

[3] Z-Noise is a trademark of Waves Audio Ltd.
[4] DeNoise (actually "Broadband DeNoise") is a component of NoNOISE, a trademark of Sonic Solutions.
[5] BNR is a component of the DINR package; DINR is a trademark of Digidesign.

processors to remove harmonic noises or unwanted transients, you end up asking too much of the broadband processor, which repays you with a signature "I've been noise reduced" sound. The trick is to identify your particular noise problem and then apply the correct processors in the right sequence and in the proper amount.

Remember, you're not mixing the dialogue at this point—save that for later. Right now you're just doing cleanups that would be too time-consuming or expensive in the dialogue premix. Don't bother with the shelving and "shaping" that naturally apply to all of the dialogue elements. Almost all of your tracks will have some low-frequency rumble, which the mixer will roll off in the premix. Don't attack these problems in your cutting room; address only the odd but exceptional noise problem there.

A Typical Noise Reduction Plan

The following paragraphs describe a typical multipass noise reduction sequence. Usually, you will work in this order:

1. Use filters to remove rumble, buzz, and hum.
2. Use interpolation processors to remove crackle that occurs when words are being spoken.
3. Use broadband processors to remove random noise.
4. Use filters again to remove remaining harmonic problems.

Rumble, Hum, and Buzz Removal Create an FFT or spectrogram of your noise,[6] and look at the low-frequency information (below 500 Hz), as shown in Figure 12-10. If you're chasing a harmonic problem like a rumble, hum, or buzz, you'll notice a distinct pattern. Look for the lowest-frequency peak in the FFT—that's the **fundamental frequency** of the noise. You should easily see harmonics occurring at multiples of the fundamental frequency. You can also analyze harmonic patterns using a spectrogram, as shown in Figure 12-11.

Write down the center frequencies of the fundamental and its harmonics, up to the tenth harmonic (or until you can't stand it any longer). Note the

---

[6] An FFT, or Fast Fourier Transform, equation is a method of studying a signal in the frequency domain rather than in the time domain (in which we live). Sonic Studio and a few other DAWs provide an FFT display for analyzing a signal. Pro Tools has no onboard means of doing this, but a number of plug-ins allow you to create a display showing the signal FFT. A spectrogram is another means of displaying frequency domain sound information.

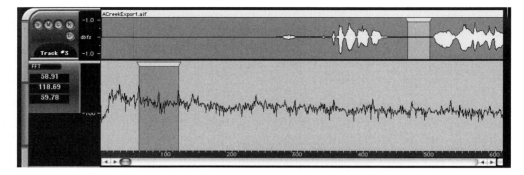

Figure 12-10 An FFT display created with soundBlade.[7] This sample shows a classic North American hum, with peaks at approximately 30, 60, 120, 240 Hz, and so on. The frequency callout (*left*) reveals that the 60 Hz fundamental measure 58.91 Hz, indicating that the original analogue recording was at some point transferred off-speed.

approximate "height" that each harmonic rises above noise floor as well as its "width." You'll use the width to calculate the Q for each filter and the height to determine the cut value. (See Figures 12-12 and 12-13.) Write all of this down or enter it into a spreadsheet (Figure 12-14), which has the advantage of doing the math for you.

Use a multiband EQ to create a deep-cut filter for the fundamental and for each harmonic (see Figure 12-15). For each filter, enter center frequency and calculate Q (center frequency ÷ bandwidth). If your processor allows you to control the amount of attenuation, set it to a couple of dBs less than the height to which each specific harmonic rose above the visual noise floor on the FFT. You'll end up with several deep, narrow filters. These aren't notch filters because they're not infinitely deep; rather, they remove only what's necessary to reduce the noise back to the level of the existing noise floor. This should effectively eliminate hum, buzz, and rumble. If not, extend the filters further to the right to eliminate harmonics at higher frequencies and recheck the FFT to make sure you accurately measured the components of the noise.

Click and Crackle Removal Interpolation noise removal tools work in two steps: identification and interpolation. They first identify telltale noises within a signal (which have an unnaturally short attack and decay) likely attributed to surface noise. These noises show little or no acoustic characteristics, so they're pretty easy to spot. Once the processor identifies the click, it removes

---

[7] soundBlade is a trademark of Sonic Studio, LLC.

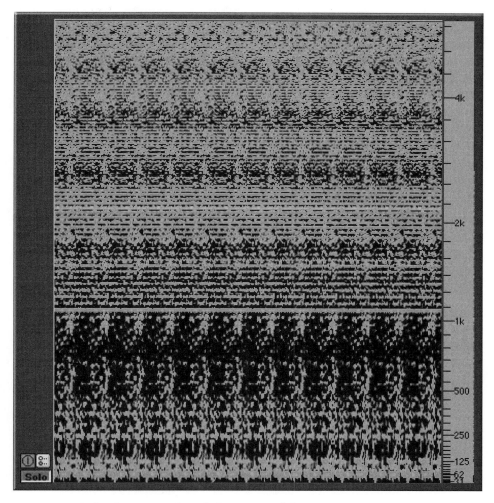

Figure 12-11 A display created with SpectraFoo[8] from Metric Halo. The pronounced horizontal line at 1081 Hz indicates a strong harmonic element.

it and then "looks" to the left and right of the event to interpolate appropriate audio to fill the hole. As a dialogue editor, you can exploit this technology to fix sharp, short irregularities such as static clicks, microphone cable noises, or *maybe* clothing rustle. Use relatively high thresholds to "protect" the unaffected portion of the soundfile, then repeatedly apply aggressive processing to the distorted/clicky/rustly sections.

---

[8] SpectraFoo, a multipurpose measuring device, is a trademark of Metric Halo.

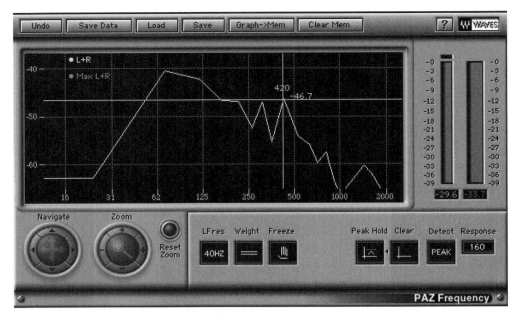

Figure 12-12 A Waves PAZ Frequency Analyzer displaying center frequency and amplitude of a harmonic.

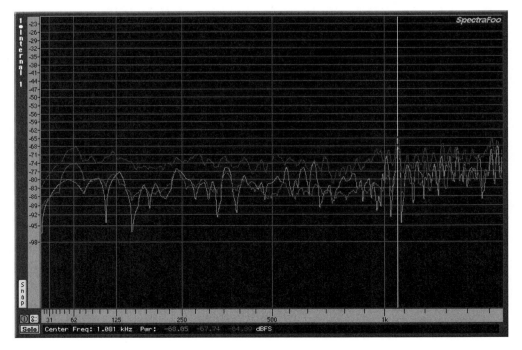

Figure 12-13 A frequency versus amplitude display of the same buzz shown in Figure 12-10; note the strong harmonic at 1081 Hz.

	B	C	D	E	F	G	H
	Freq	Gain	BW/2	BW	Q	≈Q	
1							
2							
3	61.3	12	4	8	7.7	7	
4	122.1	18	6	12	10.2	10	
5	183.4	15	9	18	10.2	10	
6	239.2	15	9	18	13.3	13	
7	301.0	12	12	24	12.5	12	
8	363.0	10	14	28	13	12	
9	419.0	15	14	28	15	14	

Harmonic Noise Calculator.xls

Figure 12-14 A spreadsheet for logging harmonics and calculating the *Q*. If the frequency pattern is predictable, you can use a spreadsheet to predict the higher harmonics.

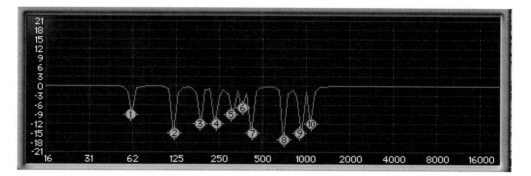

Figure 12-15 Once you determine the center frequency, gain, and *Q* for the principal harmonics, you can use a multiband EQ to remove the harmonic noise. In this case, a Waves Q10 is set to the parameters shown in the spreadsheet in Figure 12-14.

Broadband Noise Removal Many manufacturers sell broadband noise reduction processors. Perhaps because they require relatively little user interaction, or maybe because they're very sexy, they're best-sellers. The key to using them successfully is understanding what they do and don't do.

Broadband noise reduction devices work by first taking a sample of "pure noise," ideally from a pause free of any valid signal. This serves as the blueprint of what's wrong with the sound. Next they move the noise sample and signal from the time domain to the frequency domain by creating ever updated FFTs. The FFT of the noise sample is divided into 2000 (or so) narrow-frequency bins, in which the noise is reduced to a formula.[9]

When the signal is played through the processor it, too, is assessed in the frequency domain. At each of the 2000-ish bins, the formula for the signal is compared to that of the noise sample. If the match is sufficient, the sound within that bin is attenuated by a user-controlled amount. If there's no correlation between the noise formula and the incoming signal, no attenuation occurs in that bin since the dissimilar signal is likely valid audio rather than noise. This process is repeated for all of the frequency bins.

At this point there are usually control parameters for threshold and reduction. As would be expected, threshold determines the sound level at which processing begins; attenuation (or "reduction") dictates what's done within each bin flagged as "noise." If these settings are too aggressive, you'll hear very obvious artifacts. Back off first on the attenuation and then on the threshold.

After noise reduction, the signal must be recorrelated into a "normal" time domain sound. You usually have some control over this. "Sharpness" controls the slope between adjacent bins. The steeper the slope during the recombination process, the more effective the noise reduction but the "edgier" the sound. If you set the sharpness too high, you'll hear digital "swimming" artifacts, often called "bird chirping." There's usually a control called "bandwidth" that determines how much sharing occurs between adjacent bins during the recorrelation. The higher the bandwidth, the warmer (but perhaps less articulate) the sound.

Low-frequency (LF) cutoff, if available on your processor, isn't what you think: a high-pass filter. Rather, it dictates the frequency beneath which there's *no* processing. If you're attacking traffic, set the LF cutoff to zero. If all you're fighting is hiss, set it to 2000 Hz or higher and you won't run the risk of damaging anything in your audio source below that level. Many processors have a high-frequency cutoff, which normally defaults to the Nyquist frequency. Change this setting if you're processing *only* low frequencies and want to leave higher frequencies unaffected.

All broadband noise removers are shackled by the fact that as they aim for greater resolution in the frequency domain resolution in the time domain

---

[9] Not all broadband processors use FFT algorithms to transform sound into the frequency domain. Wavelets, as well as other transforms, are also used in such calculations, but for the sake of simplicity, we'll stick with FFT.

suffers. No way around it. Clever manufacturers offer options between frequency resolution and time resolution, giving you control over this dilemma.

Ambient Noise Complexity

Very few background noises have but one component. A typical noise floor will have harmonic elements from air conditioners or other machinery, ticking noises from microphones or cables if not from speech and broadband, random elements. Labeling a simple noise like air conditioning as "simple" is misleading. In addition to the obvious hissing air (solution = broadband de-noise), there'll be harmonic sounds from the motor (solution = notch filters) and perhaps clicking from ineffective isolation springs or other causes (solution = de-click interpolation). The answer is simple: Don't run straight for the broadband. Think about the source of the noise and appropriately plan your processing.

Knowing When to Stop

Aside from picking the wrong noise reduction tool for the job, the most common way to bungle the process is not knowing when to quit. When you repeatedly listen to a noise, trying to get an even cleaner signal, you inevitably lose touch with the audio you're processing. Almost certainly you'll over-process the tracks.

The antidote is annoyingly obvious: Process less. You can always do more in the mix. Also, when you're happy with the noise reduction on a file, leave it. Do something else. Take a walk and rest your ears. Listen to it later with a fresh ear to see what you think. If it passes this delayed listening test, it's probably acceptable.

To Process or Not to Process

A running battle exists between editors and rerecording mixers about processing. While there's something to be said for tracks arriving at the mix relatively clean, it's rare that an editor in a cutting room has the experience, tools, or acoustics to properly process them. Few things are more humiliating than listening to a mixer repeatedly say, "If only I could get my hands on the original tracks." In my experience, it's rare for a mixer to *like* the processing I've done in the cutting room, and more often than not my charmingly cooked tracks are greeted with disdain.

Figure 12-16 If you must perform noise reduction on a region, first make a copy. Mute this copy or place it onto a Junk track. After processing, add a suffix to the new region name that reminds you what processing you used. In this case, a 100 Hz high-pass filter was applied, as is reflected in the new region name.

Sometimes it's appropriate for the dialogue editor to process certain tracks in the cutting room. Noise reduction, as we just saw, can be one such case. Another instance may be scenes in which one side of the conversation is wildly out of balance (for instance, the generator was directly behind that actor). In such cases, it's difficult even to edit the scene without some sort of processing.

Follow these rules and you can peacefully bring (some) processed tracks to the mix:

- If at all possible, talk to the mixer. Tell him what you have in mind and see if it will fly. Ask if there's any special layout to follow when including processed tracks amid the dialogue elements. Make deals as to what you'll cover and what you'll leave for the mix.
- *Always* make an instantly accessible safety copy of each region or string of regions you're going to process. This will afford you easy A/B comparison when processing, and it will let you revert to the original with little embarrassment. The safety copy must be edited as completely as the processed region on the dialogue track so that it will be usable as a valid alternate.

As you process a region, you create a new file. When you name it, include information about the processing you did. (See Figure 12-16.)

Another bone of contention between dialogue editors and mixers is the matter of volume leveling. Every workstation allows you to adjust volume on a region-by-region basis, and most let you draw complex volume automation. How much leveling you bring to the mix depends on the rerecording mixer. I like to arrive at the dialogue premix with tracks that are well leveled and likely to contain some automation within regions. This way, the mixer needn't trouble herself with the most basic of volume issues and can more quickly move on to more interesting ones. Some mixers don't like preleveled tracks, however, arguing that the dialogue editor's manipulations get in the way. It's a matter of habit and preference. You're probably safe with basic shot-to-shot volume matching, but detailed automated volume moves should probably wait until you've spoken with the mixer.

CHAPTER 13

Production FX and Guide Tracks

Production FX

Not everything on your tracks is dialogue. Amid the words are the odd door slam, plate break, chair squeak, and car start. Occasionally, you'll encounter entire scenes with no spoken words, just action. Events without words are called production effects, or **PFX**, and they get special treatment.

There are at least two reasons to care about PFX.

- Often you want to treat a sound effect differently than you treat the surrounding dialogue. A quietly spoken line immediately followed by a loud chair squeak is a hard scene to mix. Splitting off the squeak makes it easier to control—or to replace.
- To prepare a film for dubbing into another language, you must prepare an **M&E**—that is, a mix containing all elements of the film except the words. Splitting off nondialogue sounds helps the SFX editor and mixer create the international mix.

Splitting PFX Tracks

What do you do when you encounter something you want to split off from the dialogue? If it's an entire wordless scene you want to set aside, simply move the whole thing to your PFX tracks. As the scene is premixed, it will be recorded onto PFX record tracks to be ready for both the full mix and the international version. If this wordless scene covers too many tracks to move to your PFX tracks, leave the section on the dialogue tracks but tell the rerecording mixer to bus the scene to the PFX record tracks when premixing. This way it will appear on the right fader when it's time for the international mix. Otherwise, the mixer would have to open up the dialogue **stem** to steal the scene for the M&E.

If you're splitting off a single door squeak, car start, body fall, or the like, place a cut on either side of the event, and move the event to one of your PFX

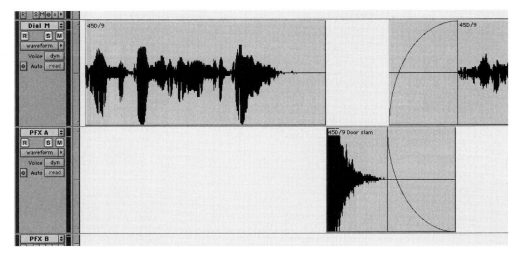

Figure 13-1 A door slam on the dialogue track was moved from Dial M to PFX A for better control in the mix. Note the −6 dB crossfade when returning from PFX A to Dial M. This construction won't allow complete elimination of the door slam because there's no replacement room tone, but it helps in managing level and color.

tracks. If the sound has a strong attack, place the beginning edit just before it starts. (See Figure 13-1.) Under such circumstances, no crossfade is necessary. If the event you're splitting off has a slow or soft attack, you'll need to find a good place to crossfade to PFX from dialogue.

Since the end of most events is harder to nail down, you'll likely need to crossfade from PFX back to dialogue. Dissolves like this must have a mid-fade attenuation of 6 dB ("Equal Gain" in Pro Tools lingo) because you're fading across identical, phase-coherent material. If you use a normal fade with a center attenuation of 3 dB, your edit will bump. (Crossfade types are discussed in greater detail in Chapter 11.)

Using Room Tone for Greater Flexibility

If the only reason you're moving the sound to a PFX track is to have it ready for the M&E mix, you're done. There are, however, things you can do with this PFX split that will give you more flexibility in the mix. You may want better control over the volume, EQ, or wetness of the PFX event. Or the SFX editor will be replacing the sound so you have to present the tracks in a way that allows the mixer to choose between the original PFX and the SFX editor's replacement.

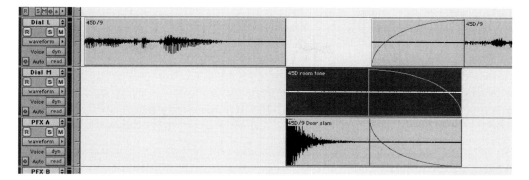

Figure 13-2 Adding a region of room tone parallel to the removed PFX provides complete flexibility. Compare the regular −3 dB fade from room tone to dialogue with the steeper −6 dB fade from PFX to dialogue.

In such cases you have to lay up a section of room tone that can be added to the mix as the level of the PFX diminishes. (See Figure 13-2.) This way the total room tone remains the same even as the level of the effect is lowered. The tone region must match the sound of the dialogue track and the dimensions of the PFX event. Only the fades need to be different: Since the room tone isn't precisely the same signal as the dialogue, you can use normal −3 dB fade linking ("Equal Power" for Pro Tools users).

Temporary Sound Effects from the Picture Edit

It's common for a picture editor to add temporary sound effects to the Avid edit for more convincing screenings, to direct the sound team, or simply to make editing easier. These effects aren't your problem, but there's a good chance that the effects editors will want to get their hands on the files. Whether merely for inspiration or actual use, the picture editor's files should provide a simple, communication-free means of transferring temporary sounds to the effects department.

One easy way to make temporary effects available to other editors is to prepare a few extra tracks in your session named something like "Temp SFX" or "For SFX." As you come to the picture editor sound effects, move them to these temp tracks. When you finish your first pass on a reel, send a note to the effects editor to indicate that your catch of temporary FX is available. The SFX editor can then import the relevant tracks, even over a network, and you can delete them from your session. Rarely is cooperation so cost-free.

Noisy PFX

Often a picture editor will add nonverbal sounds to a scene to enhance the action. From the production recordings she might glean a footstep here, a door slam there, or some extra clothing rustle. When background noise isn't a problem, these extra elements give you the tools you need to add finesse to a scene, so whenever possible use them. Because they're there for a reason, make use of them or come up with even better replacements.

Sometimes the ambient noise of a scene is so high that you can't afford the added room tone of these production effects. That subtle cloth rustle may be nice, but not at the cost of massive added noise. Likewise the sound of pouring nuts into a crystal bowl may be elegant, but that airplane in the background kills the mood.

How do you manage? Make the scene work without the added effects and write detailed Foley notes for the supervising sound editor. With good Foleys you can replicate the mood created by the picture editor without unnecessarily increasing noise. For example, door slams, gunshots, and the like are so high above the noise floor that you can often sneak them in without worry. You can also look for alternate takes or wild recordings of these effects.

Because there's no dialogue on these regions, only action, you might be able to clean the PFX with EQ and broadband noise reduction. These sections aren't carrying the room tone—that's being taken care of by the main elements of the scene—so it doesn't matter if you muck-up the underlying noise. Just remember to listen carefully to the results. The fact that there are no words is no excuse for weird equalization or noise reduction artifacts. And of course keep a copy of the original, unprocessed files.

Making Guide Tracks

When you're on a film, it's unlikely you're working alone. On the smallest of films you're joined by an effects editor, a Foley editor, a music editor, and your supervising sound editor (who often doubles as the effects editor). On a larger film, toss in more dialogue and effects editors, a background editor, more Foley people, and some assistants. No matter the number—you all have to communicate. Good paperwork from the supervising sound editor keeps everyone informed as to plans, schedules, and picture changes, but there's more to a film than paperwork. For you, the dialogue editor, this means occasionally making a mono or split-track guide track of your progress and handing (or posting if you're on the network) a copy of it to each editorial department.

Why is a guide track so important?

- Someone has to determine the sync of the film, and in most cases the dialogue editor is the best qualified to do this. As the team edits, everyone will use your sync decisions to decide precisely where to "double up" production effects, "amplify" footsteps, or replace door slams.
- It's easier to make choices when listening to a decent guide track. When an effects or backgrounds editor uses the OMF or the track from the videotape as an editing reference, the ugly and jarring shot transitions overpower subtle effects or elegant backgrounds. It's nearly impossible to make sensitive judgments, and "listening beyond" the bumps is exhausting. Even though your dialogue edit won't have EQ or other processing, the work you've done to smooth shot transitions and remove noises will greatly aid the other editors.
- As you add ADR and **group loop** lines to your edit, the effects and music editors will need to know their absolute placement. These extra bits of dialogue influence the rhythm and timing of a shot and so can alter decisions about other elements. Sometimes the opposite is true: You'll need a reference from the SFX editor to know where to place an off-screen line or vocalization.
- If time permits, a clean guide track can be prepared for the ADR recording session. This will make life easier for the actors since they'll also be hearing a "cleaner" version of the production sound.
- A guide track is a concise and transportable reference. You could give each department a copy of your entire dialogue session, but this would be an inefficient use of tracks, disk space, and DSP power.

Step-by-Step Guide for Making Tracks

The following paragraphs detail how to make a guide track that other editors will thank you for.

Step 1. Make sure you have a reference tone on the first track of your session. Don't play more than one channel of this tone while making a guide track bounce, or your reference level won't make any sense. Check that you have head and tail **sync pops** and that they're correctly placed.

If you've already edited some ADR and want to guide a track with dialogue on one track and ADR on the other (highly recommended), pan all dialogue tracks to the left and all ADR tracks right.

Step 2. Confirm that all tracks you *don't* want in your mix—work tracks, junk tracks, and the like—are muted. Make sure that all tracks you *do* want are unmuted. Getting this wrong is the most common—and frustrating—way to ruin a guide track recording.

Step 3. On one track, select everything from the beginning of the reference tone to the tail plop. The reference tone must be part of the guide track so that the other editors know how to relate to your work.

Step 4. Determine what type of file to make based on the DAW and operating system the editors are using. If you're working on a Pro Tools, select *Bounce to Disk* from the file menu. Then select the correct input path, bit depth, sample rate, and type of file.

Step 5. If you're working at 48 kHz and the rest of team is working at 44.1 kHz, instruct the DAW to make a sample rate conversion after the bounce. Choose "Dual Mono" rather than "Stereo," since this will make life easier for the others.

Step 6. When you press *Bounce*, you'll be prompted for a target folder. Create one at the root level of the main drive called "Dialogue bounces for everyone." This keeps other editors from digging around in your affairs. If you're on a network, put the bounces in a public folder.

Step 7. Pay attention. Despite the strong temptation to leave the room while the real-time bounce is happening, don't. Sooner or later you'll make a mistake and leave a work track open or fail to unmute a dialogue track. If you're off flirting during the bounce, you won't know that the recording is flawed. The other editors will hear your bounce and wonder how you got your job.

Step 8. Give the bounced file the same name as that of the dialogue session being bounced. This way you'll always know which version of your edit the others are working with. The file will have a name like "*Title*-Dial R2, ver 3, edit 4." Some supervising sound editors have their own naming systems, often using the date. Use whatever system you're told to unless it's completely silly.

In your naming scheme, think of the editors who are using your guide tracks as your proofing service. When they find some of your blunders, you'll want to know which version of your edit they're working on so that you can check the session.

Step 9. When you're finished with the bounces, tell the other editors or make a CD of the bounces for them, or put them on the server.

CHAPTER 14

Conformations

"But they told me that the picture was locked!"

You've been editing the dialogue for four weeks, and you've made thousands of detailed, interrelated edits and countless fragile overlaps. Knowing that the film was locked five weeks ago, you confidently built your editorial house of cards. Now you learn that the director and picture editor have made hundreds of "small" changes. "Don't worry," they tell you, "most of the changes are just a couple of frames each." You weigh the relative merits of poison and jumping off the roof.

It's much more common to run into postlock changes than to work on a movie whose structure is set in stone. Changes happen, and it's unimportant why. To survive these annoying reshufflings of your editorial deck, you can't take them as a personal affront; they're just part of making movies. When you get the "Oh, by the way" news that the picture editor has turned the film upside down yet the temp dub is still scheduled for Thursday, quietly throw your brief tantrum, then come up with a plan.

The Conformation Defined

The process of matching sound sessions, whether dialogue, SFX, BG, Foley, or music, to an altered picture edit is known as a **conformation**, colloquially a "confo." Since picture editors have been making eleventh-hour changes for years, there's a well-developed system for communicating those changes to the editors and assistants in the sound department.

Key to this communication are the **change notes** (see Figure 14-1)—detailed, step-by-step instructions on what to remove, lengthen, insert, or move. If you start at the top of the list and follow all of the instructions, odds are good you'll end up with the desired results. If you try to outsmart the change list, combining steps or skipping others, you'll probably run into trouble.

```
 (New)R-2_F SCS 36-67 FOR SND 7-24   (Old)R-2_D SCS 36-67  6-16 (FOR SND 6-16)
                              26 events         Old Duration  1766+00
 Picture 1                    15 insertions     New Duration  1765+08
 - Reel 2                     11 deletions      Total Change 0000+08
                               0 moves
 All Counts Are Inclusive (inside/inside)
 -------------------------------------------------------------------------------
     At This      For This                At This                        SND    Clip    Total
     Footage      Length      Do This     Record TC  Start     TC24      Roll   Name    Change
 1.  0222+11      +0000+01    Lengthen Tail  02:02:28:11 07:00:31:13 07:00:31:10  089    40-1b   +0000+01
     0222+11      00:00:00:00                02:02:28:11 07:00:31:13 07:00:31:10                  00:00:00:01

 2.  0229+12      -0000+01    Trim Tail      02:02:33:04 07:00:36:04 07:00:36:03  089    40-1b   +0000+00
     0229+12      00:00:00:00                02:02:33:04 07:00:36:04 07:00:36:03                  00:00:00:00

 3.  0359+00      -0001+07    Trim Head      02:03:59:08 05:27:29:20 05:27:29:16  087    41B-3   -0001+07
     0360+06      00:00:00:22                02:04:00:06 05:27:30:18 05:27:30:14                  00:00:01:05

 4.  0449+04      -0003+09    Delete  Shot   02:04:59:12 18:11:04:16 18:11:04:13  106    43A-11  -0005+00
     0452+12      00:00:02:08                02:05:01:20 18:11:06:26 18:11:06:21                  00:00:04:04

 5.  0449+04      +0002+11    Lengthen Tail  02:04:59:12 18:18:10:14 18:18:10:11  106    43B-11  -0002+05
     0451+14      00:00:01:18                02:05:01:06 18:18:12:06 18:18:12:05                  00:00:01:22

 6.  0454+06      -0000+11    Trim Head      02:05:02:22 18:12:00:01 18:12:00:01  106    43A-13  -0003+00
     0455+00      00:00:00:10                02:05:03:08 18:12:00:14 18:12:00:11                  00:00:02:12
```

Figure 14-1 Excerpt from an Avid-generated film change list.

Communicating change instructions was simpler when editing was done on film and mag. A conformation is a very physical process, so it was easier to communicate between one department and another when there was something real to move. Now that everyone is on a workstation, moving ether rather than chunks of film, the process has gotten more complicated and, worse, more prone to error.

A relatively painless conformation hinges on getting good information from the picture editor. An experienced editor should be able to produce an accurate change list from any professional picture workstation. On low-budget films, however, it's not uncommon that an inexperienced picture editor will hand you nothing but the new OMF and shrug when you're not impressed. If that's the case, you may need to educate him about change lists. This, of course, means that you need to learn a bit about them yourself.

Creating Change Notes in the Avid

Avid's Change List Tool[1] is accessed through the Output menu (see Figure 14-2). It works much like the Compare Document routine in Microsoft Word.[2] You point to two documents and specify how to note the differences. On the

---

[1] An excellent overview of the Avid Change List Tool is in "Configuring Avid Change Lists" by Robert Brakey, in *The Motion Picture Editors Guild Magazine* (vol. 21, no. 2, March/April 2000).

[2] Word is, of course, a trademark of Microsoft Corporation.

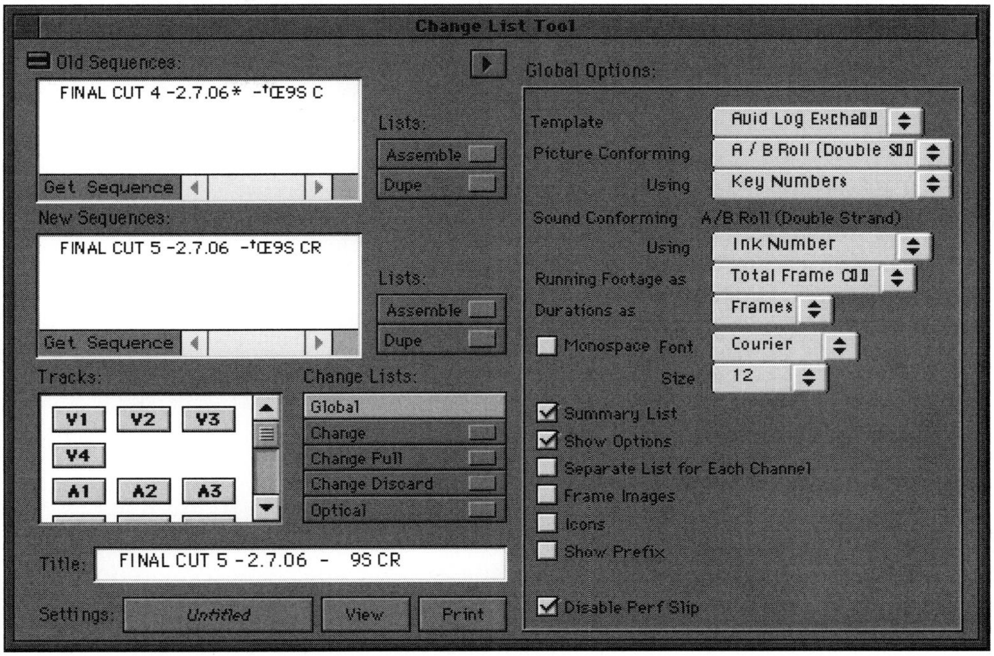

Figure 14-2 Avid's Change List Tool.

Options page, the editor or assistant chooses the desired sorting, selecting, and listing criteria, and then imports the new and old Avid sequences and performs a comparison. Differences between the two files are reported based on your preferences. This is much easier than requiring the dialogue editor to blindly find all the needles in the new session's haystack.

Normally the picture editor will prepare two change lists—one for conforming the work print and one for the sound department. Logic may tell you that all you need is the sound list, but insist on both because in regions of high track congestion or complexity the sound change list may be complicated to the point of uselessness. In such cases, the picture change list can provide just the overview you need to figure out the cut.

Make a Test Change List

Picture changes—and change lists—have a way of showing up on your desk very late at night. While you're trying to make sense of them, the picture department is at home with their teddy bears and you have no one to turn to for clarification. To avoid this frustration, convince the assistant picture editor to create a test change list a few days (or hours) before you're due to make the confos. This will give you time to digest the specifics and request alterations or at least clarifications.

Manual Conformations

You'll probably receive a new picture, an OMF, an EDL, and the change list from the picture department. If you didn't get an EDL, ask for both audio and video lists before the picture department goes home. They may prove useful later. Then:

- *Before you do anything else*, make a backup copy of your session.
- Import the new OMF tracks into your old session and save the combined session under a new name (see Figure 14-3). Confirm that the revised picture is in sync with the new OMF.
- Unhide the original OMF tracks so you can conform them along with the rest of the session.
- Reduce all tracks to the smallest size so that you can see as many tracks as possible.
- Create two edit sync groups: one containing all of the tracks of the new OMF; the other, all tracks in the old session. This includes the active dialogue tracks, PFX, ADR, and any junk tracks containing synchronous material.

Removing Material

Activate the edit group containing the old (original) session, and do whatever it takes on your workstation to ensure that your markers will move along with the audio. The cursor should span all of the tracks. Locate the session to the time or footage noted in the first event of the change list. If the event simply calls for removing material, you'll see an instruction like this:

```
at 243+04 remove 6+13
```

or perhaps

```
at 4:10:22:23 remove 4:03
```

When you type the required duration in the Length field, you'll see a selection of the correct duration crossing all tracks of the old session, including the marker region. If you're working with Pro Tools, select Shuffle mode and delete. Then immediately return to Slip mode. If you're working on another

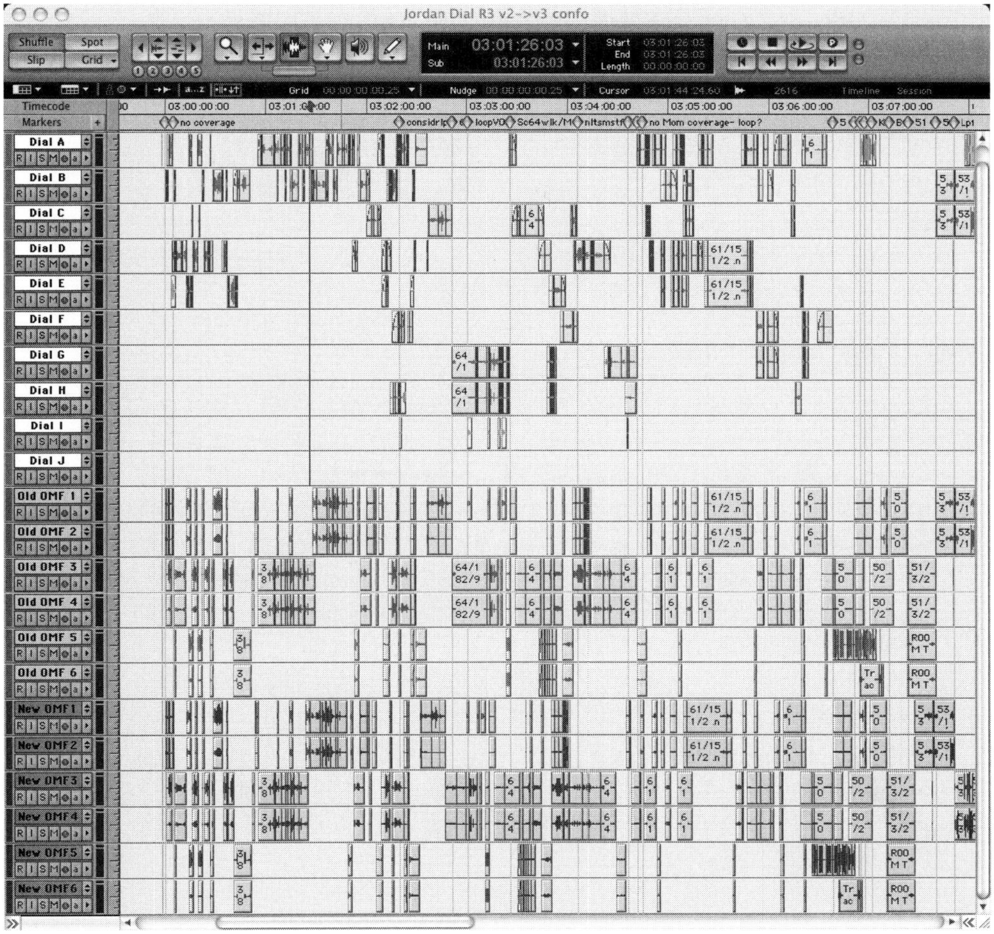

Figure 14-3 Pro Tools setup for conforming. At *top* are all of the dialogue tracks of your most recent edit; below that is the original OMF. At the *bottom* is the new OMF, which will serve as a guide.

workstation, make the edit in a mode that ripples the session when you remove material. Confirm that you've executed the move across all of the old tracks, including the old OMF copy, junk tracks, PFX, markers, and so on.

Opening up a Track

Making a shot or scene longer is a bit more complicated than removing material. The following is what you do:

- Click on any track within the group of your original session.
- Locate to the time or footage indicated in the change list.
- Make a cut across all tracks. This will undoubtedly result in some track carnage, but you can sort that out later.
- Reset the Nudge key to the time specified in the change list.
- In the "old material" edit group, select everything from the insertion point to the end of the reel. Make sure you're in Slip mode. Press the Nudge key ("+") once. Make sure you're moving your markers as well the sounds.

Changing the Order

Changing the sequence of shots or scenes is the least pleasant of all conformations because you have to juggle a lot of material. For example, changing the sequence of scenes from A, B, C to A, C, B involves these steps:

1. *Prepare B.* Before removing B, I like to add two silent, 1-frame regions on its first and last frames. These marks will travel with the scene and serve as reference anchors. When you've moved section B to its new home, these anchors should line up with the beginning and end of the picture at the new location.
2. *Remove B from the sequence.* Select the two scene B anchors and everything between them. Enter Shuffle mode and cut all of scene B. Scene C and everything after it will advance to B's old start position.
3. *Create a location to insert scene B.* Locate to the end of C, where B is to be inserted. Make an edit that will result in a cut across all of the tracks of the old session.
4. *Insert B after C.* Still in Shuffle mode, paste section B at its new location. Return to Slip mode and assess the damage.

Adding New Material

If the new version contains material not in the old session, copy these extensions, shots, or scenes from the new OMF. Wherever you insert new material, place a marker to remind yourself that you have unedited material to deal with. If the OMF audio is unacceptable (perhaps it was loaded into the Avid via analogue or has the wrong bit rate), you must recreate this section from the original tapes. This is where the EDLs come in handy.

Use your auto-assembly software or file-linking program to auto-conform the new (missing) sections of the film. Auto-assembly programs allow you to pick the EDL range that you want to conform. If this proves frustrating, open the new EDL in Word, delete all events except those you want to conform, and

Save As in a *text* format. This will leave you with a very tiny auto-assembly task. The new events can be imported into your revised session, where they ought to fit nicely.

If you follow the instructions of the change list, your session's structure should reflect that of the new picture version, but you still need to verify sync and repair damaged transitions. Use the new OMF to confirm the sync of your new assembly. Find easy landmarks, then nudge the tracks of the conformed session until the geography is identical in both old and new. You can also use Titan's "Fix Sync" to snap the new events into sync. As you repair transitions and regions damaged during the conformation, remember to look at volume automation, which will certainly have sustained some injury.

Ask any experienced dialogue editor about conformations and you'll discover the *perfect* formula for painless success. The procedures just described make up only one of many methods for matching an old sound edit to a new picture cut. Talk to enough editors and you'll develop a system that suits your personality.

Automated Conformations

Armed with a good change list, patience, and a sense of humor, you'll eventually get through the conformations and then nurse your edits back to health. However, picture changes never come at a good time but inevitably fall in your lap when you'd rather be focusing on tomorrow's temp dub or when you have opera tickets.

Thankfully, there are now several software solutions that automate conformations, among them EdiTrace,[3] Virtual Katy,[4] and Change Note Assistant.[5] All of them work in more or less the same way, by comparing an existing Pro Tools session with a change list and then coming up with a new sequence. Some interact directly with Pro Tools, turning the confo process into a player piano operation. Others work via EDLs, requiring you to subsequently

---

[3] EdiTrace is a product of Sounds In Sync (*www.editrace.com*).

[4] Virtual Katy is manufactured by Virtual Katy Development Ltd. (*www.virtualkaty.com*). Katy Wood was a sound editor on *Lord of the Rings: Fellowship of the Ring* and became famous for her ability to manage and cajole Avid change notes and convert them into human-friendly forms.

[5] Change Note Assistant is a product of Nonfiction Software, LLC. For a thorough tour of it, see "Automated Conforming Using Change Note Assistant" by Eric Stratman, in *The Editors Guild Magazine* (vol. 24, no. 6, November/December 2003).

conform your session with Titan or a similar file management program. Titan accepts a change list in EDL form and creates a DAW session.

If your workstation includes an autoconform routine, as do Pyramix and Fairlight MFX, you can import the new EDL directly into your session and then conform it. Although EDL-based conformation solutions require an additional step, they may be more appropriate if you work with a wide array of workstations, since any manufacturer's DAW can read a CMX3600 EDL.

On a typical large film, picture department changes are codified as Avid change lists or EDLs (or maybe ACLs) and e-mailed regularly to the sound department. With a good piece of conforming software and a skilled assistant sound editor, the sound can be fully conformed before the new digital picture cut arrives. All that's left is checking the conformed audio against the picture. No matter how slick the conforming process becomes, don't forget that nothing can replace physically checking the sound against the new picture.

CHAPTER 15
ADR

Sooner of later you'll get to a dialogue problem you can't repair. Say the noise interfering with a line is the same on all of the takes, so alternates won't save you, or that the actor is so annoyingly accurate that she always says the line exactly when the dolly starts to move. Maybe there's no close-up **coverage** of the off-mic wide shot you're trying to fix, or the take chosen by the picture editor really does have the best acting despite the F-15 flying overhead. There are a million reasons for rerecording dialogue.

Replacing What Cannot Be Fixed

Everybody loves original production sound, so there's no point discussing the magic of the sound from the shoot, when the actors were hyped and in character. There's always the concern that replacing the originals with studio recordings will kill the charm. Nevertheless, if you're **looping** a scene someone has accepted that it had to be redone.

What, though, are the reasons for rerecording a line, a shot, or a scene? I like to divide them into three groups based on how the lines will be used: replacement, added, and group loops.

Replacement Lines

Replacements are rerecorded lines of existing dialogue. When people think of postsync, they're what usually come to mind.

- *Noise problems.* These are easy to spot: excess general ambient noise (a scene shot in a convertible or next to a waterfall); temporary loud noises (car horns, voices, sets falling); wind. The list is endless.
- *Technical problems.* These include a wide array of screwups: radio mic breakup, hidden mic–clothing rustle, rain striking the **zeppelin**, or any other microphone-related problems; distortion; wildly underlevel recordings, and so on.

247

- *Perspective and voice quality.* Sometimes it's simply impossible to record a shot: very wide shots with lots of headroom and no place to put the boom; scenes shot in overly "boomy" spaces; weird sound reflections.
- *Acting.* Some of the worst ADR nightmares occur when the director or editor doesn't like the read on a line and wants to "improve" it. This can turn into recording hell, since the director's new idea of the "right" read may not match the gestures or acting energy of the image on the screen. But try we must.
- *Line changes.* Sometimes lines have to be changed to fix story problems. This is where you become an expert at squeezing new text into old sync shots without it looking like a Godzilla movie. It rarely works.
- *Focus control.* To isolate the characters from their surroundings you may have to rerecord their lines. Imagine you're working on a scene in which your two protagonists are surrounded by rioting, noisy Bolsheviks bent on malfeasance. In order to get inside the heads of our besieged heroines, the supervising sound editor decides to progressively peel away the sounds of the mob until nothing but the protagonists' dialogue and Foley remain. The mob's voices fade away, followed by their Foleys and then the other sounds. We're left with something far scarier than the roar of the crowd: a subjective view of the scene. Of course, to pull this off we have to loop all of the dialogue of the protagonists as well as any visible sync utterances from the crowd. Later we'll record **group loop** for the crowd.

There are many other reasons to replace a sync line. What's important about *replacement* lines is that you have to prepare the track so that the new ADR line can be mixed with the rest of the dialogue. More on this later.

Adding Lines

Not all ADR lines are intended to replace mangled, damaged, or drowned-out production lines. Some of them are added *on top of* the dialogue.

- *Story details* (a.k.a. narrative emergency surgery). If the story is foundering because a few critical facts have gone missing, well-placed clarifications might save the day, like the antagonist muttering a bit of vital information while passing behind a post. Decades of exposition have taken place during a long driving scene in buddy films. You thought those beauty shots out the window were just to celebrate nature? Not entirely; that's a great time to plug story holes, reveal details about characters, and up the tension ante. Similarly, a character who's just left the screen can yell from the exit sign that she'll be home at 8:30. This sets up the next scene: It's 12:30 and no Sally. Sally's small line adds to the drama because everyone else in the film had warned her that it was folly to go surfing during the shark warning.

- *Narration.* We're supposed to hate narration in dramatic films, viewing it as admission of narrative meltdown. But some films have it, so you've got to record it.
- *Background voices.* Imagine a scene at an oh-so-fashionable, crowded cocktail party. In the middle of the shot are our protagonists engaged in conversation, while in the background is a horde of pâté eaters, all chatting away. Occasionally walking across the foreground are other **principal** actors. During the shoot, no one made a sound save our protagonists. From the extras in the background to those crossing the screen in the foreground, everyone's superfluous conversations were mimed. (This isn't necessarily true of the nonextras. The director may choose to wire every principal actor in the scene with radio microphones, record on multitrack, and decide later how to blend the scene.[1]) In postsync you'll record any principal actors who are to be heard—whether visible as walk-bys or as added off-camera tidbits. Background action will be added as group loop.

Group Loop (Loop Group, Walla Group)

Films are full of human sounds that don't come from the principal actors: the crowd in the bar; commuters on the train or in the station; the vendor in the background selling ice cream to kids; a riotous mob. What they have in common is that they come from actors brought in during audio postproduction to add life, depth, and the occasional story detail to the soundtrack. More later on **spotting** and recording group loop.

Looping, ADR, and Postsync

Like many people, I tend to use "ADR" and "looping" interchangeably, all the while knowing that they aren't exactly the same thing. You can call it what you like as long as everyone understands what you mean. Still, it's worth knowing the differences between them.

---

[1] For an outstanding example of control over many simultaneous conversations, see Robert Altman's *Gosford Park*. Watch any of the "upstairs" scenes and you'll witness delightful control over multiple radio mics.

Looping

Long before digital audio workstations (*DAWs* throughout this book), before projectors and mag film recorders and players could move in reverse, much less "rock and roll" to repeatedly play a line, sound editors rerecorded dialogue lines by creating physical loops of film—reference dialogue (and usually picture)—of each sentence to be replaced. A film loop was prepared with beeps and visual clues to cue the actor, and because it was a loop, it could repeat continuously.

The actor would repeatedly hear a line, and then, when he was ready, recording commenced. Each time the actor heard his line, he would immediately repeat the text, in a process that continued over and over until everyone was happy. Then up went the next loop, and so on. This system was great for rhythm, since most people can manage to accurately repeat the *music* of a phrase while holding onto its spirit. You couldn't, however, conveniently check the sync of a loop during the looping session.

Enter ADR

As technology made it possible to better control mag dubbers and projectors and to preprogram the complex array of electronic commands involved in rerecording, it was all but inevitable that automatic looping would come along. Meet ADR, *automated* (or *automatic*) *dialogue replacement*, which introduced a new way of working:

- The actor listens to her lines leading up to the line to be rerecorded while watching her sync picture on a screen.
- She hears three beeps as her cue approaches. There's likely a line, or **streamer**, wiping across the screen from left to right.
- On what would have been the fourth beep, the streamer reaches the right side of the screen and the actress sees her sync picture but no longer hears the guide track.
- A cue light glows, indicating that it's time to record.
- The actor speaks her lines—hopefully in sync.
- The monitor controller switchs to playback and the actress hears the continuation of the guide track.

The process can repeat endlessly (and very quickly if the picture is on hard disk).

With gifted actors skilled in the process, ADR is a real time saver. All cue information can be programmed offline and sent to the recording studio by e-mail, and the "live" nature of ADR recording gives director, ADR supervisor, and supervising sound editor an instant indication of whether or not the recorded line is acceptable. The ADR engineer can immediately combine selected pieces of chosen takes, giving everyone immediate feedback as to what works and what doesn't.

Slick as it is, ADR isn't for everyone, nor is it for all occasions. Many actors don't like the pressure of having to perform live, in sync, all the while focusing on a good, matching performance. For them, it's best to use a modified looping technique, which I'll describe later.

Postsync

Another term you'll hear bandied about on recording stages is *postsync*. Popular mostly in the United Kingdom and its former possessions, I like this term as a general description of the whole after-the-shoot voice-recording process. If "ADR" seems too sterile but you're too much a stickler for accuracy to use "looping" incorrectly, "postsync" may be just the description you've been looking for.

The ADR Supervisor

Postsync (or looping or ADR) demands organization. Someone has to compile the postsync requests from the director, picture editor, and dialogue editor and find the problems no one else noticed. Careful planning is necessary to prepare for the recording sessions. Each line of dialogue is checked against the guide track and precisely spotted for placement. Copies of the spotting go to the recording studio for machine programming and to the production office for talent scheduling.

During the recording session, there has to be a "voice of reason" who soothes impatient actors while keeping in mind the needs of the film. And the hundreds, easily thousands, of takes generated during the postsync sessions have to be managed in a way that tells the ADR editor what to do with the fruits of all this work. It's no wonder that there's a unique job description for the person responsible for managing the ADR on a film: the ADR supervisor.

Any decent-size film will have an ADR supervisor. It's too big a job for just another crewmember. If the film you're working on has one, you can skip the rest of this section. However, many micro-budget films don't have an ADR supervisor, nor do they have an ADR editor. Responsibility for ADR is divided between the supervising sound editor and the dialogue editor. If that's your situation, read on.

Preparing for ADR

One thing that all low-budget films have in common is, well, low budgets. There's no money to waste, and everyone wants the precious funds to go into the film, or at least into the right pockets. If you're responsible for supervising ADR, remember—before, during, or after the recording sessions—that poorly organized ADR is a good way to hemorrhage money and fry nerves.

When to Record

Momentarily forgetting the film's scheduling realities (actors' schedules, recording studio availability, temp dub requirements, impatient producers), the ideal time to record ADR is near the end of the dialogue editing process. Decisions about postsync start when you spot the film with the director and picture editor, and they continue as you carefully go through the film looking for technical ADR calls. However, unless you're gifted or psychic, you won't be sure about the ADR call list until you've had a go at the dialogue. Lines you were sure you had to loop will be easily fixed with alternate takes, while many an unforeseen problem will rear its head and require looping. The later in the process the recordings are scheduled, the more accurate your list will be. Too late, however, and you squander your margin of safety.

If I have a 6-week dialogue editing schedule, I try to plan ADR recording for the end of week 4. This way I'll have three weeks of real editing to learn the tracks and a few days to prepare the paperwork. Recording ADR for, say, three days leaves ample time to edit the loops and prepare tracks for the new lines and still have time for a couple more dialogue passes.

This isn't an ideal schedule because it steals more than a week from dialogue editing. But remember, this is about saving money, and somebody has to pay. In this case it's me. Of course, the more help that's available, the less you'll be distracted from editing. A good assistant can prepare ADR call sheets and recording logs, so you'll be in less of a panic. If the supervising sound editor can cover the recording sessions, you'll have more time for editing.

But ADR scheduling is rarely about your needs alone. Actors are often not available when you want them, so special recording sessions are necessary. The film is being submitted to an important festival and certain loops have to be recorded very early in the editing process. Or maybe studio or focus group screenings mandate decent loops early on. You just have to be flexible and not resent the lost editing time.

Initial Spotting

You'll get an idea of the ADR load at the initial spotting session with the supervising sound editor, effects editors, director, picture editor, and perhaps others depending on the structure of the film team. During this meeting everyone will note problems that may require looping based on his or her agenda and needs. The director will likely provide a list of adds or changes intended to fix story problems or nurse ailing performances. The same goes for the picture editor, except that her comments may include more technical calls given her familiarity with the tracks. The dialogue editor (you) and the supervising sound editor will call attention to recording problems, overlaps, and other nasties that compromise the sound.

Take notes of the ADR requests, who made them, and why. Later you'll be glad to know why a line was called, since this will help you prioritize your problem solving.

The first meeting isn't a detailed ADR spotting session but rather a first coming-together during which the filmmaker hands off the responsibility for the film's sound to the sound department. There's much on the table besides ADR and dialogue, so the most that you and the supervising sound editor can hope for as far as ADR is concerned is to get an idea of the scope of the postsync needs and to communicate this (good or bad) news to the director and producer. You'll also learn the director's enthusiasm or reluctance regarding ADR recording, which will give you an idea of what has to be saved "at all costs" from production sounds and tell you how aggressively you should spot the ADR. Finally, you and the supervising sound editor should learn the availability of all of the principal actors during the entire sound postproduction process. This information will be vital as you plan the ADR recording.

After this first meeting, compile a list of everyone's comments. Unless you have an actor who'll soon disappear and has to be looped before everyone else, you needn't immediately concern yourself with the ADR spotting. Get on with your dialogue editing, but keep the preliminary list of ADR calls handy.

While editing the dialogue, you'll encounter problems that no one noticed during the spotting session. Most of them you'll be able to fix with bits of alternate takes or clever use of room tone, but there'll be some you can't sort out. Add these new problems to the ADR call list and move on. When you come to a production line that was called for ADR, study it, keeping in mind why it was flagged. Go back to alternate takes and see if there's anything you can do to save it. If you can rescue the line—solving the problems that brought attention to it in the first place—while respecting the spirit of the performance and delivering good sound, you may be able to remove it from the ADR call list. But not yet.

Detailed Spotting

Several days before the scheduled ADR recording, you'll need to properly spot the film and begin creating the paperwork. "Several days before" is purposefully vague. If your total dialogue/ADR turnaround time is five weeks, you can't be expected to start working on the ADR calls until the beginning of week 3 and then to provide the production with a meaningful list by week's end. This necessitates recording ADR at the end of week 4, leaving you a precious few days before the mix to cut in the lines. Such a schedule doesn't give the production a lot of time to finalize its talent scheduling, but you're not exactly handed a picnic either.

If, on the other hand, you have an 8-week schedule, you should be able to provide a decent ADR list by the end of week 4. This gives the production ample time for scheduling and will hopefully result in a bit more time for ADR editing after the recordings. Remember, you can always modify the ADR call lists you sent to the production. They only want to know approximately how many lines each actor has to record so that they can plan the recording days and schedule the talent.

By now you have a handle on your major dialogue problems. You know what will and probably won't work. On your ADR notes you've marked what you've been able to fix as well as the problematic lines you've discovered since the initial screening. Now you need to screen the film with the supervising sound editor, going over each line and confirming what's in and what's out. Show her the called lines you were able to resurrect and then decide together which ones still have to be looped. Add to the list any "add" lines you feel would be instrumental in bridging a dialogue transition or clarifying or focusing a scene. When this ADR spotting session is finished, you'll have all of the information you need to create the ADR paperwork.

ADR for TV Productions

Find out if there'll be a special mix for tamed-down language. A TV version often requires special loops, not needed in the full mix, to replace potentially offensive exclamations, blasphemies, and steamy pillow talk. You, the supervising sound editor, and perhaps the director will become skilled at creating nonsense nonprofanities that match the mood of the scene and the sync of the shot. These special lines are recorded at the same time as the full-mix ADR, and their code names carry the suffix "TV."

Organizing ADR Paperwork

There's a lot to ADR: microphone selection and placement, room acoustics, dealing with actors, and knowing when you have the best take. Fortunately, the technical issues are rarely your concern—that's what the ADR recording engineer is for. But you're still left with the huge responsibility of managing the vast amount of information generated by the ADR process. An ADR recording session is a very busy, reasonably expensive event. In the studio or control room are the talent (who easily may prefer not to be there), the director (who's probably agitated for one reason or another), perhaps the supervising sound editor, at least one engineer, and of course you, on whose shoulders all of this rests.

Getting through an ADR session without blowing it or "blowing a fuse" requires outstanding organization. By carefully spotting the ADR cues and organizing the data in a way that's comfortable for the production company, the engineers, and the talent, you'll streamline the session. When you clearly have your act together, the talent will be more relaxed and you'll have greater power. Being able to control a session is vital because you—more than anyone—know what you need to complete the dialogue. If you've earned the respect of the actors and the engineer, you'll be able to fight for those extra takes or those few minutes beyond quitting time.

Remain aware of everyone's reactions to each take so that you can later decide just how hard to work to get the line right. Never forget that by the end of ADR recording you'll have accumulated thousands of takes. Remember, too, that you'll have very little time to edit the ADR into your dialogue. Except in extraordinary cases you have to decide in-session which is the best take (or the takes you'll combine to create a good performance). That's why great note taking is critical.

Paperwork Overview

Here's a summary of the paperwork you'll need to prepare, both before and during the ADR session. Later we'll look at each form in more detail, so don't worry about the nitty-gritty yet.

- *Before the recording session.* Compile the ADR calls, breaking down each long line into manageable lengths and precisely noting its start and stop times. From this you create a master **ADR cue sheet** (sometimes

ADR call list)—a list of all ADR lines in film order. Each line carries a unique ID number, which may include the character name. Count the lines each actor needs to record and inform the production company. Based on an average pace of about ten lines per session hour, the production secretary will use this information to schedule the talent. The call list, the Bible of ADR calls, is what you'll use to create printouts of each actor's lines—simplified, easy-to-read scripts the actors will use during the recording session. Also from the master ADR cue sheet you'll make the **ADR recording logs**, which you'll use during the recording session to keep track of what's going on.

- *During the session.* The code names and numbers you assigned to each line will become the names of the corresponding soundfiles created in the recording session. During the session, use the ADR recording logs (or "session reports") to take notes about each line and each take. Note which takes are acceptable and which take is the preferred "buy" (or "print" or "go" or even "hero").
- *Back in the editing room.* Use the ADR recording logs to figure out what to do with each line. This way you won't need to listen to all of a cue's takes unless the ones you selected don't pan out. Place a check mark on each ADR recording log as you successfully edit the line into your film so you know what has—and hasn't—been edited.

The ADR Cue Sheet

The ADR cue sheet (ADR call sheet) is the master document, containing all of the ADR lines in the film in chronological (film) order. (See Figure 15-1.) As with all film industry forms, the details of the paperwork vary by region and film culture. If at all possible, adapt your paperwork to the style of your local film industry so that people are comfortable with the forms and you don't come across as a hick or a pedantic jerk.

Because absolutely every phase of the ADR process can be automated by computer, in this day and age it's pretty silly to type, and retype, all iterations of the ADR sheets. You can do most management using Excel. I prefer File-Maker Pro,[2] but there are also plenty of good comprehensive ADR management programs available.

The ADR Cue Sheet in Detail As you can see in Figure 15-1, the information at the top of the cue sheet is pretty obvious. One item, though, will hunt you

---

[2] FileMaker Pro is a trademark of FileMaker, Inc.

ADR Call Sheet

Client: Nessie Prods	ADR Supervisor: Sancho Panza		Date: 15/03/2005
Title: "Lost in Jordan"	Reel: 3	Version: 2B (11/03)	Page: 2 of 9

CODE	CHARACTER	A/R Call	START STOP	TEXT
REB 309	Rebecca	R AG	3:04:36:02 3:04:40:05	It's cold. Aren't you cold?
BEA 310	Beatrice	A AC	3:04:37:16 3:04:42:23	This was the brilliant idea of Alfred.
REB 311	Rebecca	R AC	3:04:41:00 3:04:44:18	You'd think for someone who lives in Jordan you'd be freezing
BEA 312	Beatrice	R JP	3:04:44:23 3:04:47:17	To find work when he was unemployed
BEA 313	Beatrice	R AC	3:04:52:00 3:04:53:02	You're not?!
REB 314	Rebecca	A JP	3:05:37:22 3:05:39:11	What did he decide?
REB 315	Rebecca	R JP	3:05:44:04 3::05:45:01	Mmm. (polite reaction)
			: : : :	
			: : : :	
			: : : :	
			: : : :	

Figure 15-1 Excerpt from one page of a typical ADR cue sheet.

down and make you cry if you ignore it. This is "Version," which refers to the picture version you used to spot the ADR. It's perfectly normal for the picture department to keep making "improvements" long after picture lock and even after you spot the ADR. If you don't know which picture version your spotting refers to, you won't know which tape to take to the ADR session. If the recording studio preprograms the ADR cues—beeps, streamers, monitor cues, and the like—based on your detailed instructions and then you show up with the wrong tape, who looks stupid?

In the main section of the call sheet, each line represents an ADR line.

- *Code.* Each line of ADR bears a unique code that follows the cue from spotting to mixing. The first digit of the code reflects the reel number and the subsequent two or three digits are the serial ID. I like to prefix the number code with a three-letter abbreviation of the character's name, so Rebecca becomes REB and Hanna becomes HAN. This helps me keep the lines straight while I edit, and since the code numbers will appear on the computer-generated rerecording cue sheets, it makes life easier in the dialogue premix. It also makes for easier sorting by character. ADR lines recorded specifically for a TV mix should carry the suffix "TV," so the TV version of Hanna's line, "HAN 304," becomes "HAN 304-TV."

- *Character.* If you use name abbreviations in the code, you don't need a separate column for the character name, but including it in the master makes the list more human friendly. Some film cultures insist on it.

- *A/R (Add/Replace).* This tells you if the line will replace an existing production line or just "sit on top" of the dialogue. Original lines being replaced with ADR require special preparation.

- *Call.* Whether recording or editing ADR, I like to know who requested that a line be recorded. You may have to drop certain lines if there's just not enough time, so it's useful to know if a line was requested by the director or the dolly grip.

- *Start.* This is the line's *exact* start time: If that's an audible breath, Start falls there. (If during the recording session you find the actor is having a tough time getting the timing right with cues that start with breaths, drop them; record some wild breaths and begin each take with text.)

- *Stop.* This is the end time of the cue, plus about half a second for ringout or a late delivery.

- *Text.* This is pretty obvious. Less obvious is how long a line should be. If the loop line is one short sentence, that's a natural duration. But what about longer text, say a whole paragraph? Remember what you're doing. The actor needs to memorize the line and its rhythm, so the spotted lines shouldn't be unduly long. However, overcutting results in an unnatural recording process and can be very time consuming. Plus, you lose the text's flow if it's been recorded in very tiny bits. There are a few rules of thumb to remember when dividing text for ADR:

– *Break at the end of a sentence.*
– *Break lines at breaths.* Unless an actor is a pearl diver, a breath pause is a pretty natural place for a break.
– *Break at an inflection.* Most sentences are composed of clauses offset by changes in inflection. Read the sentence aloud and you'll usually know where to break it.

- If a line isn't sync but rather off-camera, behind the back, or in another such hidden place, you can usually spot a longer ADR replacement. Most actors prefer to record complete sentences if there's no concern about lip sync. Plus, you'll likely save time in the session.

The Actor's Script

Each actor will need a list of his lines in film order. Of course, you could merely provide a sorted copy of the ADR call sheets, but these aren't the easiest things to read, especially in a darkened recording studio. It's better to provide a stripped-down version of the ADR calls, with a minimum of clutter. (See Figure 15-2.)

ADR Recording Report

You have to take notes and keep track of your takes during the ADR recording sessions. Period. If you don't, you'll face a Herculean ADR editing task. And, since there's no time in the session to prepare for efficient note taking, you have to enter the studio ready to write. That's where your prepared ADR recording reports come into play.

Here you'll mark all acceptable takes (the ones at least worth considering when editing) with "Hold," and for the best take or takes, you'll check "Buy" (or whatever term your local film culture uses to indicate *the* take). In the comment region for each take you can indicate things like "good ending" or "middle section OK" or "director likes this, I don't." At the bottom of the page is a section for notes to the editor (even if it's you), where you can explain complicated combinations such as "Use first three words from TK 7; middle section from TK 1; end with TK 2." (See Figure 15-3.)

ADR actor's lines

"Lost in Jordan"

Character name: Rebecca

Actor: Amalia Sedley

Record date: 03/04/2005

page 1

Code	start TC	Text
REB 2•01	02:00:17:12	Yep.
REB 2•07	02:02:15:00	It was terrible watching the television float away.
REB 2•08	02:02:18:23	And she slowly began to walk as the TV screen dimmed. (breath).
REB 2•09	02:02:23:09	Walking and walking and walking and. . .
REB 2•10	02:02:30:04	And then (sigh) no more TV.
REB 2•11	02:02:37:16	It was sad.
REB 2•13	02:04:13:19	Oh, here's the turn off.
REB 2•14	02:05:10:17	How come you speak Armenian?
REB 2•15	02:06:48:08	You'll be fine.
REB 2•16	02:06:59:23	That's what you said. I didn't say that.
REB 2•17	02:07:10:13	(sigh/exhale) You'll be fine. You'll be fine.

Figure 15-2 An actor's ADR lines for a recording session. Only the line code number, start timecode (or footage), and text are shown.

ADR recording log

Company: Nessie Productions   **Video version:** Ver 1-ADR

Production: "Lost in Jordan"   **Version date:** 21/03/2005

Loop Code
REB 2•11

Sample Rate: 48 kHz   **File Format:** BWF   **Record date:** 03/04/2005

Start TC: 02:02:37:16   **Location:** INT car drive

End TC: 02:02:38:22   **Mic used:** 416

Duration: 00:00:01:06   **Frames:** 31   **Actor:** Amalia Sedley

Text   It was sad.

sync

Take	Comment	Hold	Buy
☐		☐	☐
☐		☐	☐
☐		☐	☐
☐		☐	☐
☐		☐	☐
☐		☐	☐
☐		☐	☐
☐		☐	☐
☐		☐	☐
☐		☐	☐
☐		☐	☐
☐		☐	☐
☐		☐	☐
☐		☐	☐
☐		☐	☐

write additional takes on back

Editing notes

Figure 15-3 Sample ADR recording log. Use one sheet for each ADR line.

Automating ADR Paperwork

If you don't have a typing maven for an assistant, it's not hard to see the advantages of computerizing your paperwork. Find out what commercial ADR management programs are used in your film community. Failing that, Use Excel or create a custom database, with FileMaker or another database program, that will spit out all the forms you need.[3]

The ADR Data-Entry Page Figure 15-4 shows the data-entry page I use to program ADR. After compiling an ADR wish list with the supervising sound editor and director, I fill in pertinent information about each line. Then I can report what's there in any number of ways to provide lists for the engineer, the actors, and the production company. I also use this information to create the ADR recording logs. Much of what's on the form is automatically entered, so data entry isn't as overwhelming as it appears.

Other important information you'll want to keep track of:

- *Sync.* I like to know if a shot is sync or not. Even before seeing the picture during the recording session I can start planning whether to record the shot wild or to picture. Knowing the balance between sync and wild shots for a recording session can aid in scheduling, since the off-camera lines inevitably take less time.

- *Location.* If the ADR recording engineer knows in advance the locations he'll be matching into, the session is more efficient. Many ADR studios have wet (reverberation possible) and dry (no reverberation possible) areas to match interior or exterior locations, so the engineer may want you to sort the list by location to make for a slicker session.

- *Microphone.* The ADR engineer likes to know what microphone was used during the shoot to be able to better match the texture of the production dialogue. You can usually find this information in the sound reports. If not, ask the production mixer.

Whether by hand or on the computer, you'll need to produce one set of ADR call lists sorted in film order and another sorted first by actor and then by film order. (See Figure 15-5.)

---

[3] To perform timecode calculations in FileMaker Pro, you'll need the "Timecode for FileMaker" plug-in. This shareware product is available from Belle Nuit Montage (*www. belle-nuit.com*).

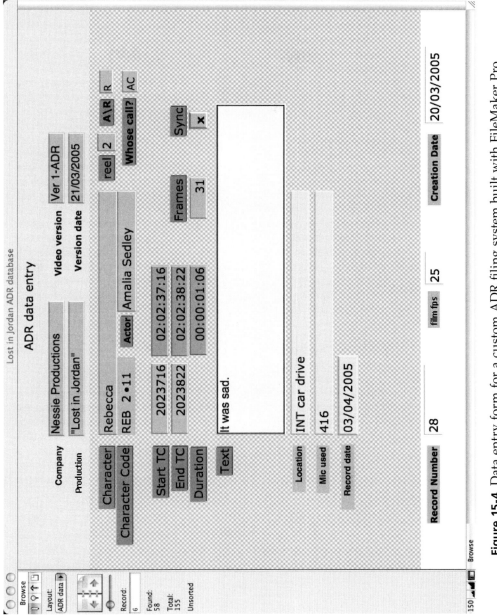

Figure 15-4 Data entry form for a custom ADR filing system built with FileMaker Pro.

ADR call sheets
"Lost in Jordan"

Code	in	out	Text
REB 3 •21 Ver 2 AC sync	03:09:18:01 00:00:02:13	03:09:20:14 INT car driving.	You're in the used TV business?
REB 3 •22 Ver 2 AC sync	03:09:36:23 00:00:03:16	03:09:40:14 INT car driving.	I was hoping for something a little bit more romantic.
REB 3 •23 Ver 2 AC sync	03:09:42:21 00:00:07:19	03:09:50:15 INT car driving.	Maybe a trip to Las Vegas.
BEA 3 •082 Ver 2 AC	03:11:11:14 00:00:01:15	03:11:13:04 INT car driving.	Thirty thousand dollars.
BEA 3 •083 Ver 2 AC	03:11:27:13 00:00:03:00	03:11:30:13 INT car driving.	Take a left at the next corner.
BEA 3 •084 Ver 2 AC	03:11:36:19 00:00:02:08	03:11:39:02 INT car driving.	(sigh, exhale)

Figure 15-5 An excerpt from an ADR call sheet generated by FileMaker Pro. Note the additional information provided: version, whose call, duration, and scene description.

The ADR Recording Session

ADR sessions were once pretty standardized. You might loop in one studio and record ADR-style in another, but the technology was predictably similar. Today, the workflow in most serious ADR studios is fairly interchangeable but the tools used can differ wildly.

Studio Technology

At the top of the ADR studio food chain, you'll find dedicated controllers such as Taker and SoundMaster that control the streamers, beeps, and monitors as well as the record and safety functions. You'll also find automatic voice slates that slug scene and take numbers into each soundfile, and picture being played on one of many types of nonlinear video recorder/player. Very few studios still use tape or mag as their primary recording format, so the recorder can be anything from Fairlight to Pyramix to Pro Tools.

At the other end of the ladder you'll find systems built entirely around Pro Tools, in which beeps are prerecorded soundfiles the ADR engineer places in the session prior to recording. Likewise, monitor switching is managed through clever editorial preparation of the guide track. The picture may be on tape or hard disk.

More and more software-only systems are on the market. Most of them will manage your ADR from spotting to printing and all the way to recording and conformations. One, ADR Studio from Gallery Software, sits on the same computer that houses Pro Tools and provides many of the ADR management tools available in external hardware devices.

Working with the Studio Thankfully, you needn't be overly concerned with the ADR technology that a particular studio boasts. If the studio has a decent reputation for getting the job done and the ADR recording engineer has the experience and talent to capture a good sound match, it's not that important that the equipment is the most modern. People have been successfully recording postsync for a long time. Besides, a dialogue editor doubling as an ADR supervisor usually has little say in the matter of studio selection.

As with the mix, the key to a successful recording session is communication with the ADR studio and particularly with the engineer. Find out how best to organize the cues. For example, do they want you to separate interior from exterior recordings? How much time do they need to program the ADR information? In what format do they like to receive notes? Can you send them by e-mail or do they have an FTP site? What about picture format? If the picture needs to be digitized for nonlinear playback, the studio will need time to load it.

Specify the audio file format you want to leave with (BWF, SDII, AIFF, etc.) and tell the studio manager if you need to take the material with you on the day of the session. Bottom line: Communicate with the studio, whether the engineer or the client services liaison.

Learn a bit about the actors you're going to loop. Any weird habits? Do you have to provide Pop Tarts? Does he drink only Italian bottled water? Does she insist that you not be in the studio with her but rather in the control room? Let's not go nuts, but it's good to know whom you're dealing with.

At the Session: The Talent, the Recording Engineer, and the Director

Get to the session early in order to spot-check the programming of the ADR cues and go over the sound issues with the ADR engineer. When the talent arrives, keep your cool. If you're dealing with a "star," be neither star-struck nor unaware of the imbalance of power. Introduce yourself. Explain what you'll be covering. Find out how the actor likes to work. Sitting? Standing? Does she prefer to work ADR-style or looping-style (or, better yet, a combination of the two depending on the line)? Don't waste too much time "making everything comfortable."

The best way to size each other up is to get to work. After a few lines you'll begin to understand how to get the most out of the actor. Listen more than talk, but don't be afraid to speak your mind. You're the one who'll have to make all of this material work. Remember the goal and keep at it until you're happy.

Don't assume that the actor and the ADR engineer have your interests at heart. Yes, they have a job to do and most likely want to do it well, but everyone is looking to you to know when it's good enough.

When you begin an ADR cue, find the corresponding ADR recording log, which will already include text, timecode, and other recording information. Use it to note your impressions of each take. Also note the director's reaction to each take if she's involved in the session.

Working with the Talent If an actor has particular difficulties on a certain line, don't beat it to death. Move on. When you finish the other required lines, go back to the problematic ones and try again. Odds are he'll do a better job this time, when there's less pressure. If you're not completely happy with a performance, flag it on the ADR recording log. When you've finished the mandatory lines, go back and try again, this time recording it using looping style on the reprise if you were using ADR the first time around. The results might be interesting.

Be gentle with actors. Never forget that acting ADR lines is horrifically hard stuff. Try it sometime. It's not easy to walk into a role months after the shoot, and many actors don't react well to seeing their scenes for the first time—they don't like the way they look or they hate the editing—and you may have to absorb some of their disappointment. Be patient and don't buy into the actor's frustration or anger. Your job it to get the line, more or less at all costs, and getting flustered rarely helps. Be kind and polite, but don't let the talent get the better of you. You're in charge.

It's not unusual for an actor to try to talk you out of certain loops. Remember, for her ADR may be as much fun as dental surgery. She'll try to convince you that the underlying noise problem isn't really so bad (tell her that she can't hear the noise on headphones) or that the line requested by the director is stupid (use all of your charm to get her to record it anyway) or that she has no problem understanding the corrupted line (say that she's a gifted listener but that the Average Joe isn't). Lie, cheat, flatter. Don't be coerced out of a line that you need.

If you're responsible for directing the actor, remember that you're not directing a movie; you're mechanically replacing lines. It's about listening to the guide track—really listening—and getting the actor to mimic it. Rarely do you need to provide method acting instructions, although at times it does the trick. Give the actor specific, detailed instructions, usually referring to the guide track. Very often an actor can't hear the nuances of the original performance as well as you can, so you'll occasionally have to remind him to listen again. Point out the details of the original performance he's missing.

Working with the Recording Engineer ADR recording engineers can require a bit of work, too. Of course, they take it seriously and, yes, they're pros. But it's not their film, so they can't be as enthusiastic as you are. Don't be afraid to coax them along. When you question a microphone position or the exactness of a sound match, don't give up if the answer is "Oh yeah, it's fine." The engineer is likely to know more about recording ADR than you do, but it's your dialogue.

Never be impolite or behave inappropriately, but if something is telling you that it's still not right, *listen*. Trust your gut, even in the face of a more experienced engineer. He may prove that everything really *is* all right, but don't give up too quickly. Tomorrow, he'll have another film to work on while you'll be back in the cutting room, kicking yourself for having accepted a microphone position that you knew was inappropriate.

Working with the Director If you're recording a loop line because the director wants a different reading, it's best for him to be around. If not, make sure you have a very good understanding of what's wrong with the original dialogue and what he wants in its place.

Recording Takes

When you start a new scene, test how well the new ADR fits into the production dialogue. Record the first line. Once you have a good take, tell the actor to relax for a few minutes. Ask the ADR recording engineer to sync the buy take and fill the hole in the production track with room tone from the guide track. Now play the dialogue section against the picture. Listen to the way the ADR "sits" in the dialogue. If necessary, ask the engineer to equalize the line or add reverb to improve the match. Decide whether this recording setup will work or whether you need to move the microphone, change the acoustics in the room, move the talent, or change the mics.

This is a good time to ask the engineer's opinion. Even though you're in a hurry, spend these few moments to obtain as good a match as possible. If you can't get an almost perfect match between dialogue and ADR in the recording session, you'll never achieve a perfect match in the mix.

Pay special attention to the cadence, the "music," of a line. It's very common for everyone in the studio—actor, director, engineer, and editor—to be convinced that the actor is "nailing" the line when in fact he's misinterpreting its cadence. If the original line is "How now, BROWN cow" but the actor is consistently reading "How NOW brown cow," the mistake can easily go unnoticed until you're editing the ADR line, but by then it's too late.

Recall the listening skills you had to force on yourself when watching the Avid cut of the film for the first time, how you had to occasionally tear yourself from the narrative so that you could assess the sound. Use that same discipline to listen to the music of the line being read. If all else fails, try a trick you used while editing alternate takes—making up nonsense phrases to describe the cadence and essence of the line to the actor. The lack of content reduces the line to pure rhythm and tone, and the silliness adds a bit of levity, which can help you get your point across.

When you finish recording all the lines, review your notes. If you're unsure about a line or two—and you still have time—ask the actor to try those lines again. Ask her if there are any lines she'd like to review. Now that the heat's off, you may get surprising results. When you return to a line, be sure to note the new takes on the appropriate ADR recording log.

ADR File Names

Each studio has its own method of managing ADR recording sessions and naming soundfiles. At the top of the heap are sophisticated ADR management programs like ADR Studio that automatically assign line/take names to recorded cues. Other software/hardware options afford complete control over the ADR spotting and recording processes. Regardless the method, the code names with which you christened each line on the ADR cue sheets will become the names of the soundfiles created during the ADR session. Usually, the code number becomes the "root" name of the new file, and the take numbers are added automatically.

If your studio is on the budget end of the spectrum, you can assign soundfile names by temporarily renaming the record track with the root name of the line, leaving it to the DAW to create take numbers (see Figure 15-6). Run a few tests to make sure that your names won't be obliterated or changed when you create new regions from the recorded soundfile.

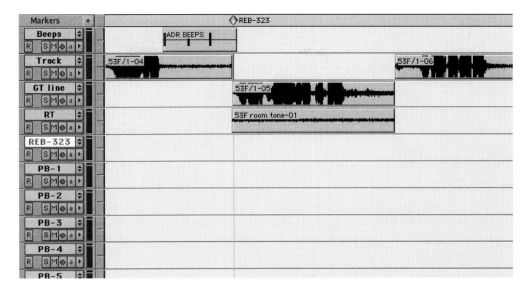

Figure 15-6 A typical Pro Tools recording setup. Notice that the tracks have been renamed for ADR recording. The record track carries the cue name, automatically identifying each take with name and take number. Production playback is on two tracks: "GT line" is for the production tracks that have to be replaced; "Track" is for the pre- and postroll of the line. Below the removed GT region is room tone (RT), which is used to replace the removed dialogue when testing recorded ADR lines. On the top track is a beep sequence to cue the talent.

Rich or poor, remember that it's imperative that the the soundfile names reflect the original ADR call names, and that the scrupulous notes you took during the session reflect the realities of the recordings. It's worth the investment to ensure that the names and take numbers on your well-planned paperwork relate to something real.

Soundfile Backup

Finally, back up all of the ADR files when you get back to your cutting room, or have the studio do it. Even with a large number of files it's no longer the gargantuan task it once was. It's absolutely certain that all of your ADR session recordings will fit on one DVD-R.

Preparing Dialogue Tracks for ADR

Dialogue has room tone. ADR doesn't. When you remove the original (to be replaced) line from the dialogue track, you have to fill the resulting hole with something, typically room tone and motion. Say the shot you're replacing consists of one person sitting quietly in a chair or standing still. Since there's no movement, there's no need to fill the space with motion from alternate takes (footsteps, clothing rustle, loose coins rattling in a pocket, etc.). Just add a bit of clean room tone and you'll be fine.

However, if the shot that was replaced included body motion, talk to your supervising sound editor about whether it will be replaced with Foley or whether you should try to fill it from alternate takes. In general, replacing the missing action with dialogue elements will give you a better fill.

Because a successful dialogue premix depends on flexibility and your ability to move quickly back and forth between the original line and the ADR replacement, you can't simply fill the hole in the dialogue track with room tone (see Figure 15-7). Such a layout affords no flexibility. Instead, you have to construct the tracks so that original dialogue, tone fill, ADR, and X are on their own tracks and you can calmly switch between them during the premix. (See Figure 15-8.)

In Figure 15-7, notice that all material removed from the dialogue tracks is placed on the **X tracks** (X, Y, and Z), which are used exclusively for material

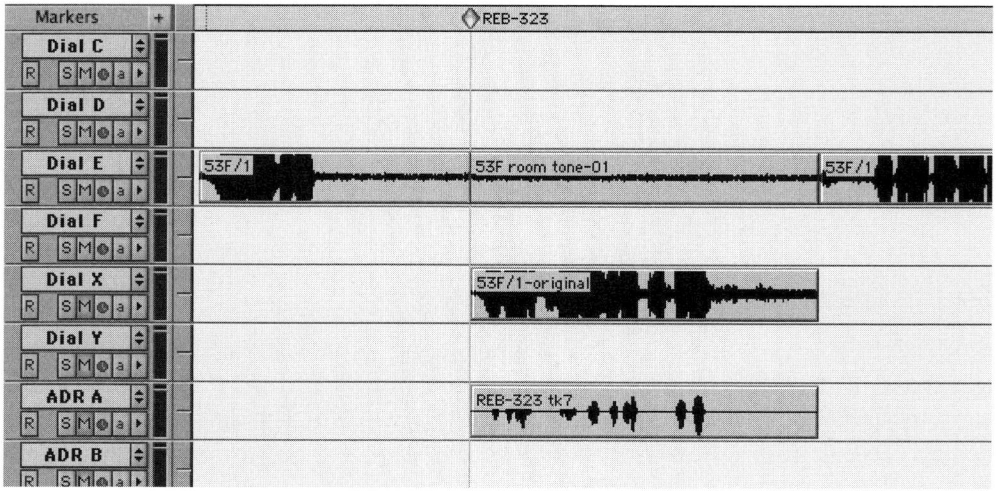

Figure 15-7 Incorrect same-track tone fill. The hole caused by moving the original line to an X track was filled with room tone on the same track. This provides no flexibility and will ultimately cause problems.

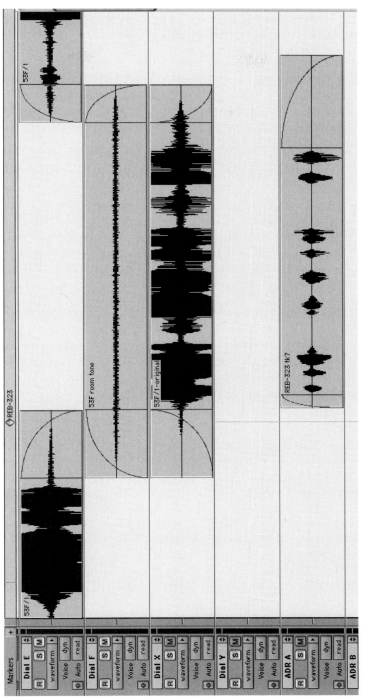

Figure 15-8 Room tone isn't on the same track as the hole it's filling. Notice that the fades between the original dialogue and the X tracks are –6dB "Equal Gain" since these edits are in essence perspective cuts. The room tone edits are standard –3dB "Equal Power" since any fade between the dialogue and the room tone isn't phase coherent.

removed for ADR. Before moving to the next edit, audition this new construction with both playback options:

- Original dialogue → tone fill → original dialogue. Once the ADR is added, this is the "normal" playback for when you want to use the loop line.
- Original dialogue → X track → original dialogue. This option will result in the line in its original form.

It's important that the fades for each option work properly, since you never know which option you'll use in the mix.

ADR Editing

Even on a small film, you can easily end up with thousands of ADR takes. Combine this with the fact that you rarely have enough time to edit, and you begin to appreciate the importance of organized paperwork. There are many ways to import, choose, edit, and manipulate ADR recordings.

Preparing for ADR Editing

Open a reel of your most current dialogue session and perform a Save As with a new name. Beneath the active dialogue tracks (for example, Dial A → Dial M), open four or more new mono tracks—label them "ADR A → D." These will be your final, edited ADR tracks. How many depends on the density of the ADR, the number of characters, and the preferences of the mixer. Below the new ADR tracks add about ten new mono tracks, labeling them "ADR Work 1 → 10."[4] (See Figure 15-9.) These are the tracks onto which you'll initially open your ADR lines—safe places to work without endangering the active tracks. You can delete them when you finish editing the ADR.

Organize your note-filled ADR recording logs in film order. (You had them arranged by character for the recording session.) If specific characters haven't been recorded yet, remove those logs from the pile. Locate your dialogue/ ADR session to the timecode of the first ADR cue. Note which takes were indicated as "Hold" and "Buy." Import these cues into your session.

---

[4] As you saw in Chapter 9, I use a convention in which all tracks to be used in the mix—the "active" tracks—are sequenced with letters (Dial A → M, ADR A → D, etc.), whereas temporary tracks are identified with numbers (junk 1 → 6, work 1 → 4, etc). This makes it easier to identify tracks during editing and allows anyone who knows my system to prepare my session for a mix. This isn't a "standard" system, but it works well for me.

Figure 15-9 A detail of the tracks used in ADR editing. Use the ADR work tracks to open cues, perform "dangerous" edits, and maintain some degree of order.

Choosing Takes

If an ADR line has a clearly indicated buy take, spot the line onto an ADR track or ADR work track. If you spot the region by its timestamp, it will position itself at the timecode at which it was recorded (see Figure 15-10). Unless you're working with a different version of the picture than was used in the recording session, the line will be more or less in sync (remember, the version number is indicated on the ADR recording log). If the picture version has

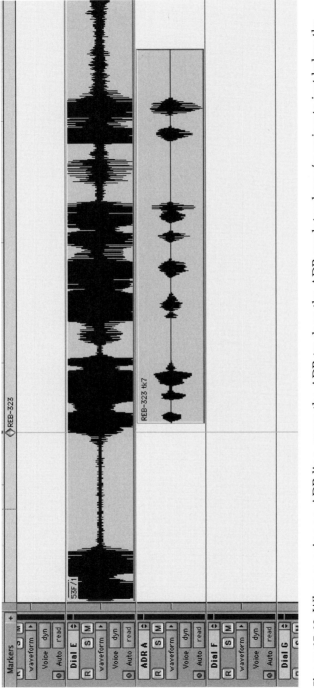

Figure 15-10 When syncing an ADR line, move the ADR track or the ADR work track you're using to just below the reference dialogue track. Notice that track ADR A is temporarily sandwiched between Dials E and F.

changed, drag the ADR region until it's lined up with the original dialogue line, forgoing timecode.

"**Top and tail**" the cue, leaving just the line and a bit of ringout afterward. Move this trimmed region to a track just below the dialogue element you're replacing. You may have to temporarily rearrange your tracks.

Sometimes you can align the beginning of the dialogue cue with its ADR replacement and begin making sense from there. Other times the initial attack isn't sufficiently clear to be used as a reference. In such cases, analyze both waveforms and look for notable landmarks. Plosive consonants such as B and P are usually easy to spot, as are stop consonants such as T and K, because they typically rise above the rest of the waveform, begging to be used as guide posts. Find common landmarks in the dialogue and ADR regions and align the two regions from either head or tail, whichever suits you. If they align well for their entire length, you can move the cue to the desired ADR track, "Get Out of Jail, Collect $200," and consider yourself very lucky. (See Figure 15-11.)

Listen to the reference and the ADR replacement and make sure the meaning, melody, and attitude of the loop match that of the original. Then watch the replacement line for sync. Watch it again. If you're still happy, move on. In the ADR recording log, mark that the line is finished. Prepare the dialogue line to accept the ADR (discussed in the previous section), and remember that you got off easy this time.

Combining Takes

More than likely you won't always be so lucky. Most ADR lines need editing, often necessitating a combination of takes, time expansion/compression, pitch shift, and other tricks. It seems a formidable task to compare numerous outtakes and combine them in a way that honors the spirit of the take that you or the director selected in the recording session. Yet with a standardized plan you can extract the best parts from each take without creating a soulless Frankenstein.

Arrange your tracks so that just beneath the reference dialogue track is the target ADR track (ADR A, B, C, etc.) and below that are your ten or so ADR work tracks. (See Figure 15-12.) Compare the chosen ADR take to the original dialogue. Figure out why it was selected and why it's not working. Is it a sync problem? If so, where does the ADR line fall apart? Does the ADR cue regain sync after the sync-defying irregularity? Find out how much of the chosen ADR take you can use and how much will need to be replaced from alternate takes. This will limit your search.

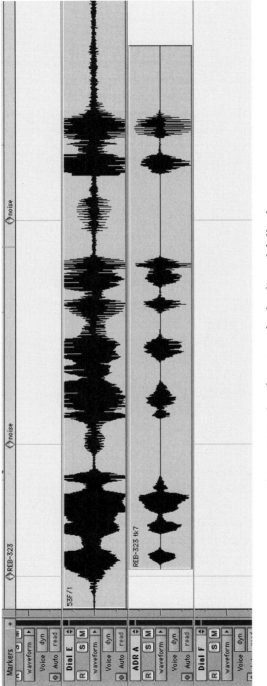

Figure 15-11 An almost perfectly aligned full take.

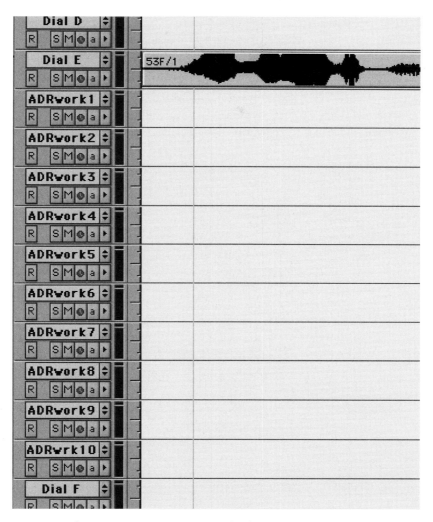

Figure 15-12 It's often easier to compare multiple takes by moving the ADR work tracks directly beneath the dialogue reference track.

If the buy take suffers from more than just a sync problem (maybe a section of bad diction or perhaps a vowel held much too long or not long enough), decide what if anything you can salvage from it and note what you're looking for. You might be looking for a "brown" in which the vowel is held while the pitch rises or perhaps an unusually short "now."

"How$_{now}$, BROO^{OOW}N cow."

Find the qualifying alternate takes. (See Figure 15-13.) Before importing candidates, listen to them and cull the ones that don't have what you're looking for. No point clogging up your session.

Line up all your alternate takes onto the work tracks beneath the reference dialogue line. Listen once to each take just to make sure that your recording session decisions were sound. Maybe, just maybe, one of the alternates will have everything you need. Probably not, but you might as well listen.

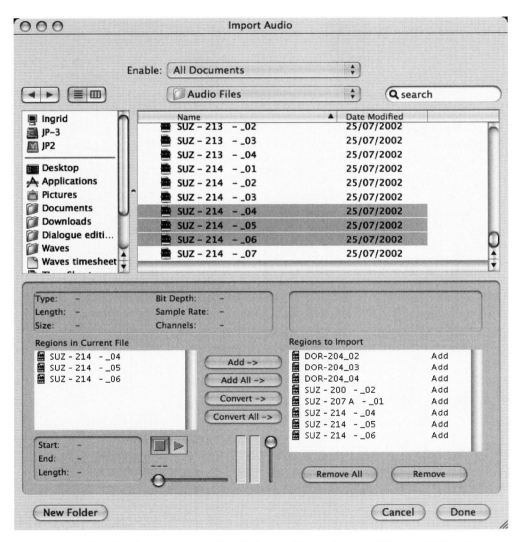

Figure 15-13 Pro Tools Import Audio dialogue. Note that qualifying ADR takes are selected for import into the session.

When you're piecing together a line from alternate takes, it's best to sort out one problem at a time. Otherwise, you'll easily lose focus and fall victim to the fantasy of quick fixes. From the information provided by the waveform, pick the most plausible candidates for the word you want to replace and listen to each. Select the most likely candidate and edit it directly onto the buy take. See how well this works. Next you must find a way to splice the replacement into your line.

Where to Edit

In one way or another, the sounds of every language consist of vowels and consonants. Generally, vowels are created with an open vocal tract and consonants are the result of some sort of constriction in the mouth or throat. Understanding a bit about vowels and consonants can be helpful when you're trying to squeeze takes together to form a replacement sentence or when you need to tighten or loosen a phrase.

For the most part, it's the vowels that give you trouble. They're usually longer than consonants, so they have more opportunities to wreak havoc, and being open they tend to be more tonal, more musical, than their percussive consonant cousins. It can be frustratingly difficult to cut within vowels. In fact, unless you're totally without options, don't try it. You'll likely create a bump since the complex tonal elements of the vowel won't line up properly at your cut. And if you try to smooth the edit with a crossfade, you'll create a double voice. Approach vowels as respected adversaries. Avoid them as best you can and focus instead on consonants.

Most consonants are useful landmarks for lining up alternate takes against a reference. Those like *D*, *P*, and *T* tend to show up quite clearly in a waveform, so they're ideal beacons for navigating through a sentence. The only problem with short consonants is that they're, well, short. The very attribute that makes them useful for alignment lends them little flexibility. You can't really stretch time by making a *T* sound longer. You can, however, play with the space *around* it. Don't be afraid to lose a tiny bit of time before a *T* or buy a little more pause after a *P*. Just don't expect to gain a lot of time.

Editing within Words If the vowels are too dangerous and the short consonants are good as markers but not the least bit flexible, where can you edit within words to change the length of a sentence?

- *Cut in the pauses when possible.* You can make up a lot of ground by pulling a frame here and there from the spaces between words, but there aren't always real pauses in a sentence or it sounds unnatural when you tamper with them. Be careful not to hurt the breaths.

- If a vowel is terminated with a sharp consonant sound, you might be able to *shorten the end of the vowel* using the attacking consonant sound to mask the vowel glitch. Try it; it just might work.
- *Look for a shorter or longer vowel sound from another take.* This isn't the fastest approach, but it may give you just what you need.
- *Use sibilants.* Sibilant sounds are the "hisses" created by consonants such as *Sh*, *Ss*, or *Ch*. They inhabit an enchanted land between vowel and consonant sounds. Like other consonants, sibilants are easy to spot; in fact, their familiar pursed-lip shape is the most obvious of all waveforms. Unlike normal consonants, however, sibilants are long-lasting so there are usually many opportunities to make them longer or shorter. Very tonal vowels are all but impossible to splice, but sibilants are more like white noise than music so you're rarely punished for editing them. In fact, you can do (almost) anything: cut, fade, loop—all within reason, of course. When you're anticipating a difficult ADR editing session, hope for lots of sentences like "Sally sells seashells by the seashore." Of course, as convenient as sibilants are, you'll pay for that convenience in the form of de-essing during the dialogue premix.

Tools for Fitting ADR

Most of the sound shaping for matching ADR into the dialogue (EQ, dynamics, reverb) happens in the dialogue premix, so you needn't bother with that just yet. When you're working with good ADR tracks, your concern is mainly intonation, matching performance, and sync.

Intonation When combining takes, you may find that one is pitched higher or lower than its neighbor. The result is an unconvincing sentence that doesn't make sense, but it's one that can be fixed with pitch shift. Select that part of the phrase whose pitch you want to change. Take a bit more than you need by pulling out the handle and selecting so that you'll have a pitch-shifted handle available for crossfades.

Keep in mind that a little pitch change goes a long way, so experiment with the parameters until you have the intonation you want.[5] On most

---

[5] One reason to be cautious when changing the pitch of a line is that most pitch-shifting processors change the formants along with the pitch. Formants, the peaks in the vowel spectra caused by the various articulators in the throat and mouth, enable recognition of vowel sounds and hence language itself. Pitch variations in a voice can be quite substantial, yet the formants will remain consistent. A small change in formants will make a recording sound like the wrong vowel.

plug-in pitch-shift processors, there's a button called something like Speed Correction. If you want to change the speed and pitch simultaneously so that the processor works like an analogue tape recorder (faster speed with higher pitch or slower speed with lower pitch), deselect this option. Remember, if you don't like the initial results, go back to the original (unprocessed) file. Leave an already processed track alone to avoid accumulating artifacts.

Speed and Length If you need to change the duration of the inserted word, there are a few ways to go about it. *TimeFlex, TimeFx,* and *Timestretch* are three of the many names for utilities that change the duration of a file or region (and hence speed) without changing its pitch. Time expansion/compression processors don't necessarily work linearly, and as we saw in Chapter 12, they represent a constant compromise between sync and rhythmic consistency.

Sometimes you need glitch-free processing and can forgo a bit of rhythmic honesty. Other times cadence is everything, so you might be willing to endure a glitch here and there. One way to get around this unsavory compromise is to break the original region into smaller sections. When you dissect a sentence like this, you'll find legato sections and staccato sections, and you'll also realize that there are probably stretches that require no processing; they're just surrounded by words of the wrong length. Don't process the sections that don't need it, and treat the staccatos differently from the legatos. Piece together the results and, odds are, you'll have a glitch-free line that has good local rhythm.

Here's one way to safely and systematically use time expansion/compression to make the inserted alternate word (in our case, the word "now") a bit longer:

- Move the replacement ADR word's region—in sync—to a free track. This is the region you'll process with the time expansion/compression plug-in. (See Figure 15-14.)
- Copy this region—again in sync—to yet another track. It's useful to have an unprocessed copy standing by.
- Expose a bit of handle from either side of the region you plan to process. Since AudioSuite plug-ins create a new soundfile, you'll want to process more of the region than you need. Without handles, your editing and crossfade options will be very limited.
- Select the region and open the time expansion/compression plug-in. There are scores of these available, and there's a good deal of debate as to their relative merits. Ask around, experiment, guess. Or just use the

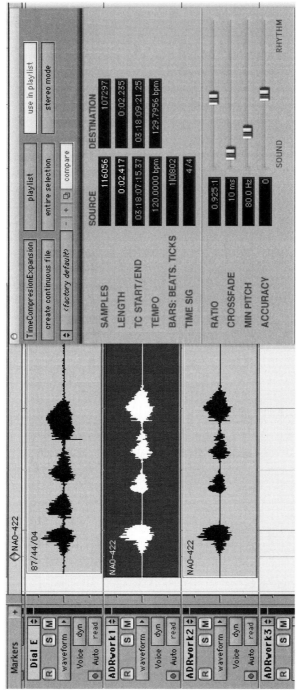

Figure 15-14 Preparing for time expansion/compression. Below the dialogue reference track, place at least two copies of the take you want to manipulate. In this example, the highlighted line on ADR work track 1 is being processed; the copy below is the virgin.

one that's in the computer you're working with. For what we're doing, most of them are pretty good.

- Choose a time expansion or compression ratio to change the length as needed. There are two schools of thought on how to calculate the ratio desired. By switching the workstation time display from *timecode* to *minutes and seconds*, you can accurately compare the length of the original phrase with the ADR line you're time-stretching. Then you can calculate the ratio that you'll type into the "Ratio" cell of the time expansion/compression plug-in. Frankly, I find all of this a bit tedious. I prefer to guess at a ratio, give it a try, line up the result, and undo if my guess was wrong. It's not a very scientific method and may be just a little rebellion from an otherwise disciplined dialogue editor. Either way, come up with a ratio that works for you.
- If your chosen ratio works well for one part of the word/phrase/region but not for another part, you might have to perform several time expansion/compression operations. This is where the safety copy you created comes in handy. Once you've created a time-flexed region, don't reprocess it. Let's say you expanded a region by 4 percent to match the original. It's a good speed match except for a short section in the middle that's running slow. You'll be tempted to time-flex that section since it's sitting right in front of you. But then you'll be processing an already abused soundfile. Time expansion/compression is a nasty business hardly free of artifacts, so instead of recooking the processed region, go to the safety copy and see if it solves the problem, given that part of the ADR line may need no time expression/compression at all. If you need to squeeze specific parts of the line at different ratios, this original region will give you far better results.
- If things aren't working out, go back to the other acceptable takes. Once you've started down the processing path, it's easy to forget that better, low-tech options may be available.

If you're satisfied that you resolved the first problem (in our rather simple example, the word "now"), move on to the next issue ("brown"). Follow the same steps. Rarely do you need to go word by word, and it's preferable to find the longest workable word strings to create a more natural flow, minimize the chance for weird edits, and lessen your work. Still, sometimes you have to tackle a line a word at a time.

Piece together all of the resulting regions—newly processed sections intercut with pieces of the ADR buy take. You may encounter some bumps, so don't be afraid to move the edit points a bit earlier or later than the obvious word beginnings. Music editors often use the downbeat (in our case, the beginning of a word) as an alignment reference point but make the actual cut someplace else. In dialogue you can use word beginnings as sync reference points but you may find that cutting at other, less obvious places gives you better results. Greater flexibility with edit points is the payoff for having pulled out some handle from the region before you performed the time expansion/compression.

Throughout this syncing process, periodically listen to your creation. Waveforms are helpful for syncing and matching, but film dialogue is about sound. It's quite possible that you'll put together a collection of regions whose waveform pattern perfectly matches that of the reference, but the result will be nothing familiar to humans.

Word Fitting Once you're happy with the construction, you can give the whole phrase a pass of word fitting, using a program like Wordfit[6] or VocALign.[7] These programs work like time expansion/compression but automatically and on a much smaller, more dynamic timescale.

Word fitting enables you to automatically match an alternate dialogue take or an ADR line to a reference phrase (almost certainly the original). All you need to do is select a processing range on the reference and replacement regions; the program then compares the respective waveforms and locally lengthens and shortens the replacement, ultimately producing a new soundfile, in sync, on a different track.

Today a favorite word-fitting program is VocALign, available as a freestanding application or as a plug-in for a number of workstations. It's a great product—I use it myself—but I have the same reservations about word-fitting tools that I have about workstations in general. Great kit, no doubt. Yet scary things happen when inexperienced or lazy editors blithely charge forward with such tools or when miserly producers use them as an excuse for cheapness.

Sorry VocALign, I mean you no harm. But I repeatedly see inexperienced editors opening the ADR take chosen by the director and then, without really listening to or understanding the material, "VocALigning" it, with results that can be anywhere from satisfactory but uninspired to totally unusable. Then, somehow, the director and producer decide the Emperor's Clothes really aren't so bad, and standards slip by another notch. Of course, the pro-

---

[6] Wordfit is a trademark of DAR.
[7] VocALign is a trademark of Synchro Arts.

ducer is happy because this operation takes little or no time. But the next time a comparable film is out for bid, the expectation is that ADR "editing" will be equally quick, so the winning bid will be even lower than before. Once standards have dropped, it's all but impossible to bring them back up.

So, how do you effectively use VocALign? First you edit, constructing the best possible, most natural-sounding phrases. You're probably (but not necessarily) better off building a line from several takes than heavily processing the one selected. If you need to expand or compress a line or part of one, do so. (I'm not claiming that time expansion/compression sounds better than VocALign; it doesn't. It's just that doing your homework first allows VocALign to do its best work.) Piece together the best possible sentence and *then* apply VocALign.

The processor will do some nice "nip and tuck" that you couldn't do yourself, and since you're not asking it to do the impossible you ought to get tight sync without artifacts. (See Figure 15-15.) Newer versions of VocALign offer control over landmarks within the reference and the dub, so you may get by with less preprocessing editing, but don't get lulled into thinking that any plug-in can do your work for you.

Be sure to intelligently name the resulting region beginning with the ADR code number. Also, place the pre-wordfit string of ADR edits—muted—on a track that will travel with you to the mix. You never know when a previously unheard processing artifact will surface in the mix or when, as you watch your manicured ADR construction for the first time on the Big Screen, you'll realize that a word is out of sync. Having the unprocessed string immediately available will make for faster fixes.

Editing ADR on a Noisy Scene

Looping a very noisy scene is hard work. The scene may be so noisy that even transcribing the original lines for your ADR call sheets becomes a test of patience and hearing ability. And the recording session will be difficult because the actor has trouble hearing herself in the guide track, which certainly gets in the way of artistic expression and results in frayed nerves.

Unfortunately, the headaches don't end with the recording session. When you can't hear well and can't discern details within the waveform, you're working with at least one hand tied behind your back. The same goes for word-fitting processors. If the signal-to-noise ratio on your reference track is so bad that the processor can't make wise decisions, the results will show it.

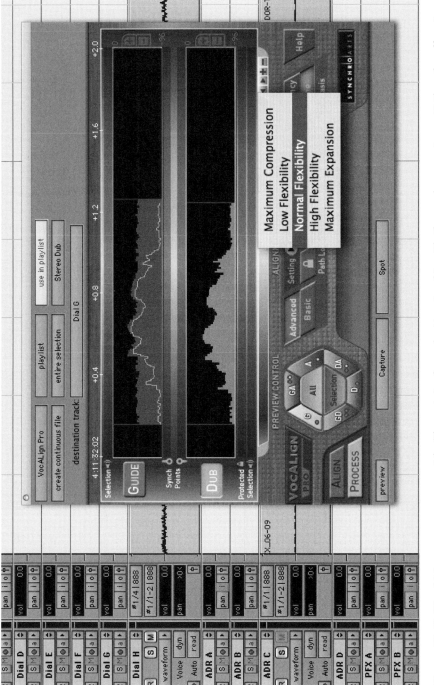

Figure 15-15 VocALign compares a guide (the original production track) with the replacement cue. It then locally nips and tucks to create a new soundfile that generally matches the sync of the guide track. You can choose sync points for comparison and select different types of processing along the "quality-vs.-rhythm" continuum.

Soft transients—the gentle beginnings and ends of phrases—will suffer the most.

To better hear and "see" the reference track, process it with a high-pass filter and perhaps also add a boost at around 2 kHz for better voice articulation. Be brutal. You don't care what the reference sounds like; you just want better resolution to increase the signal-to-noise ratio and provide more detail in the waveform. Ugly, maybe, but you should be able to hear more voice information and VocALign will be able to match waveforms more accurately.

Naming New Regions

As you dissect and process ADR takes, the region names will become increasingly indecipherable. Each time you edit a region, you add a suffix, and every process that creates a new soundfile appends its suffix as well. By the time you've pieced together the best takes and then pitch-shifted, time-stretched, and VocALigned, the region names have been reduced to unreadable hieroglyphics.

For each region, you have to keep track of the code and take number. If later on you or the director wants to know which take was used—or not—you've got to be able to divine that information quickly. Beyond that, there's room for even more diligent naming. When I perform a process on a region, I like to give it a name that describes that process (see Figure 15-16). Thus, if I time-stretched a region to make it 7 percent longer, I add "+7%." Same goes for pitch changes and EQ. If I use a high-pass filter to remove some wind rumble, I include the filter's frequency. It doesn't take long, and the information can be very valuable later.

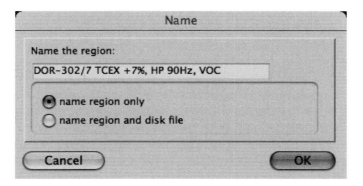

Figure 15-16 If you have the time and patience to create a "paper trail" of ADR or alternate take regions, you may save time in the mix if changes are necessary.

There's another reason for sensible naming of regions. Computerized cue sheet (rerecording log) programs name a string of regions (such as an ADR line constructed from a number of manipulated regions) based on the name of the first region in the string. If the first region, however short, bears a name unrecognizable to humans, the cue sheets will faithfully use it for the entire line. It is better to name the first region something meaningful. (More on this in Chapter 18.)

Group Loop

Not all postproduction dialogue recording involves principal characters. Often you need to record the other voices in a scene, whether to enhance the plot, to say more about a principal character, or to add mood and texture. This process is called group loop, and it involves contracting voice actors and a supervisor to study each relevant scene, come up with appropriate dialogue, and record the result in a studio.

Group loop recordings can roughly be divided into three types:

- Walla
- Specific group loop
- Callouts

Walla

Walla is the American term for the indistinct "buzz" created by a background group (in the United Kingdom it's sometimes called "rhubarb"). The classic example is barroom chatter. Imagine your two main actors sitting at the bar having a beer and discussing the meaning of life. Behind them, seen and unseen, is a crowd of fellow drinkers doing whatever you do in a bar. During the shoot, the extras are only mouthing their lines lest they interfere with the principals' dialogue, so aside from the words of principal actors in the foreground, the raw scene is eerily quiet.

You've already looped any critical lines from the principals. What's left is to fill in the background and define the mood—how big and rowdy the crowd and perhaps some clues about class or region. For this, a group loop supervisor will spot the scene with the supervising sound editor to find out what's important in the background sound. Are there any critical plot issues that need to be dealt with through off-camera commentary? Are our protagonists noticed by the crowd? Are there comments? What's the mood? This process continues for all relevant scenes. The group loop supervisor will come up with a plan for each scene and then hire a group of actors, each of whom can play many roles. Obviously, the group loop talent can't be any of the principal actors in the film, as their familiar voices would confuse the viewer.

During the group loop recording session, there'll be stereo passes for the general walla of the scene. The group can be made larger by recording successive passes in each of which the actors change their positions and voices enough so that in the final multipass recording you don't hear them standing simultaneously in several places across the screen.

Group walla is largely improvisational. In our barroom scene, the group loop supervisor might instruct the actors to talk about an imaginary game between the Cowboys and the Redskins or about how much they hate politicians or to complain about this year's corn crop. It doesn't matter as long as it doesn't interfere with the film and it won't become dated quickly.

The supervisor has to balance the actors as a conductor balances an orchestra. For example, if one or two actors' voices rise above the crowd, it's distracting and makes the track hard to recycle—the ideal walla track should be a relatively smooth din. And if the group is speaking in a language neither you nor the supervisor speaks, you have to find a native speaker to do a "stupidity check" to ensure that the seemingly benign walla isn't filled with "I curse your ancestors" or "I really hate this movie."

Specific Group Loop and Callouts

While much of group loop consists of background chatter, there are occasions for specific mono group loops. The waitress bringing a beer to the customer at the table behind our protagonist might utter, "Here you go, hon." There may be offscreen lines for the bartender or for the couple who walks past. All of these lines have to be written and assigned to a member of the loop group, and they're recorded much like normal ADR or as wild lines. Group loop supervisors often develop superhuman skills in reading lips or making up lines that match an actor's actions. On occasion, a real lip reader will be called in to figure out what a background extra is saying so that a sync line can be written.

Callouts are yells mixed into the track at a very low level in order to make an environment feel bigger. Hearing a disembodied voice from way down the beach yelling, "Hey Chico, throw me the ball!" enlarges the space and livens up the atmosphere.

Editing Group Loop

Editing individual group loop lines, such as those of our friendly waitress, is no different from ADR editing, except that you'll rarely have a reference track. Since extras on a shooting set usually don't make any sounds—their lips just flap—you can't rely on the guide track for sync or for content. Also, with group loop you'll rarely encounter the detailed paperwork that accompanies ADR.

- Open all takes for the individual line you want to edit.
- Line up all takes on ADR work tracks, one under the other.
- Listen to all takes and pick the performances that best suit the shot. There's no point in syncing, editing, and processing a bad take.
- Find your take, or takes, and look for landmarks in the picture—those easy-to-spot, hard, short consonants. Match them to corresponding sounds in the dialogue track and see where you stand. If the text heard and seen is the same, use the ADR syncing tricks to force the line into sync. Remember that you can combine takes to create a better, more in-sync line.
- If there are two or more versions of the line, both believable in terms of sync, consider editing them both so that the director can choose.
- Find out if the mixer wants these specific group lines to be on the ADR tracks or to share space with more general group elements.

Getting the Most Out of Group Loop

To do justice to group walla, you need to keep a couple of things in mind. First, just because the crowd recordings were taken in a certain order, you don't have to use them that way. Some sound events have to be in sync, such as the cheer of the barroom crowd when the Cowboys (or Redskins) score, but many of them can be used in any way you like. Listen to the dialogue and find appropriate moments for that small burst of laughter or the muffled "Damn governor, he's a crook!" in the background.

You can use these lines to enhance the rhythm of the dialogue or to motivate an actor's twitch or even to make an omniscient commentary. At the same time, if an event in the group loop conflicts with the dialogue—one voice that sticks out above the crowd or a shout that hits at just the wrong time—either move or delete it. If you're cutting the group loop, it's yours to play with. Keeping the tracks exactly as recorded is boring and wimpy.

You may have to repeat a group recording to make it last longer. As when editing backgrounds, you can't merely copy and repeat but have to open the recording onto to a work track and from there build a new sequence. Much of the sequence can be random, but pay attention to what's going on with the picture and in the dialogue to most effectively use the recording. If there are any recognizable beacons, such as a telltale laugh or chair squeak or a recognizable bit of background dialogue, don't use that moment more than once, even in different scenes.

Don't lose touch with the desired size of the crowd. Groups often sound better, richer, when "doubled up"—that is, when several takes are piled atop each other. If this works, great. However, if there are only 8 people in the small restaurant, it will sound weird when you overlay four group takes, resulting in a crowd of 30 or more.

ADR and Group Track Layout

It's important to know what the mixer expects from your ADR track layout. Should you prepare alternates? If so, how many? Should they be on "active" tracks or hidden away? How should you handle ADR to be panned? There's no such thing as "the right" way to lay out your ADR; it depends on the production, the budget, the supervising sound editor, and the mixer. There's only one "wrong" way: not asking what to do.

CHAPTER 16

Editing Production Sound for Documentaries

If dialogue occasionally assumes a supporting role in dramatic film sound editing—quietly toiling away in the shadow of its sexier sound effects, music, and Foley colleagues—it's at center stage when it comes to documentary films. *Documentary* is a hopelessly broad genre, including anything from straightforward news docs to wildly stylized films that are largely re-creations, from concerts to *cinéma vérité* glimpses into someone's life. Nevertheless, although they cover a wide spectrum, documentaries are for the most part overwhelmingly dialogue driven. Many have soundtracks that consist of little more than production sound, however edited it may be.

Documentary Sound Challenges

Dialogue editing is dialogue editing, so documentaries require the same basic sound editing tools as do dramatic features. You have to organize the tracks to understand the material and create the circumstances for an easy mix. You have to smooth the transitions between shots to create the impression of a living scene that feels real. And you have to remove unwanted noises and anything that calls attention to the filming process.

Still, documentaries present a variety of special challenges for the dialogue editor.

- Often there'll be few or no backgrounds or SFX added to a scene, so the dialogue must carry the entire soundtrack, which places it under much greater scrutiny.
- Rarely are there second takes in a documentary, so finding alternate material to fix overlaps, remove noises, and correct improperly terminated sentences is more difficult.
- Documentary film editors regularly construct voiceover sentences from disconnected sections of an interview, leaving it to you to make them sound like normal language by repairing cadence, pitch, and energy with very limited resources.

- Depending on the type of documentary, there may be various ethical restrictions on your language manipulations. Overwhelmingly, these fall on the picture editor, but in certain cases you may be required to document the source of the "fakes" you used to make the film sound like a film.
- Documentary structure differs from dramatic structure. Narration and interview/voiceover material and scenes, or **B-rolls**, are each handled in their own way, so you have to adapt your workspace to let the tracks speak to you and to prevent a confusing mess in the mix.
- Because of the way documentaries are filmed, the region names in the OMF session will probably be of less use than what you'll find on dramas. Sound reports also will likely provide less information than you're used to.
- Most documentaries have tighter budgets and schedules than dramatic features, so you have to get used to working more quickly and managing the mix with greater efficiency.

The Documentary Workspace

There's no such thing as a "typical" documentary, so it's difficult to create a session template to suit all types. But I'll try.

Imagine that you're working on a documentary consisting of interviews, occasional omniscient narration (a.k.a. "Voice of God"), and scenes that show what everyone's talking about. Most of the story is handled by interviews or by voiceovers derived from them. The narration carries additional exposition and background information, and the "scenes" are either freestanding and follow the rules of drama or are simply illustrative **cutaways**.

When you receive the OMF, it's likely that all of the dialogue elements will be jumbled together, so your first task is to sort out the mess. Just as with dialogue tracks for dramatic films, it's impossible to make sense of what's there before you organize it. So, too, is it useless to wade through documentary sound elements until you can put each one in its proper place.

Note that *narration* is defined as text spoken by an omniscient speaker who is usually not one of the film's interview subjects. **Voiceover**, on the other hand, is dialogue derived from interviews but temporarily disconnected from the talking head who uttered it. Usually narration is recorded in a studio, generally close-microphone recorded, and read from a script. Being part of an interview, voiceover carries with it all the characteristics of location sound.

Table 16-1 Suggested Track Layout for a Documentary Film

Track Name	Contents	Description
Narr A	Primary narration	If there's only one narration voice, recorded in the same setting, use only one narration track.
Narr B-?	Other narration	If there are two or more narrators, or if the single narrator was recorded in more than one (different-sounding) session, assign additional tracks.
Intv A-? (or Info A-?)	Interview/voiceover	This is where all interview-based information is placed. Use as many tracks as you need, but usually five or six of these will do.
Scene A-?	Scene/vérité material	Use these tracks for noninterview material: B-roll action or cutaways to illuminate the voiceover; full scenes of character action; montage constructions. Usually five or six scene tracks are sufficient.
Music A-?	Musical performances or other music stripped from the OMF	Use these tracks for production music (e.g., the band is playing or the string quartet is practicing) or score or acquired music that you inherited with the OMF.

You can organize your documentary tracks as shown in Table 16-1. Of course, since each documentary has its own style, you'll have to adapt your track plan to the needs of the film, filmmaker, and mixer.

Once you've organized your tracks, place memory markers on all scene boundaries. You do this for the same reasons you mark scenes in dramas: to indicate where to cut dialogue and later backgrounds; to ensure that all scene cuts are of a desired and predictable length; and to create an easy way to find scenes and perspective cuts.

Cutting Scenes and Narration

You cut documentary scenes much like you cut dramas. The *vérité* material (or *vérite scenes* or *B-roll material*, depending on whom you ask) behaves much like a dramatic scene, so use the same rules of track organization and shot transition. Within a scene, split shots by character, shooting angle, noise problems, or whatever else makes sense. Also split off unusually loud or noisy elements for easier mixing.

Narration shouldn't carry appreciable room tone, so you needn't think about filling between regions. You'll probably want to fade the tops and tails of the narration segments to avoid clicks and to smooth what little room tone there is. However, just as with dialogue, never fade during words.

Narrator's breaths are a touchy subject. Many editors argue that the narrator's omniscient, God-like point of view requires that mundane human breaths be removed. Certainly vulgar, unsavory, or loud breaths get in the way of the film and call attention to the reader rather than the writer of the narration. These must go, as must page turns and other silly sounds. At the same time, a long string of text without any breathing can leave listeners gasping. It just doesn't sound right. Usually, I like to begin a paragraph with a small, delicate breath and then eliminate all intervening breaths. But it just depends.

If the film is narrated by a known personality, who's serving as an activist or endorser, you're likely to keep more breaths because she's humanized by her role. If, on the other hand, the narrator is an anonymous voice, you'll probably want to lose more breaths to maintain a respectable distance.

As with ADR or dialogue editing, you needn't use a sound just because it's there. Narration is nothing more than someone reading into a microphone. It's not sacrosanct. If there are flaws—pops, diction problems, mouth noises, and so on—don't be afraid to dig into alternate takes for solutions. Of course, save the original—in sync—on a nearby track so that you can get things back to normal if the director dislikes your changes.

Talking Heads and Voiceovers

You'll likely spend most of your time working with interview material or voiceovers derived from interview footage. After all, this is where most documentaries tell their stories.

Start by organizing the interview regions by shot origin, which normally means splitting first by interviewee and then by location. If in one scene you have talking head and voiceover material from three characters, split the regions onto three tracks. If a character in a scene appears in material originating in more than one filming location or from an additional audio source (such as an audiocassette recording), split this material onto additional tracks. If you need more tracks to solve cadence or shot-matching problems, use them.

In short, follow the rules and logic of dramatic editing and you should make the right choices. Normally you don't need to split a character based on on-camera versus off-camera, since you usually want a continuous flow between a character's talking head and his voiceover.

With a limited number of characters and interview filming locations, you may be able to place your subjects on dedicated interview tracks for the duration of the film. This allows for very easy mix organization, but works only if you have very few characters and locations. Talk to your mixer before pursuing this approach. (See Figure 16-1.)

Figure 16-1 With only a few interview subjects whose shooting locations remain the same throughout the film, you can dedicate individual tracks to them. If not, or if the background location sounds are inconsistent, stick with track names like "Interview A → Interview F" and move things around as you see fit.

Now that your interview tracks are organized, you have to begin making sense of the sentences the picture editor put together to tell her story. Aside from familiar chores like balancing room tone and removing noises, you face two common documentary frustrations: (1) cadence problems caused by assembling sentences from different parts of an interview or constructing phrases based on text rather than sound; and (2) incorrect terminations caused by a sentence chopped off before the phrase actually ends, resulting in an unconvincing ending inflection.

Cadence and Voice Matching

It makes sense for documentary filmmakers to transcribe their filmed interviews. By studying the text of an interview, they gain a foothold on mountains of footage. Documentaries are famous for their small budgets, so some filmmakers use transcripts to organize the film's backbone—the stories derived from the interviews—long before the picture editor comes onboard. The result can be more efficient editing, even if the transcription separates the picture editor from some of the footage. And in investigative, political, or **vox pop** documentaries, transcripts are essential in proving the authenticity of the footage in the event of a libel lawsuit. Overall, then, transcripts are an important part of much documentary filmmaking. However, problems arise when interviews are edited in a word processor rather than by an editor working with both the interview and its sounds and images.

When a producer or director (or worse, a committee) constructs dialogue by cutting and pasting words from transcripts, the results are completely content driven. The filmmaker has a story to tell, she has before her all the words spoken by the interviewee, and she soon learns how to make him talk. Even though what's produced may be the sought-after story, when the film editor tries to impose the director's text-based vision on the footage, the resulting sentences may have inflection problems, rhythm irregularities, and misplaced breaths. The time/date recorder on your answering machine might sound more like English than many voiceovers edited this way. A decent documentary film editor will reject the worst of the atrocities and find workarounds for others. But you'll still inherit much impossible but pivotal dialogue.

What can you do? First of all, find the transcripts so that you can use the same tool that built the mess to sort things out. When you encounter a bumpy string of words that you can't massage with your normal dialogue editing tools, look for solutions within the transcripts. "But why," you may ask, "will the transcripts help me find a solution to the transition problem when the director, producer, and editor had the same document and only made matters worse?" The answer is that they were looking at content. You're looking at sound.

Listen to a bumpy edit between two regions and identify the sound transition. It might be a long vowel moving to a sharp consonant or perhaps a stop, like a *T* followed by a vowel. Whatever it is, look through the transcripts to find similar-sounding transitions, although not necessarily the same words. The film editor may have overlooked a good sound transition because she was concerned with meaning, which requires longer word strings, while you care only about transition sounds. Naturally, you'll begin by looking for exactly the same words in combination to get the most natural results.

Sometimes you have to time-stretch parts of a region to create a better cadence. Remember to save the original region in case your efforts fail or you need a clean starting point for a single region that requires several kinds of time squeezing. Also remember to open up the handles of the original region before changing the speed or duration of the file, since this will give you greater flexibility when you splice the new region into the sentence. You may need to selectively change the pitch of certain regions for the string to make more sense.

Whether adjusting length, speed, or pitch, don't reprocess an already processed soundfile. If you need to fine-tune your parameters, you're far better off returning to the original and modifying your settings, as discussed in Chapter 15. All of these processes are unfriendly to sound quality, so repeatedly process a soundfile if what you want is a horrible line of dialogue.

When the editor hands you a string of voiceover edits that just don't fit together, don't be shy about replacing words with more sound-appropriate alternates. Keep the original regions in case you or the director is unhappy with the new construction, but be as bold as necessary to recreate believable sentences. Remember, the director and editor created these strings by assembling dismembered words, so you're under no greater obligation to honor the integrity of their unworkable assembly than they were to honor the integrity of the dailies. Just make it work.

Termination

It's common for a documentary filmmaker to chop off a sentence in order to bend its meaning. "It's true: I shot him as he was running toward me with a chainsaw" may be too fact-laden for the filmmaker, so he'll turn his villain's words into an easier to understand "It's true: I shot him." Period.

The fact that this turns justice on its head isn't your problem, but you're left to fix the mess and turn "I shot him" into a strong, believable declaration. In its current state, the sentence is bound to sound unconvincing because the **liaison** between "him" and "as" will corrupt the ending of the new phrase. Plus, a statement as direct as "I shot him" deserves a confident ending. You have to find a strong, terminal "him" spoken by this character in the same interview environment. If you do find such a sound, consider yourself lucky and don't ask too many questions.

It's more likely, however, that you'll have to settle for a terminal *m* sound and then splice that onto your existing "him." Given enough time and will, you can usually find an adequate ending. Sometimes though, you won't be able to solve the problem by editing. In such desperate circumstances, use pitch shifting, time expansion, and clever addition of room tone to generate the best termination possible. Use whatever sound effects or Foley gimmicks are appropriate to mask the edit.

Production Sound Effects

Whether because of ethics or because of the filmmaker's artistic or philosophical concerns, your production soundtrack may end up being the sole sound element in a documentary film. No added sound effects, backgrounds, Foley, or music—just production sound. This puts far greater pressure on your tracks to tell a complete story, maintain a steady and interesting room tone, and flawlessly move from shot to shot with nothing to hide behind.

Thankfully, audiences are far more forgiving of sound bumps in documentaries than they are when watching dramas. Documentaries are, by definition, real, and suspension of disbelief is almost a forgone conclusion. Thus, bumps that would destroy the effectiveness of a drama scene are readily overlooked.

But if you're responsible for the entire soundtrack, you'll have more on your hands than just smoothing out the picture editor's cuts. You'll need effects, backgrounds, and perhaps wild voice elements to bring scenes to life. Look through the sound reports, if they exist. If you're lucky, they'll tell you something about the shooting sequence and where room tone, wild recordings, and backgrounds are hiding. If you don't have sound reports, which is often the case with documentary sound recording, go to the last recording for each shooting location, where wild elements are the most likely to be.

Don't be afraid to ask the film editor—she's far more familiar with the footage than you'll ever be. And if you're in contact with the production during the picture editing, ask the editor to set aside important wild sounds, room tones, backgrounds, and the like. It's enormously easier for her to drop these treats into an Avid bin as she finds them than for you to blindly wade through the original tapes.

If the location recordist provided some stereo backgrounds, use them. Real, appropriate stereo atmosphere will add a great deal of depth to your production tracks. Be on the lookout for small sounds like footsteps and body motions that can play the role of Foleys. And find doors, cars, and other PFX within the original recordings that you can use to beef up the track and enhance the reality of the scenes.

CHAPTER 17

Preparing for the Mix

By the time you finish your final pass on the dialogue, the tracks are as good as they'll ever be. Now it's time to take off your editor's hat and put on the hats of office manager, secretary, and shipping clerk. In the days remaining before the mix, you'll have to deal with the following details, or at least make sure that someone in the production office does.

- Confirm that the dialogue sessions are in sync with the newly arrived answer print telecine. If you make sync changes, pass along this information to the supervising sound editor or other editors.
- Print (or draw) and annotate the cue sheets.
- Prepare your materials. Confirm the drive type (including connector) that the mix facility prefers. If your OMF, auto-assembly, and other elements are spread over several drives, consolidate them onto one FireWire drive. Find out if you will play your files from your own drive or if you have to copy them onto the mix room's. Allow time for copying once you get to the mix.
- Make sure that each reel's session is made up of the same tracks, in the same order. Disable and hide any tracks you don't want, such as your work tracks.
- Make sure the head and tail sync plops are correct. Check them again.
- On each reel, copy your 1 kHz reference tone onto all tracks that will be active during that reel. This will ensure that the output of the playback workstation is accurately patched into the console and help identify broken connectors or shorts. If a track won't be used *at all* during a reel, don't copy a reference tone on that channel and do deactivate the track, so that the mixer and her assistant will know that the channel isn't engaged for that reel.
- If there are some truly unique sounds in the dailies, make a copy of them for yourself. The sound effects editors will undoubtedly have done the same thing. Even though you're a dialogue editor, you never know when the sounds of a 1927 Quadrant motorbike or a 1966 Susita

sedan or the background sounds of NASA's Mission Control will come in handy.

- Arrange shipping of your material to the mix facility. Find out how and when the mixing stage will receive it if you're not taking it yourself. Although you no longer have to deliver mix elements in a truck—a gym bag suffices—you have to make sure that everything that must travel does. Of course, this is much more hair-raising when you're traveling to another city or country.
- Talk with the studio manager to find out when your setup will take place.
- If you're never coming back to your cutting room after the mix, box up what's yours and what belongs to the production. Grab the things you care about, since by the time you've finished with the mix, someone else will be in "your" room.
- Archive your project. Make backup files to take with you plus one copy for the production office.
- This may sound a bit pessimistic, but make sure you get paid. Overwhelmingly, most producers pay their bills, but if you've been having trouble getting money throughout the gig, it's naïve to assume that things will get better once you're done and can contribute no other value to the production.

Check the Answer Print

While you're sprucing up the dialogue, the picture is undergoing its own metamorphosis. At lock, the picture department made a video EDL and a cut list for the negative cutters—those people with the white coats, gloves, scissors, and nerves of steel, who located each piece of original negative and reconstructed the picture editor's creation. When they were through, they shipped it off to the lab where it became the first answer print, which the director and the director of photography use for making decisions about the look of the film. They'll eventually spend many hours at the lab, adding a bit of cyan here and a little magenta there and doing other painterly magic.

Meanwhile—on a film with a reasonable budget—the picture editor is checking that the film is in sync or, more bluntly, whether the negative cutters made a mistake. On a very low-budget film, the picture department will be long gone, so you'll inherit this responsibility. Actually, it's not so hard. You just need to synchronize *a copy of* your session to the telecine of the answer print and watch the movie. Take into account the name of the new video version when you name the "Save As" session. If you notice a scene slightly out of sync, make a note, but don't change anything yet. When you finish the screening, go back to the "regular" session, the version of the final Avid cut. Check each of the noted shots for any apparent sync differences between the Avid output and the answer print. If you find any, let the production office know.

Normally, the supervising sound editor will want all editors to resync their edited tracks to the answer print so she can mix against that rather than the ugly Avid digital dumps. In this case, reopen your new "Save As" session and watch the answer print. You'll probably need to "nip and tuck" the dialogue sync. You've been looking at an Avid digital dump over the course of your dialogue editing, so there are likely things in the shot that you've never seen before. Now that you have a much higher resolution image, you can clearly see the lips past that walrus moustache or the footstep on the dark marble floor.

Keep track of what you offset: what you moved, how much, and in which direction. This information will tell the other editors what you did and prevent sound effects built on top of production sounds from getting gooey. Also check both ends of any region you move. You may have displaced the region enough to damage your transitions.

Resyncing Tips

Blindly syncing your session to a new cut will wear you down, and you'll never be totally confident that you're in sync. Sooner or later you'll have to trust your eyes, ears, and gut to fine-tune the sync of a print, but don't start there. Instead, use the countless landmarks a reel provides.

When you get your first Avid digital dump, and with every new video version thereafter, make a log of a few landmarks for each reel. The few minutes this takes will pay off when it comes time to resync to another version. Table 17-1 describes the benchmarks I use.

Armed with this information, you can quickly determine if the new version is behaving correctly and you'll have a number of sync locations for calculating offsets. If this level of list making is too much, then always—at the very least—record the start mark, head sync pop, first internal cut, and LFOA. Don't start resyncing your session until you've measured the LFOA and calculated the reel length. If the old version and the new version aren't the same length, there's no point in continuing.[1] Something is terribly wrong and

---

[1] This is a good time to have a timecode/footage calculator. There are many good ones out there, and because the players change regularly, there's no point in recommending one. Do a Web search for "TC calculator shareware" and you'll be rewarded with many options.

Table 17-1 Benchmarks in a Reel for Confirming Sync

Benchmark	Description
Start mark	Timecode of the leader's picture start mark
Sync pop	Timecode or footage of the head leader's sync pop
FFOA	Timecode or footage of the first frame of the reel (unless it's a fade from black)
1st cut	First internal picture cut
2nd cut	Second internal picture cut
2nd to last cut	Next to last internal picture cut
Last cut	Last internal picture cut
LFOA	Timecode or footage of cut from the last frame of action to the tail leader
Tail pop	Timecode or footage of the tail leader's pop (if there is one)

it's definitely a picture problem. Note the problem, tell the supervising sound editor, and get out of the way.

If the film begins in sync but sound and picture progressively drift apart, it's not a negative-cutting mistake; rather, the film was running at the wrong speed in the telecine. Stop. There's nothing you can do, and if you try to sync to this version, you'll learn a hard lesson that you'll never want to repeat.

Cuts inside a scene are usually more reliable sync references than are the scene boundaries, which is one of the reasons you measured the first two internal cuts. Synchronize within a scene, and the reel will follow suit. It's an easy fix if the beginning of the scene is a bit longer or shorter.

Long ago, when you began editing this project, you added markers to indicate scene changes and used them to identify scenes for easy access and to control scene transitions. Now you can use them to resync a new version. The markers may be exactly a half frame early or late because of the telecine pulldown sequence, but the cuts should hover around them. If you encounter a scene change in the new version that doesn't match the session's scene marker, you'll know that the picture change occurred between the last marker you checked and your current location.

Sync is elusive. The more you analyze a shot, the more you advance and retard a region, the greater your focus on a shot, the less likely you are to get anywhere. If you're having a tough time nailing the sync, leave the room, do something else, come back later. Bring flowers. Chances are you'll do better with a fresh head. Some shots (and some actors) simply never seem to be in sync. Do the best you can and try not to look at them during the premiere.

Cue Sheets (Rerecording Logs)

When film sound was edited on mag, mixing was a very physical affair. The day before the mix was scheduled, the sound "units"—roll after roll of mag stripe and sound fill—arrived by truck. When it was time for a reel to be mixed, the machine room crew threaded its sound units onto countless **dubbers**. These were interlocked playback machines, controlled by the rerecording mixer, that moved synchronously with the projector and were each patched to a channel strip on the console. If you needed to change the sync on one track, you could disengage the dubber holding that track, slip the sync, and reengage.

Many facilities had controllers that allowed the mixer to slip the sync on individual or groups of dubbers—all from the comfort of the mixing desk. If an editorial problem spanning several tracks cropped up, the elements had to be taken off the dubbers and either fixed "on the bench" in the machine room or sent back to the cutting room for repair. Given the hourly rate for a mixing room, such scene overhauls were wretchedly expensive for the production and humiliating for the editor.

In those days there were no visual cues to tell the mixer what to expect from the scores of tracks playing in the back room, so the cue sheet, a matrix displaying each track and its contents against time, was developed. (See Figure 17-1.)

For each track, a typical dialogue cue sheet will display an event's start and stop time, the cue name, including the character name, and often the first and last words spoken during the cue. This information allows an experienced mixer to navigate through the morass of tracks you've presented. Track overlaps are easy to spot, so the mixer knows how much time is available for crossfades. ADR and alternate take options are clearly indicated.

Information-rich, easy-to-read cue sheets that show off their maker's creative flair and aesthetic penchant have long been a source of pride for assistant sound editors. Even when computer-generated cue sheets became available, many crews turned to them only as a source of information, hand drawing the final versions for greater legibility. It took a long time for mixers to accept cue sheets printed by computers.

Cue Sheets in the Digital Age

In today's dialogue premixes, almost everyone plays mix tracks from a workstation. There's a monitor right in front of the editor and probably another in

Title: **Lost in Jordan**

Dialogue Premix rerecording logs (mix begins 26 June)

Elements: R1 Dial AP Offset 24/03 #2 (Pro Tools)

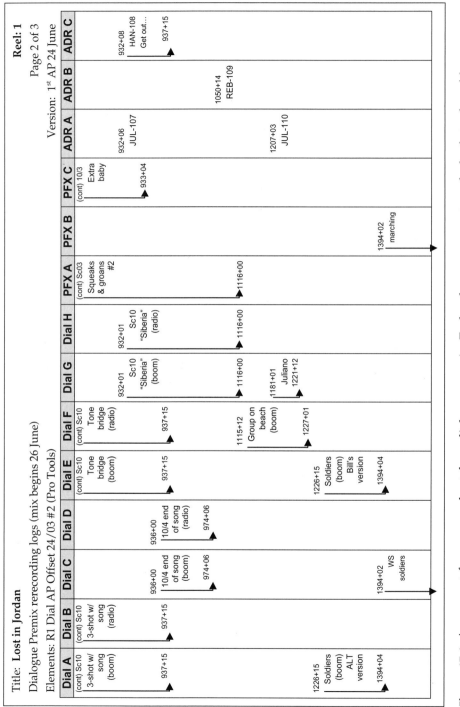

Figure 17-1 An excerpt from a cue sheet for a dialogue premix. Each column represents a playback track and hence a fader on the console. The timeline can be shown in timecode or in feet+frames.

front of the mixer. Workstations allow tracks to scroll while playing and so in many ways would seem to take the place of cue sheets. Taking cues from them is easier than reading cue sheets because you can see events as they approach the play head, which gives you much better timing information. You can zoom close to a transition or a line of dialogue to make detailed corrections, and you can zoom out very wide for an overview of a scene.

So, why bother with cue sheets? Simply because you can write on them, noting valuable information about the cues and the mix, something you can't do with a workstation's display.

Some very good automated cue sheet programs are available, and many workstations have built-in utilities to create detailed rerecording logs. Still, there's still nothing like a hand-drawn cue sheet to get your point across to a mixer. Color coding, illustrated fades, unambiguous cue names, and clear word clues are just some of the reasons to draw your own. On the other hand, time and money are the obvious reasons to have the computer do this for you.

Tracking Your Premix Record Tracks

Whether you hand-draw your cue sheets or print them from a computer, you can use this graphic display of your tracks to help plan the mix. As I said earlier, the dialogue premix has a twofold purpose: to smooth, focus, and de-noise the dialogue; and to organize the mixed tracks for maximum flexibility and comfort in the final mix. Drawing a rerecording plan on your cue sheets before you begin the premix will ensure that this purpose is fulfilled. (Chapter 18 discusses managing the dialogue premix.) Even if the mixer changes your premix recording strategy, the time you spent planning will help the mixer make wise decisions.

During the premix, keep track of the *actual* recordings by writing the record track numbers directly onto the cue sheets. If dialogues A, B, and C were mixed and then recorded onto record track 4, draw a circle around those events in Dials A, B, and C and write "4." This will help in the mix and prevent accidental recording over tracks.

Packaging and Backup

The fact that you can carry your tracks on a hard drive the size of a cigarette pack is a mixed blessing. Not needing a hand truck is undeniable progress, but that precious little drive is attractive to thieves, easy to lose, easier to drop, and much more likely to break than are box after box of mag elements. For these reasons, always have a sensible backup plan.

FireWire drives are becoming cheaper by the day, which is why I use them for backing up my files during editing. I use two large drives: one for editing and one for daily backup. Before the mix I consolidate my sessions and store them in a new folder called "For Mix," or something equally clever, which I copy onto both drives so that I have two identical options for the mix.

By far the cheapest way to make a final archive is to copy this folder onto a DVD-R, which is nowadays nothing more than a big floppy drive. You probably won't be able to copy your entire film project onto one disk, so break it down by reels. If your system doesn't allow reel-by-reel filing (that is, if all of your dailies are in one huge folder), find a workaround that makes sense.

The beauty of archiving onto DVD is that the 12 cm disks are light and very easy to ship or carry, and although not completely robust, they'll still withstand a tumble or a bath better than your FireWire drive. Make one DVD-R backup for yourself. This will be the copy you slip into your bag and carry to the mix just in case. When the mix is finished, keep it for your records. It's good for future reference and will come in handy if you ever decide to write a book about dialogue editing. Pack up the other one with the rest of the editing room materials and give it to the production office.

The end of the editing process is a bad time to be without an assistant. Not only do you have to prepare for the mix on your own, but you also need to pack up and inventory the cutting room. Thankfully, a modern dialogue job can be stowed away in a matter of minutes. As you box up all the materials—DATs and videotapes, paperwork, and any special equipment that belongs to the production—make a log of what's in each box. Tape the log to its box and send copies to the production office. Keep one for yourself. This is a minor hassle, but it can protect you if you need to find something later or if the production office claims you took their Kensington mouse.

CHAPTER 18

The Mix

A gymnast will spend years preparing for a 3-minute Olympic performance, a pianist will endure months of 12-hour practice sessions in preparation for a competition, and firemen repeatedly drill for something they hope will never happen. In comparison, dialogue editors have it pretty easy. Still, like the gymnast, for the past few weeks you've been preparing for one brief, intense experience: the dialogue premix.

Over the course of a few days, you'll find out whether your editing decisions were sound and whether you constructed your tracks in such a way that the mixer (whom you may never have met) can quickly move beyond "making it less horrible" to using your work to breathe life into the film.

Each day during the premix, the producer will spend far more than a week's worth of your salary, so the pressure to perform is high. There's a balance between getting it done well and getting it done at all. Moments when you think you're a genius are sideswiped by self-doubt when you realize that you misjudged a scene.

It's your last hurrah, and there's never, ever enough time. In short, the experience is thrilling, rewarding, scary, and overwhelmingly enjoyable.

Premix Goals

Two conflicting goals guide the premix: One, to see that scenes are smoothed, perspectives are established, sound is shaped, and ADR is matched; and, two, to ensure that important, volatile elements aren't forever merged with the rest of a scene. Options must be held open for the final mix, when all of the other sound elements are available for comparison. That's when the director absolutely, positively must make decisions—when the buck finally stops.

Given its schizophrenic mandate, what exactly are we hoping to accomplish in the dialogue premix?

- Establishing a smooth flow of room tone within each scene.
- Establishing a warm, pleasant color for the voices in a scene.
- Removing unpleasant vocal sounds, most notably whistling sibilants.
- Removing excess ambient noise both from the entire scene and from specific shots to eliminate imbalances between takes.
- Adding focus and perspective to shots.
- Controlling dynamic range. This doesn't mean "flattening" each scene but rather containing what's there within sensible limits while keeping the scenes dynamic and interesting.
- Matching the ADR to the rest of the scene.
- Controlling the level and treatment of PFX.
- Recording the results in a way that preserves options.
- Preparing good notes of how the premix tracks are recorded to facilitate the final mix.

With all these objectives, you have to become part artist, part traffic cop, and part perpetual cheerleader and facilitator. There are as many flavors of dialogue premix as there are films, dialogue editors, and mixers. Sometimes you'll be a major player in the process, and sometimes you'll be little more than a pair of hands. But the objectives remain the same.

Working with the Mixer

Why are you in the mix? You're there for three reasons:

- You're the human representative of the tracks, so you have to make sure they're allowed to do the talking. If you did your job well, the premix should be pretty straightforward. Speak for the tracks only when they're having a hard time expressing themselves.
- You shepard the film. You know it well, whereas the mixer is likely meeting it for the first time. With all the junctures in your tracks that can lead in unforeseen directions, you have to guide the mixer in moving the sound narrative in the direction you want it to go. At the same time, the mixer's freshness and experience will result in new, exciting options you may never have considered.
- As the representative of the production, you see that the premix is up to par. This is the tricky part because it involves egos and personalities. The way to negotiate this is to present yourself as a supporter rather than a supervisor. If you're not getting what you want, seduce

the mixer into that extra mix pass rather than demand your rights as a client. Get him on your side. Whatever you do, don't "pull rank." You might win this battle, but with a disgruntled mixer you'll most certainly lose the war.

Getting the Most Out of the Mix and the Mixer

The rerecording mixer has the skill, experience, and (hopefully) taste that your dialogue tracks need to make the film work. He also runs a very complicated room, without which you cannot finish your job. But mixers are human like all of us and occasionally require a bit of maintenance.

Figure out right away how to get the most out of the mix and mixer. On one hand, you represent the client, so you have power. On the other, the mixer sits at the top of the audio postproduction food chain, far above the dialogue editor, so you may experience some insecurity and intimidation. None of this need be a problem if you keep two goals in mind: (1) finishing the dialogue premix more or less on schedule and (2) getting what you want from it.

Don't be too shy to say, "That was really great, but I know you have it in you to do it better" or "It's just not working. Let's see what's keeping this scene from being what I thought it could be"—or words to that effect. You worked hard on your dialogue and it's your reputation that's on the line. Push as hard as you reasonably can and give in only when you're convinced that the tracks just don't have it in them.

Still, there'll be times when you feel the tracks aren't getting the love and attention they deserve, and that the mixer isn't addressing all of the problems. You have to deal with this, or you'll never rest.

- Talk to the mixer. She's probably more experienced than you, so her opinion is valuable. Try to determine whether the problem is sufficiently solved for the premix stage. Find out whether the backgrounds, effects, and therapeutic efforts of the final mix can fix the problem. If not, go back and try again.
- Use charm to get the mixer to reexamine a troublesome section. If that doesn't work, come back to it later. A fresh view may be all it takes.
- Only under the most desperate of circumstances have your supervising sound editor, or even the producer, talk to the mixer or studio manager. Getting what you need from the tracks is more important than being buddies with the mixer, but it can take days to get the mix back on track once you've gone over someone's head.

You will have several days together with the mixer to figure out how to get what you need from this high-octane situation. It's vital that you apply the same skill and creativity that went into your editing to get the most out of the dialogue premix. There's a magic within all rerecording mixers waiting for you to discover and make use of.

The rerecording mixer has the skill, the experience, and (hopefully) the taste that your dialogue tracks need to make the project work. In addition, it's a very complicated room to run, without which you cannot finish your job. It's vital that you apply the same skill and creativity that went into your editing to get the most from the studio and the most from the mixer and the mix room assistant. Unless you are very unlucky, you'll find that you can benefit from all their skills.

Planning the Premix

Before you begin, spend a few minutes with the mixer to concoct a plan for the mix. Compare what you have to accomplish with the number of hours available, and decide what you must have in the can at the end of each day. The first reel will undoubtedly take longer than the rest, since there'll be a certain amount of unfinished setup as well as some stabbing in the dark for the best way to address the tracks. So count the first reel as two reels' worth of work when making up a schedule.

Mix Out of Sequence

Just as I prefer to edit dialogue out of film order, beginning on an interior reel and working my way out, I like to premix the dialogue out of sequence as well. If you don't have a lot of time, you won't be able to return to your first mixed reel once you've cracked the film's code. In that case, don't cut your teeth on reel 1, since it's during the picture's first few minutes that viewers decide if it's worth watching.

If you start on a middle reel—but not the one where you began your dialogue editing—you can hide some of your learning curve in a "softer," less exposed section. Of course, if you make a huge mixing discovery on your second or third reel, you'll have to go back to your first finished reel and apply your new wisdom. Even so, by mixing in a sequence different from the editorial sequence, you'll diminish the weaknesses of the "first-off-the-rack" reels.

Mix Groups

Within a scene, there are processing issues that all of the elements have in common. Overall noise reduction and sound shaping are more or less the same for all tracks, so they can be treated together. Conversely, each track has small, or not so small, quirks that will usually be individually sorted out in the console with the EQ and dynamics processors on each channel strip. For the "common" problems, the entire scene is usually bussed to an auxiliary mono chain that may be routed back into the console or to an external processor such as a Dolby Cat.43, a Cedar noise suppressor, or a Urei dipper.

Recording the Premix

As we saw in earlier chapters, finished dialogue is overwhelmingly mono. Nevertheless, you'll premix it to 6 or 8 or 16 record tracks. Remember, a lovely dialogue mix is only one of your goals. The other providing quick, easy, logical options for the final mix.

A week or so before the mix, talk to the mixer or supervising sound editor to find out whether you should plan the recording strategy yourself (before the mix) or if the mixer will map it out. If you're not responsible for engineering this strategy, read no further, but if you are, you need to understand the logic behind record tracks.

During the mix, you'll be playing your 20-odd dialogue tracks from a workstation. Each output—analogue or digital—will be patched to a channel input of the console, mixed, and finally recorded onto hard disk. Let's say you're recording onto 14 record tracks. There are many ways to design these tracks, and unless you have a very good reason to object, defer to the mixer—he's the one who'll have to live with the consequences. Table 18-1 shows an example of what he might come up with.

The wider you spread the dialogue premix recordings, the more flexibility you'll have in the final mix, but you'll pay for it in the time it takes to reroute the mix to different record tracks, especially if your outboard processing equipment is limited. It's easy to print to separate record tracks when all of your processing is within the console. Just route each channel to the record track you want and record everything in one pass. (In some premixing models, the number of record tracks is the same as the number of playback tracks.)

If, however, you're matching shots using the console's EQ and dynamics but bussing the entire scene through one Cat.43 or digital noise reduction device, you'll have to print each record track separately. This is time consuming and a common birthplace of mistakes. What's the "right" number of record tracks? Of course, the only answer is "It depends," so talk with the mixer and the supervising sound editor. The following are a few guidelines.

Table 18-1 Dialogue Premix Record Track Design

Record Track	Record Track Name	Description
1	Dialogue 1	The primary record tracks. Some mixers use Dialogues 1
2	Dialogue 2	and 2 for the bulk of the work, saving Dialogue 3 for
3	Dialogue 3	off-screen or "weird" sounds that may cause trouble
4	Dialogue 4	in the final mix. Track 4 might be saved for the odd "to-be-panned" dialogue event.
5	PFX 1	The production effects tracks, which the mixer may
6	PFX 2	choose to separate at this point to facilitate the international (M&E) mix.
7	ADR 1	Postmixed ADR, which whenever possible is recorded
8	ADR 2	onto separate tracks. Two ADR characters talking to
9	ADR 3	each other shouldn't be recorded onto the same
10	ADR 4	premix track so as not to diminish the final mix options.
11	ADR reverb return 1	The ADR's reverb return, often not mixed with the ADR
12	ADR reverb return 2	but recorded separately. Splitting ADR reverb return
13	ADR reverb return 3	onto several tracks provides more options in the final mix for changing or deleting loop lines.
14	Dialogue reverb return	Mono reverb return, used to match dialogue shots to each other, isn't mixed into the dialogue track but kept separate.

- *Scene by scene.* At the very least, checkerboard one scene against the next. It's entirely possible to mix a whole scene onto one record track, and it makes sense as long as the scene is straightforward, with no great uncertainties, perspective changes, or production effects. But don't put the next scene's mix onto that track. Doing so will rob the mixer of the final mix flexibility he needs to adjust the level, EQ, or other processing of two adjacent scenes.

- *Foreground from background.* Say you're working on a movie about a garage band. In one scene, there's foreground conversation between two band members while the drummer is banging away in the background. If you received separate tracks of the background drumming and the foreground conversation, keep them separate until the final mix. Naturally, there'll be drum sound on the boom covering the foreground chat, but if you keep the drum set's dedicated microphone out of the dialogue until the last minute, the mixer will have greater control.

    Consider another example: Back in Chapter 11 we saw Hamlet and his mother arguing in her room with Polonius listening behind the curtain. Here you would print Hamlet and Gertrude onto two tracks—one with their close perspective and one with Polonius's POV—and put Polonius's breathing, mumbling, and production rustle on a third track.

- *Strange, loud, or otherwise troublesome sounds*, such as screams, shouts, and crying. If the track might need further processing or control in the final mix, split it.
- *PFX*. You went to the trouble of separating the production effects from the dialogue. If these elements are recorded to a dedicated set of record tracks, the M&E mix (for the international version) will be greatly simplified.
- Anything else for which flexibility is prudent.

As always, ask the mixer how to plan the recordings. Even if he decides to take care of the routing and track-arming plan, your input on how to efficiently record the dialogue premix will prove helpful because you know the film and probably have some pretty strong ideas about the focus and depth of its scenes. You also likely know the director better than the mixer does, so you have a better idea of where to cover your bases. Write your premix plan directly onto the cue sheets, as discussed in Chapter 17.

Forgoing the Premix

Newer, bigger, and more glorious digital consoles allow mixers to automate every fader move and every EQ and dynamics setting. That's because the outboard kit linked to the console via MIDI, MADI, or Ethernet can be included in an automation session. With this power of recall, some mixers forgo premixes altogether, instead stringing up all the film's tracks and interactively mixing one section with another. They argue that because all film sounds are interrelated, any change in one section of the mix necessarily affects all others.

This is undoubtedly true, but I'm still a holdout when it comes to diving headlong into the final mix. For me, the dialogue premix is about focusing on the details. It's when you can really dwell on the tiniest of matters, without the burden of the rest of the film weighing on you. This is your chance to find those sublime moments that are rarely directly heard in the final but that collectively make up a masterpiece. During the final mix, everyone is more concerned with balance than with detail, with telling a story than with minutiae. And during the print master stage, there's a further step back, to flow and the overall subtle changes that give the film its polish and integrity.

If the mixer insists on "going straight to final," try to persuade her that a single mixer can't open up all of the tracks and give them the attention they deserve. We have only two hands and two ears. This is a good time to try to get the producer to argue your point. If persuasion doesn't work and you find yourself supervising the "dialogue part of the final mix"—whatever that is—your job will be to ensure that the dialogue isn't shortchanged and swept under the carpet of backgrounds and effects.

Getting Approval

It's just as well that most directors find observing the dialogue premix akin to watching a printer set type. It's much easier on all concerned if you keep her out of the daily blow by blow, bringing her onto the stage only when you've finished a reel. If possible, ask the director to remain quiet and take notes while you play an entire reel. If you're always stopping and starting to address her issues, you'll never get a feel for the reel and you'll never finish. Ask her to attach timecode or footage to her notes since it's difficult to tell a machine control to "cue to the shot where Roxanne coughs."

When you've finished screening the reel, listen only to the opinion of viewers who have any business spouting one. If you can, keep ex-spouses, accountants, boyfriends or girlfriends, and personal trainers out of the screening—one tiny bomb dropped by an outsider can poison an evaluation and the damage may take hours to rectify. Take good notes on who says what, and review them before dismissing the audience. Look for any conflicts, such as the director wanting scene 3 more blue and the producer wanting it more red. Don't let anybody go until you have a plan for the fixes you intend to make.

As you address complaints, decide with the mixer which ones are for final mix and which require getting back into the premix. Normally, most issues raised by the guys in the back of the room are of the "Louder here, softer there" variety, which can be addressed in the final mix.

The Final Mix

It's likely that you won't be at the final mix unless you stick around for your own enlightenment (a good idea from time to time). Even if you aren't there, it's important to know what happens to your work down the line, after you've left the job, just as you had to know what happened to the dialogue tracks before they got to you.

Dialogue is almost always the first premix, since on most narrative films it serves as the backbone of the soundtrack, with other mixes referring to it. In the premix of the other elements of the film, as well as during the final mix, the 8, 12, or 16 multitrack recordings you created during the dialogue premix become playback tracks. Typically, they'll show up on individual console channels and will be slaved to one or more master faders to make life more sane for the mixer. Global dialogue adjustments (for example, "Make it louder!") can be controlled from these master faders, whereas individual dialogue premix tracks will be controlled from their channel strips, whether for reequalizing an ADR line or lowering a PFX door slam.

The number and sequence of premixes depend on the film type, the console size, and the mixer's habits. Obviously, an action film will demand a lot of time on SFX and Foley, whereas on a dialogue-heavy film, with only atmospheric sound effects, the mixer may bring the nondialogue elements directly to the final mix. Giant consoles with ample automation allow premixing of any element without having to record anything. This is the best of all worlds because the mixer can focus on detail during the premix without commitment.

The final mix is where all elements finally meet each other. Music, more than likely already mixed at another facility, will appear as a set of LCRS (or wider) elements, and sound effects, backgrounds, and Foleys will show up raw or as multitrack premixes. As you would expect, monitoring the final mix depends on the format it's being prepared for. A Dolby SR mix will be monitored on LCRS; a Dolby Digital mix, in 5.1 channels and SDDS, on five behind-screen speakers plus surround. The final mix is not only about story, style, balance, and emphasis, but also about sound image.

Just as the premixes were recorded "wider" than necessary to allow for flexibility in the final mix, so the final is mix recorded onto discrete multitrack groups called **stems**, which provide yet more flexibility. As the mix progresses, the final mixed dialogue is recorded on LCRS stems (or wider stems depending on the format), either on hard-disk or on 35 mm magnetic film. The same goes for SFX, BG, Music, and Foley—to preserve flexibility during the final pass and, more important, to facilitate the creation of print masters in various release formats.

Print Master and Special Mixes

When the mix is finished, two tasks remain. First, it must be mastered in a format that enables the shooting of an optical negative to hold all of the channels for the release print. From this optical negative, a soundtrack can be printed onto film.

Dolby SR The only surviving analogue format, except for mono, is Dolby SR; it requires the most exotic mastering process. During the mix, and later in cinema playback, it's a 4-channel format but the four channels are stored on the film print as a 2-channel analogue optical track. In North America, this 2:4:2 print master format is called "Lt/Rt" for "Left Total/Right Total." In Europe, it's called SVA, for "Stereo Variable Area."

Since this encoding process uses phase information to guide sound to the correct channel, the mixer has to listen to the playback of the decoded Lt/Rt to make sure there are no unexpected imaging gifts. Many mixers will mix the entire job through the Dolby matrix so that they'll always be certain that all sounds end up where they should. A Dolby SR Lt/Rt print master is usually recorded to a DAT or DA-88, depending on the needs of the lab that will shoot the optical negative. Dolby Digital is a discrete format, so no matrix is required. The print master is recorded to a Dolby-owned magneto-optical recorder. SDDS and DTS each have their own special mastering requirements, so if a film is to be distributed in several release formats, separate print masters are needed.

International Version (M&E) Once the native language mix is complete, it's time for the international mix. Wherever possible, this is a combination of SFX, Foley, and music stems, plus whatever you were able to extract from the dialogue during the premix. Many dialogue-based sounds in the final mix can't be salvaged for M&E, usually because the dialogue steps on them (how ironic that dialogue editing requires excising nonverbal sounds from the track, while in the international mix it's the words that ruin everything). The sound effects editor will undoubtedly have to add many new effects to cover the loss.

It's much more efficient to create the M&E mix just after the main mix rather than weeks or months later. The sound crew is still assembled, the elements are easily available, and the supervising sound editor and mixer are familiar with the film's quirks. Moreover, the automation is still loaded in the console and whatever outboard kit was used for the main mix is still connected.

There are times, however, when the international mix has to wait, usually because the production has spent its last cent on the mix and the lab, and they're waiting for a foreign distributor to commit to the project. Only then will the M&E mix take place. It's an inefficient way to work, but at times it's the only option.

TV and Airplane Versions Most films will eventually make it to television, and in the United States there are some unusual laws and conventions about film language. Even if a film meets FCC standards for violence and nudity, it could still require dialogue cosmetic surgery to play, for example, in Peoria. Anticipating this, the ADR supervisor recorded alternate TV versions of all problematic dialogue while tracking the primary loop line. You added these alternates when you prepared the ADR for the dialogue premix. You didn't need them in the regular dialogue premix, but you or the supervising sound editor will now use them to replace the offending lines. This new, aseptic dialogue will be folded into an otherwise acceptable final mix.

The airplane mix is the most castrated of all sound jobs. The way the airlines see it, going to a cinema is a choice and you can walk out if the movie offends you. Likewise, you can always turn off the tube if you find a film objectionable for you or your family. However, it's pretty difficult to ignore the screen on a 15-hour flight from New York to Tokyo and harder still to keep the kids from watching *Lenny* while you sleep.

So, according to some rather draconian standards for film content, an airplane version will undoubtedly have undergone picture censorship, which means that you'll be faced with a new print version. You will have to make the full-mix stems conform to this new print, and any ADR language expunging that's beyond the scope of the TV version will have to be mixed in too.

Afterword

You've been through the whole process of dialogue editing. You've taken a film, whose narrative was complete but whose sound structure was a mess, and turned it into a clean, clear gem that has focus, point of view, and tension. You've sought out the very best of the sounds recorded on the set and folded them into the story without compromising the director's vision. You've removed from the dialogue the telltale artifacts of the filmmaking process as well as the annoying noises that everyone makes while talking.

Then you presented all of this to the mixer in a way that ensured a quick, productive, artistic mix. In short, you've successfully presented the moviegoer with the cleanest, smartest, most appealing dialogue sounds possible. This is no small feat, and it warrants real congratulations.

I've shown you my approach to organizing and editing dialogue. This system works well for me, but you'd expect that. Take from this book what works for you, look to others for more advice, and figure out the rest. Your own personality and way of thinking will mold your way of editing.

I love this job. Despite its pressures, frustrations, and occasional tedium, I can't imagine doing anything else to make a living. My tracks are my babies: I find them in a totally undeveloped state and I slowly raise them to stand on their own. The final tracks speak with their own voices; I merely help them to find themselves. But within each of "my" tracks is a bit of me. When I see a film I've worked on and I listen to the dialogue, I feel like a proud parent watching my grown children telling their stories.

Like all trades, cutting dialogue is at times nothing more than a job. Of course there are days I'd rather be at the beach or playing with my cats. There are times when I want to choke the editor or the director, but then I remember that it's not my film, and whatever pressure I feel is much, much worse for them. Too many times the thought of *one more screening* makes me want to scream. But most of the time, I am amazed that I actually get paid to do what I so love to do.

Dialogue editing combines a knack for storytelling, a decent ear, some technical knowledge, better-than-average organizational skills, a head for *process*, and a good chair. Mostly, it's a love of movies and the knowledge that, through your subversive contributions, you can have a huge impact on the cinematic success of a film that makes the job so satisfying. Most people won't notice what you've done, but your *footprint* is huge. Dialogue editing is truly the invisible art.

APPENDIX A

Dialogue Editing in a Nutshell

Regardless of the shooting format or the video standard, all dialogue editing follows more or less the same path. Only the details vary depending on style, budget, and schedule.

This outline of the steps involved in editing dialogue for a theatrical dramatic film should help you plan your work and track your progress, whatever your project. Don't consider it etched in stone but rather as a reminder. Keep in mind that the type of film being edited determines whether all steps will be required or if some will be replaced. For example, documentaries generally don't need ADR, and shorter TV schedules eliminate some steps because of time constraints.

Depending on the project, you probably won't perform all of the tasks outlined, particularly much of the setup for editing, which is traditionally handled by the assistant sound editor (indicated by an asterisk,*) or by the assistant picture editor (indicated by a double asterisk,**).

Of course, on very small-budget jobs, the entire process usually falls into your lap.

Preparation

1. *Meet with the picture editor and watch a few scenes of the offline edit before the film is finished.* (Chapter 5)
   1.1. Understand how the editor thinks and what "traps" await you.
   1.2. Ask the assistant picture editor to set aside important wild sounds or alternates if possible. It's often easier for him to find this material than for you to look for them in the dailies.
   1.3. Listen to a few scenes to see if the OMF sound is acceptable. Find out how the sound was digitized into the Avid so you can decide whether the OMF is usable or if you have to use the original field recordings.

1.4. Determine the quality of the tracks and estimate how long you'll need for dialogue editing. Knowing what the big problems are will come in handy at the spotting session with the director, editor, supervising sound editor, et al.

2. *Make sure the picture editor cut the film into 2000-ft reels, or no longer than 21 minutes.** (Chapter 5)
    2.1. Make sure reel breaks occur at sensible places.****
    2.2. Ensure that "sync pops" (or "plops" in the United Kingdom) occur two seconds before the first frame of action on each reel. See that the picture editor has attached tail leaders with corresponding sync pops.****
    2.3. Make sure the picture is "locked" before you begin!!!

3. *Perform OMF conversion and/or auto-assembly from original tapes.** (Chapter 5)
    3.1. Extract OMFs from the Avid and convert to Pro Tools sessions. Or use the OMF import routine of whatever DAW you're working on.**
    3.2. Create CMX3600 EDLs from the Avid session. Make separate EDLs of audio-only edits and video edits, by reel.****
    3.3. Clean the EDLs in preparation for autoconform (auto-assembly) or file linking.**
    3.4. Autoconform or file-link on one reel of the project (if you plan to autoconform the film).**
    3.5. Listen to a reel of the OMF, then to a few minutes of the autoconform. Compare the two to see if there's any advantage to autoconforming the entire project. Decide if you're using the OMF, the autoconform, or both. Dialogue crews on feature films almost always reload and resync the original sound elements. Low-budget films often rely on the OMF audio files because of money/time constraints.

4. *Set up your editing workspace.* (Chapter 9)
    4.1. Open the session you created with the OMF translator.**
    4.2. Open about 14 tracks above the OMF or the autoconform tracks (for a total of about 30 tracks). Label the first 10 *blank* tracks "Dial A," Dial B," . . . "Dial J." Label the 11th and 12th tracks, "work 1" and "work 2." Before you set up your track workspace, talk to the rerecording mixer about track preferences.**
    4.3. Create three new tracks called "junk 1," junk 2," and "junk 3." These are for regions you remove from the active tracks but want to keep just in case.**

4.4. Label the original OMF tracks: "OMF 1," "OMF 2," . . . "OMF 8," and so on.*

4.5. Label the original autoconform tracks: "Conf 1," "Conf 2," . . . "Conf 8" (depending on how wide your autoconform was). Or call these auto-assembly tracks "Assy 1," . . . "Assy 8." You'll add other tracks for ADR, X and Y, and PFX later. No point clogging up your session so soon.*

4.6. Adjust the DAW outputs to match your monitoring setup. A truly hip cutting room will provide L,C,R monitoring so that dialogue can be monitored in true mono rather than phantom center.*

5. *Set up a sensible saving/naming plan for the project.* (Chapter 6)

6. *Import and sync the film if you're working to a digital picture file.**

6.1. Obtain a "hard copy" (e.g., Betacam) of the final picture rather than just a QuickTime or AVI movie. This allows you to recreate a video file, if needed, and gives you more control of the information superimposed onto the digital movie.

6.2. When you create your video file, create a timecode burn-in of the record time. If possible, place the timecode window outside of the image area. Make it as small as possible and don't cover up other windows (placing the timecode burn-in at the top or bottom is an issue for you and the other members of your crew to decide).*

6.3. Record audio and video when you make your digital movie file. This audio guide track will help you to determine if your tracks are in sync with the edited work track but won't necessarily ensure sync with the picture.*

6.4. Sync the QuickTime video with the audio timeline in the DAW.*

7. *Check the sync of the OMF against the guide track. Get the entire project in absolute sync before beginning to edit.* This way you won't have worry about it for the rest of the project. (Chapter 9)

7.1. Create an edit group for the OMF tracks.

7.2. Open the movie's audio guide track onto a track outside the OMF edit group, in sync with the movie. Lock the track so that you don't inadvertently move it.

7.3. Solo the movie's audio along with the OMF group and play the session. If the two are in sync, you'll hear phasing. If not, the OMF track will have to be nudged to bring it into sync. Usually, the OMF is either in dead sync or out by half a frame.

7.4. Set the *Nudge* value to 0.25 frame (10 ms in PAL, 8.3 ms in NTSC). Select all OMF tracks and nudge them in ¼-frame increments until they phase against the guide track.

7.5. If you're working against Betacam or DV or other tape-based video, make a mono guide track (with timestamp) from the videotape. Place it on the top track of your session and lock it; then follow the preceding steps for syncing.

8. *Check the sync of the autoconform or relinked files (if used) against the guide track.* Use the same technique as with the OMF. (Chapter 9)

9. *Keep a copy of the original OMF and autoconform tracks, disabled and hidden away.* If you inadvertently delete a track, knock a section out of sync, or delete the wrong side of a split-track file, you can refer to a copy from these original tracks. (Chapter 9)

9.1. If you've opened an OMF and created an autoconform, decide which one to use for editing. If you have both OMF and autoconform and you won't be editing with the OMF tracks, disable and hide them.

9.2. Select everything on the tracks you're planning to use, then "copy/drag in sync" to the topmost dialogue tracks (Dial A → Dial?). On Pro Tools the command is CTL+OPT+drag (Mac) or right click+ALT+drag (Windows).

9.3. Disable and hide the original tracks.

10. *Delete level and pan automation. Pan all tracks to center, volume to zero.* It's much easier to edit the dialogue without the picture editor's automation. Remember your reference copy in the hidden original OMF tracks, which you can use to figure out what sort of level automation was done in the picture cutting room. (Chapter 9)

11. *Hold a spotting session with director, picture editor, and other sound crew members when the OMF or autoconform is complete and in sync.* (Chapter 7)

11.1. Note ADR requests (if there's no ADR supervisor on the film).

11.2. Determine the director's pet dialogue and ADR concerns.

11.3. With the rest of the sound crew, come up with a plan and a schedule.

12. *Remove unnecessary regions.* The elements you receive from the picture department in an OMF or autoconform will likely be on two tracks, regardless whether the material is stereo or split track or dual mono. To get a better idea of what you need to do, to avoid phasing or distortion, and to have a "lighter" session, decide which element pairs are dual mono and delete one side from each. *Never simultaneously use more regions than are absolutely necessary.* (Chapter 9)

12.1. Use phase cancellation to determine if a pair of regions are identical. On each odd-numbered track containing dialogue, insert a zero-latency plug-in that can reverse phase.

12.2. Click the phase reverse button (ø). Don't touch anything else on the plug-in.

12.3. Turn off level automation.

12.4. Solo one pair at a time. One track will be in phase; one will be phase reversed. If the material is *exactly* the same, you'll hear little or no sound. Use the track level adjustment to tweak the cancellation. You'll know you have phase cancellation if you mute one track and the sound becomes louder and more robust. Once you know that the tracks are identical, delete *one* of the regions. It doesn't matter which one because they're similar enough to phase-cancel.

12.5. If you don't have phase cancellation, the tracks aren't identical. *Do nothing*, even if one side is significantly "better" than the other. You don't know enough about the scene yet to make this choice.

12.6. Continue for the rest of the regions; then cancel the inserted plug-ins and turn on automation.

12.7. Click *Save*.

13. *Mark and name the scene boundaries for the entire film.* This will allow you to navigate through the reel and make quick, easy scene transitions. Do it now before you get busy. Also mark obvious perspective changes within scenes if you're feeling industrious. (Chapter 9)

14. *Organize the regions within each scene.* This will give you better control of the scene, to facilitate an easier mix, to allow for sensible perspective control and processing, and to set up scene transitions. Well-organized tracks also make editing much faster. (Chapter 10)

14.1. Split by source angle—not at each picture cut but at the camera angle the soundfile "belongs to." Think of this as splitting by boom angle or shot. Under normal circumstances, use the shot information within the region name to organize the tracks. If you're working on scene 31 and the shots are 31A, 31B, 31C, and 31D, place the A shots on one track, the B shots on another, and so forth.

14.2. If necessary, split by "sound problem." Even from the same angle with the same actor, one shot may have more traffic, air conditioning noise, etc., so split accordingly.

14.3. Split by perspective. This relates to picture edits, *not* source angle.

14.4. Split for production effects (PFX) you want to save for an international version or for better mix control. Split off doors, slaps, bangs, and other sounds. If there's dialogue or breathing within a PFX region, leave it on the dialogue track.

14.5. Split weird or very loud sounds—anything that might need extra control in the mix.

14.6. Consider the rerecording mixer who'll have to make sense of your edits. Talk to her about her splitting preferences, and give her what she wants.

Editing

15. *First pass.* The most important phase of the process, where you'll do most of your work and where you'll learn what has to be replaced via ADR. (Chapter 10)

15.1. Repair using room tone.

15.1.1. Make tone transitions between regions.

15.1.2. Remove production noises.

15.1.3. Make the scene "seamless."

15.2. Repair using alternate takes. Use the EDLs and the sound reports to find other takes. Go back to the original sound recordings.

15.2.1. Repair or replace off-mic dialogue and overlaps.

15.2.2. Fix or replace "bad" dialogue (poor diction).

15.2.3. Repair or replace words corrupted by noises.

15.3. List items you can't (or won't) fix. You'll have another opportunity to fix these items.

15.4. Periodically record a dialogue guide track for the other sound editors (SFX, BG, Foley, music). Update this track when you make major dialogue changes.

16. *ADR.* (Chapter 15)

16.1. As you edit, note dialogue problems that can't be fixed and must be replaced for various reasons.

16.1.1. Off-mic sound.

16.1.2. "Stepped-on" dialogue (overlaps).

16.1.3. Bad acting (usually a dangerous fix).

16.1.4. Text changes (bad idea; sometimes accomplished during over-the-shoulder shots or when character is off-screen).

16.1.5. "TV-safe" alternate lines (none of the seven deadly words).

16.1.6. Very high ambient noise.

16.1.7. Distortion.

16.1.8. "Additional" lines requested by the director (off-screen, exposition, explanations).

16.1.9. Additional breaths, smacks, sighs, and so on to enhance drama or action.

16.1.10. Group loop (background walla, specific background action, pages and announcements, other crowd sounds).

16.2. Spot ADR.

16.2.1. Break lines into short segments and assign each segment its own code number. Usually the code consists of the first three letters of the character's name followed by a series number; this will become the "root" of the soundfile name during ADR recording.

16.2.2. Spot the exact timecode or footage start and stop. Scrub to the *exact* beginning of modulation to get the precise start time. Generally add ½ second to the out time to allow for decay.

16.3. Prepare for recording session.

16.3.1. Make a list of lines for each character. Type everything.

16.3.2. Prepare the ADR recording report forms.

16.4. Prepare the recording sessions (beeps, track names, locate points) if you're recording to a workstation. If you're using another process, work with the ADR recording engineer to streamline the session. *Record ADR.* You probably won't record the ADR, but instead provide information for the ADR supervisor or supervising sound editor. Use the paperwork to make notes about the recording session. (Chapter 15)

17. *Second pass.* Edit the ADR/group loop (unless there's an ADR editor), improving your first-pass edits, repairing items you didn't get to in the first pass, and better organizing the tracks. This is another chance to talk to the rerecording mixer about track layout. (Chapter 15)

17.1. Edit ADR. Use the ADR recording reports to tell you which take to use, how to put together complicated ADR sections, and to check off the ADR call as completed.

17.2. Tackle unfinished dialogue problems.

17.3. Remove remaining production noises.

17.4. Rethink your editing philosophy and redo any bad work.

17.5. Check your track geography for the best layout.

17.6. *Screen the dialogue* to the director, picture editor, producer, and so on.

18. *Final pass.*

18.1. *Adjust sync* to match the answer print telecine (film projects) or online (video projects). (Chapter 17)

18.2. *Make final repairs.* Review the comments from your screening with the director, producer, picture editor, etc., and your own. Fix what you can; apologize for what you can't.

Prepare for the Premix

19. *Preparation.* (Chapter 17)

19.1. Print cue sheets and add any notes for the mix (bussing assignments, instructions for the mixer, etc.).

19.2. Reconfigure DAW outputs to match the mixing environment. Check voices.

19.3. Make sure each track has a reference tone at the correct level (e.g., $-18\,dB = 0\,VU = +4\,dBM$, or $-20\,dB = 0\,VU = +4\,dBM$).

19.4. Make sure that Dial A has a head sync pop at the correct place on each reel.

19.5. Add the tail pop to match the answer print tail leader.

19.6. Archive all work material.

APPENDIX B

Track Template for a Typical Small Film's Dialogue

It's impossible to create a track setup that works for all small- to medium-size films, but when you're setting up your workspace you have to start somewhere. I suggest you build a template with the tracks shown in the following table. Keep it on a USB keychain or a CD that you can take from job to job, and save it in the lowest version of Pro Tools (or other workstation) that's available in your market so you can open it anywhere you work.

I prefer to use letters in naming the tracks I take to the dialogue premix (e.g., dialogue, PFX, X, ADR) and numbers in naming the tracks that don't interest the mixer but just make my life easier (e.g., work and junk tracks, etc.).

Initial Tracks	Initial Source	Audio Format	Comments
Dial A → L	Mono, from original field recordings	Mono and/or dual-mono	Used to hold most of your production sound edits.
Work tracks 1, 2, 3 +	Blank for now	Mono and/or dual-mono	Used as safe places for opening files, making complex edits, and using Shuffle mode.
Junk 1 → 6	Blank for now	Usually mono	Used for anything you don't want in your active tracks yet don't want to delete. Also useful for storing alternate take regions. Keep these tracks in sync (unlike work tracks, where there are no rules). Use for storing room tones you create for a scene.

(continues)

Initial Tracks	Initial Source	Audio Format	Comments
PFX A → D	Blank for now	Mono	Production effects are used to sync sounds from the field recordings that you want to separate from the dialogue, either for use in the international mix or for better mix control.
For SFX 1 → 4	Blank for now	Mono/stereo	Used for all nondialogue elements, such as temporary music and SFX, removed from the OMF, so that SFX and music editors can retrieve them without entering your session.
ADR A → D +	Blank for now; later you'll add mono or two-microphone files from the ADR recording sessions	Mono or dual-mono (and some stereo elements if you use ADR tracks for group loop)	Used for holding ADR. The number of tracks depends on the ADR complexity of your film.
Dial X, Y, Z	Blank for now	Mono	Known as "X tracks"; used during ADR editing to hold lines that have been replaced and completely edited. A dialogue track holds a tone fill that matches a replaced line on an X track so that the rerecording mixer can conveniently A/B between the original line and the ADR line.

Glossary

There are many outstanding film sound glossaries. David Yewdall's *Practical Art of Motion Picture Sound,* Third Edition (2007), contains a glossary with concise, no-nonsense definitions useful to sound editors and designers. Another, Larry Blake's "What's a Binky?"—a legendary collection of film sound terminology—was originally published in *Mix Magazine;* it is now available on a number of web sites. This is one of the most comprehensive film sound dictionaries ever compiled and offers a refreshing glance of what things are really called in the working world. For a massive glossary of film editorial terminology, see Norman Hollyn's *The Film Editing Room Handbook;* for a narrative-treatment glossary with a historical bent, turn to *Film Sound: Theory and Practice* edited by Elisabeth Weis and John Belton.

This glossary isn't as comprehensive as those just mentioned. Instead, it focuses on terms specifically applicable to dialogue editing and other concepts that affect those who edit dialogue. Some terms fall into the realm of picture cutting or mixing, but they're nonetheless part of the basic vocabulary of dialogue editors.

A/B reel   A reel of film not longer than 2050 feet (about 22 minutes). When movies were edited on film and mag, picture and sound editors worked in reels no longer than 1000 feet. After the premixes, these reels were joined to form 2000-ft lengths. Today, most sound editors work directly in 2000-ft lengths, since the inconvenience of large film units on a flatbed or upright editor is no longer an issue.

ADL (AES31 audio decision list)   The ADL is a file format for exchanging information between different types of workstations, both sound and picture. Its format offers far greater detail and accuracy than the conventional CMX edit decision list, which it's gradually replacing. See *EDL.*

ADR (*automated dialogue replacement* or *automatic dialogue replacement*, depending whom you listen to)   An electronic means of rerecording dialogue lines that combines machine control, monitor switching, and cues for talent and naming. The term *ADR* is often used interchangeably with *postsync* and *looping*, although there are mechanical and procedural differences between the three.

ADR call sheet (ADR cue sheet)   A detailed list of the lines that need to be rere-corded in a studio to repair damaged lines or add new information.

ADR recording log   A log of recording of an ADR cue that contains information about each take, including whether it's the "buy" (the one chosen), as well as instructions to the ADR editor. Also referred to as a "session report."

ADR spotting session   A screening of a film to determine which dialogue lines will be rerecorded. After the screening, the ADR supervisor makes detailed, standardized notes concerning each ADR cue.

A-frame   The first of five frames in a complete cycle of the *3:2 pulldown*. During a telecine transfer from 24 fps film to NTSC videotape, certain film frames are repeated to maintain correct speed. Knowing which is the A frame is vital when establishing a direct relationship between film frames and video frames—some-thing you must know when cutting negative.

ALE (Avid Log Exchange) file   A type of *telecine log* used to manage film negative information and ensure a solid relationship between film negative frames and video frames. Similar to a *FLEx file*.

Alternate take   Any take of a shot (setup) other than the one chosen by the director and picture editor. Alternate takes are valuable sources of replacement dialogue and room tone, which is why dialogue editors spend so much time going through them.

Answer prints   These are the first prints to emerge from the lab after negative cutting and before mass duplication. The answer prints are used to correct the final look of the film and to ensure that no mistakes were made during negative cutting. The *first answer print* provides the dialogue editor with the first real chance to see what the film looks like and to solve lingering sync problems.

Assembly   In the picture editing process, the first meaningful stringing together of selected takes in script order. Often very long, the assembly allows the picture editor and director to understand the material and to begin a meaningful rough cut.

Auto-assembly/autoconform   The reconstruction of all audio events within the picture edit, using the EDLs, original tapes or files, and software to control the process. An auto-assembly recreates the picture editor's work with original sounds, in contrast to an OMF, which uses Avid or FCP soundfiles. Also called *PostConform* (a trademark of Digidesign).

Batch digitizing   The picture workstation equivalent of an *auto-assembly*. Most com-monly, batch digitizing takes place at the end of the picture editing process to create a high-resolution version of the final picture cut.

Bin (Avid)   A folder in which files are stored in the Avid workstation. A dialogue editor without access to original recordings can convert the Avid or FCP bins to *DAW* sessions (via *OMF*) to make alternate takes and wild sound available.

B-roll   In news-style documentaries, the supporting or illustrative footage. Contrast this with *interview* or *talking head* footage.

BWF (broadcast wave format)   An improvement on the wave (.wav) soundfile format. In addition to audio information, a BWF file can carry shot descriptions, technical logs, and timecode.

Change notes   Information provided by the picture department to describe changes made to the film after picture lock. The audio tracks must be conformed to match these changes. Change notes can be handwritten or automatically generated by the picture workstation.

Changeover   On a multireel film, the switch from one projector to the other during a reel change. Nowadays, few films are projected on two projectors, but rather are spliced into one continuous string and stored on a horizontal platter. Nonetheless, due to the displacement between the projector gate and the sound head, care must be taken when preparing print masters. Approximately the first 20 frames of a subsequent reel must be copied to the tail of each reel. This extension is called a *pullup* or a "changeover tail."

Channel mapping   An audio-routing matrix used when performing an *auto-assembly* (*PostConform* or *autoconform*). The audio channel relationship between an event's description in the *EDL*, the source material, and the target channel can be set while preparing for an auto-assembly. This is particularly valuable when loading sounds from a 2-channel medium into a multichannel session.

Clean edit list   Required for auto-assemblies, an *EDL* free of illegal events, unnecessary information, non-Latin fonts, and legacies from previous edits. Today, this is rarely an issue, since nonlinear picture editing machines automatically generate a clean list.

CMX   Initially the result of a partnership between CBS and Memorex, it was the pioneer in machine controllers for online editing. The CMX3600 edit decision list, which describes and stores editing information, is still the standard means of communicating event information between picture and sound departments. See *EDL*.

Color timing   The adjustment of a film's colors and brightness in the lab, which usually occurs while the sound department is editing. Also called "grading."

Comment   A line or lines of information beneath the event line on a CMX edit decision list that can be used to insert scene/take data into the region names in the dialogue editor's session.

Conformation   Any change made to a reel after picture lock. Sometimes unavoidable yet loathed by the sound department.

Coverage   The manner of shooting a scene to provide sufficient material to work with. A scene that lacks the takes/angles needed to piece together a decent assembly is wanting of coverage.

Crossfade   A transition in which one sound element fades out as another fades in. In dialogue editing, a crossfade should usually be "level neutral" so that there is neither an increase nor a decrease in level over the course of the transition.

Crossfade linking   A control within the fade parameters of a digital audio worksta-tion (*DAW*) that links the characteristics of the two sides of a crossfade: the fade-out and fade-in. Under normal circumstances, crossfade linking ensures fade symmetry. Care must be taken to select a mid-fade attenuation of −3 dB when crossfading "normal" (not phase-coherent) material, and −6 dB when crossfading a sound against itself, as in *perspective cuts*.

Cross-modulation test (cross-mod)   A series of exposure, processing, and printing tests used to ensure the best results when preparing an optical soundtrack. The tests calibrate the film stock and equipment at the sound facility that shoots and develops the optical negative with those of the film lab that prints the *answer print*.

Cue sheet (rerecording log)   A tabular chart showing the layout and contents of the tracks brought to a mix.

Cutaway   A picture editing technique in which a shot is briefly interrupted by another, usually to hide a piece of main shot, to adjust timing, or to change from one take to another. Cutaways are commonly used in documentaries to hide sound edits within an interview.

Cut list   Similar to an *EDL*, a list that contains all of the information needed for the negative cutter to conform the film's original negative to the final locked edit. In the modern world, the cut list is generated more or less automatically by the picture workstation. In the days of sprockets, this list was prepared by hand.

DAW (digital audio workstation)   A nonlinear electronic editing platform used for music and audio postproduction editing.

Destructive editorial processes   Any electronic sound editing process that alters or destroys an original sound file. Examples include any recording in which old takes are overwritten, and certain noise reduction processes that permanently alter the soundfile.

DigiTranslator (a trademark of Digidesign)   A utility for converting *OMFI* 2.0 files into Pro Tools sessions. No longer offered as a standalone utility, DigiTranslator is now packaged within the Pro Tools application.

Dolby SR (a trademark of Dolby Laboratories)   (1) A noise reduction system, intro-duced in 1986, offering much better performance than its predecessor, Dolby A. (2) The standard analogue format (Dolby Stereo) on film release prints, provid-ing left, center, right, and mono surround channels encoded into a 2-channel analogue optical soundtrack. (3) Dolby SR-D (or Dolby Digital), introduced in 1992 as a 5.1-channel digital format whose data are stored between the sprockets of 35 mm prints. Dolby Digital uses AC3 coding for data compression.

Double system   (1) A type of film projection in which image and sound are on separate media. Interlocking a mute answer print with a soundtrack on a DA-88 or workstation is an example. (2) A location recording technique, such as shoot-ing film or tape and recording sound to a DAT or hard disk recorder. Contrast this with recording sound directly onto videotape, an example of *single-system* production.

Dual-mono Two parallel audio channels containing exactly the same information. Compare with stereo or split-track recordings, where the two channels contain different information.

Dubber A playback-only mag machine used to reproduce sprocketed sound elements during a mix.

EBU (European Broadcasting Union) A standards organization (and more) for European radio and television. "EBU timecode" refers to the 25 fps timecode used in *PAL* (phase alternate line) and SECAM (*séquentiel couleur à mémoire*) countries.

Edit group A function in digital audio workstations (*DAW*s) that allows you to link a number of tracks so that they behave as a group. Mono, solo, and editing commands on any track within the group will affect all of them.

EDL (edit decision list) A list generated by nonlinear film workstations and offline video editing systems that describes each event in an edited film reel, TV program, and so on. The information it contains includes the source of each shot and its location within the program and possibly an identification of scenes and takes. EDLs are vital tools for dialogue editors looking for alternate takes of a line.

Exhibition print The mass-produced prints of a film shipped to theaters for public viewing, comprised of reels of approximately 2000 feet (about 600 meters) in length.

FFOA (first frame of action) The first frame of meaningful picture of a reel of edited film. In other words, the first frame past the head leader.

Final mix The ultimate combining of a film's sound elements. Typically, the mixing process begins with the dialogue premix, followed by other premixes if deemed necessary and the budget allows. The final mix uses the premixes as playback sources, along with remaining unmixed sound elements, to create a finished soundtrack.

First answer print The first print made of a film after negative cutting. In most cases, this print is mute. In some film cultures, this silent first answer print is called a "blacktrack answer print."

FLEx (Film Log EDL Exchange) **file** Developed by da Vinci Systems, a file protocol for transferring film-related information to and from videotape and nonlinear editing systems. With FLEx (or Avid's *ALE*) files, data on film negative, telecine transfer, audio, and the like (all forms of *metadata*) can be stored for later use in negative cutting, retransfer, and sound finishing.

Focus group A "man on the street" public audience assembled to watch and comment on an unfinished film. The focus group is becoming increasingly important in determining the direction, if not the fate, of a film.

Foley "Live" sound effects recorded sync-to-picture and later edited for finesse. Foley effects commonly include footsteps, clothing rustle, and chair squeaks, but may include mechanical sounds, door squeaks, and unrealistic sounds.

Fullcoat This is 35 mm magnetic film that's completely covered with oxide on one side. Depending on the head stack used, you can record up to six channels onto one fullcoat.

Fundamental frequency   The lowest frequency in a harmonic series and almost always the lowest frequency present in the pitch of a note made by a musical instrument. Also called "first harmonic."

Genlock   A system allowing vertical, horizontal, frame, and color synchronization of two or more video devices such as cameras. In audio applications, the most common genlock reference is black burst, which synchronizes all digital audio devices in a chain to each other and to the video devices within the facility. Genlock provides speed and timing information so that multiple machines play at the same speed and their frames begin at exactly the same time. This provides synchronization accuracy of much less than a frame (when combined with another synchronization protocol such as MTC, LTC, VITC, or Sony 9-pin).

Group loop   The recording of extra, nonprincipal voices during postproduction to add mood and texture to a scene, to enhance the plot, or to provide other information.

Guide track   (1) A field recording under impossible circumstances with less than ideal results. Knowing that the track is needed for reference but useless for sound, the location mixer labels the track "Guide track." (2) A temporary mono (or wider) mix provided by one sound editing department to another as an editing aid. A dialogue editor will periodically provide a mono guide track of his or her progress to the SFX and BG editors so that they can make better judgments than when working against the unedited *OMF*.

Handle   Extra sound material extending beyond the visible (and audible) boundaries of a region. Handle duration can be determined during OMF creation or *auto-assembly*. As a rule, dialogue editors want handles to be as long as possible. See *load spacing*.

Harmonic   An integer multiple of a fundamental frequency. For example, a string vibrating at a fundamental frequency of 100 Hz will have a harmonic at 100 Hz intervals. The harmonic structure of a musical note is what gives it its color. The harmonic nature of buzzes and hums is what makes them so hard to clean.

Headroom   (1) The area in a shot between the top of the frame and the subject. Shots with a great deal of headroom are often difficult to mic with a boom. (2) The available dynamic range between the reference signal level and distortion or digital zero.

Keykode (a trademark of Eastman Kodak)   A machine-readable barcode printed onto a film negative during its manufacture that provides an automatic method to capture key number information during telecine transfer. This information is stored in *telecine logs*, such as FLEx or ALE files, and is vital in negative cutting. The term "keycode" is used sometimes when referring generally to machine-readable code on film.

Latency   The delay imposed on an audio signal by a processor. It can become significant when using a series of plug-ins during a mix.

Layback   The last step in a videotape-based project for which the final mixed audio is recorded onto the online, color-corrected master tape to replace the old offline tracks. After the layback comes the party.

LCRS (left, center, right, and [mono] surround)   The four decoded channels of Dolby SR.

Leader, Academy   A leader placed at the head of and tail of each reel. From the start mark on the head leader to FFOA is 12 feet, and there's a countdown ending 3 feet from FFOA. Each countdown number represents 1 foot (16 frames), and the final "beep" frame reads "3," meaning 3 feet.

Leader, SMPTE Universal   Similar to the Academy leader: From the start mark on the head leader to FFOA is 12 feet, and there's a countdown ending 3 feet from FFOA. Each countdown number represents 1 second (24 frames) and the final "beep" frame reads "2," meaning 2 seconds. Remember, 2 seconds equals 3 feet at 24 fps.

LFOA (last frame of action)   The last frame of picture before cutting to the tail leader. When you're working on videotape or with a nonlinear editing system, LFOA is measured while looking at the first frame of leader rather than at the last frame of picture because a video EDL "out" is the same number as the next "in."

Liaison   The fusion of sounds across word boundaries, making it difficult to perform clean dialogue edits. (More accurately called *sandhi*.)

Lip flap   Any movement of the lips not supported by sound. It could be the result of the picture editor using a shot without sound or an actor miming speech during a shot. Lip flap can also be completely natural in its origin—maybe an actor moved his lips and no sound came out. Whatever its source, this inconsistency is usually disconcerting in films, so dialogue editors often add appropriate "lip fill" to cover the flap.

Lined script   The shooting script of a film on which the script supervisor has indicated the *coverage* of each scene. Setups and actions/events during the shoot are indicated as vertical lines drawn over the text, hence the name.

Load spacing   During *auto-assembly* of original sound, the term refers to the minimum separation between two sources before the two events are loaded as a single soundfile. When two source events in an *EDL* are closer than the load spacing setting (including handles), they are digitized as a single file on disk because (1) it's faster and (2) it causes less wear on the load deck because the machine doesn't have to stop, rewind, and cue up again. See *handle*.

Locked picture   A finished, final, "ain't gonna change" picture edit. Just kidding.

Lt/Rt (left total/right total)   An encoded 2-channel track that contains four channels of film channel information (*LCRS*). When the mixer completes the final surround mix for a film to be distributed in Dolby SR, he processes the film through a Dolby DS4 processor (usually in the presence of a Dolby consultant). The result is a 2-channel print master ready to be converted into an optical soundtrack. In Europe, this 2-track encoding is called *SVA* (*stereo variable area*). See also *LCRS*.

LTC (longitudinal time code)   Timecode stored as an audio signal on videotape or audiotape; often not reliable at nonplay speeds.

Mag stripe   This is 35 mm magnetic film with only a narrow strip of oxide and a smaller balance stripe. When a film is edited mechanically, analogue field recordings are transferred to mag stripe, synced, and coded for editing.

Mains (or utility) **frequency**   The frequency at which alternating current electrical power is transmitted from the power plant to the end user. In most parts of the world, it's 50 Hz; in the Americas, it's usually 60 Hz. Used often in analogue recording and postproduction as a convenient means of maintaining proper speed and of interlocking several machines. As digital recording and playback devices supplant analogue machines, mains frequency, as a synchronization tool, is generally being replaced by video reference or word clock.

Married print   A film print that contains both picture and optical sound.

M&E (or international) **mix**   A mix used for foreign language dubbing of a film. It contains all of the sound contents of the original mix except for the language elements of the dialogue. When a film is sold to a foreign distributor, usually all that will be required to create a localized mix from the M&E is the addition of local voices.

Media wrapper   A file carrier that standardizes how different devices obtain the information they need from a file to facilitate the interchange of audiovisual material, data, and metadata.

Metadata   Simply put: data about data. In audio postprodcution, it describes the contents of an audio file, such as timecode, scene/take, sample rate/bit depth, and the like, which can squeeze into the metadata area of a file.

Negative cutter   The individual in the lab who conforms the camera original film to match the picture editor's edits. The negative cutter uses the *cut list* to locate and assemble the correct sections of negative. A copy of the digital dump (*output tape*) is used as a reference.

NTSC (National Television Standards Committee)   (1) The color television standard for North America and a smattering of other places. (2) The standards body that long ago set the NTSC standard—525 interlaced vertical scan lines at a frequency of 59.94 Hz results in 29.97 frames per second (fps)—which is occasionally lovingly referred to as "Never Twice the Same Color."

Nudge value   A user-definable value in any DAW that allows the editor to offset a region or a selection by a fixed amount.

OMF   See *OMFI.*

OMFI (Open Media Framework Interchange) **format**   A translation language that allows material to move (relatively) easily from one platform to another. In dialogue applications, the OMFI allows complete access to sounds for films edited on a variety of nonlinear picture workstations. Usually shortened to "OMF."

One light transfer   A quick *telecine* transfer from original negative film to videotape. Normally, processed original camera film is developed and then transferred to videotape prior to digitization into a nonlinear picture editing workstation. When shot-specific color correction is needed, a *timed* or *graded* transfer is necessary.

Optical camera, optical recorder A recording device for converting sound from a final mix (whether on *DAT*, mag, hard disk, or in another format) to an optical negative track. An optical camera works much the same as an analogue tape recorder, converting an electrical signal into a print analogous to the sound wave. Unlike a tape recorder, which stores information as a magnetic "snapshot," an optical camera stores the sound information as visible lines of varying density and width.

Optical soundtrack The soundtrack on a finished film *exhibition print*. When passed through a projector's optical reader, the soundtrack's squiggly lines alter the voltage generated by a photo cell. This voltage is then amplified and decoded to play as sound. Prints with digital soundtracks carry digital information as well as analogue tracks. The digital information is stored in the form of small dots—a high-density type of barcode. Both digital and analogue soundtrack information is printed with the picture to reduce costs.

Output tape (or digital dump) The video output of a nonlinear picture workstation recorded to videotape, which becomes the work picture tape the sound crew will use when editing the film's soundtrack. Once the negative has been cut, printed, and transferred to videotape, the output will be replaced with the much more attractive first answer print *telecine* tape.

Overlap In dialogue editing, an interruption by an off-mic character of an on-mic speaker, which inevitably ruins part of the take.

PAL (phase alternating line) A color video system used throughout much of the world that consists of 625 lines per frame, interlaced. In the PAL environment, the frame rate is 25 fps and EBU timecode is used for production and postprodcution.

Perspective cut Organizing dialogue tracks in a manner that allows easy manipulation of the sound at a picture cut. Often used to enhance physical or psychological separation between characters, to focus on a specific element of a shot, or to enable two simultaneous conversations, as in a *phone split*.

PFX (production sound effects) Tracks within a dialogue session that contain nonverbal events removed from dialogue tracks. PFX may be split off from the dialogue for better control or manipulation, or to facilitate creation of an *M&E* mix.

Phone split A type of perspective editing that allows for easy control of both sides of a telephone conversation.

Pilot tone A very stable tone used to keep a sound recording device in sync with a camera. Synchronous analogue recording devices, such as the Nagra series of field recorders, need a means of ensuring that original recordings are played back at precisely the same speed at which they were recorded. On mono Nagras, this is accomplished by recording a 50 Hz (60 Hz in the Americas) sine wave along with the location audio. The pilot tone is generated by a crystal within the recorder. When the location tapes are played back for transfer to mag or another working format, a *resolver* compares the pilot tone recorded on the tape with a reference and slews the tape to match the recording speed to ensure accurate sound sync. The original Nagra pilot tone was replaced with Neopilot tone, which consists of two out-of-phase sine waves. On later Stereo Nagras, a high-frequency FM pilot signal is used. Timecode Nagras are resolved with EBU or SMPTE timecode.

Plop (sync pop, beep) A 1-frame-long tone used to synchronize soundtrack with picture. Temporary plops can be used anywhere within a reel for temporary sync references, but the final plops are placed 2 seconds before *FFOA* (9 feet after the start mark) and 2 seconds after *LFOA*.

Point of view (POV) A shot from the perspective of one of the characters, as though the audience is seeing the scene as he does. A POV shot is more subjective than the normal coverage of a scene's shots and thus may receive special sound treatment.

PostConform (a trademark of Digidesign) An application for *auto-assembly* (auto-conform) that uses edit information from the picture editor's EDLs to automatically extract and conform sounds from original field recordings. The result is a Pro Tools session containing the picture edits recreated with original sound material. Currently, it is supported only in Mac OS 9.

Premix (predub) A mix (dub) preceding the final mix in which like elements (usually elements from an entire department: dialogue, SFX, BG, or Foley, etc.) are mixed and organized to facilitate a more efficient final mix.

Preroll (1) In linear video editing, the amount of time programmed to allow all video machines to properly synchronize before the edit point. (2) In sound editing and mixing, preroll usually refers to how much program you want to hear before the sound you're focusing on.

Principal (actors) The core ensemble of actors through whom the film's story is told. Other actors may play secondary roles or serve as extras.

Print master A finished mix encoded into a distribution sound format used to create an optical soundtrack.

Pulldown (1) In the transfer from film to *NTSC* video, the process that slows the film chain by 0.1 percent to accommodate NTSC's 29.97 noninteger frame rate. (2) Material added before the *FFOA* of mixed reels to facilitate joining of reels for platter projection. The final 24 frames (usually) of the previous reel are copied to the head of a reel. This practice is not common.

Pullup (1) The speeding up of the film chain by 0.1 percent when transferring from NTSC video rate to "full" film rate. (2) Material added after the *LFOA* of mixed reels to compensate for the offset between a projector's gate and sound reader when reels are joined. The minimum pullup is 20 frames, which are copied from the head of the next reel and added to the tail of the current reel. To properly add pullups, you must know *FFOA* and LFOA for each reel.

Reconform   The manual assembling of original sound or video elements to match an offline edit. Compare this to an *auto-assembly,* which is largely an automatic process.

Reel, editing   A reel of no more than about 1000 feet. When films were edited on Moviolas or flatbed editing tables, the longest reasonable length of film editors could work with was 1000 feet, so traditionally, dialogue and other elements were edited and premixed in 1000-ft loads. After the premixes, the recorded reels were joined into 2000-ft double reels for the final mix, which was how the completed *married* print was distributed to theaters. When reels 1 and 2 were joined, the resulting reel was referred to as "Reel 1 A/B"; reels 3 and 4 became "Reel 2 A/B," and so forth. In today's electronic world, films are almost always sound-edited and mixed in 2000-ft reels.

Reel, exhibition   A 2000-ft reel of film for distribution to theaters.

Resolver   A device for controlling the playback speed of a tape recorder. Typically, field recordings have a *pilot tone* or *timecode* embedded into the signal. A resolver compares the recorded pilot tone signal with a known reference, possibly *mains frequency* or a crystal, to precisely recreate the speed of the original recording.

Ripple mode   An editing function in which changes to the edit point result in corresponding changes to the rest of the timeline to the "right" of the edit. A delete ripple edit closes the gap of a selected area, advancing all subsequent material on that track. Inserting in the ripple mode delays all subsequent material by the amount of the insert. Pro Tools calls this the Shuffle mode.

Room tone   The "air" of a location recording. Remove all words, movements, and noises from a dialogue recording and this is what's left. It's the dialogue editor's most valuable tool for removing noises, bridging mismatched shots, and inserting *ADR.* Room tone is not the same thing as backgrounds or atmospheres.

Scrubbing   A method of precisely locating a specific spot by listening to modulations while slowly moving the sound head (or the cursor in a *DAW*) over a track. It is very useful for finding ticks, pops, and other short-duration noises.

Shot (setup)   A single camera position (or lighting setup) during a shoot. Dialogue editors organize sessions based on shots, since it's logical for different setups to carry distinct sound characteristics.

Single system   A recording or projection process in which sound and picture are on the same medium. Sound recorded directly onto videotape is an example of single-system recording; a married film print is an example of single-system projection.

SMPTE (Society of Motion Picture and Television Engineers)   The professional standards organization that developed the SMPTE timecode standard for *NTSC* video: 29.97 fps, drop or non-drop frame.

Sound report   Created by the location mixer, a description of the contents and details of a field recording. It is essential in dialogue editing when looking for alternate takes and wild sound.

Sound roll   The original field sound recording media, whether ¼-inch tape, *DAT*, or hard disk. Each sound roll is accompanied by a sound report that describes the contents of the tape.

Source time   In an *EDL*, the timecode that indicates the location within the original field recording that corresponds to an event in a session.

Spot   (1) A *DAW* function that allows you to position an event to a specific timecode location. Spotting is useful for returning a region to its original location. (2) The process of determining where to place *ADR* lines or production effects.

Stem   The final components of a film mix, usually *LCRS* or wider. Typically, there are stems for dialogue, SFX, backgrounds, Foley, and music, each containing the *final* decisions made by the mixer. When the mix is done, the stems are combined—hopefully without further alteration—to form the print master.

Streamer   A visual cue, usually in the form of a vertical line moving from one side of the screen to the other, that tells an actor when to begin an *ADR* line.

SVA (stereo variable area)   See *Lt/Rt*.

Sync pop   See *plop*.

Talking head   An onscreen interview element in a documentary film. When the picture editor cuts from the subject to other material (*B-roll* or *cutaway*), the subject's disembodied audio track is referred to as *voiceover*. Picture editors cut from talking head to voiceover for illustrative purposes and to allow for editing of the voice track.

Telecine   (1) A device used for transferring film to videotape or digital files. (2) The process of transferring film to videotape or digital files. Once called a *film chain*.

Telecine log   A record of a telecine session used by the picture department and the negative cutters to maintain a solid relationship between the film negative and the videotape. The log can also carry audio metadata. Proprietary telecine log formats include *FLEx* and *ALE* files.

Temp mix (temp dub)   A preliminary mix of a film usually made for a specific screening. The reasons for temporary mixes include focus groups and studio screenings, festival submissions, whims of the executive producers, and so on.

Temp music   Music added during the picture edit to set a mood, increase drama, enhance the story, and/or facilitate editing. When picture editing ends, a composer will create music in the spirit of the temporary music, or a music consultant and music editor will acquire appropriate music, which then must be licensed.

3:2 pulldown   A method of transferring film running at 24 fps to NTSC video running more or less at 30 fps, without changing the speed of the film. One frame of film is transferred to two successive video fields; the next film frame goes to three video fields, and so forth. Also called 2:3:2 pulldown or 2:3 pulldown.

Top and Tail   The removal of unnecessary silence or extraneous material from the beginning and end of a sound clip (dialogue, SFX, BG, ADR, etc.). The resulting clip is ready for use.

VITC (Vertical Interval Timecode)   It is inserted into the vertical interval (blanking) of a video stream. You can occasionally see VITC as dancing white dots and bars at the top of a television picture. Unlike *LTC*, VITC can be read at nonplay speeds, even when the tape is stopped, which makes it useful for scrubbing to a location on a tape to spot an event. Most timecode translators automatically switch from LTC to VITC at nonplay speeds and then back to LTC once picture lock is achieved.

Voiceover vs. narration   In documentary sound editing, voiceover is a disembodied voice derived from character interview material. Narration is usually studio-recorded and not directly linked to a field recording. A character in the film can also be the narrator, but the field recording material is still called "voiceover," whereas studio material is always called "narration." Voiceover carries the legitimacy of the film's characters, while narration is usually omniscient, sometimes known as the "voice of God."

Vox pop (*vox populi*—Latin for *voice of the people*)   Film interviews in which members of the "general public" are asked their opinions on a certain topic. These interviews are intended to appear spontaneous and unrehearsed and to reveal the opinion of the "man on the street."

Wild sound (wild track)   Any sound recorded on the set with no associated picture (as opposed to "sync sound"), including wild dialogue, *room tone*, effects, atmospheres, and more.

Work track   A "safe" track in a dialogue session that contains no useful program material. Work tracks provide a comfortable environment for recording or opening extra material, editing in a sync-destroying mode (such as Pro Tool's Shuffle), or doing other work tasks that can damage material sharing the track.

X (X, Y, Z, and more) **tracks**   Tracks housing dialogue lines removed from the dialogue tracks because they were rerecorded (*ADR*). X tracks aren't mere trash bins—lines moved to them must be fully edited and prepared for the mix in case the loop line is unacceptable in the mix or the director decides to keep the original line.

Zeppelin   One of many humorous names for the fuzzy, energy-absorbing microphone covers seen on location shoots.

Bibliography

Aaton, s.a. *Aaton Audio: Post Chain, v11.* February 2006; see *www.aaton.com.*
———. *Aaton Audio: Post Chain, v10.* January 2005; see *www.aaton.com.*
Argy, Stephanie. "Roll, Cut, Print: A Conversation Between Sound Professionals from the Set, the Edit Room and the Mixing Stage." *The Motion Picture Editors Guild Magazine* 1(25), January/February 2004.
Audio Engineering Society. See *www.aes.org.*
Austen, Jane. *Mansfield Park.* London: Penguin Classics, 1994.
Brakey, Robert. "Configuring Avid Change Lists." *The Motion Picture Editors Guild Magazine* 21(2), March/April 2000.
Chalmers, Richard (EBU Technical Department). "The Broadcast Wave Format—An Introduction." *EBU Technical Review,* Fall 1997.
Cook, David A. *A History of Narrative Film.* New York: Norton, 1981.
European Broadcasting Union. "BWF—A Format for Audio Data Files in Broadcasting." *EBU Technical Specification,* June 2001.
———. "Broadcast Wave Format (BWF) User Guide." See *www.ebu.ch.*
Franklin, Ron. "Workstation File-Format Interchange." *Mix Magazine* 1, October 2002.
Harris, Brooks. "Advance Authoring Format and Media Exchange Format." *The Motion Picture Editors Guild Magazine* 24(3), May/June 2003.
Hollyn, Norman. *The Film Editing Room Handbook, Third Edition.* Los Angeles: Lone Eagle Press, 1999.
Library of Congress. "The Thomas Edison Collection." See *www.memory.loc.gov.*
Meyer, Chris. "Designing for HD: An Essential Checklist." See *www.filmmaking.com.*
Munro, Chris. "Multi-Track Production Recording: Using Digital Disk Recorders to Improve Quality and Simplify Post Production." *The Motion Picture Editors Guild Magazine* 1(25), January/February 2004.
Murch, Walter. *In the Blink of an Eye, Second Edition.* Los Angeles: Silman-James Press, 2001.
Murray, Douglas. "PAL Basics: Film Sound for the Rest of the World." *The Motion Picture Editors Guild Magazine* 23(2), March/April 2002.
Phillips, Michael, et al. See *www.24p.com.*
Robjohns, Hugh. "The Ins and Outs of Interfacing Analogue and Digital Equipment." *Sound on Sound,* May 2000.
Seckel, A. *The Art of Optical Illusions.* London: Carlton Books, 2002.
Stratman, Eric. "Automated Conforming Using Change Note Assistant." *The Motion Picture Editors Guild Magazine* 24(6), November/December 2003.
Stratmann, Erich, and Benson, Phil. "Metadata & Metaflow." *The Motion Picture Editors Guild Magazine* 24(3), May/June 2003.
Turner, Bob. "A Reflection/Eulogy." *SMPTE/New England Newsletter,* January 1998.
Ulano, Mark. "Moving Pictures That Talk—Part 2: The Movies Are Born a Child of the Phonograph." See *www.filmsound.org.*
de Vries, Tjitte. "The Cinématographe Lumière: A Myth?" *Photohistorical Magazine of the Photographic Society of the Netherlands,* 1995; see *www.xs4all.nl.*
Weis, Elisabeth, and Belton, John, eds. *Film Sound: Theory and Practice.* New York: Columbia University Press, 1985.
Wheeler, Paul. *High Definition and 24p Cinematography.* Oxford: Focal Press, 2003.
Yewdall, David L. *Practical Art of Motion Picture Sound, Third Edition.* Boston: Focal Press, 2007.

Index